EX LIBRIS
NEW YORK INSTITUTE
OF TECHNOLOGY
NEW YORK INSTITUTE OF TECHNOLOGY
SCIENCE
TECHNOLOGY
HUMANITIES

Community and Regional Planning

Melvin R. Levin

The Praeger Special Studies program—utilizing the most modern and efficient book production techniques and a selective worldwide distribution network—makes available to the academic, government, and business communities significant, timely research in U.S. and international economic, social, and political development.

Community and Regional Planning

Issues in Public Policy

Third Edition

PRAEGER SPECIAL STUDIES IN U.S. ECONOMIC, SOCIAL, AND POLITICAL ISSUES

Praeger Publishers New York London

Library of Congress Cataloging in Publication Data

Levin, Melvin R 1924-
Community and regional planning.

(Praeger special studies in U.S. economic, social, and political issues)
Bibliography: p.
Includes index.
1. Local government—United States. 2. Regional planning—United States. 3. Program budgeting—United States. I. Title.
JS341.L4 1977 352'.96'0973 76-12862
ISBN 0-275-23690-0
ISBN 0-275-85740-9 student ed.

PRAEGER PUBLISHERS
200 Park Avenue, New York, N.Y. 10017, U.S.A.

Published in the United States of America in 1977
by Praeger Publishers, Inc.

789 038 987654321

Printed in the United States of America

For Dolly, Georgie, and Dave

ACKNOWLEDGMENTS

This collection of studies prepared and assembled over a period of years owes much to the author's callous presumption on past friendships. My former colleagues, Norman Abend, Joseph Slavet, and the late George Blackwood, have been mercilessly exploited for review, criticism, editorial assistance, and ideas. Their patience and forbearance have been much appreciated.

Reflections such as these on government organization inevitably tend to take on an autobiographical tinge. In cases where discretion seemed to be called for, names of persons and agencies have been carefully omitted out of kindness and cowardice. Nevertheless a number of anonymous benefactors, some of whom may read this book, deserve my thanks for their unwitting assistance.

My thanks are also due to *Planning,* published by the American Society of Planning Officials, for permission to use three articles which appeared in the November 1974, January 1976, and September 1976 issues under the titles "There's More to This Job Than Coloring Maps," "Conscience of the Planners," and "Why Can't Johnny Plan?" "The Big Regions," in an earlier incarnation, appeared in the *Journal of the American Institute of Planners,* March 1967.

As a last note, the author wishes to assume full responsibility for errors of fact, poor judgment, and bad temper that may offend the learned, wise, and sensitive reader.

CONTENTS

Chapter

Chapter

LIST OF ABBREVIATIONS

ACIR	Advisory Commission on Intergovernmental Relations
ADP	Automatic Data Processing
AEF	American Expeditionary Force
AIP	American Institute of Planners
ARA	Area Redevelopment Administration
ARC	Appalachian Regional Commission
ASPO	American Society of Planning Officials
BLS	Bureau of Labor Statistics
BPR	Bureau of Public Roads
BRA	Boston Redevelopment Authority
CED	Committee for Economic Development
COGs	Council of Governments
CRP	Community Renewal Program
DES	Division of Employment Security (Massachusetts)
DOD	Department of Defense
DOJ	Department of Justice
DOT	Department of the Treasury
EDA	Economic Development Administration
FAA	Federal Aviation Administration
HEW	Department of Health, Education, and Welfare
HHFA	Housing and Home Finance Agency
HUD	Department of Housing and Urban Development
LEAA	Law Enforcement Assistance Administration
MBTA	Massachusetts Bay Transportation Authority
NASA	National Aeronautics and Space Administration
NRPB	National Resources Planning Board
NYC	Neighborhood Youth Corps Program
OCS	Officer Candidate School
OEO	Office of Economic Opportunity
PPB	Planning Programming Budgeting (System)
R&D	Research and Development
ROTC	Reserve Officers' Training Corps
SMA	Standard Metropolitan Area
SMSA	Standard Metropolitan Statistical Area
SSRC	Social Science Research Council
TVA	Tennessee Valley Authority
USES	United States Employment Service
VISTA	Volunteers in Service to America

INTRODUCTION

George Blackwood

PLANNING: FROM NEW NATIONALISM TO GREAT SOCIETY

Throughout the history of the United States, we have paused now and again—all too infrequently as it turns out—to appraise how well the spirit and purpose of our society are working out in the machinery of government. The ends of such examinations are evident: modifications, improvements—new directions if you will—for a new generation. The underlying assumption is that there must be a series of progressive changes to meet conditions that are shifting here as rapidly as anywhere in the world, if not as spectacularly.

In this book, Melvin R. Levin, with the background and perspectives of the planner, examines social trends and needs within American society. In a series of chapters concentrating on specific aspects of governmental relationships with society during the last third of the twentieth century, he elaborates three central themes:

First, hesitantly, and up to this point without adequate and skillful use of its most vital resource—brains—the national government and to a much smaller extent state and local governments have begun to recognize and adapt to the pressing needs of society. This has come about amid much conflict, and difficult transitions in thinking lie ahead. But the needs are now beginning to be recognized; and Dr. Levin suggests that the tools are at hand at least to meet the most urgent.

Second, there is a very substantial gap, and therefore a very real dilemma for democracy, between a leadership elite that grasps the necessities of planning or experimentation with the new urban forms and ideas and a large although restless mass that is not at all sure precisely which actions it should endorse. All too often, programs for actions have been presented on paper—and then left there. Planners, economists, and social scientists in general have observed, analyzed, and criticized, but all too often they have presented grandiose and unrealistic schemes that have not respected politicoeconomic realities. The relationship between talent and pragmatic common sense has therefore all too often been inverse and one that creates disillusionment and frustration. Careful management of programs by agencies concerned with the quality of life in the United States can help close the existing gap.[1]

Third, the kind of inflated rhetoric so often encountered in public affairs makes coordination more difficult, especially when combined with a bureaucratic orientation that stresses quantity of governmental personnel in a neat organizational chart rather than quality of staff and administrative practices. The lack of adequate foresight in planning and the frequent resistance to intelligence and innovation, as for instance the failure to properly use universities as sources of ideas and talents, has fostered a "deadlock and drift" type of psychology within the governmental structure and among clients of government agencies. Certain social trends (such as talent migration) strip some areas of their capacity to act intelligently and forcefully even though such failures are often obscured by the cloud of rhetoric and the fog of bureaucracy.

The author of this book is especially concerned with the rise of a number of new professions that are vital to the future, and he stresses the role of education in American society. To planners, he addresses a special plea: It is now almost universally recognized that narrow economic and land-use perspectives are not sufficient, and a "social planning" dimension is as inevitable as it is overdue.

One caution to the reader before he proceeds further: This book is concerned with America's domestic future, and those who seek answers for our international problems should look elsewhere. American democracy, especially since World War II, might be thought of as a giant sandwich, in which a thin slice of bread at the top covers a rich variety of foods supported by another thick slice of bread at the bottom. The thin slice is the elite or leadership; the thick, of course, the general populace; the foods in the middle, public policies of all types. What the author has done is cut down the middle of the sandwich, separating domestic matters from international and examining the state of the former.

Basing his assertions on a wide-ranging knowledge of recent developments in federal and state governments, Dr. Levin suggests that the present era in domestic affairs can be considered the reverse of (yet somehow parallel to) the Great Depression. Then, as now, positive political-economic action was necessary as traditional patterns proved inadequate. Then, as now, experimentation on a broad scale seemed to be warranted. The difference is more than a generation in time, however. The problem of an affluent society may well be that it thinks in simplistic Depression terms, that scarcity of talent (combined with a viscous bureaucratic machinery) has replaced scarcity of employment as a basic social ill. Since the Depression, we appear to have learned a great deal about what *not* to do and only a little about what *to* do.

However, some recognition has begun among social thinkers of what A. F. K. Organski has called the "politics of abundance"—greatly increased productivity in a peacetime economy, better technology and economic organization for warmaking, generally high scales of living surrounded by pockets of poverty, and an economy that requires a labor force possessing increasing and diversified skills.[2] The implications of the revolutionary economic changes that have taken place are not fully grasped by many people inside *or* outside government. For example, the structure of American federal government is fundamentally the same as it has been for many years, but the *substance* today is different; we still have sharing of power between the central government and the state governments, but the actual workings of their relationships are vastly different today from 1933, for example. This has been brought about largely by the pressure of social needs translated to political realities. It is not the result of a "conspiracy in Washington"—no matter how much Birchites and their fellow travelers swear to the contrary.

Awareness of the kinds of problems to which this book addresses itself is not new. In the early 1900s, Herbert Croly, later the founder and first editor of the *New Republic,* wrote: "The way to realize a purpose is not to leave it to chance. . . . The problem belongs to American national democracy, and its solution must be attempted chiefly by means of official national action."[3] The problem to which he referred was how to bring the "promise of American life" —abundance for all, the good society standing on the bedrock of freedom— to fruition. His suggestion was that the government needed to substitute purposive planning for the drift which he believed to be its main characteristic. Croly's doctrine of the positive state moving to meet social problems as they arose was adopted by Theodore Roosevelt as the theme of his 1912 campaign for the presidency and put forward under the theme of the "New Nationalism." Essentially, this embodies the idea of the reconstruction of society through strong governmental intervention in the economy. The general idea had been advanced by Lester Frank Ward in his *Dynamic Sociology,* and it penetrated the Progressive movement and its thinking; but Croly (and Roosevelt) had pinpointed the place where action needed to be inspired most—Washington, rather than the state capitals which were the focus of much Progressive thought.

In 1912, Roosevelt confronted not only the incumbent president, William Howard Taft—whom contemporary historians regard as not nearly as "standpat" as his associates did—but Woodrow Wilson. Wilson, the ultimate winner, stood staunchly on the traditional Jeffersonian platform of small government for small action. But within a brief time of his inauguration he began to take halting steps toward the Rooseveltian ideals—so much so that Croly turned from skepticism about Wilson to a mild enthusiasm. Still, however, Croly felt that planned action by the Wilson administration was lacking, and he wrote: "The planning department of the democratic state is created for action. . . . It plans ahead as far as conditions permit or dictate. It changes its plans as often as conditions demand. It seeks above all to test its own plans, so as to discover whether they will accomplish the desired result."[4]

By this test, Wilsonianism was deficient. But if this was the case with the Wilson administration, the 1920s were a positive disaster, at least from the standpoint of government action. Furthermore, the gap between the social sciences and practical applications to society widened rapidly. Social scientists and planners, like most intellectuals, found themselves increasingly in what seemed to be an alien land;[5] but rapid advances were made in internal organization of the social sciences and in new theoretical concepts, and progress was made on the development of planning as a coherent discipline within the general framework of the social sciences.

There had, of course, been fragmentary and somewhat abortive efforts to use the techniques of governmental analysis to improve existing government machinery, the most notable private group being the Institute for Public Administration in New York. A significant step forward came in 1924, when Charles E. Merriam founded the Social Science Research Council (SSRC), a federation of various academic societies covering the major social sciences: economics, political science, psychology, sociology, and history. As a recent study points out, Merriam's basic hope was "to place academic research at the disposal of the government."[6] This hope was not to bear fruit for some years; but one accomplishment of the SSRC was as a force in helping to persuade President Herbert Hoover to appoint a Research Committee on Social Trends in 1929. The report of this committee, on which the noted sociologist William Fielding Ogburn served as chairman with Merriam as vice-chairman, resulted in little concrete action, but, it demonstrated in exhaustive detail to what extent research techniques in the social sciences (in some cases, with such tools as computers and input-output analysis not yet available, rather rudimentary) might be used by governmental agencies to gather information.

However, most concrete advances in the thinking and techniques of the social sciences in terms of adaptations to society, as of 1930, had taken place on the local level rather than the national. A significant breakthrough toward thinking on a broad national scale, with due attention to the problems of governmental units at all levels—federal, state, and local—came with the founding of the Public Administration Clearing House in 1931. Not only did this organization, with Louis Brownlow as its director, soon become a major center for information about governmental administration, but it also became the core of a cluster of organizations specializing in governmental research and advice in policy making. This cluster of groups, often known as "1313" from its street address—1313 East 60th Street in Chicago—soon began to play a role as a significant source of expertise in government which has continued down to the present.

At about the same time, planning as a conceptual field of analysis and training had begun to "jell" as an aspect of the social sciences. As in the field of governmental analysis and public administration—where the first significant advances had been in the formation of municipal bureaus of research, an American invention which by the 1930s had spread as widely as Japan and Ireland[7]—planning had first of all concerned itself with the city. Between 1920 and 1930, as Robert A. Walker points out, the leaders of the planning movement had made important contributions to city planning, and by the latter year, practically all the larger cities in the United States had official planning agencies (on paper at least).[8] Practitioners of planning were numerous enough by 1917 so that the American City Planning Institute (now the American Institute of Planners) was created, and the first school of city planning was founded at Harvard, in 1929. For the most part, city planning at this time was not only narrow in focus but tied closely to landscape architecture as a field of study in the few institutions that had created academic programs. One broadening step was taken in the late 1920s, when regional planning for urbanized areas began to come into focus. Governor Alfred E. Smith initiated a subregional planning study for New York state; by 1929, the Committee on Regional Plan of New York and Its Environs, working closely with social scientists at Columbia University, published a series of volumes dealing with population movements, industrial development, public services, and many other facets of the various regions within the state. These pioneering efforts stood alone, however, until well into the 1930s.

The coming of the Great Depression brought about a major shift in the position and perspectives of planners, economists, political scientists, and other social scientists. Participating in a series of social experiments during the New Deal, they were perhaps more scorned than applauded. But from the vantage point of the present day, it is clear that much of the criticism was misdirected. The real problem of the New Deal was a lack of broad-gauged coordination, a failure to develop and use the talent at its disposal with sufficient skill. Nonetheless, the 1930s marked a distinct step forward in the relationship of the new techniques and perspectives of the social sciences to government.

For one thing, planning began to break out of the straitjacket of city (or more accurately, simple land use) planning toward new horizons that were of course still limited. In retrospect, perhaps the most important measure of the New Deal was the creation of the Tennessee Valley Authority (TVA). Going beyond the production of electric power, flood control, rural electrification, and related goals, the act carried the significant language that the TVA was to advance "the economic and social well-being of the people living in the said river basin." There has been much debate about the accomplishment of the TVA, but it provided a domestic pattern—an aborted pattern, but one which was to be revived and extended in the 1960s—for future development of regions concerned with long-range economic and social planning.

The role of planning in government developed rapidly in other respects as well. Unfortunately, a substantial part of the development was verbal rather than substantive, and for a time the word "planning" was as romantic for thinking Americans as "resistance" was to be for adventurous Frenchmen a few years later. "Planning" was everything; accomplishment, nothing. For a brief Indian Summer in the 1930s, 47 of the 48 states had created planning boards (a number seem to have had primarily a paper existence) concerned with the best use of state resources. Over 1,000 city planning departments could be found, and 400 counties could boast planning boards. One of the early activities of one of the "1313" agencies, the Council of State Governments, was to sponsor commissions on interstate cooperation. Twenty were in operation by September 1937, and it was assumed that planning would have a high priority on interstate agendas. Already, regional planning boards stretched across state boundaries, including the Pacific Northwest Regional Planning Commission, the New England Regional Planning Commission, and the Ohio Valley Regional Planning Commission. These commissions, however, seemed to enjoy little popular or legislative support and understanding; in 1938, for instance, a modest request from Governor Charles F. Hurley of Massachusetts for $10,000 to be allocated to the work of the New England Regional Planning Commission was quickly sliced out of the state budget by the hostile legislature, which was angered at the governor for other reasons.[9]

Within the national government, the National Planning Board, established by executive order in 1933, became the National Resources Board in 1934 and the National Resources Committee in 1935. Even with these changes in name and much uncertainty of functions, this body marked a signal change of direction in Washington. Originally concerned with the preparation of a national public works program under the direction of Secretary of the Interior Harold L. Ickes, the National Resources Committee by 1935 was engaged in some aspects of comprehensive national planning. Since it was evident that federal programs required cooperation from the states, it was decided that state plans could be financed from federal funds available for emergency relief. The result was that with the exception of Delaware every state set up an official planning agency, which usually had some power over public works projects in the state. In many instances, these agencies had just begun to function, carrying on research and planning some assistance to local governments, when the federal momentum caused by the Depression began to slacken. By 1939, several states had quietly cut back their planning agencies, and by 1942 very little was being done across the country. Significantly, in a number of instances state planning boards merged with agencies concerned with industrial development.[10]

The National Resources Committee was in a strategic enough position within the governmental structure in 1935 so that when Charles Merriam and Louis Brownlow suggested a study promoting more effective organization of the executive branch, the committee's approval was essential in arousing President Roosevelt's interest.[11] The recommendations that were made as a result of the study included strong emphasis on planning through a permanent National Resources Board. Brownlow, the chairman of the committee appointed by the president (the other members were Merriam and Luther Gulick), assembled a group of social scientists as the research staff; the general desire of the committee and the staff was to set up an agency that would "serve as clearing house of planning interest and concerns in the national effort to prevent waste and improve our national living standards," and they asserted that "the universal aspiration for economic security and the increasing enrichment of human lives may be forwarded by substituting the results of careful scientific study for uninformed judgment and political expediency as the basis for the formulation of government plans."[12]

The committee's proposal to establish a National Resources Planning Board—together with most of its other proposals—encountered a difficult time in Congress. The Army Corps of Engineers stoutly resisted incursions on its domain of river and harbor development, and western senators succeeded in inserting a provision that two of the five members of the board come from west of the Mississippi. Conservatives were openly fearful of a dictatorship through planning via a New Deal sovietism. The result was a rather weak board located in the executive office of the president from 1939 to 1943, when it was quietly abolished.

During World War II, other facets of applying the social sciences to governmental activities came to the fore, while planning faded. Economics had undergone a rapid evolution in the 1930s, with the two most important developments (which were related) being the impact of the thought of John Maynard Keynes and the rise of a new system of national accounting centering on "input-output analysis." Keynesianism provided the theoretical base for the national accounts system devised by Simon Kuznets and others, a system to measure the aggregate content and the changes in national production. This was now applied by government economists, who used as a base the summary figures of gross national production. One economist active in this endeavor later wrote that the new system of economic analysis was a weapon whose "bearing on victory was considerably greater than that of atomic energy," because in England and the United States it was much clearer than in Germany what was being produced, what proportions were going to military and civilian use, and how resources were allocated between immediate use and investment.[13] This meant that the Germans were simply mobilizing economic resources less wisely than their major opponents, despite the vaunted efficiency of Nazism.

Two other wartime developments should also be noted: The immense growth of technology and productivity demonstrated that the country could mobilize its resources to achieve hitherto undreamed of levels of living if it so desired; and the central organizing mechanism, carrying on in a different way the fight against the Depression, was the federal government. The vast expansion of the federal government indicated another step in significant alteration of state-federal relationships. At the same time, however, there was also a trend toward deterioration in the quality of government personnel that appears to have begun during or shortly after World War II; this was noted by James M. Landis in late 1960.[14]

Under President Harry S. Truman, wartime economics techniques were institutionalized under the aegis of the Council of Economic Advisers, created by the Employment Act of 1946 and designed as a central mechanism in governmental planning for the stabilization of the economy. Another area in which the Truman administration moved was in expanding the role of the Bureau of the Budget; this bureau, through increased powers of decision making for the president, became in a limited sense the "allocation planner" for the energies and activities of the government.

Since the administrative structure of the government had expanded enormously under the impact of depression and war, much attention was concentrated in the 1940s and 1950s on efforts to "streamline" and reorganize it. The First and Second Hoover Commissions and the Kestnbaum Commission were the most ambitious attempts to do this—with limited success, especially with respect to the Kestnbaum group in 1955. Probably more important, at least in its subtle effects, was the fact that major elements of American business came to accept the concept of economic and (to a limited degree) social planning on the part of the government. The major instrument in this "reconciliation" of business and government was the Committee for Economic Development (CED), a group of about two hundred corporate executives and educators who have sponsored numerous studies to help formulate policies leading to "full employment at higher living standards." Sometimes described as "progressive conservatives," CED leaders formed a seminal group around President Dwight D. Eisenhower: Robert Anderson, Marion Folsom, James D. Zellerbach, Meyer Kestnbaum, and others. All had been chairmen of the CED, and even Eisenhower himself had been a trustee of the organization while president of Columbia University.[15]

Although many liberals felt frustrated during the Eisenhower years by what seemed to them to be a stultification of progress in the meeting of national problems, legislation that bore great import for the future was passed. In the field of housing, for instance, the Housing Act of 1954 introduced the "urban renewal" concept. This extended the principle of the Housing Act of 1949, which provided funds for public housing and redevelopment conforming to planned programs for entire communities. The 1954 act included neighborhood conservation and rehabilitation as well as redevelopment. It required the submission of comprehensive plans by eligible communities in the form of "workable programs" before they could qualify for federal financing. A most important part was section 701, which provided funds (on a matching 50–50 basis) to state planning agencies for assistance to smaller communities or for planning work in metropolitan and regional areas. This still did not provide planning aid for the larger cities, but later amendments broadened the act.

Another area of public policy affected by the Eisenhower Administration was highways. The Highway Act of 1956 provided billions of dollars for a 41,000-mile system of superhighways crisscrossing the country, with the federal government paying 90 percent of the cost. A little-noticed section of the act expanded 1934 highway legislation setting aside up to 1.5 percent of the combined state-federal highway expenditures for use in nonengineering planning studies in connection with road building, to relate economic and social patterns to the new roads. As was the case with housing legislation, the highway acts were fundamentally narrow-gauged in dealing only with one area of public policy and ignoring the far-reaching ramifications for society of a sudden thrust in one specific segment of the national economic policy.

On the state level during the late 1940s and 1950s, similar trends were evident. While rapid urbanization was taking place, state and regional planning lagged behind. Perhaps the only type of planning that could be readily grasped by executives and legislators (or at least financed in proper fashion) was that related to economic development—especially the attraction of industry. This type of "smokestack" planning (which also embraced the tourist) usually stressed colorful promotional efforts; because not a great deal was done to study the appropriate relationship between a planning agency and a development, the latter tended to overshadow the former. One result, however, was all to the good: The competition for "smokestacks" meant an increasing demand for persons with a number of different types of skills such as industrial geography, market analysis, population movements analysis, and transportation expertise. The trend toward fragmentation increased, but there was at least the unifying theme that state and regional planners engaged in industrial development could tap a broader range of talents.[16]

With the inauguration of John F. Kennedy, social scientists and planners assumed new importance in the federal government. Spencer Parratt pointed out at an American Society for Public Administration convention that "the people who are doing the most for metropolitan planning are sitting in Washington," and he stated a confident belief that the near future would witness greater federal activity.[17] Kennedy's acceptance of Richard Neustadt's concept of strong presidential leadership is well known, as is his rapport with many intellectuals. Soon after his inauguration, Kennedy proposed several measures advocated by various types of social scientists, and two were passed in 1961. The existing program of federal aid to housing was broadened, with an expanded urban renewal program, subsidies for private rehabilitation of slums, additional public housing, and more aid for metropolitan planning, open space development, and community facilities. The other major Kennedy innovation was legislation providing aid to urban and rural areas with substantial unemployment rates. This proposal, first put forward by Senator Paul Douglas of Illinois (the only professional economist in Congress) in 1955, had attracted Kennedy's interest with special intensity during his campaign in West Virginia. For such areas, federal loans and grants became available to build or reconstruct industrial buildings, modernize water systems, and establish training programs for workers with no skills or outmoded ones. Subsistence for the workers during the training period was also provided. The legislation was later broadened into the Public Works and Economic Development Act of 1965 and included public works project authorizations for areas with chronic unemployment and provision for planning on a broader regional scale.

In 1962, Congress passed the Manpower Development and Training Act; this directed the federal government to assess national manpower needs and to develop training programs to equip unemployed or underemployed workers to fill the needs. After Kennedy's death, several of the projects he initiated came to fruition. In 1964, the Economic Opportunity Act was passed; it provided for the Job Corps, work-study programs, the "Domestic Peace Corps" or VISTA, and community action programs, sometimes called the heart of the fight against poverty in the United States. Community action programs were to be designed locally, with representatives of the poor being enlisted in planning and operating the programs.

The Appalachian Regional Development Act of 1965 provided $1.1 billion in federal funds, four-fifths of it to be used for highways in the region, the remainder to be used for such varied projects as multicounty health centers, mining area restoration, and vocational education facilities. Perhaps the most important tool in the program is the one that cost the least—the Appalachian Regional Commission. With a rather small staff, this commission is headed by a federal member appointed by the president and a state member elected from among the 12 Appalachian governors. Projects were to be designed by the states, approved by the regional commission, and executed with federal funds. In general, the approach underlying the Appalachian bill was not to meet the region's immediate needs for money but rather to improve the economy of the region. The people of the region were to increase their purchasing power through basic economic development rather than through welfare. The theory and its explanation by President Lyndon B. Johnson and his associates were attractive enough to Congress that a program covering only 12 states received the votes of at least one senator or representative from 48 states; the bill passed 62–22 in the Senate and 257–165 in the House.[18]

In March 1965, when the act was passed, per capita income in the area was almost 40 percent below the national average, and unemployment was about 50 percent greater. The region as defined by the act extends from Lake Erie to northern Alabama; with 17 million people in 182,000 square miles, it is roughly the same size and has about 15 percent less population than California. The difficulties and achievements of the Appalachian Commission are significant for observers of so-called creative federalism. While still too early to render a judgment, the hope is that new patterns of cooperation between the federal and state governments and combination of resources beyond the boundaries of single states will emerge.

While Appalachia represented a new concept of federal-state relations on a regional basis, urban renewal and redevelopment represented a novel federal-local planning enterprise. Initially authorized under the Eisenhower administration in 1959, the Community Renewal Program (CRP) became a major factor in such planning in 1962, with about a hundred communities receiving federal grants covering two-thirds of their cost. The general idea of CRP was comprehensive planning for city renewal rather than the project-by-project approach previously followed.

From the academic standpoint, the most important developments of the 1960s lay in the rapid growth of urban specializations within the social and behavioral sciences. The new field of urban economics emerged, generated in large part by the Ford Foundation's supported group, Resources for the Future, which has also stimulated research into "regional accounting." Sociologists and political scientists more critically and analytically began to examine phases of urban and metropolitan life; among them might be counted Edward Banfield, Robert Dahl, Herbert J. Gans, Nathan Glazer, Scott Greer, Daniel Patrick Moynihan, and Robert C. Wood. Computer science also developed into a major tool for the social scientist concerned with the type of problems dealt with in this text.

By the mid-1960s, the trends were clear: Concerns at all levels of government with overriding urban and regional problems were combined with new techniques and tools of social scientists and planners. Two new cabinet departments, Housing and Urban Development, and Transportation, were set up in 1965 and 1966 respectively. In analyzing the evolution of public policy with respect to urban renewal, Lowden Wingo, Jr., wrote that the policy focus had moved

> from the slum area to the neighborhood, the central city, and ultimately the region; from limited policy power concerns with the lower housing strata to the total housing stock and currently to the state of the physical plant of the region; from a policeman-and-policed relationship between local governments and parts of the private housing sector to an intricate net of intergovernmental public-private relations into which are drawn neighborhood organizations, financial institutions, welfare agencies, local interest groups, and the complex array of housing, planning, land use, and transportation agencies from every level of government.[19]

One final note may be added to this already lengthy introduction. Because the text looks toward the last third of the twentieth century, it should be noticed that the author lays much stress on the role of the young within society. This is part of the point about the colleges and universities—they are places where to a surprising extent the young teach the old (although it is presumed to be vice versa). Those in constant contact with youth know that each generation of college-going youth look with new eyes and new ideas at the world around them. As is evident in several of the chapters presented here, a major task of the social sciences in our society is to teach young people realistically about the obstacles in the path of immediate constructive change—without dimming their enthusiasm for progress. This is a noble goal and difficult of accomplishment. But the young are, of course, not only the key to the future but the best road to an understanding of the present, because society shaped them to its own ends while supposedly training them for productive future careers. The migration of talented youth from backwaters to scenes of action, the need for careful structuring of educational patterns in order to provide a broad cultural base while creating fruitful specialized skills, the need for society to keep the channels open so that the economy and the polity can be geared to incorporating the talents of youth—these are only a few of the points that can be made about the role, relationships, and needs of the younger generation within our society. In a real sense, therefore, the underlying theme of this book is a constant invocation to keep the young in mind in framing policy and implementing programs.

NOTES

1. For some cases applying this general principle, see Robert Morris and Robert H. Binstock, *Feasible Planning for Social Change* (New York: Columbia University Press, 1966).

2. A. F. K. Organski, *The Stages of Political Development* (New York: Knopf, 1966), pp. 186–91.

3. Herbert Croly, in *The Promise of American Life,* Arthur M. Schlesinger, Jr., ed. (Cambridge, Mass.: Belknap Press of Harvard University Press, 1965), p. 24.

4. Herbert Croly, *Progressive Democracy* (New York: Macmillan, 1914), pp. 370–71.

5. Richard Hofstadter, *Anti-Intellectualism in American Life* (New York: Vintage, 1963).

6. Richard Polenberg, *Reorganizing Roosevelt's Government* (Cambridge, Mass.: Harvard University Press, 1966), p. 12.

7. John M. Gaus, Leonard D. White, and Marshall E. Dimock, *The Frontiers of Public Administration* (Chicago: University of Chicago Press, 1936), p. 24.

8. Robert A. Walker, *The Planning Function in Urban Government,* rev. ed. (Chicago: University of Chicago Press, 1950), p. 35.

9. Boston *Post,* September 4, 1937; Boston *Herald,* April 3, 1938.

10. Albert Lepawsky, *State Planning and Economic Development in the South,* report no. 4 (Washington, D.C.: National Planning Association, Committee of the South, 1949).

11. Louis Brownlow, *A Passion for Anonymity* (vol. 2 of his autobiography) (Chicago: University of Chicago Press, 1958).

12. U.S., President's Committee on Administrative Management, *Report of the Committee* (Washington, D.C.: U.S. Government Printing Office, 1937), p. 28.

13. John K. Galbraith, *American Capitalism* (Boston: Houghton Mifflin, 1952), p. 80.

14. James M. Landis, *Report on Regulatory Agencies to the President-Elect* (Washington, D.C.: U.S. Government Printing Office, 1960), p. 11.

15. R. Joseph Monsen, Jr., and Mark W. Cannon, *The Makers of Public Policy* (New York: McGraw-Hill, 1965), p. 47.

16. Council of State Governments, *Planning Services for State Governments* (Chicago: Council of State Governments, 1956), p. 27.

17. New York *Times,* March 26, 1958.

18. U.S., *Congressional Quarterly Weekly Report,* March 13, 1965.

19. Lowden Wingo, Jr., "Urban Renewal: Objectives, Analyses and Information Systems," in *Regional Accounts for Policy Decisions,* ed. Werner Z. Hirsch (Baltimore: Johns Hopkins Press, 1965), pp. 7–8.

CHAPTER 1
PLANNERS AND THEIR PROBLEMS

INTRODUCTION

A reviewer of the second edition of this work commented quite accurately that it reflected the concerns and problems besetting the profession in the late 1960s and early 1970s. In a sense this volume updates our afflictions. This is not to suggest that it is a semantic rechristening of old diseases—consumption becoming tuberculosis, the pox renamed syphilis—but there are perennial ailments that carry on from one generation to the next. One of these is the wobbly position of the planning profession, its uncertain status and role in a troubled urban society that seems to listen more carefully to other professions. For this reason there has been a continuing concern with planners, their selection, education, prospects, and career crises.

This first chapter is devoted to these topics. It begins with an overview of the context of global problems within which planners are (and have been) assigned a minor role. It continues with an exploration of career dilemmas which nag at the planners' conscience. And it concludes with an exploration of one of the root causes of career vexation, the capture of professional planning education by nonprofessional academics.

The sections in this chapter entitled "Beyond Land Use There Be Dragons" (originally entitled "There's More to This Job Than Coloring Maps"), "The Conscience of the Planner," and "Why Can't Johnny Plan?" (which has been revised) are reprinted with permission from *Planning*, the magazine of the American Society of Planning Officials, 1313 E. 60 St., Chicago, Ill., 60637.

BEYOND LAND USE THERE BE DRAGONS

As a profession, planning has never strayed far from its land use beginnings. During the last generation there have been flurries of interest in economic development, the poor, transportation and communications, and, more recently, the environment and energy. But most planners continue to cultivate their garden: land use planning.

In the future, however, it may be necessary for planners to come out of their relative isolation into the larger world. For there are issues of national (and even international) scope which affect what planners do, but which they rarely take into account. Perhaps it is time for planners to stop concentrating on land use and consider other, larger problems.

Planners and their clients know well enough that land use planning has not been an unalloyed history of triumphs. Indeed, accusations that the profession has been the willing, learned servant of entrenched privilege have been uncomfortably close to the mark. It is true enough that very few planners are outright thieves, in a nation where real estate is the primary generator of millionaires: nevertheless, it can be argued that the profession's standard of social ethics has been considerably lower than its personal incorruptibility. Only the tiniest handful of planners have been bribed outright. Perhaps there was no need to step outside the law. It is possible that planners in sensitive positions earned their salary by justifying and validating the things that others had to be bought to do. Like lawyers, planners have been ready tools for the price of their salary or consulting fee: like lawyers, planners are retained to do a client's bidding. But, unlike lawyers, planners need no elaborate rationale to the effect that all clients deserve professional help. In a real sense, the professional planner sees himself as judge, advocate, and jury.

Much of the public breast beating and private job jumping of planners in recent years stems from the belief that most planners prefer to see themselves as something more than narrow professionals. The planner views himself as guardian of the public interest, closer perhaps to the teacher or social worker than to the attorney.

In this context, there is no difficulty in finding the world in his back yard. Any small suburban town fighting to retain low-density zoning offers a microcosm of the problems and complexities confronting an urban nation: How much change and what types of change should be permitted without injuring the fabric of the community? How should conservation and environmental protection be weighed in relation to housing needs and economic growth? How much resistance to development is racial bigotry and class prejudice and how much is legitimate concern for real or perceived danger? How can widely differing life-styles be accommodated?

In the small world as in the great, choices are simple enough for the simple-minded. Both those who view the struggle for suburban zoning as an exercise in opening up opportunities for the hard-working poor against barriers erected by vicious, narrow-minded fat cats, and their opponents, who see the battle as a heroic defense of America's dwindling number of safe and decent neighborhoods (sans muggers, school dropouts, and welfare cases), find life a matter of clear-cut alternatives: light against darkness, good against evil, us against the crazies. For the planner cursed with binocular vision, land use decisions are not that easy. The choices range from bad to worse to worst. The operative word is trade-off. Only the fierce partisan can afford to ignore the desperate complexities of people, plans, causes, actions, and consequences.

Clearly, the task of becoming sensitized to the broader implications of land use planning or larger issues is vexatious. Yet there is every reason to believe that new perspectives are in order. Along with the rest of the nation, planners are faced with painful choices in a difficult era, an American version of a Time of Troubles.

It has been said that crises have a half-life of nine days to nine months. In the last decade, poverty, race, the environment, crime, and the energy squeeze arrived, agitated the nation, and faded into the background. This does not mean that anything has been resolved. On the contrary, it is as if a man afflicted with arthritis were to discover that he also suffers from colitis, dropsy, dyspepsia, and Parkinson's disease, but the really bad news is that his heart may go at any moment. Planners have been engaged on some of these fronts. But the big issues, such as inflation, national economic policy, and federal taxation, are left to other professionals, especially the ubiquitous lawyer-politicians. Therein lies the first major dilemma of the planner and the planning profession: Should planners embrace economics and inject national economic planning into our academic curricula and professional efforts?

Robin Hood Is Alive and Well

Consider the following facts: For the past generation planners have based their thinking and their decisions on the Cornucopia Theory—that America is rich and getting richer and that all we need is a reordering of priorities. Therefore, the United States need not engage in nasty class struggle: the government need not play Robin Hood, taking from the rich to help the poor.

In fact, the United States has always done it the other way: co-opting, buying off, or subsidizing the wealthy in return for their contribution to public purposes—manufacturing armaments, building public works, or operating Job Corps camps. Today, the situation is even worse: the Horn of Plenty has run out. Growth is minute, resources are finite and costly, prices manipulable and always higher. The gap between aspirations and income is growing wider, and the people in charge of the economy do not seem to know what to do. The mood seems defensive: pull the wagons in a circle, keep the Indians out.

This suggests a number of things. First, planners must be remarkably persuasive if they are to claim an increasing share of public expenditures or even to hold their own. Second, there is more need to experiment with techniques such as the transfer of development rights that do not require public funds to achieve public purposes. Third, basic reforms are in order for the sake of amelioration, including serious efforts at income redistribution through tax reform, job creation programs, and national health insurance. Fourth, and equally important, is the need for fundamental structural reorganization to improve morale, efficiency, and equality.

One area badly in need of reorganization is the land use system. In the past, planners have used their talents to enrich developers as a means of achieving such public goals as generating new housing, industry, and commercial space. We probably can assume that most land will remain in private ownership and that future development will not be very different from what it has been in the past. Nevertheless, an age of scarcities and changing demographic patterns resurrects the ghost of Henry George. Urban development is increasingly nodal—garden apartments, townhouses, and PUDs* —reflecting higher site and infrastructure costs, smaller families, and energy and transportation pressures. The detached single-family home, like live-in maids, is becoming an expensive luxury.

In an optimistic era, the creation of instant real estate millionaires is not particularly offensive. When money is tight and a dab of multifamily orange on a land use map means riches for a happy few, however, there is always a suspicion of favoritism or granting of undeserved rewards. This poses something of a moral dilemma: How much should private entrepreneurs profit at public expense when most people are facing harder times? This raises a new version of Henry's Georgian question: How can a substantial proportion of such conferred gains be recaptured by the public without obliterating developer initiative? Shouldn't there be an analogy to the recapture of excessive profits made in wartime military production, whereby developer gains accruing from permission to build at very high densities should be subject to built-in government partnership?

The discussion so far has concerned the planner's responsibilities and opportunities in his traditional bailiwick, municipal land use planning. At the national level a much more profound issue of priorities, allocations, and growth policy confronts the profession. Since the national economy is not growing much now and may not be growing much in the future, there is a great need for planning at the national level to strike a balance between develop-

---

*Planned unit developments. These are large subdivisions in which shopping and service facilities have been planned and constructed to accompany and serve residents.

ment, resource conservation, incomes and national budget policy, and international economic relations. The economists and the political leadership are quarreling and groping for answers. It is time that planners express informed opinions rather than motherhood pomposities on the need for a national land use policy and more housing for the poor. We need a planning voice, a professional posture in national economic policy. Simply stated, we as a profession must do what we can to head off another major depression.

Progress Through Deportation?

Based on recent vital statistics, there is good news from the maternity ward. Lower birth rates mean less school construction, less juvenile crime, less pressure on resources, less danger of wall-to-wall people. Given another few years of lower-than-replacement birth rates, particularly among the educated and affluent, we will be due for sermons and exhortations concerning Sodom, hedonism, the fall of Rome, selfishness, the danger of being heavily outnumbered by the Chinese, and the hazards of a nation dominated by old people and retardates. Despite such Shockley treatment, the trend toward personalism—late marriage, few (if any) children—seems likely to continue if only because the cost of supporting a child from conception through college is over $100,000 and climbing fast. Without the need for family farm helpers or mom-and-pop retail labor, children are all expense (minus a pitiful IRS deduction). Hence we can expect more high-density apartments, more singles and sunset-years villages, more empty schools, more politicized gays. Planners will be required to do their bit to make parenthood less wearing: Oscar Newmanish safe play and residential areas; more compact, low-rise development for families; better sound control.

So far, so good. The dilemma comes with the foreigners. The ecologists' dire predictions of an age of famine by the mid-1970s seem all too accurate. One reason for the poverty and economic stagnation in developing nations, where children are the only form of social security and sons are considered proof of virility, is their inability or unwillingness to reduce birth rates. With its dwindling birth rate, the United States represents an increasingly enticing target to the hungry, particularly because America's domestic supply of labor for hard, low-paying jobs is drying up. For example, Mexico, with only one-fifth the U. S. population, is increasing at a rate three times faster than the United States. The same fecundity is present in other parts of Latin America and the Caribbean. These are developing areas from which migration to the United States is not too difficult or expensive and for which there are established urban beachheads to shelter both legal and illegal migrants.

The nation's long history suggests that in good times there is not much resistance to immigration. In bad times, however, the labor unions in particular have demanded an end to the influx of competing, lower-paid foreign workers. And the newcomers, once acclimated and Americanized, are among the first to call for stiffer quotas on immigration—from all nations but their homeland—lest their precarious position on the social and economic ladder be jeopardized.

So, the United States of the 1970s and beyond must answer some tough questions. What debt does the fortunate, industrious ant owe to the unlucky grasshopper? What is the responsibility of the United States to a fast-breeding, starving Third World? What is our obligation to foreigners who suffer, in some measure, because of pro-natalist government policy? What is America's obligation when scarce government funds in some developing nations are allocated to prestige armaments instead of fertilizers? What do we owe to nations with dysfunctional social systems which permit domestic resources and foreign aid to be siphoned off by corrupt officials? And what about innocent children who go hungry because America's food is swapped for high-priced oil?

To carry the problem closer to our doorstep, what should government immigration policy be if jobs are scarce or if adequate housing and services for immigrants cannot be provided reasonably? Suppose (and not so much supposing is necessary here) tens of thousands or hundreds of thousands of illegal immigrants cram themselves and their families into already overcrowded slum apartments. Strict housing and health code enforcement would reduce the supply of available housing for such persons; continuous roundups by the Immigration Service would substantially reduce the financial and social burdens on the cities. Surely such tactics are abhorrent; but, with an estimated 5 to 10 million illegal aliens already in the United States and another million or so slipping across the border each year, when does the American lifeboat start to list? When does a most painful choice become inevitable? And can the planner stand aside from this dreadful tangle of energy, food, people, and political systems?

Face to Face with Big Bureaucracies

Most planners are employed as bureaucrats in weak government agencies. Most are "liberals" in that they support a substantial public sector. They tend to dismiss fulminations against big government as the programmed ravings of reactionaries opposed to federal supercession of what planners see as venal, incompetent, and bigoted state and local governments.

In recent years some of this sentiment has faded away because of a new emphasis on decentralization, advocacy planning, and concern about the social consequences of traditional physical planning. A modest number of planners are now working for citizen groups and poverty agencies or as consultants for poor clients fighting city hall. But the present employment pattern does not adequately mirror the change in outlook of the profession. Disenchantment with much of the urban renewal program is at least a decade old; mistrust of the typical torpid, sclerotic planning agency is widespread. The mere mention of HUD in a gathering of planners is likely to trigger a spirited exchange of horror stories.

Yet many in the profession have missed the larger significance of the national mood. Like many liberals, they have failed to grasp the message—a deep, quasi-populist revulsion against bigness and most particularly against being pushed around by government agencies.

In its simpler, professional manifestations, the trend toward miniaturization is likely to alter the job picture, with more planners working outside conventional agencies. The polite, gentlemanly crust of professional courtesy will be pierced, as technical warfare erupts between factions of experts. It has been, after all, many years since master plans were accepted as holy writ. Once the schismatics begin to leave the mother church, sectarianism becomes a way of life.

A step or two beyond decentralization are other enticing counters to arrogant bigness. Ombudsmen, knowledgeable newsmen, Nader investigators, special commissions—all are peering at, poring over, criticizing, and casting doubt on the work of planners. Would 20 percent of your staff really be missed? they ask. Justify your agency, they command.

A pronounced distaste for sheer size is not the only reason for the distrust of big government agencies. City bureaucracies have gotten out of hand. In many cities, salaries, fringe benefits, and pensions are higher than in the private sector. The quality of services is often unsatisfactory; agencies are inert and unresponsive; and public employee unions stand ready to bring cities to their knees to extort more for less. Too many cities are served by fossilized agencies, run by and for their employees, insulated from outside criticism, and barely tolerant of their clients.

There is another, possibly even more serious, consideration. While the federal payroll has remained stable in the past decade, state and municipal employment has bulged enormously, particularly in the schools and in other service agencies, such as sanitation and police. During every business recession there is a frantic rush to join the government service. Nearly one of every five persons in the nation's nonagricultural work force is a government employee; in some cities the proportion is one in three. (In fact, counting welfare clients, some cities have a third or more of their total population living directly on government checks.) Perhaps the tip-off to the danger ahead occurred in the 1960s, when right-wing Republicans stopped attacking a favorite bugaboo, "payrollers" fattening on the public purse. When the most benighted political candidate talks about "dedicated men and women in the public service" because there are too many votes to be lost by spouting that old-time religion, there is a clear sign that things are getting out of control.

So we have a dilemma. Planners are probably more aware of the need for muncipal reform than other professionals, if only because so many hopes for city stability and upgrading have been shattered by the almost total inability to deal with ossified police or school bureaucracies. There is a large and growing literature of disillusion: exposés of city school systems, police departments, auditors' offices, transit and sanitation departments, welfare agencies. The potholes in the streets are the visible manifestation of more serious troubles. The problem is that it is virtually impossible to terminate agencies or civil service staff for cause. Only the cosmetic layer at the top can be replaced.

Many planners have been active in struggles for urban decentralization, advocacy planning, and planning with people. Yet most planners are not entirely comfortable with the realization that governmental miniaturization, the dismantling of existing agencies, and the creation of bypasses to the bureaucracies will require a head-on confrontation with the municipal labor unions and the bureaucrats. As government employees themselves, as political liberals, as pleasant people who prefer to avoid vicious battles, planners are reluctant to join in close combat to overturn, split up, or create alternatives to the big agencies. There are those who fear the alternative: little, homogeneous constituencies, petty kleptocracies, and mini-police states—more tyrannical, more corrupt, more bungling, and more bigoted than existing agencies and governments. They point out that being groined by a spiteful pygmy is equally as painful as being stepped on by a giant. But as professionals who have a special stake in making government viable, planners do not have much choice in the matter, despite the very real dangers.

Some planners, such as consultants or professors in quiet universities, can postpone confronting the issue. But city planners and planners as a profession with a stake in the cities must face up to the big agencies. Indeed, it is more than likely that the issue cannot be deferred: by the 1980s the United States may be emulating Uruguay, where so large a porportion of the working population is employed in unmanageable, unproductive, unresponsive, government agencies that the process is virtually irreversible. Nothing, including attempts at reform through the ballot box and bombs, seems to be effective. In any event, as a profession whose efforts rest on the assumption that urban government works tolerably well, planners also have a duty to confront the bureaucracies which ensure that cities work very badly.

Confronted with such burdensome problems, planners will undoubtedly be tempted to evade, postpone, deny, obfuscate, or counterattack. In America, as elsewhere, premature Cassandras are never taken seriously. Only when crisis strikes do we act. So it was (and is) with the ecologists warning of famine, depletion, pollution, and poisoning. But, if we believe in planning principles —rationality, serious investigation, objective presentation of alternatives, and delineation of probable consequences—our approach will be different. Moreover, there is a built-in obligation that goes with the territory: planners are professionally duty bound to act as an early warning system.

What does this mean for planners in terms of the three principal dilemmas identified here: the future of the national economy, immigration policy, and municipal government? Since planners are not a monolithic group, it is useful by way of clarification to discuss these problems within the context of their four actual roles. These are working professional, member of a professional association, public educator, and informed citizen.

As working professionals, our involvement with national economic policy is likely to remain limited. As the money runs short, most planners will grumble and make do, arguing that planning, housing, and land use deserve more than they are getting. Under any circumstances, it is inconceivable that more than a handful of working planners will be in a position to serve as high-level advisers on monetary policy, energy programming, foreign trade, minimum wages, or price controls. On the other hand, there is no reason why planners as a profession, acting through professional associations, cannot take a responsible stand on these and related issues. This means doing some homework in unaccustomed areas, broadening the scope of university planning curricula, and enlarging the content of professional conferences—in short, returning to the breadth of perspective characteristic of part of the profession during the New Deal 1930s. Moreover, there is no reason for trepidation. Economists and businessmen are painfully, openly wallowing in ignorance and uncertainty. Planners can keep these poor chaps company, perhaps adding new insights. This is also a task for the planner in his role of informed citizen, acting, one would hope, as a spirited participant in the political process.

The task is much the same with respect to national immigration policy. There is one major difference, however. This field has not been staked out by the equivalent of the economics profession, replete with arcane mathematics, esoteric discussions of cyclical theory, bloc convertibility, and balance of payments. In fact, the ebb and flow of people is a highly complex phenomenon that traditionally is discussed in simple, understandable terms. It is perfectly suited for energetic intervention by planners. Since much of what passes for political discussion in this area has been a blend of emotive nativism, atavism, and misinformation, rational discussion would constitute a refreshing change. Once that discussion has begun, planners should not be timid about making their collective opinions known. This advocacy posture would be in line with the precedent established by strong professional planning association resolutions on civil rights and the Vietnam war.

The daily professional duties of a substantial number of planners bring them into contact with the immigration problem. To varying degrees, they can act directly on the scale and character of immigration into their community by their influence on housing and health codes, land use programs, municipal economic development, and tax policy. There is no ducking this problem even if we wish to do so.

Finally, there is a great need for informed planners to pursue their role as public educators. This requires amplification. More than most professionals, planners are continually engaged in the process of oral and written persuasion, in conjunction with colleagues, planning boards, civic associations, the media, interest groups, engineers, lawyers, and the general public. In a real sense, planners spend much of their working day conducting adult education programs. Planners also conduct classes for civic and professional groups, have speaking engagements, conduct interviews, write articles and speeches, and serve on advisory commissions and task forces. In these latter activities the planner-educator carries the expert's word to audiences with limited technical background.

There is another aspect to education. In view of the lack of interest of most planners in running for significant political office and the singular lack of success of the few who have made the attempt, planners might try another tack. Perhaps the attempt of one or two planning schools to train *eminences grises* to serve as high-level policy advisers will bear fruit. Possibly we can recognize an even greater opportunity by injecting planning courses into law-school curricula to exert some influence over the next generation of politicians.

Although planners are marginal actors in national economic policy, they have a more direct role in municipal agencies and are deeply involved in the advocacy and decentralization movement. But, as was suggested earlier, there is some distance to go before planners—as a profession, in their associations, and in their roles as public educators and active citizens—will be ready to take a professional stand on this issue.

These are what I believe to be some of the major problems being overlooked by the planning profession. They pose dilemmas which, in my opinion, place greater demand on the planner, specifically, involvement in aspects of national policy on a scale and direction unknown since the 1930s. The planner's choice is made even more agonizing by the inevitable confrontation with traditional loyalties and constituencies—fellow municipal employees, advocates of open immigration, and proponents of unrestricted food and energy policies. But because alternatives are difficult does not mean they can be avoided. They can only be postponed. It is now time for open discussion of the issues.

THE CONSCIENCE OF THE PLANNER

In recent years much of the blame for the decay of the cities and the sprawl of the suburbs has fallen on the planning profession. In a way, this attention is flattering. After all, there are only about 15,000 professional planners in the nation—less than 50 percent of the number of architects and only five percent of the number of doctors and lawyers. They earn only 60 percent as much as lawyers and half as much as doctors. Planners have been neglected in serious fiction and the mass media. Where are the novels or television series illustrating the drama of zoning referrals, the romance of subdivision control, or the comic relief of floor-area ratios?

Planners have by no means closed ranks against outside critics. In fact, planners are their own severest and most persistent critics. The self-flagellation which characterized the profession in the latter part of the 1960s was attributable in large measure to the planners' role in the wholesale clearance of slums for urban renewal and highways. This era was the planning profession's Vietnam. We have never quite recovered the certainty, the tendency toward ex-cathedra prescriptions (concealing vast areas of ignorance) that was ours in the fifties. The profession is racked by doubts concerning its legitimacy, its honesty, its mission, and its effectiveness. For the sake of convenience, these moral dilemmas can be grouped under five main headings.

The Little Tin Box. From time to time a planner surfaces in news stories as a party to land fraud or as an influence-peddling defendant in a zoning scandal. Planners have taken some comfort from the fact that such reported cases are rare. But there is more to the story than meets the press. Certain consulting firms are notorious for their success in operating in corrupt environments. Outright bribery, kickbacks, phony subcontracts, dummy partners, tips, and laundered fees are all part of the game.

This business of sticky fingers is not as simple as it may appear, however. It is not uncommon for many, if not most, employees of consulting firms to be unaware of the financial calisthenics taking place in the upper echelons. Indeed, it is common practice to seal off the fixers and bag men from the rest of the firm; partners and senior staff are careful to avoid any direct knowledge of the shady side of the street, so that they can plead ignorance in the event of legal action. Under these circumstances, morality is often divorced from efficiency; and staff planners, unaware of the sordid details of contract procurement, can perform their duties as competent professionals.

So far as the big money is concerned, however, most planners are no closer than rumor and suspicion; they lack the opportunity. Like the good folk of Mark Twain's Hadleyburg, most planners are honest because no one has offered them an alternative. Since critical decisions are made outside their jurisdiction, they are rarely considered worth corrupting. In money, as in sex, the appearance of virtue may be due to a lack of good offer.

Most planners have to settle for lesser spoils—typing paper, colored pencils, paper clips, personal calls on the office phone, and minor expense padding. This is kid stuff. So is goofing off on the job, occupying space, drawing a salary but doing nothing productive. Some planners may comfort themselves with the notion that they are learning their trade. But much of this is self-delusion and comforting rationalization. Like the rest of the army of useless public and private bureaucrats, far too many planners are engaged in this most costly game.

Why does a professional engage in conduct that even by charitable standards is demeaning in its vacuous triviality and utter waste? To be sure, hard times may be partly responsible: even a dull job is better than no job. And there are civil service benefits, security, on-the-job socializing, generous vacations and sick leaves and pensions. But there are still a horrifying number of presumably professional planners clinging year after deadly year to positions that, except for salary, are one step above work relief.

The Bully Boys. Some planners are shoved around by supervisors they heartily dislike and fear; others linger on in a work environment they detest. Many others are pushed into nasty practices—favors for chosen developers, political shenanigans (including forced contributions to favored candidates), concealment of data and reports embarrassing to big-money operators.

It is possible for planners to mature and ripen (or more accurately, sour) into satraps, responsive to corrupt pressures and given to vicious and tyrannical behavior with their subordinates. There is an excellent reason for rough treatment of junior professionals in agencies whose directors have established cozy working arrangements with the boodlers. Rudeness is an effective way of chastening idealists who want to poke their young, inquisitive noses into important business matters.

There are far too many docile, browbeaten planners working at jobs that hurt both their pride and their conscience. Equally sad is the fact that we have produced our share of obsequious servants to networks of the powerful and corrupt who simultaneously are despicably mean-spirited bullies to their subordinates.

The Benign Cabal. The practice of conferring in private to make plans for the benefit of client-constituencies is a feature of most bureaucracies, including planning agencies. Most planners are aware of the dangers inherent in paternalistic, class-biased, traditional planning and are theoretically and emotionally in favor of broad public participation and informed feedback. In practice, however, their commitment is substantially weakened by political and administrative realities.

As a practical matter, the public has limited time and technical expertise at its disposal. Attempts to secure a wide spectrum of citizen participants usually fail. As a result, citizen participation generally takes on a representative character: trusted volunteers or paid experts represent the interests of the hitherto neglected segments of the population. In contrast, effective mass participation usually occurs only as a negative response to a specific proposal, such as the construction of a highway through a residential neighborhood.

There is always the risk that citizen representatives are virtually self-appointed rather than truly representative. Only 5 percent of the potential voters turn out for certain elections. As a result, citizen participation may turn out to be a dialogue between a handful of ambitious, young activists and the technical staff. Some of the Young Turks may even be co-opted into well-paying establishment jobs. The aged, housewives, children, and the institutionalized population have little voice in planning decisions.

By its very nature, give-and-take with different citizen groups is a time-consuming, frustrating process. A crafty administrator wedded to the status quo can easily restrain attempts at reform and innovation by requiring painstaking checking and rechecking with the various citizen groups and government agencies. In most cases broad citizen participation leads to paralysis and stagnation. Some planners feel that process is more important than product—that participation, even if it means only wheel spinning, is its own reward. Others expect concrete results; and if it means using a significant number of secret, private conferences, they are prepared to let part of their conscience trouble them. They know, too, that the agency that spends its time "participating," not writing reports, may be left at the funding post.

Finally, there is a serious, vexing, and unresolved issue involving potential conflicts between the democratic system and planning decisions. The battle lines are clear. In the mid-1970s many democratically elected political figures faithfully reflect the sentiments of their constituents in their strong resistance to desegregation of any kind. By and large planners support desegregation. Some have deliberately conspired with like-minded lawyers, newspaper reporters, and federal agencies to sabotage and overturn the exclusionary policies of democratically elected public officials. They have, in fact, sought to bypass a public sentiment that obviously reflects a participatory consensus, albeit one that they find unacceptable.

This dilemma seems to impose little strain on the planner's conscience. Apparently many planners view themselves as agents of a larger community. Hence, a lapse from their professed adherence to the principles of participatory democracy is not troublesome when, as in this case, the consequences are considered inappropriate.

Professor Beware, or The Doctor's Dilemma. For many fortunate folk, academia offers one of the most pleasant working environments conceived by man. But even in paradise, there are worms in the apples.

Take the case of the tenured freeloader. Given a light teaching load for the purpose of scholarly research and publishing, he is incapable of either. Even so, the tenured professor has one cheering thought. He is in the education business; and, if he is unable or unwilling to serve at the front, he can train tomorrow's combatants. Depending on his talents, that may be a significant contribution.

Then there are the academic snipers. In the mid-1960s it became fashionable and profitable for academicians to perform autopsies, biopsies, and occasional lobotomies on government reform programs. A number of youngish professors directed their criticism to deficiencies in the public sector rather than the private sector. In the process, they helped to kill off a number of marginal, useless, or counterproductive programs; but they also helped to poison the climate for reform. From the comfort and safety of the academy they not only criticized, maligned, and ridiculed well-meaning, if often inept, government efforts but also soured the prospects for future programs. The upshot is a scholarly contribution to conservative standpattism, reinforcing a fairly widespread public sentiment that government is always wrong and always incompetent.

The snipers seem happy in their work. After a barrage of criticism from a group of unsympathetic academics, one of the nation's outstanding planning directors asked, "Am I the enemy?" From their viewpoint, perhaps he was.

Hired guns are another type. A lot of dyed-in-the-wool academics who have never worked for a planning agency are in great demand from developers and lawyers skilled in busting zoning laws. For sizable fees they lend their academic prestige to all sorts of proposals, often after only cursory study of local planning needs and objectives.

This illustrates a basic difference between the legal and planning professions. Most lawyers see themselves as clinicians selling their talents to any client who can pay their fee. Planning faculty or planning consultants who do this are regarded as conscienceless guns for hire. This is another example of the planner's tendency to be judge and jury as well as advocate. The legal profession applauds a brilliant performance in the service of a shoddy client. In contrast, the planning profession castigates such efforts as pandering to greedy developers.

Political Gamesmanship. Some planners appreciate the intimate relationship between planning and politics. But many planners, aware only of the surface outcroppings of the political landscape, view political activity as an ecology of friendly games—preparation of reasoned policy statements, polite calls on legislators, adoption of high-minded resolutions, financing full-page newspaper advertisements. They dismiss the active subterranean movement as either worthless or demeaning.

If it can be assumed that political influence rests primarily on the ability to muster votes or money, planning ranks far, far behind such professions as medicine, law, or education. Since the kind of high-minded pageantry in which the profession is now engaged has not worked, other methods—coalition building, infiltration, or bureaucratic maneuvering—are worth trying. They all seem promising until one examines their implications.

Fashioning effective coalitions is a task calling for considerable energy, shrewdness, tolerance, patience, and a willingness to compromise. The most politicized members of the profession, however, are hot-blooded, dogmatic sectarians who are convinced that compromise is tantamount to selling out. They do not find it easy to work with a variety of groups with differing viewpoints, and they are constantly on the lookout for signs of backsliding on the part of their colleagues. On balance, it is likely that the planning profession's role in political coalitions is likely to be that of endorser and validator, adding a professional imprimatur to a reform candidate who has already marshaled his resources elsewhere.

Planners do not seem to be much better at infiltrating the inner temples of power. In the first place, planners are perpetually astonished by the mendacious, venal, rough-and-tumble tactics of harder-working, ruthless, public administration or business types slavishly devoted to serving their masters. The planner who breaks through to the inner circle is likely soon to become indistinguishable from his bright, tense colleagues. For a time, he may feel a few twinges of conscience as he jettisons some of his past values and beliefs in favor of the criteria of political realism that now govern his actions, but planners must exhibit the same degree of adaptability as other staff if they are to survive.

If he is indeed one of the lucky survivors, he may be awarded with an upper-echelon appointment in a planning agency. He then discovers that he has been promoted into a supergrade target for invective, misrepresentation, and vilification. His fate hangs on the fortunes of his political sponsor, and he may be sacrificed as a liability.

Even if he lacks outstanding ability, all is not lost for the upper-level planner. Should there develop a consensus that the planning agency must be retained but must not pose a threat to the power structure, then there is a very good chance that an impressive-looking but not very aggressive planner may be used as a kind of front man. He serves as a screen to hide the real decision making. Bland, solemn, and pompous—it helps if he is bald or at least graying —he dignifies conferences with his persona, drawing a high salary for his services.

And so we come to the final twist of the ethical pretzel. Like the young and useless occupant of a desk and title, there are some in the profession whose consciences do (or should) trouble them, not because of peculation but because their talents have grown rusty from disuse in a planning job that calls for the presence of ectoplasm rather than substantive effort. If there is contempt for thieves, there might also be a modicum of sympathy for the pathetic molluscs who have thrown their professional lives away for tenure, salary, and pension.

This examination of the state of the planner's conscience suggests that in outlook planners are perhaps closer to ministers and social workers than lawyers or businessmen. That the profession is its own severest critic is a compliment to both its principles and the quality of the people it attracts. But how is the profession to grapple with the restless stirrings of ethical disquiet? Surely laceration in print is not the answer, even if the pummeling is performed by academic moralists, quick to consign their colleagues to the thumbscrew, rack, and stake. We need a better method.

One possibility is the equivalent of the religious retreat, a prolonged change of scene, a year or so of sabbatical to permit the kind of perspective and understanding that can only be achieved through a substantial period of service in someone else's shoes.

Meanwhile a great debate on the proper role and ethical function of planners can continue.

Foremost among the topics for debate is the role of the planner within the broad sweep of economic, social, and technological convulsions that have ripped the urban landscape to shreds. In some respects planners are akin to social workers, restricted to tinkering with symptoms rather than causes. They are not attracted to pure scholarship as a career. They want to help shape urban patterns and trends; are frustrated by their lack of influence; and, pinched by conscience, often consider dropping out in favor of a career (like law) that seems to promise a closer relationship between energy input and tangible output.

Yet, despite the unquenchable optimism of many planners and the purblindness or callousness of others, there is a nagging, persistent, and fundamental question: Is planning in the United States irrelevant? Are we no more than marginal professionals, spear carriers in the urban drama, fit—"to swell a progress, start a scene or two . . . an easy tool, deferential, glad to be of use, politic, cautious, and meticulous. Full of high sentence but a bit obtuse; at times, indeed, almost ridiculous "?

Did T. S. Eliot know any planners?

WHY CAN'T JOHNNY PLAN?

The trouble with America's graduate schools of planning is that they are not teaching young people to be planners. This is not the same as saying that the curricula are "irrelevant," to repeat that much-overused phrase from the 1960s. The schools seem to be going out of their way to be with it. No, I am not talking about the focus of professional education. I am saying that planning-school graduates have not been given sufficient technical training of any type to make them employable in today's tight job market.

Much of the blame for that failure must fall on the planning-school faculties. They cannot teach planning because they have not spent enough time in the real world of planning agencies and consulting firms. They have given their energies to earning Ph. D.'s and writing scholarly tomes, not drafting and implementing zoning ordinances. If they cannot teach their students how to do the practical work of a planner, it is because they have never been real planners themselves.

A quick look at the trends in planning education shows how this remarkable situation has come about. Twenty years ago only the rare planning-school graduate could have complained of having insufficient training in practical work. Graduate programs were run by land use planners, most of them without Ph. D.'s, but possessing extensive agency and consulting experience. Like their fellows in architecture, the planning faculty operated an extensive consulting practice, including long-term, comprehensive planning contracts with nearby communities. To help churn the work out, the faculty hired students to take care of the mundane parts of the job.

Even in this golden era, there were problems. In many cases the planning departments were simply grafted on to architecture schools. They became warped or stunted as a result. Many of the faculty were resistant, even hostile, to change. As the immutability of the Eisenhower years yielded to the rapid change of the early 1960s, the sentiment grew that planning curricula—and the Old Guard who devised them—were too rigid and narrow-minded. The verdict came down that many of the Old Guard had to be replaced. The new troops were a different breed.

The first assault of doctorate-bearing academics into the planning schools was made by technocrats whose first love was mathematics. They thought of planning in terms of measurements, planimetrics, models, and regional science. They filled the technical literature with formulas and charts—indeed, for years the *Journal of the American Institute of Planners* looked more like a math text than a planning journal.

Then came the Great Society, Model Cities, and the racial upheavals of the 1960s, all of which had a profound effect on planning education. Rallying round the banner of "relevance," students demanded a share in departmental governance and a focus on the planner's role as a "change agent" in the service of oppressed minorities. As curricula shifted toward the problems of race, poverty, and other social concerns, university planning departments began to draw heavily on a second wave of academics from other disciplines, particularly political science, sociology, economics, and the law.

This is not to suggest that this changeover in faculty was universal. Some smaller planning departments, particularly those linked to schools of architecture, virtually ignored the new wave. Others made token changes by adding a course or two in "hot" areas. But most departments were thoroughly altered in character. In a few instances the emphasis on the technocratic and social change role was so profound that these newly hatched planning departments never bothered to develop a serious land use component.

The new breed of faculty was not only different, it was antagonistic. For the most part these young faculty possessed Ph. D.'s. Moreover, there was a deep sense that the old gang were abysmal failures, ignorant of math, lackeys of the establishment, blind to the nation's social problems, and not very bright. True, the Old Guard had published a great deal, but these were simple-minded technical reports for communities, just one step above a cookbook in profundity.

None of this is meant to suggest that the new regimes were barren of accomplishment. In contrast to the seat-of-the-pants operations of the Old Guard, the academics helped to provide a solid base of research and theory capable of being transmitted to students and working professionals. What was missing was a base of planning practice.

Hopes that government programs and private foundations would create a permanent market for the new breed of planning change agents proved overly sanguine. As a result, academically oriented faculty found themselves in the anomalous position of attempting to train planning students in skills they were not really prepared to teach for service in agencies they held in low esteem.

The capture of planning schools by the academics led to a growing mandarinism in planning education. This is a reference, of course, to the civil-servant class of nineteenth-century China. These elite workers were masters at calligraphy and knew all the classics, but they were totally ignorant of industrial arts or weaponry. They were bright people who possessed none of the skills or knowledge needed to prevent China from being taken over by foreigners.

The academic mandarins also live in a closed world not unlike that of nineteenth-century China. They have developed a careful pecking order, an impenetrable jargon, and an all-around aloofness, not to say arrogance, toward real-world practitioners. They live, if not in an ivory tower, in a kind of hothouse, visible to the outside world, yet insulated from it. The mandarins have chosen a world where they can flourish without any outside interference.

But in the larger academic universe, planning departments occupy a lowly position. The reason is simple: the loyalties of the new breed lie with the academic departments from which they received their Ph. D.'s. They share the view that planning is an ersatz discipline like unto home economics rather than economics, an Elba on which the sociologist, economist, political scientist, or lawyer is condemned to live in exile until a triumphant book or a stroke of luck will enable him to return to the real academic world. Planning departments are in fact full of people who dream of returning to home base at some prestigious—that is, nonplanning—department. They yearn to play for the Yankees, but are stuck for now with the Wichita farm club.

The domination by mandarins has had a profound impact on professional training in planning departments. To begin with, unlike other professional schools, many planning department faculties are composed of people who have not missed an academic step from kindergarten through the doctorate. Certainly there is no hint of any substantial field experience or even much sympathy with those who possess it. Taking two to five years away from one's academic career line for the purpose of picking up substantive experience with a planning agency is viewed as a form of insanity. Career progress in the academic world depends on academic credentials, degrees, and publications, not one's success in drafting a planning proposal, having it adopted, and supervising its implementation.

What does the mandarin think of planners? Some comments culled over the years from various planning faculty are instructive: "We're training students for dull jobs so we (the faculty) can have interesting jobs." "Cindy is too bright to be a land use planner. I told her she should go on for her Ph. D." "I've met only one planner with real conceptual ability." "Tom is much too good to remain a planner. I've recommended law school." "If you want to teach, stay around and finish your dissertation. A job would only sidetrack you and slow you down."

These are the merest tip of a very large iceberg. What they suggest is that a large proportion of planning faculty have little or no experience as practitioners, despise people who do (including their students who are ostensibly being trained as practitioners), and are incapable of providing usable professional training. It is clear that something has to be done to correct an educational system which is not doing its job.

It is, of course, tempting to do nothing. Students do learn, if not as much as they should, enough to go on learning. Often the first year or two on the job is spent in picking up material that should have been included in the curriculum. But details are not really important. The purpose of law school, for example, is to teach bright young people to think like lawyers, to know how to look things up, and to marshal a line of argument in an organized, convincing fashion. How much can be crammed into a handful of courses? No law firm is complete without a tax specialist or two who learned the trade with only a few law school courses as a foundation, and the same holds true for other specialties like maritime law, international law, labor law, and so forth.

Assuming that planning students are as intelligent on the average as law students, how are they trained to think? Is there the kind of rigorous preparation for careers that most law schools offer? It is precisely this, I submit, that constitutes the problem.

One can discount the complaints that are traditional in many professions to the effect that the new breed of graduate is overpaid, spoiled, lazy, and arrogant. The refraction of memory serves to distort the past as well as the present, and middle-aged planners are as prone to swap hard times stories as other professionals. More attention, however, must be paid to specific charges relating to the lack of immediate professional capacity. Whereas a typical law school graduate can be counted on to do serious research and to prepare a near-professional brief suitable for litigation, all too often planning school graduates are incapable of turning out work of a professional caliber. By this I mean well organized memoranda and research relevant to the needs of planning agencies.

Why this deficiency? We can start by examining the curriculum and faculty. A student can learn all there is to learn from a course that covers the political spectrum from Marz to Marcuse and can develop skills in manipulating data, yet when presenting himself (or herself) to an employer, he may be quite useless for a period of a few months to a year. The reason is simple: the planning student is not taught to think like a professional planner because he is not taught by planning professionals. Moreover he is taught by academics who have a very low opinion of the day-to-day work that most planners do.

Given this state of affairs, what is the planning graduate fit for? From the agency standpoint he is a junior trainee, an intelligent and quick learner no doubt, but nevertheless an apprentice. He must be given a crash course in reality: agencies, planners, politics, budgets, the art of persuading citizenry and other professionals, and dealing with the press. Equally important, he must develop a sense of patience, discretion, and the capacity for sustained bureaucratic effort.

If the planner is not a quick learner and shares the essentially negative attitudes of his faculty toward the profession, the results can be most unpleasant. The planning graduate who carries a chip on his shoulder and whose principal skill is in devising a social critique from computer esoterica is not easily employable without a severe wrench.

In effect, we are witnessing an unusual, perhaps unique, example of controlled professional schizophrenia in a field where graduates are taught by many faculty members alienated from professional practice. The planning student is therefore confronted with the choice of lingering, perhaps permanently, in academe if he can qualify for the Ph.D.-faculty route, or else learning the ABCs of practical planning on the job, putting aside the bulk of his classroom knowledge in the process of adjustment.

Mandarins in Action

To say that academics have a low opinion of practitioners is not to say that they will not work for them as consultants, for pay. Based on these confrontations and judging by various field and university activities of the professors, in some instances taking on academic mandarins may be akin to inheriting a serious, albeit nonfatal, disease. One can anticipate adding to agency staff, depending on the luck of the draw, one or more of the following:

The Wallflower Critics. These are academics who would like very much to work as consultants but who, from the agency standpoint, have no usable skills. Consequently they do all their consulting for foundations or other nonagency purveyors of support. Their research topics are often scathing critiques of agency programs as incompetent, fraudulent, and, depending on their political persuasion, as con jobs on the poor or the taxpayer. Having one or more of these professors on one's staff as consultants may be equivalent to sitting on a porcupine. Many fit into the category of academic sniper discussed earlier in this chapter.

The Morale Builder. There are academics who are demonstrably delighted and astonished to find intelligence in unexpected places like government agencies. They spend much of their time asking staff the classic cathouse question —What's a nice, bright person like you doing in a place like this? The implication is that the employee has made a pact with the Prince of Dullness to sell talents and soul in return for a career of crass mediocrity—on your staff. One or two rounds of staff visitations tend to lead to frustration, gloom, and resignations.

The Academic Miracle. This is a person of minor discernible talents. Some are triple-threat nonentities at research, teaching, and administration; many fall into the category of tenured freeloaders, since they occupy space in academia without performing useful labors and may be counted on to do the same for you. Their chief career function is to serve the same exemplary role as a dull-witted Caucasian in a ghetto school, that is, visible evidence that honkies can be more stupid than deprived minorities.

The Academic Blabbermouth (A). A certain amount of confidentiality and reliance on trust is built into the world of agencies and bureaucratic politics. Among academic mandarins, however, there is every incentive to publish a learned work naming names, dates, and places, vilifying your hosts. If there is something to be said on behalf of the scholarly blackguard, it is that he is a bit slow. A one-year delay in publishing in an academic journal is fairly common, and a two- or three-year publishing time for a book is the norm. The dust may long since have settled by the time the text appears, and one can live with largely unread insults in obscure publications.

The Academic Blabbermouth (B). Much more dangerous is the tattletale intriguer and panic monger who talks and tells to the staff, to other agencies, and to the press. The danger signal is usually a flow of malicious, unsolicited confidences detailing scandals relating to colleagues past and present. One of life's traumas is to observe an academic adder-tongue in a lengthy and animated telephone conversation, voice lowered to a confidential level as you approach, eyes sly and shifty. A growing apprehensiveness is later confirmed; on the other end of the telephone was an experienced news reporter skillfully milking the professorial fangs for a witch's brew compounded of naiveté, envy, and malice.

Eminence Grise, or Richelieu on a Bad Day. A few academics, more eloquent and possessed of more influential friends than their academic colleagues, have darted in and out of high-level commissions and delivered themselves of policy advice which, when followed, has usually resulted in bleeding ulcers. To the advice taker it has been suggested that blood is the consequence of intelligence applied without wisdom even when the Best and Brightest are involved in the process. In a number of remarkable cases the advice givers have shifted their views in an extraordinary fashion, but they have two admirable traits: they are always impressively glib, and they are always absolutely positive that this latest model or recommendation is It. Given this temperament and their isolation from the implementation process, such persons never admit to culpability, confess to failure, or admit error; they give ulcers but do not get them. On numerous occasions they have written research papers dissecting the disasters for which they themselves were partly or largely to blame—without once owning up to their share in the wreckage. In brief, if one adds them to one's staff, it is always critically important to remember that this breed of academic—eloquent, thoughtful, sincere—for some reason is almost always wrong in assessing the consequences of policy recommendations. The only consolation (as one surveys the disaster) is to reflect that at least no one was killed because they were asked for advice on foreign affairs.

The Super Specialist. Some advanced academic specimens seem to have mislaid their English and picked up an incomprehensible language of systems, mathematical symbols, and esoteric patter that does not register with most mortals. Surprised that any agency official can function without a working knowledge of queuing theory, they cover blackboards with formulas, explaining your job to you, informing the agency as to how it really functions, all in a bewildering display of lines, signs, and numbers, quickly altered and as quickly reformulated. Furthermore, they tend to use mandarin talk—a terminal case of heuristic dysfunctionalism aggravated by paradigmatic regression analysis.

The Ideologue: The Agency as Sexist Racist Capitalist Exploiter. To the academic ideologues, a small but active group, your agency is guilty, by definition, of a multitude of social crimes. At best it can only try humbly and contritely to atone for accumulated past misdeeds. With such a person on the staff there is need for an active array of lawyers, hearing officers, and special committees to disprove allegations. Productive work becomes an incidental item on an agenda increasingly composed of briefs, counterbriefs, hearings, and appeals.

Professor Loyalty. One of the most difficult agency problems arises with the academic who understands and claims to participate in the reciprocal network of mutual obligations that characterizes the political and bureaucratic world. Early on, he outlines his personal ledger, a bank of debits and credits in which the agency is a welcome depositor. There is, however, one minor surprise: When it suits his convenience, his promissory notes are marked, in invisible ink, "good until cashed." This kind of behavior is, of course, far from unknown in the political arena or the agencies. However, in these worlds one does tend to be wary of an accumulating reputation for slipperiness. In academia it does not seem to be a handicap.

The Young General. Occasionally a youthful professor with bold and positive ideas will be given his heart's desire, the opportunity to mold an organization according to his administrative blueprint. There are remarkable successes from a few of these academic Alexanders and Napoleons, but as a rule the results are disastrous. Often it becomes evident that the radical young commander is a closet young fogey. Since he mistrusts older persons and denigrates past experience, he tends to hire even younger, nonthreatening versions of himself. While he condemns himself to painfully reinventing the wheel as he repeats avoidable past errors, he breaks new ground in making mistakes which could never have been conceived of before his coming.

Taken as a whole—if any agency is so minded—the prospects for retreading mandarins may be less for mutual enlightenment than for the importation of a useless nuisance at best and a pestilence at worst.

Prof in the Manger. It is difficult to conceive of a profession which harbors —and honors—as many loonies as academia. So long as a professor possesses paper credentials and meets his classes, he is free to indulge in behavior that borders on the certifiable. Not surprisingly, the most common ailment is a self-fulfilling paranoia which is fed by a realistic appreciation of the fact that universally detested people are, more often than not, detestable. In practical terms, the mentally ailing academic is usually a bulldog for committee work, an indefatigable nurser of grievances, and prone to endless, humorless tirades on woolly subjects. Frequently the burden of the discourse revolves around a specialized interpretation of reality in which only he, Dr. Paranoid, is the possessor of firm ethical principles and is ever alert for violations of academic morality. As a rule these involve hostile behavior on the part of conscienceless enemies who continually try to ignore his abilities, evade his counsel, and otherwise seek to reduce their contacts with him to the barest minimum.

The paranoid professor has two major impacts on the university and governmental agencies. From the viewpoint of government clients or potential clients, he represents an incredible phenomenon—unreal, ridiculous, yet menacing. In their view, there are a few weirdos in government, but sheer survival in most agencies depends on smoothing off most of the rough edges. Full-blown nuts are rare, and it is not surprising to find government reluctant to welcome abrasive aberrants from academia to work with them on their problems. As if this were not sufficient, on his home grounds the paranoid prof plays dog-in-the-manger, doing his best to prevent other academics, often for a period of years, from developing fruitful institutional programs, contracts, and contacts. The net result is to shift, hamper, or destroy the possibility of official university efforts in favor of fragmented or personal ad hoc consulting.

Under these circumstances it would be foolhardy to suggest that terminal mandarinism can be cured by exposure to operating agencies. In far too many cases, an agency head would be foolish to assign substantive responsibility to one of these academics and insane to take their advice.

Hope for Reform?

In most unhappy situations there are two avenues for change: either reform is internal or it comes about as a result of outside pressure. Unfortunately, history indicates that bureaucracies rarely reform themselves, and in the case of academic mandarinates, the tendency for self-perpetuation is as marked as in other bureaucracies. Under the current ground rules, as one established faculty member put it, "You do no one a favor by hiring someone without a doctorate. They'll never get tenure without it." Since unfortunately there is no experiential equivalent currently valid as academic currency, the dilemma is clear. Since most new academic appointments must be made at the lowest assistant professor level and, since a Ph.D. is virtually required, the odds are in favor of mirror-image hiring: The mandarins hire young Ph.D.'s in their late twenties or early thirties—by definition, marinated academics. Hybrids who combine academic credentials with substantial experience are not only rare but are usually long in the tooth with a background of serious family responsibilities and hefty salaries. On this count alone, they are not likely to be suitable candidates for $11,000 to $13,000 assistant professorships.

Occasionally a department chairman will attempt to alter the composition of a faculty by hiring experience without the advanced degree, but he quickly discovers that the days of hiring new faculty in twos and threes ended with the 1960s. In the 1970s he is lucky to add one new appointment every couple of years. And there is no reason to hope that ill health or premature decease will clear away any of his tenured academic deadwood. Like a judgeship, faculty appointment seems to be a passport to longevity. Aside from one or two alcoholics and a few cases of obesity, the vices to which faculty are prone are not conducive to truncated tenure. No one ever perished of pomposity or expired of Byzantine intrigues. Indeed, venom appears to be a preservative ensuring its bearer a long and waspish life. Moreover, a chairman's function is to protect rather than attack his faculty. It seems clear that nothing short of a brutal assault will do for basic reform and that the chairman cannot be expected to perform surgery on his intimates.

In normal circumstances an overhaul is not likely to be forthcoming from deans, provosts, or university presidents. From an administrator's point of view, it does not pay to borrow unnecessary trouble. If the planning department seems to rank reasonably well with its peers, the obvious temptation is to leave well enough alone. Only when there are obvious signs of trouble, like a paralytic, draining civil war (of which there are several examples), do university administrators feel impelled to act.

How about the students? In the 1960s and early 1970s they were seething with discontent, but by the mid-1970s mutiny had been transformed into sullenness. They may feel that they are being had, or have been had, but students are a transitory group, preoccupied with papers and exams, gone in the summers, and disappearing in two years. Furthermore, they depend on faculty for grades and job recommendations. Few students are likely to attempt to alter the composition of planning faculty. And when they try to do so, it is generally in the direction of demands to hire more eloquent alleged change agents—more of the same, only worse.

Who is left? The last card left to play is the profession itself, the practitioners, the agency heads and the consultants who hire (and grumble about) the product. If there is to be reform, it will have to come from this quarter.

Belling the Cat

It is not likely to be easy. Some of the professionals are in awe of planning academics. They may suspect them of patronizing arrogance and charlatanism; they may be absolutely certain that they and what they teach is irrelevant to their needs; but they nevertheless tend to defer to titles, Ph.D.'s, and publications. Others, often some of the more outstanding practitioners, may themselves have their eye on a Ph.D. or a part-time teaching assignment. They, too, are unlikely candidates for a serious critique.

The answer seems to lie in a carefully selected, small blue-ribbon commission, beholden to no one and composed of respected consultants and senior agency officials. Quite possibly they would have to be from out of state, outside the normal web of friendships and favors. Such a panel could operate under the aegis of state AIP chapters with a clear mandate to determine: the extent to which planning departments are governed by academics with little or no practical experience; the manner in which graduates of these schools and their employers are suffering therefrom; and the necessary corrective action. How is such a commission to gain legitimacy and authority? Only by going over the heads of the departments, not to the dean, but to the university president-trustee level. Further, there must be an assurance that a lack of cooperation will have unfortunate, real consequences in terms of a diminished market for graduate placement. Paper tigers get paper responses.

Assuming that the university administration agrees that planning faculties should have practical experience, what is to be done? The primary need is to fashion a new reward-penalty system under which faculty are required to have stipulated amounts of field experience as part of the hiring-promotion-tenure procedure. It should also be one in which the agency official's comments on the quality of the academic's field performance carries weight.

One point should be made clear at the outset: curriculum descriptions are less important than the teachers. It would be tempting to get bogged down in fruitless discussions involving curricular semantics, specifics, and alternatives. Certainly it is true that planners probably need fewer courses in esoteric computer analysis and theory and more in land use, finance, and administration. But the curriculum is a secondary issue because it is internally malleable, depending on the instructors; core requirements and course descriptions are not the critical issue. The critical element is the faculty. Who is it who teaches?

It may be that the only way to get rid of the mandarins is to transfer them to the "pure" disciplines they so love anyway—sociology, economics, political science. That may be the only feasible way of disintegrating the hard core of mandarins to the point where they no longer control the planning schools.

One thing seems clear—the profession cannot afford to drift along on the assumption that there are more pressing problems than the reform of planning education. We must resolve never again to permit a fissure between the practice of planning and the teaching of planning. Not only should new faculty be required to have substantial practical experience, but the criteria for hiring, promotion, and tenure should be revised to give substantial weight to agency and consulting background.

The working professionals have to take charge of planning education. The job is too important to be left to the educators themselves. It will be tough and time-consuming, but it must be done.

CHAPTER

2

INTELLECTUALS IN STATE AND MUNICIPAL GOVERNMENT

GOVERNMENT BY REJECTS?

Shortly after government in America began to be tolerated as a necessary evil—about the time of the Revolutionary War—it became necessary to staff the growing bureaucracies. At the upper reaches, there was some continuity with the all-star cast of intellectuals who had drafted the noble set of documents and laid the solid conceptual foundations for the world's longest lived, large democracy. Below the very top layer, some of the staff was conscious of being involved in a gentlemanly, leisurely calling. Hawthorne's and Melville's stints as civil servants were very much in the international tradition; the civil service had long been an unwitting patron of the arts and numbered among its successful authors Dante (government shipyard), Kafka (unemployment compensation), Trollope (postal service), and Chaucer (customs service), among many others, past and present.[1]

In an era of modest responsibilities it was not surprising that government employment came to be regarded as a sinecure for the privileged, a storehouse of good, steady jobs that should be opened to the masses. By the 1830s, victorious Jacksonian democracy was able to act on the belief that sound common sense rather than formal education was qualification enough for a government position. Following the native Jacksonian precedent, succeeding waves of immigrants, with the Irish often in the vanguard, conquered the municipalities and moved on to penetrate many state and federal government strongholds.

Up to the New Deal 1930s, the civil service, below the very top echelons, fully reflected the background of its employees and the low esteem in which it was held by the middle and upper classes. Most government jobs paid badly, but they offered the security treasured by new immigrants and by the more impoverished segments of the domestic population. They were not scorned by blacks, poor whites, or many of the newly arrived Europeans. To a degree, this sentiment still prevails. There seems to be an endless supply of applicants for jobs that hardly qualify as prestige laden in the context of the late 1970s (such as street cleaners).

The New Deal was clearly a watershed in the civil service as it was in so many other aspects of the nation. Excitement, an outlet for idealism and ambition, decent pay, and security were all obtainable in government agencies. In contrast, the private sector seemed stodgy, ingrown, and dull, and the corporations were not doing much hiring. As a result, for over a decade, the civil service at all levels of government was able to skim off much of the cream of the college graduates. After World War II, however, there was a significant fork in the road. By and large, the federal civil service succeeded in preserving continuity with the 1930s; despite reductions in force, McCarthyism, and an unfriendly press, federal agencies were able to inject a steady stream of bright young people into the bureaucracy. On the other hand, except for a few mutants like New York, Wisconsin, California, and a handful of others, the states, along with most municipalities, regressed a good deal of the way back to the practices of the 1920s and earlier. As a result, in many state and local bureaucracies the thin layer of depression-era talent was nearing retirement in the 1960s, and below them was darkness.

Two explanations for the difficulty in attracting well-qualified professional talent to government service were advanced by Tocqueville in the 1830s. The first is the tendency to pay relatively low salaries for relatively scarce and hard to obtain upper-echelon jobs, as opposed to comparatively generous pay scales obtainable at the lower levels that are within reach of the voting majority. The second is that historically in the United States, private employment consistently offered much greater opportunity for the ambitious man than did the government service. Tocqueville was accurate and prescient in his observation that only during depressions, when commerce and industry are checked in their growth, does "place hunting" become generally followed.[2] To a very great extent, this remains a valid description of the current situation in state and local civil service. What makes this situation dangerous as well as absurd is the growing responsibilities confronting these levels of government—solutions to problems of the schools and the cities among others. Major sums to improve the environment and the quality of life can be made available, but the cutting edge of the programs is often blunted in the states and cities. Tocqueville could virtually ignore state government, and big cities, but a century and four decades later, this was no longer a realistic possibility.

Thus, the return of the intellectual to state and municipal government, after the hiatus of the 1940s and 1950s, is a subject worthy of exploration. It is beyond dispute that weakness in the staffing of state and local agencies is a major handicap in implementing programs, particularly the innovative efforts that call for substantial competence. Of course, some states and cities are well equipped to play an equal partnership role with the federal government. Unfortunately, the majority do not have the talent-in-depth to act as anything other than passive, clumsy responders to federal initiatives. The same observation applies with even greater force to all but a relative handful of cities. (In fact, the disparaging references to state government in this chapter are equally valid for municipal agencies and staff.)

One facet of the problem deserves careful study, namely the frictions, difficulties, and general expendability of intellectuals employed in state and local government either in a staff capacity or as hired consultants. While this discussion by no means purports to present a full statement on the situation in all states, in the generation of the mid-1940s a large proportion of the states, municipalities, and county governments have tended to be inhospitable to college-trained professionals.

There is some dispute over the causes for the unfortunate condition of state and municipal civil service, but there is a general consensus that standard party labels have little relevance; neither long-term domination by Republicans or Democrats nor a change in control of the state house or city hall seems to have much correlation with the quality of government employees. One authoritative view ascribes many of the difficulties to the outworn rural, small-town ideology prevalent among state political leaders and the Jacksonian antipathy for intellectuals which many states share with municipalities. The gerrymandering that dominated state legislative apportionment in past years was thought to reinforce a "consecrated negativism" dedicated to simplicity, conventional wisdom, and a mistrust of trained professionals.[3] A slightly different approach is the distinction that has been drawn between the immigrant ethos focused on patronage, job security, and hostility toward many professional standards with the "middle-class," "public-regarding" ethos centered on efficiency, reform, high quality of services, and friendliness to trained specialists.[4]

Both views seem to be deficient as explanations. Hostility to professionals and a high regard for tenure at the expense of quality are as prevalent in states that have barely seen a foreign immigrant as they are in the northeastern quadrant of the nation. Many rural courthouse gangs, thoroughly native in ancestry, that traditionally have dominated political life in the South and Midwest, are equally adept at hanky panky, and their government appointees are fully as incompetent as the civil servants in northeastern cities and urban states. Nor can the answer be found in nostalgically clinging to an outworn, small-town ideology. If one is searching for true parochialism and a paranoid attitude toward the professional, he can find it in full bloom in the central cities among our urban villagers.

Perhaps a more useful dichotomy may be found in conflicts between town and gown, traditional in communities containing sizable universities. There one finds the political machinery and the civil service dominated by the townies, who are unsympathetic to college radicals, immoral smart alecks, and snobs, and are generally uninterested in such college-type concepts as reform and the public interest. There are obvious grounds for friction—conflicts over collegiate highjinks, parking spaces, and taxes. But these rather minor *casus belli* are only outward evidence of a wide chasm between two antipathetic life-styles. The collegiate community mistrusts townie politicians, despises most local government employees, and is thoroughly frustrated by what it sees as a stupid, regressive governmental structure. On their part, the townies view the collegians as overeducated, overpaid, impractical, radical, immoral, and parasitic.

It may be suggested that, in a sense, much of the conflict in American state and local government can be explained as a tense, prolonged struggle between town and gown life-styles. This is far from an income or class phenomenon—there is much overlapping. A number of wealthy contractors, lawyers, undertakers, bar owners, realtors, professionals, and businessmen, many of them college graduates, are found in the town camp, while among the gown people there are numbers of relatively poor folk. Some of the latter are in temporary poverty (such as graduate students), but some (such as school teachers) may earn less than townies in the building trades. Obviously, the differentiation is sometimes hazy, but this categorization does seem to present a recognizable view of reality, particularly in state and local government, where academic types tend to be as identifiable as albino Congolese.

In Anthony Downs' bureaucratic taxonomy, "townies" would likely be found among cautious "conservers," while academics would be more heavily represented in the ranks of hot-eyed zealots. Either group can furnish partisan "advocates" or harbor officials who display, on occasion, broad statesmanlike loyalties.[5] Similarly, Bertram Gross would classify more townies as "stickers" rather than "climbers," as "oldtimers" rather than "newcomers," and certainly as "locals" rather than "cosmopolitans." He would find many grandstand players among temporary project staff and consultants, rather than among townie personnel; and townies quite probably would shelter more "nay-sayers" than "yea-sayers," more "rule-enforcers" than "rule-evaders" compared to outsiders with a strong academic background.[6]

There are clear differences between the townie civil servant who is probably not a college graduate and the gown-oriented government employee. The former has no (or believes he* has no) alternative employment available, and partly because of this entrapment he often evinces much verbal loyalty to the system. He has found a haven, and, as a rule, he is not actively looking toward

---

*"He" may also mean "she."

professional advancement on the outside. Rather, he hopes for gradual escalation through tenure and/or political influence within the existing system; consequently, he is violently resentful when degree-holding outsiders or "foreigners" are recruited. The latter are viewed not only as threats to the townie's promotion but as an insult to the way of life he has chosen. On the other hand, the intellectual-professional marches to a different drummer. His employment horizons and ambitions usually transcend agency and system, and he reaches out to his professional peer group. Since the 1950s, the number of alternative opportunities has been steadily growing, and he feels that his future lies in an adherence to professional standards and a willingness to relocate as opportunity beckons. This tends to create certain frictions with the entrenched townies. Partly as a result, the gown people tend to become disillusioned quickly and move on to friendlier climes. The agency is thereby left in the care of the townie, who has nowhere else to go.

At this point it is useful to clarify a few definitions. For present purposes, an "intellectual" is defined as a college graduate who holds a responsible professional position with a life-style that differs significantly from that of most state employees in terms of job horizons, professional standards, speech patterns, reading habits, and thought processes. The existence of such an identifiable disparity in state and local government may surprise persons familiar with federal agencies or corporations, organizations in which the upward-bound collegian and even the master's degree are commonplace. However, a prevalent, nonintellectual environment among executives still exists in certain lagging, corporate enterprises in which men promoted from the shop or other holders of diplomas from the school of hard knocks remain dominant.

As late as the 1940s there was much discussion of whether an ambitious young man helped his career more by spending four years in gaining practical business experience or in going to college. For the most part, the question is no longer asked because the issue has ceased to exist. Even in a few quaint industries such as some of the railroads and various family concerns, collegians are "in," and ungrammatical, old-shoe types are "out." It gets harder every year to find executives in private industry who boast about their lack of college education. At their executive levels, state and local governments therefore possess authentic antique qualities.

If there were a market for governmental memorabilia, a dealer could become a wealthy man by stuffing, preserving, and auctioning off the quaintly preserved tableaux in state house and city hall that have remained steadfast under the inroads of college-trained executives. There is a reason for this paralysis: It has proved possible to create a new breed of university townie. A generation of people with college degrees has moved into state and local government, but their interests, outlooks, and life-styles are close to those of the old-guard staffers. The source of this new breed of college graduates who manage to retain a considerable share of working-class orientation is the larger third-rate colleges and universities in the big cities and their backwater brethren in small, parochial communities. In faculty, course orientation, and student body, these institutions have reproduced, on a slightly more intellectual plane, the accent and outlook of local high-school systems. They faithfully reinforce rather than challenge the inbred background of their students. This is, of course, an exaggeration, since in recent years, at any rate, intellectual stirrings are very much in evidence even in the remotest institution or the most insulated college. But it nevertheless is a fact that the two societies—along with much fence jumping—embrace two different kinds of college input. Town and gown are often matters of allegiances, aspirations, and reading habits, rather than of class, income, or amount of formal education; but there are relatively few graduates of first-class institutions among the townies.

The built-in friction between town and gown is as much in evidence at the national level as at other governmental echelons. Secretary of Defense McNamara's experience with certain congressmen, angered, baffled, and yet unconvinced by his smooth intellectual performance, is an excellent example. Although he was far less abrasive, obnoxious, and openly contemptuous of inferior intellects than were others in the presidential stable, there were enough rough edges to irritate the townies:

> His [McNamara's] habit of marshalling a dazzling array of statistics to support his case in Congressional testimony has dismayed and irritated the Southern Conservatives on the Armed Services Committees. Many of these men . . . are anti-intellectuals and superpatriots who have vigorously resisted changes and who have been particularly disturbed by McNamara's unceasing efforts to reform and modernize the Reserves and the National Guard. "They listen to him rattle off all those facts and figures which they can't comprehend and they can't answer and they say to themselves, 'you smart son of a bitch, you're too goddamn smart. I'm going to take you down a peg,' " one associate of McNamara's said. "And when they try and they don't succeed, they get a little bit madder."
>
> What the Secretary's colleague did not mention is that the anger is sometimes justified when the Congressmen later discover they have been hoodwinked by McNamara's tactic of supporting a weak argument with an adroit combination of statistics and sophistry.[7]

Having established a working definition of town and gown, we can examine the intellectual in state government from three standpoints: employment as regular, permanent staff; employment as "temporary" project staff; and employment as a consultant-firm contractor. It is recognized that the dividing lines are often blurred: individuals often move out of project jobs into staff positions and vice versa. Nevertheless, the distinction is generally valid; the inert mass of long-service employees who occupy most of the chairs in the state and local agencies can easily be differentiated from the three types of intellectuals.

IN THE FIRM: THE HOUSE INTELLECTUAL

Reference has been made to the injection of talent into state and local government in the 1930s. Insights into the problems of the gown wearer can be gleaned from the history of these pioneers. Many have had notable careers in government, either at the state or local level or after moving into the federal agencies. A substantial number apparently regretted their career choice and either left government service in the 1940s or 1950s or retired as early as the relevant pension laws and regulations permitted. The larger share remained on after World War II. In part they were interested in protecting pension rights; counting military service, many had a ten-year investment in sizable retirement benefits. There was also the fear on the part of a depression-battered generation that the prosperity of the 1940s was ephemeral and that a recurrence of mass unemployment was just around the corner. The recessions of 1948–49 and 1953–54 were interpreted as reasons to hang on to the civil service life jacket. Also, by the late 1940s, they had accumulated seniority and status, and the thought of risking a step or two backward by moving to outside employment was unwelcome.

In general, the intellectuals of the 1930s made several types of adjustment to their surroundings. More intelligent and better educated than their seniors, the entrants of the 1910s and 1920s, and brighter than the later recruits of the 1940s and 1950s, many rose to high positions, although, as was suggested earlier, a large number quit or retired early. Those who became department and division heads adjusted, chameleonlike, to circumstances. Some became virtually indistinguishable from their superiors and employees, hiding their talents under a self-imposed discipline. The adjusters became accepted, to a degree, as right guys "once you get to know them," experts in baseball and bowling, tolerant of minor foibles, and respected by co-workers and politicians. Sometimes they were transformed into sleazy intellectual "pols," pliable hirelings who resembled nothing so much as the shyster lawyers who congregate in the men's rooms of city halls. Others have existed for years in seething frustration, witnesses to buried reports, distorted recommendations, and treated like intellectual Uncle Toms, trotted out for ceremonial occasions. Often they became office sages, repositories of agency history and accumulated wisdom, respected confidants, and problem solvers for agency and personal difficulties. Their chameleon reaction to the prevailing local color parallels the career patterns of policemen with southern or central European ancestry who, after a few years of service, take on some of the Hibernian flavor that permeates many big city police departments. Many an intellectual in northeastern state and local government becomes an honorary Irishman, an occasional guest at wakes and clan picnics, and a knowledgeable participant in political tribal gossip. In the Midwest and South, they become honorary hicks and rednecks, conversational sportsmen, football rooters, and basketball boosters.

Some intellectuals have sought to master their environment by imposing their own standards. They too were respected, but in their case overt deference was mingled with covert fear and hatred. Lacking political protectors, they used their brains, or more accurately, their tongues. Like the frail, elderly ladies who terrorize entire family clans unto the third generation, a number of intellectuals in government have carved out positions of power with the weapon of biting sarcasm. They are, after all, surrounded by relatively slow-witted, inarticulate people, most of whom have had traumatic experiences with sadistic schoolteachers. Under these circumstances, they can assume the waspish role of correctors of spelling errors, covering papers with stinging ridicule, singling out some unfortunate for scornful treatment. One technique is to return submitted memoranda with sarcastic comments in red ink; another is to ridicule the target openly, at staff meetings on early Monday mornings (the choice of time is significant, since the prospect can ruin a weekend and the reality can blight two or three working days). There is no need to fear resistance: re-creating powerful childhood memories can cause a man in his fifties to revert to the status of classroom dunce, the butt of his frightened colleagues in the atmosphere of apprehension, themselves thankful at having been temporarily spared. Bullying, toadying, flunking examinations, and subordination can be re-created in a government office. The masterful, pungent individuals capable of reducing their colleagues to a state of palpitating terror tend to be rarities, however. As a rule, the house intellectual risks developing bleeding ulcers under the day-to-day psychological abrasion involved in the wrenching conflicts and compromises demanded by an alien, often hostile environment. In contrast, the graduate of the third-string college is immediately at home among a family of friends, peers, and colleagues.

In the late 1950s and early 1960s, however, the picture changed substantially in one respect. Taking into account the utter hopelessness of getting much done with the regular troops or of upgrading the civil service structures, the states and localities were allocated federal funds to employ large numbers of technical mercenaries in the form of project staff or consulting-firm personnel.

PROJECT STAFF: KING FOR A DAY?

The passage of the 1954 housing act was a landmark in intergovernmental relations. Although the practice was far from new, the 1954 legislation marked the initiation, on a large scale, of the use of federal matching money in combination with local funds for the purpose of undertaking complex planning and renewal tasks. Many communities performed the job with regular staff, while others hired consulting firms. Much of the planning, however, was conducted with the use of temporary project staff, employed for a one- or two-year period at premium salaries. The justification was the big-push theory. There is no reason to expand the permanent payroll to undertake a single massive job, it was argued—far better to hire highly skilled technicians, even at high salaries, to complete the job quickly and then move on without benefit of tenure, pension rights, or civil service protection.

This argument loses some of its force when short-term projects stretch on into three years, five years, or longer. Many projects can be classified as temporary only by the greatest stretch of the imagination, particularly when some project personnel may be employed for longer periods than many regular staff. Moreover, the existence of a permanent group of highly paid project personnel offers a constant source of friction with the relatively poorly paid regulars. An additional distraction is the blurred borderline between the regulars and the temporary personnel where there is much shifting back and forth, as permanent staff enlist in projects for a year or two at higher pay, and project people are taken on into the ranks of the regulars.

The federal government has had serious second thoughts concerning the use of project staff. While well-trained project professionals can usually get a job done in the sense of turning out the stipulated paper work, there is no guarantee that they will leave much in the way of permanent residue. If the project is separated and insulated from the existing structure, it is not likely to produce a postproject staff of regulars versed in the planning process, capable of carrying out project recommendations and updating plans as time and events require. For this reason, the federal agencies have tried various techniques aimed at involving regular staff in temporary projects. One method is personnel matching.

In the 1960s states and municipalities were encouraged to use a barter system to pony up the local share of urban-renewal projects. Public improvements, including construction by nonprofit institutions, have been used to pad out the local share. Taking this approach a step further, regular staff salaries could be allocated, in fact or fiction, and in whole or in part, to provide the local matching share for comprehensive planning operations of various types. This means that an official who could not rely on his permanent staff to undertake difficult tasks could match the salaries paid to his force of incompetents, at a two-for-one—or even a three-for-one—ratio, to obtain funds to hire competent project personnel.

There is one minor danger—the regular staff had to be certified as actually participating in the operations to which their work time or a portion of their time has been pledged. Revolts in the mortuary have been known to occur. Staff regulars ordered to stay out of the way have refused to be a party to a fraud; on moral grounds they will not agree to sign in as matching project participants until they are bribed with promotions and pay raises.

By and large, the hope that project staff would educate the regulars in the course of the project has not been realized. The two groups are oil and water, differing in everything from pay scales to background and speech patterns. The project and its attendant staff tend to be regarded as a necessary evil but, fortunately, a transient one. Like the old-time regular army noncoms who cordially detest the disruptions of wartime, including the officers produced by the ROTC and OCS, the permanent staff eagerly awaits the return of peace and normality.

The hostility of the regular staff toward project personnel is one of the causes for subsequent disappointment with the temporary projects. The well-paid consultant, often a foreigner (from out of state), is regarded as an overpaid alien, short on common sense and primarily interested in extending his period of lucrative employment. Before ascribing all of this cynicism and bitterness to ill-mannered envy, it must be admitted that on numerous occasions project staff hired with attractive advance billing have proved to be poor performers, weak in pragmatic, administrative, and technical skills, naive and inept in the political arena, and purveyors of windy, expensive inanities disguised as learned research. There are instances when project staff have insisted on displaying the accuracy of Mark Twain's adage concerning certain collegians to the effect that one can send a jackass to 40 universities and load him with degrees, but on his deathbed he will bray. In short, as in the case of McNamara and the Senate, there is, unhappily, ample cause for mutual disenchantment.

Setting aside the problem of the peripatetic project nitwit, there can be serious obstacles to accomplishing much even with an outstanding temporary staff. The project staff's path is strewn with hazards as it attempts to intrude new, unsettling concepts involving sensitive policy and operating issues into a recalcitrant, skeptical, or downright hostile bureaucracy. The prospects are far from favorable in many federal agencies; but subject to many exceptions, the number of unfriendly Yahoos increases proportionately with hierarchical distance from Washington. In some states and smaller cities, the figure approaches near unanimity with barely a glimmer of intelligence in evidence. This fact seems not to have penetrated among ideology-bound conservatives who attack the federal bureaucracy as unresponsive and muscle-bound and either laud local and state government or imply that lower-echelon failings are relatively minor compared to the federal monster agencies. But as is usually the case, prejudice is impervious to contradictory reality.

There are two ways in which the project staff person may find himself in hot water. After an initially warm reception from a representative of the top echelon that he is subsequently likely to feel is composed of intellectual giants compared to middle management, project staff may fall afoul of the bureau chiefs, old-time technicians, and ingrown professional cliques. A special problem arises from the resistance of strong, professional, ingrown groups—educators, generals, welfare workers, or physicians—to outside performance evaluators. There are frequent charges that the aliens have failed to grasp the elusive essence of a program, are incapable of understanding prevailing local mores, and otherwise are unqualified to perform services that in effect entail judging the performance of the controlling insiders. In addition, the old-line agency regulars tend to interpret each probing question by project staff as a threat, a judgment on their past and present performance, a risk to their chances of promotion, and a potential loss of power over their empire. For these reasons, the agency administrator is clearly of two minds in welcoming the intrusion of potentially unsettling project operations. Any project worth its salt involves a hard look at existing agency operations, but as Peter Rossi suggests: "Practitioners and policymakers are apprehensive; they want evaluations of program effectiveness, but they are afraid of what might be shown."[8]

There is further cause for disquiet in that a project is seldom narrowly defined; with comprehensive planning very much in fashion, the fact that the project staff is employed by one agency will not prevent it from analyzing interface areas involving the activities of other agencies. The latter are frequently competing for funds and power with the agency to which the project staff is under contract and understandably tend to react with hostility and alarm to those on the payroll of a rival. The project staff finds itself in sticky situations in which its agency employers vacillate between supporting and disowning its efforts, depending on which counsel predominates at the moment.

Another type of problem arises when the project staff is involved in internal program evaluation and research. Given a mandate to forage around the agency, to establish performance measurements, and to produce critiques of their colleagues, the project researcher is likely to find himself regarded with about as much affection as a police commissioner's personal investigating team assigned to ferret out evidence of corruption at the precinct level. But there is a further problem involved in that the investigators are also looking into the commissioner's activities; it is difficult to confine a research professional to scrutiny of subunit performance.

The requirements of objective research and analysis may be difficult to sustain within the context of a fast-moving action program. The in-depth gathering of material considered necessary by the project staff to provide an adequate basis for program formulation may involve substantial costs and lengthy delays. Furthermore, as suggested, there may also be a basic internal friction within the agency because of the very different orientation between the administrator and the program planning and evaluation staff. The experience in one government operation is indicative:

> Research directors chafed at the inconsistency and incoherence of much that was done, the programme directors were equally impatient of pretentious methodology and theoretical preoccupations which failed to answer their needs. In practice, if not in theory, the claims of research and action were hard to reconcile.[9]

The researcher involved in an evaluation project can ordinarily expect to uncover much disturbing information. He will discover that the process of program review and feedback is tenuous at best and tends to conclude that the project staff has a sacred and unique mission to complete a task that the regular agency personnel cannot possibly undertake.

A research director will argue that:

> There will be no genuine analysis of program impact unless the researcher leads the way [and that] once the impact model is formulated, the researcher must continue to remain within the environment, like a snarling watchdog ready to oppose alterations in program and procedures that would render his evaluation efforts useless.[10]

Permanent program personnel are usually allergic to this type of autonomous and uncontrollable research empire within the agency. Furthermore, the agency regulars are rarely in a position to preserve the purity of social science experiments or to tolerate delays to slow-moving research processes. The research project effort must either result in immediate payoffs in terms of providing guidance for pressing, unpostponable decisions or else be relegated to a low-priority status. The project researcher, on the other hand, has a divided loyalty—a fidelity to professional standards which is linked to his long-term career goals, as well as a commitment to his current employer. Also, by temperament he is more often contemplator than man of action. There is, therefore, considerable potential for mutual disregard between jarring points of view that may either negate or vitiate the value of the project or may lead to a premature termination of project-staff contracts.

From a program standpoint, there is something to be said on both sides. The task of satisfying intermediate and long-term project research objectives cannot be permitted to overshadow the administrator's need for immediate help in choosing between alternatives, bringing to bear such information as can be secured with a reasonable investment in time and cost. The project staff must decide between retaining its scientific purity and engaging in action-oriented research that may be "disreputable" from a scientific and professional standpoint. On the other hand, most government agencies find it difficult to mount a significant program evaluation effort under the pressures of day-to-day agency needs and the frequent crises that absorb the limited talent at their disposal. Though project staff researchers are usually uncomfortable in recommending action without a full panoply of research studies, Marris and Rein propose a compromise. The agency project staff should be less a "snarling watchdog" protecting the sanctity of its domain, poised for departure the instant its prerogatives are threatened, than an amiable retriever at the service of the administrator, "uncovering whatever he can usefully use." The project staff "should and can, if necessary, improvise a well-informed evaluation."[11]

Another dimension to the problem of divided loyalties arises because the project staff tends to include a few intellectuals who write for publication. There are temptations to publish frank, critical memoirs and scathing analyses of agency operations. In contrast, it can be assumed that a career official is aware that the publish-or-perish relationship may have a different sequential link in government service as compared to the university. The intellectual employed on a temporary project arrangement may feel he has a duty to his profession, but his enraged former hosts may consider him a hypocritical, unethical ingrate if he broadcasts sensitive inside information. One must be aware that this is one of the reasons that the intellectual is regarded with suspicion in some quarters. While oral gossip and newspaper speculation are the meat and drink of government, an intellectual on the staff is regarded as an individual who is continually tempted to kiss and tell for the sake of scholarly prestige and/or financial reward. Few governmental units are willing to permit access by scholarly blabbermouths to sensitive information if this material is likely to be translated into print for history books or periodicals.

Another source of danger to the project intellectual is negative reactions emanating from hypersensitive client groups. Adverse criticism from the black community cut short Kenneth Clark's activities as a program "participant-observer" in Harlem.[12] Similarly, Daniel Moynihan's report stressing the weaknesses of the black family was violently attacked by black leaders as well as some civil rights liberals.[13]

Moynihan has identified one of the dilemmas that confront a social scientist whose research may provide ammunition for his enemies and the enemies of his allies and clients:

> Knowledge is power, and in contemporary society social scientists are often in the position of handling power in an almost absent-minded way. Professional ethics, at least as ideally defined, can lead them to hand out the very best arguments to those whom they would consider the very worst contenders.... All concerned with the development of a system or urban social indicators [must] be prepared in advance to find themselves accused of having been betraying some of the very causes with which they have been most allied.[14]

It should not be thought that vicious attacks on researchers are the prerogatives of seething minority groups. Peter Rossi adds some sobering thoughts on the limited possibility of implementing unpopular recommendations even by supposedly highly intellectual and rational organizations. He notes that when the report of the National Opinion Research Center concluded, contrary to the sponsor's belief, that fellowships and scholarships had no appreciable effect on either the student's selection of a field of study or in deterring promising Ph.D.'s from entering a field,

> the first reaction of the sponsors was to attack the researcher's methodology leading to the coining of the aphorism that the first defense of an outraged sponsor was methodological criticism. Policy remained unaffected. I do not know of any action program that was put out of business by evaluation research, unless evaluation itself was meant to be the hatchet.[15]

The intellectual retained by a governmental agency to undertake the delicate task of pioneering in the sensitive area of goals and performance measurement (opposed to service as either advocate or executioner) will probably be required to display almost superhuman qualities of patience and understanding. He may in fact discover that the continual reassurance and therapeutic counseling that his clients seem to require absorb a larger share of his time than the technical task for which he was ostensibly hired. However, even if his temperament is unusually resilient, he may conceivably find himself regarding his clients with some small measure of distaste, especially when he discovers himself abandoned on an unsupported limb. There is an understandably human but nevertheless regrettable tendency for agency chieftains to renege on verbal agreements and to deflect criticism from themselves by forcing the temporary project staffer who has faithfully been carrying out their instructions to defend their decisions against subsequent outside attack.

Is the project staff as helpless as all this sounds? In most cases one would have to give an affirmative answer: the agency belongs to the people who live with it rather than the visitors, no matter how intelligent they may be. This is not to suggest that project staff, particularly the director, is a forlorn object of scorn and a passive target for his enemies. On the contrary, if he dares to play them he actually has extremely strong cards in his hand. First and foremost, he is the key to the federal treasury. Persons who can, in William Lee Miller's vivid phraseology, forage for the cities "through the nation's bureaucratic jungles, extracting the meat from Titles I and II are rare specimens. It is not enough that the Federal government pass city-helping laws; there must also be hunters for the city who can make their way through the Titles I and Titles II to find the meat."[16] But finding sustenance is not enough. Administrators who can cook the meat when they bring it home are rarer still.

If by some mischance, however, the federal tap is turned off and a project director can no longer perform the feats of financial legerdemain that have insulated him from the local long knives, he may find himself playing the lead role in a nine-part scenario. With local variations, the following sequence of events is observable in a number of federal grant-in-aid programs:

1. A strong project director makes a favorable impression on federal agencies, secures wide local backing, and receives a large federal grant.

2. But the executive has moved far and fast, his salary is large, his staff is sizable and well paid, and he has made local enemies. Unhappy with some

aspects of his program, local rivals and detractors journey to Washington to demand that the flow of future federal funds be made contingent on a radical alteration in agency policy that strips the administrator of much of his power. Naturally this disturbs the project director who

3. is alarmed by the extent of local opposition and even more by the favorable hearing his opponents seem to be receiving in Washington. The director canvasses for backing among his political masters. He does not find much support, because he has come to be regarded as a political liability. He also discovers that he is now controversial and hence no longer regarded as a favorite son by his federal sponsors who

4. have arrived at a new consensus: their erstwhile favorite is now viewed as an empire builder, a troublemaker, a frightening czar who is misusing or who may misuse federal largesse to ride roughshod over his clients and peers. He is also receiving too much personal publicity for operating their program. Lower-echelon regional and headquarters staff whom he has bypassed in securing Washington approval for his program agree that he must be taught a lesson and be made aware that his behavior has fallen below federal standards.

5. A furor follows when the press gets wind of the story. Press coverage stresses the element of drama and conflict, how low are the mighty fallen, and so on. Media sympathies do not lie with the local executive who has offended local interests, who threatens the flow of federal funds, and who offers a convenient peg for a stream of behind-the-scenes stories emanating in part from his enemies and in part from disgruntled and ungrateful staff.

6. At this point, faced with the prospect of no federal money for program commitments, the local executive discovers that all of the local politicians have deserted him; from the chief executive on down, their overriding objective is a minimum of fuss and a maximum of federal funds. In addition, townie politicians have made demagogic capital from his out-of-state origins and his alleged arrogance and callousness to local interests. The director has become a lightning rod to absorb punishment and a source of embarrassment to his political superiors.

7. This is the moment of truth when the director approaches the critical choice: a threat of resignation that he may be called on to make good or knuckling under to pressure. Surprisingly, if he chooses to do battle, the coalition of enemies often collapses; the federal bureaucracy, paper tigers, gives him his funds. More often he surrenders, partly out of loyalty to "his" program, partly out of hope of better times—vindication when his enemies hang themselves with federal rope and rend themselves with jealousy and rival incompetences.

8. If he compromises, the director usually discovers that partial surrender is the first step to removal. Sensing weakness, federal officials, local enemies, and the mass media move in for the kill. A broad consensus develops: his

removal is alleged to be essential for the progress of the program. The director's powers grow weaker; he is blamed for all the misadventures of his staff (who rush to desert his sinking career) and for the accumulated and inherited errors of federal, state, and local government.

9. If this occurs, his position becomes intolerable, and the director resigns.

It may be submitted that this sequence of events is descriptive of a number of bloody dramas in the war on poverty (where executive casualties were inordinately high), and of other operations. Moreover, it can be predicted with gloomy confidence that the advent of community development and the growth of other experiments in creative federalism will engender increasing numbers of similarly depressing episodes. In short, there is a fundamental tension inherent in pioneering programs that is directly correlated with the dynamism of the local executive responsible for implementation. Federal agencies are repeatedly faced with the alternatives of continuing to finance the chosen commander of the local army or choosing instead to support the disgruntled guerrillas who seek to overthrow him. Often, despite claims to the contrary, the federal executive seems ill at ease in the presence of strong, independent talent. Like social workers who are alleged to reinforce dependency by stifling individuality and independent judgment among their clients, some federal executives seem to prefer passive, mediocre executives—safe men who make no waves, neither causing discomfort to federal guardians of program funds nor producing much of consequence. In contrast, strong local administrators pile up a host of federal as well as local enemies in their whirlwind progress. Predictably, local opponents will journey to Washington to sever the financial administrator's jugular, and often Washington executives, irritated by the local baron, seem eager to wield the axe. However, experience suggests that executions on living organisms require a relatively helpless victim—an executive who chooses to submit rather than fight. Those who dare to risk all in a test of nerve may emerge stronger than ever, dictating terms to a chastened federal bureaucracy and to sullen, but no longer dangerously mutinous, local opponents. In time, however, disenchanted with what they view as ingratitude, disloyalty, and needless wear-and-tear on the nervous system, it is not surprising to find that forceful executives seek alternative employment and leave the field open to residual talents. Indeed, if their antennae are sufficiently sensitive, they may leave before the cheering stops, aware that stormy seas lie just over the horizon.

The project staffer who proceeds to undertake a task on the basis of what he regards as logic, intellectual honesty, and faithful adherence to professional standards may unwittingly raise storms all around him. At worst, his services may be abruptly terminated; at best, his recommendations may be heavily diluted if not relegated to the graveyard maintained by every agency, in fact if not in name, to bury unwise, untimely, or dangerous suggestions.

One question that comes to mind concerns the growing impact of revenue sharing on this scenario. A shift to no-strings bloc grants tends to alter the sequence by removing one set of actors from the playlet—the Feds—while leaving untouched the wretched confrontations between star-quality, arrogant project staff, suspicious, jealous, or otherwise unsympathetic locals, nervous politicians, and a sensation-seeking press. What we are likely to find is a pattern exemplified among short-tenured school superintendents; the scenario of rise and fall can be enacted on a very small stage.

HOW TO BE A RICH CONSULTANT

Unquestionably, hiring consultants is the least effective of the three methods of injecting expertise into state and local government. As compared to either permanent or project staff, the consultant is usually an instrument rather than a craftsman—a tool of power rather than a wielder of power. (The reference here is to consulting firms that work on temporary contracts, rather than to individuals who may be employed as consultants on long-term personal service contracts for periods of time comparable to regular civil service staff.) There are certain defects in using consultants to solve agency problems. From the agency's viewpoint, the studies are frequently expensive; they are often conducted by persons unfamiliar with local conditions; and much of their value is lost in translation because the agency often lacks the requisite staff capability to follow consultant advice. The difficulty is that consulting is often misused as a substitute for rather than a supplement to agency personnel. After the consult-and-run operation is completed and the final report submitted, there is often little permanent residue in the form of augmented staff expertise, persons who have mastered the research substance and are fully capable of implementing study recommendations. These widely known deficiencies in the consulting-firm approach have led some federal and state agencies to adopt a jaundiced view toward use of consulting firms as a means of avoiding employment of permanent or project staff.

Yet agencies are still tempted to hire consulting firms, partly because a good staff is not easy to assemble. The consultant approach has another advantage: It is a means of decelerating agency empire building because it permits large jobs to be tackled without adding to permanent staff. Equally important, the consultant presumably has a qualified organization in readiness to complete projects on schedule. Agencies attempting to take on sizable projects are often faced with serious time and staffing problems. Presumably the consultant has reserve personnel capacity, or, if he does not, he can more easily hire new people because he can offer them the prospect of continued employment on other projects while the agency can offer only a limited-period contract to attract project staff. For these reasons, more and more consultant firms are being hired by government agencies.

The above may suggest that the title of this section has been used in a playful spirit of irony. This is not the case, however, for the fact is that consultants, like staff, come in two main varieties: There are pet consultants, friendly firms chosen in a back room more for their connections than for their talent, who can indeed wax fat on contracts with government. A state or municipal agency can have at its disposal a stable of consulting corporations with anonymous, generic names implying a worldwide practice from Lhasa to Monaco but actually with only one captive client. Such firms have been known to charge top prices for their used stencils, purveying canned products, warmed over slightly, for repeat sales. A "political" architect can place the same blueprints on the block perhaps a dozen times over, charging a standard fee for each building. Under these conditions, consulting can be a profitable trade, but in places where this kind of arrangement is customary, it tends to generate certain problems for the other, second variety of consultant—the firm that enjoyed a substantial professional reputation before that unhappy day when it decided to devote its talents to uplifting the quality of state (or local) government.

In areas where "consulting" has become a synonym for crooked incompetence, the professional firm finds itself the object of instant suspicion; it risks being crucified between two thieves. If the agency that has recently hired the firm has had a long, dismal, and well-publicized record of employing shady, third-rate firms, the day may come when a legislative investigating team takes over the files, and the newspapers print long alphabetical lists of consulting firms, some of which have been previously accustomed to being singled out in public solely for praise and prizes.

The traumatic impact of the press allegations is exacerbated by a press that appears all too ready to gloat over the plight of the razzle-dazzle, hot-shot professional and by a public which is always prepared to see rich, smart-aleck brains get their comeuppance. Moreover, the consultant-on-the-griddle can expect little sympathy from colleagues whose consciences have been troubled by his self-righteous moralizing. This latter point requires explanation.

In the initial honeymoon phase of its labors, the professional consulting firm that has recently signed a contract is prone to preachments on the moral rectitude of working for necessitous near-at-hand agencies rather than restricting one's talents to federal and private clients. Other firms that have not followed this noble example tend to be skeptical, but quite often their conscience has been disturbed. Subsequently, when trouble develops, the thankful, nonparticipating firms loose a chorus of muted "I told you so's" mingled with a trace of *Schadenfreude* at the discomfiture of their friends and rivals. A vow by the consultant to avoid similar hazards in the future is by no means unusual —with a resultant diminishing of the pool of talent available to the states and localities.

The consultant—second category—may also experience extreme difficulty in getting paid. Although agencies may retain a consulting firm, they do not have to cooperate with it or pay it; by virtue of incompetence and/or misrepresentation, an agency can delay payment and processing contracts until the consultant is close to bankruptcy.

As a rule, the firm does get its money, in time, but it may have to finance its operations on IOUs for many months, absorbing the bank-interest payments as part of its lesson on choosing clients. There can be several reasons for delay in payment: An agency shell-shocked by legislative investigations may simply hold up all payments; the staff may feel that, under the circumstances, approval of outgoing checks entails a degree of risk and that, because the agency cannot be sued for lethargy, administrative caution is preferable to adherence to a stipulated contract time schedule. Added to administrative timidity, Murphy's Law may also be operative. This law (anything which can go wrong, will go wrong) was once thought to govern out-of-town tryouts of Broadway plays and ill-fated military adventures. However, variations of this law have been discovered in many fields. In the present instance, for example, consultant bills can be wrongly routed, lost, returned for verification, or otherwise snarled in the machinery.

The mundane but vital matter of payment has been alluded to rather briefly. Like the sex of the hippopotamus which is chiefly of interest to other hippos, payment schedules for consulting firms are a matter of concern only to other consultants. However, it does assume a wider importance by contributing to the pervasive distaste for taking on state or local contracts. The point is that the threat of serious financial harm is added to the trauma of public insult.

Consultant in Action

It is no secret that consulting resembles other professions, and particularly the law, in its wide range of extracontractual services. Just how broad the scope of activities for the consultant can be is a matter of conjecture. For example, in terms of the state client, a senior consultant may find himself practicing psychiatry without a license as he listens to insoluble woes and offers advice on careers and human relations which the client is totally incapable of adopting.

Frequently, a consultant finds himself employed as a hired audience, regaled for hours with anecdotes and philosophy by clients who have apparently been starved for intelligent conversation. If the consultant contract calls for a payment on a per diem basis, being transfixed as a captive listener may eventually become nothing more than an irritant. However, this role may have a disastrous impact on a consultant's earnings if he is paid for a product and the chitchat interferes with the progress of his research.

Other unobvious burdens are heaped upon the consultant's shoulders. Unlike project staff or civil service regulars, a senior consultant is expected to look intelligent and rather prosperous—unless he chooses to look intelligent, tweedy, and moderately seedy, which he may do if he is a college professor. In part, he has been hired as an ornament, a token of the agency's entrance into the great world. News of private opinions and advance information on unpublished research, secret information, gossip retailed by the *cognoscenti* but concealed from the masses are all part of the unstipulated services that the agency may think it is purchasing from its consultants. To a degree, this orgy of name dropping and alleged information leaks can be manipulated as both threat and promise. In corporate counseling, one financially successful operator used his hypothetical connections with the New York "money men" and what they allegedly did or did not view with favor to browbeat simple-minded midwestern clients. Variations of this practice are not unknown in government consulting.

It is, however, apparent that the senior consultant has one enormous advantage over other types of intellectuals in state government: He need not strike a mucker pose. An interest in books, sailing, skiing, the theater, and even ballet is wholly acceptable, even desirable, as long as he does not exhibit signs of being weird or queer. After all, he does represent a tangible prestige item for the official who selected him. The savage, ulcerating struggle to empathize, communicate, and live with the townies is not part of his job. For this reason, one must temper one's sympathy for his plight. The intellectual in permanent service or on a long-term project is the deserving case; the soldier who holds the line is more worthy of sympathy than the visiting correspondent who writes eloquently of the mud and blood before returning to base for his booze and warm bed.

In some respects, consulting for state government is not much different from consulting for private enterprise. For example, the consultant more often than not finds himself a white chip in a high-stakes poker game. He is thrust on stage in a minor supporting role, a player in a half-understood melodrama full of strange passions and ferocious in-fighting. The consultant normally experiences an adverse reaction to playing a bit part in an obscure, squalid, and unpleasant scenario in which his technical counsel has the most marginal relevance to events and decisions. The consultant is frequently used to reinforce his employer's position, to second guess a previous consultant whose work is regarded as suspect or whose recommendations were unacceptable. The consultant may be a weapon of offense or defense, prompted by his employer to add weight to decisions already agreed upon and that lack only the consultant's imprimatur, or to challenge another faction or another agency. In this highly charged atmosphere, the consultant may find himself wooed by opposing parties eager to capture or at least neutralize him. Whatever his personal qualities, the consultant discovers that he has more than a few enemies, some inherited from his employer and others conjured up in the research process as his probing questions succeed in generating alarm and dismay.

Only adequate financial remuneration can compensate the consultant for his mounting irritation and frustration. One particular cause for dismay is the dawning suspicion that he and his study are being used as an outright smokescreen, with barely a nod in the direction of professional counsel. Initiating a high level consultant study is a common ploy to placate an irate press and public and to head off brutal savaging by political wolf packs. Not infrequently the baying wolves will be tossed a bone or two in the form of minor research studies in lieu of meatier substance. Subsequently, his forebodings often prove justified; the consultant discovers that a clause in his contract, written in invisible ink, calls for him to serve as a layer of asbestos, insulating employers from the hot blast of criticism. The consultant may be especially angered to find that, as the fires grow hotter, he is disowned by his employers despite the fact that he has faithfully followed their written and verbal instructions. Prior to his service with the state or locality he may have thought that the expendable employee who ascends in trial balloons is a prerogative of the presidency, but alas, it is not. The consultant finds that minor bureaucrats in minor agencies expose their hired men to vicious, undeserved attacks to save themselves minor embarrassment. A consultant may be fully capable of swimming in dangerous waters, and when matters of great import are involved, he may be willing to risk his professional skin. Often, however, he may begin to doubt the necessity of scuba diving among the resident piranhas when he may be sacrificed for inconsequential reasons.

The consultant soon learns that others besides himself question the need for service under the state banner. On occasion, he discovers that idle discussions initiated by his agency employer concerning the rewards and hazards of consulting tend to evolve into an ill-disguised attempt at job hunting. If the consultant is an academic off on a foray into consulting, the agency bureaucrat may make overt, wistful, embarrassing attempts to penetrate the professorial elysium as a nonpublishing faculty member. In either case, the consultant must express his high regard for a client whom he nevertheless feels is lacking in the essential qualifications for crossing the consultant barrier.

The amount of admiration for his client's abilities may decline precipitously if the consultant discovers that his firm has been retained to undertake a last-ditch, desperate effort. The consultant experiences premonitory qualms as his smallish research study is more and more frequently referred to by his employer as holding the answer to all sorts of accumulated agency ills. The call for miracles may occur in the case of an agency that has frittered away virtually all of its financial reserves and is facing a deadline with a major report still to be produced and little money left in the till. It will seek to employ a prestigious, productive consultant to undertake instant salvation, the agency naturally absolving itself of blame for any weaknesses in the final report. This situation can arise in federally financed, lethargically run projects that call for a massive final publication. The bulk of the project funds can be drained away by unqualified and/or political consultants, expended on unproductive staff, or misused by allocating a competent staff to urgent nonproject duties. The consultant is then asked to take the compost heap of ill-assorted materials dredged up by his predecessors and to spray the manure pile with an opaque deodorant material bearing his professional signature.

It is rumored in the consulting world that somewhere there exists a well-organized client who, when honestly baffled by a problem, proceeds to hire a qualified consultant. In a brisk and clinical fashion, the consultant signs a contract, proceeds with the study, produces recommendations, and lives to see his advice either accepted or rejected on plausible professional grounds. No accurate statistics, however, are available concerning the relative prevalence of this type of client in various levels of government, or in private corporations for that matter, but they are by no means common.

A consultant who sees his role simply as that of an impersonal purveyor of expert opinion is likely to be disappointed by state government, but it is a matter of degree; the smoothly running organization that knows how to choose and use consultants is rare in any sphere of activity. The problem is that the potential for being run through the meat grinder for no significant purpose seems to be so much greater in state government than in other areas.

A CONCLUDING NOTE: E FLAT

State and local government can be viewed as an underdeveloped nation of the kind that has baffled the United Nations Technical Assistance Program and the successive American foreign aid agencies. Sorely in need of technical aid, the states are not properly equipped to absorb it because they do not have adequate staff and cannot make good use of in-house or outside consultants. The future of the states rests in large measure in their ability to change their spots. As inhospitable places for intelligence—barring a few notable exceptions—the states will remain ciphers in the creative federalism equation unless they can somehow offer a lot of bright young men promising long-term careers and attractive service as short-term project staff. State and local governments will also have to become the kind of clients that interest the consultant who has sufficient reputation to be selective. In brief, states cannot hope to be taken seriously as social laboratories, or as effective governments for that matter, until they make substantial progress in closing the intelligence gap.

NOTES

1. Some of the authors bit the hand that fed them all the way up to the elbow. Dante's Hell bore an uncomfortable resemblance to the shipyard, Kafka's works portraying labyrinthine bureaucratic nightmares drew heavily upon his experience, while Trollope's pictures of government agencies provided ammunition for demanding deep budget cuts. Perhaps an international civil service federation should take certain appropriate steps.

2. Alexis de Tocqueville, *Democracy in America* (New York: Vintage, 1954), vol. 2, pp. 263–64.

3. See Charles Press and Charles R. Adrian, "Why State Governments Are Sick," *The Antioch Review,* Summer 1964, pp. 156–57.

4. Edward C. Banfield and James Q. Wilson, *City Politics* (Cambridge, Mass.: Harvard University Press and M. I. T. Press, 1963).

5. Anthony Downs, *Inside Bureaucracy* (Boston: Little, Brown, 1967), chap. 9.

6. Bertram M. Gross, *Organizations and Their Managing* (New York: The Free Press, 1968), chap. 10.

7. Neil Sheehan, "You Don't Know Where Johnson Ends and McNamara Begins," *New York Times Magazine,* October 22, 1967, pp. 131–32.

8. Peter Rossi, "Evaluating Social Action Programs," *Trans-Action* 4, no. 7 (June 1967): 51–53.

9. Peter Marris and Martin Rein, *Dilemmas of Social Reform,* Institute of Community Studies (London: Routledge and Kegan Paul, 1967), pp. 181–207.

10. Howard E. Freeman and Clarence C. Sherwood, "Research in Large Scale Intervention Programs," *Journal of Social Issues,* January 1965.

11. Marris and Rein, op. cit., pp. 101–02.

12. Kenneth Clark, *Dark Ghetto: Dilemmas of Social Power* (New York: Harper and Row, 1965).

13. See Lee Rainwater and William Yancey, *The Moynihan Report and the Politics of Controversy* (Cambridge, Mass.: M. I. T. Press, 1967). The Moynihan study, like other research which generated an unexpected amount of protest, was eventually disavowed by political superiors.

14. Daniel P. Moynihan, "Urban Conditions: General," *The Annals* 371 (May 1967): 160–61. See also his article, "The Moynihan Report and Its Critics," *Commentary* 43 (February 1967): 31–45.

15. Rossi, op. cit.

16. See William Lee Miller, *The Fifteenth Ward and the Great Society* (New York: Harper and Row, 1966), p. 154.

CHAPTER

3

YARDSTICKS FOR GOVERNMENT: THE ROLE OF PPB, ZBB, ETC.

THE NEW SUPER X-RAY CALIPERS

It is said that once upon a time, a truth-obsessed beauty-contest judge resigned in disgust because he would not be party to a fraud. It was impossible, he said, to reach definitive conclusions on the basis of exterior evidence. Forbidden to probe down to the fundamentals, His Honor refused to be forced to lend his good name to a potentially inflated royalty.

Under certain circumstances, it is conceivable that absolute verification could be obtained to satisfy the rigorous standards not only of the learned bench but of the losing contestants. The situation becomes much more complicated when the object to be measured is a government program, complete with history, promises, varying levels of staff performance and impact, and obscured in mists of raw data and self-praising reports. It is, in fact, the growing suspicion that the visible dimensions of many programs are synthetic and illusionary that has prompted much of the interest in various types of program biopsies. These include the traditional stand-bys, the legislative investigation, the budgetary review, the audit by a central agency, and more recently, a systematic effort to match investments and results known as Planning Programming Budgeting System—PPBS, or minus the S, PPB, and ZBB, Zero Base Budgeting, a further refinement of budget-program analysis.

In practical terms, the movement toward clarifying objectives and measuring results has not come too soon. Judging from the vigor of the congressional trouncing given to the model cities and poverty programs, the widespread attacks on urban renewal, in-town expressway construction, and other domestic ventures, moralizing rhetoric is losing its utility in securing continuing support for governmental programs, even from long-standing, liberally oriented allies. The tendency to subject these programs to informed criticism has demonstrated their vulnerability to inconoclastic Ph.D. candidates, let alone to dour appropriations committees. In short, more plausible proofs of performance are now required than has been the case in past years, particularly when the annual budgetary moment of truth rolls around.

In the 1960s under McNamara's guidance, the Department of Defense (DOD) made well-publicized progress toward relating goals to quantifiable measures of achievement. Under prodding from the Bureau of the Budget, the techniques pioneered by large private corporations, notably DuPont and Ford, and adapted by the DOD began to percolate through the federal establishment. In August 1965, President Johnson announced that the PPB developed by the Department of Defense would be extended through the other federal agencies. By early 1966, the Bureau of the Budget issued appropriate instructions to the executive departments. The system was to be applied immediately in the largest agencies and 18 other agencies were "encouraged" to adopt formal systems.[1] In practice, progress has been slow: PPB is easier to discuss than to apply, and by the early 1970s much of the earlier interest had waned.

PPB, ZBB, and such allied decision-informational technologies as operations research, cost-benefit analysis, and systems analysis represent an attempt to develop a flow of useful information about programs that center on whether discretely measurable and presumably attainable objectives were in fact achieved. However, as we shall see, the road has been strewn with obstacles. The most serious are attributable to the fact that highly sophisticated techniques such as PPB and ZBB call for cadres of talented technicians and sympathetic and decisive executives. Not surprisingly, these are in extremely short supply at every level of government, and the few who are capable of formulating and implementing new-style budgeting are usually hard at work on day-to-day program management and the normal run of agency crises.

According to reports, the processes of formulating goals, measuring performance, and arriving at choices on the basis of the results were highly successful at DOD. Applying the technique to the civilian agencies was another matter. It is interesting to note that doubts as to just how effective PPB actually is in the Department of Defense seem to grow in proportion to the amount of strenuous grappling with this technique on the part of the other federal agencies.

It has been argued that performance standards in government agencies can serve as a partial substitute for the market mechanism that weeds out the inefficient businessman or the test of combat that eliminates weak military leaders. Forays by legislative investigations or press exposés on vulnerable government agencies are the traditional means of forcing agencies to change direction because bureaucracies tend to find self-analysis and overhauling difficult to contemplate, much less to effectuate. Changes, when they do come about, are small and incremental unless the heat is on from the legislature, chief executive, and/or the communications media. PPB and ZBB offer a continuing, rigorous, and systematic method of improving agency performance without the violent upheaval of the congressional investigation and the presidential directive—in short, improvement without trauma. This movement to clarify, measure, and evaluate government operations may have certain real dangers to the public safety in addition to its implicit threat to complacent bureaucrats. The vagueness, imprecision, and inconsistencies that abound in private enterprise and familial life as well as in governmental programs are not solely attributable to dullards or incompetents. Secrecy as to salary levels, wills hidden in lawyers' offices, and program-reporting systems that fail to make a full disclosure of their impact share an important characteristic. A little fuzziness around the edges provides the insulation between interest groups, heirs, and employees; cloudiness tends to muffle dissent when people are not entirely clear about responsibilities, rewards, and punishments.

In contrast, precise identification of controversial issues and extreme clarity in analyses of program impact can sometimes be an invitation to conflict. To cite one outstanding example, a substantial amount of bureaucratic inefficiency and legal entanglement can mute class and race disputes by miring potential contestants in a glutinous sea of red tape. It can be argued that perfect knowledge of governmental inconsistencies, inequality before the law, and differential treatment for communities and neighborhoods augment rather than diminish intergroup suspicions. Positive verification of exactly how various groups are shafted—and by whom—is not likely to promote community harmony. Knowing in detail just how badly one is treated as compared to one's neighbors can have lethal consequences.

While an absence of hard facts can be dangerous, the high-minded verbiage of the type found in preambles to new legislation and political speechmaking has traditionally served as a placebo for impatient zealots. This is not necessarily the cynical process that it appears. Flowing rhetoric has been deliberately used on occasion as an effective method of placating agitators while avoiding immediate struggle on too many fronts, meanwhile preserving the reformer's political capital for a riper, brighter day when successful action becomes feasible. In brief, for several valid reasons, lofty expressions of good intent and vigorous speeches unrelated to subsequent action are indispensable to the workings of democratic society.

The fact that the layers of fine words are being stripped away from administrative operations may therefore offer some cause for alarm by exacerbating societal conflicts. This is a policy question that will be confronting us more frequently as we learn more about how our programs actually work. Clearly, the intrusion of slide rules that measure or purport to measure the effectiveness of government operations can have a devastating effect on the administrative equilibrium, and not all administrators have been enthusiastic about innovations in goal setting and program evaluation. Some have reacted negatively, suggesting that numbers are soulless, meaningless, or misleading because they fail to capture the intangible, vital spirit that animates a meaningful program. The attacks on McNamara's "whiz kids" in the DOD launched by disappointed generals and admirals fall into this category. However, this objection has been countered by demands that the bureaucrats get to work on standards of performance which do have meaning. And this is precisely the point at which the trouble begins.

To begin with, there is room for long and inconclusive wrangling at every stage of the process, over goals, performance criteria, the nature and quality of the judges, and measures of achievement. The agency administrator is likely to be extremely sensitive on each of these issues. He may feel that PPB or ZBB can help him in bringing a sprawling agency operation under control, but it also entails the risk of exposure. The immediate defense to criticism is to ascribe all the recently highlighted agency ailments to one's predecessor. However, only up to a point can bureaucrats blame dunderheads in the previous administration; this tactic tends to wear thin as time passes and the new appointees can no longer evade responsibility for error.

Despite the administrator's natural and wholly understandable reluctance at venturing into those stormy seas, the voyage is inescapable. Systematic analysis of government programs is here to stay. Although computers are popular and important, there is far more involved than simply new technology. There is a pervasive dissatisfaction with choice of goals, with the allocation of priorities, and with the apparent difficulty in translating objectives into reality. Most of all, there is irritation, frustration, and resentment over requests for more funds for programs that do not seem to be working very well. The public and the Congress seem to echo Lincoln's response to General McClellan's demands for more troops. Under McClellan's leadership, giving the Army of the Potomac more troops was "like shoveling flies across the room"—a most descriptive comment on men and programs that seem to be, in equal measure, insatiable and unproductive. Certainly the bureaucrats' belated ex post facto admissions of ignorance on such basic matters as the reason why the educational process is operating so badly in slum schools, how a reasonable urban land use and transportation pattern can be achieved in a nation married to the automobile, or how many blacks are unemployed in city ghettos have not diminished the growing skepticism. In short, as has happened before in history, public sentiment and technological innovation have come together to make life miserable for government agencies that have been operating comfortably and quietly on the basis of hitherto unquestioned assumptions.

New Tools: PPB

The technique of introducing an energetic new broom to clean out old stables is as old as history. Faced with a complex, ectoplasmic mess, the traditional approach is to locate a strong-willed, effective administrator and to turn him loose. What PPB offers is a possible means of economizing on virtuosos. It offers a new way of systematizing program management.

PPB is a method for analyzing programs in terms of outputs as related to expenditures.[2] Properly designed, it can be an important tool in the selection of alternatives because it can help to evaluate relative results from different kinds of public investments. The design of an effective system is predicated on two very critical assumptions. The first is that a substantial, reliable flow of timely information, probably through a computerized system, will be available to program administrators. The second and even more basic prerequisite is the existence of a program design that organizes information in a meaningful framework for decisions because it is of little consequence to have access to a vast amount of marginally relevant material that cannot be put to use in answering critical questions. One can be sympathetic to those who suggest that the problem is not generating more information because administrators are already swamped with more data than they can profitably absorb and that, anyway, most important decisions are political and judgmental.[3] However, while there is obviously far too much statistical trivia on hand and the computers will generate a lot more, there remains a clear need for relevant information on program impacts. Further, there is insufficient accurate follow-up information on programs in which the payoff is necessarily delayed as, for example, in education and health. Just as important, there are inadequate data that can be used to weight various programs designed to achieve similar objectives, as, for example, alternative manpower training programs. A critical distinction must, therefore, be made between masses of marginal data and the important information, much of which is not currently available and must either be forcibly excavated from a reluctant bureaucracy or generated through new research. As one observer suggests, we produce much data, but at least in the vital field of education, it does not tell us what we want to know.

> When we survey the voluminous, yet unsuitable, data now available for assessing the products of education, we must conclude that practically none of it measures the output of our educational system in terms that really matter (that is, in terms of what students have learned). Amazement at the revelation of the tremendous lack of suitable indicators is almost overshadowed by the incredible fact that the nation has, year after year, been spending billions of state and local tax dollars on an enterprise without knowing how effective the expenditures are, or even if they are being directed to stated goals.[4]

One prerequisite of PPB is that program objectives must be clearly defined, and the questions to be answered and the measures of performance must be part of a plan extending over a period of several years in the future. While there should be no suggestion that dubious programs be permitted to run on and on in the hope of long-term results or, even worse, of doubling expenditures for unproductive programs on the ground that results will then surely follow, PPB does not eliminate the need for a strong common-sense judgment on what constitutes a reasonable input of time, funds, and effort. Given this vital prerequisite—good sense—PPB offers a way to evaluate systematically the relationship between ends and means. Properly used, it offers the possibility of escaping some of the biases injected when information is filtered through the prisms of existing agencies and current programs. For the administrator, PPB can be an almost unprecedented method of clearing away, conceptually at least, the dense accumulation of underbrush that often obscures the paths between present programs and possible goals.

Despite these obvious advantages, there is an important caveat. If it can be said that the navy is a machine "designed by geniuses to be run by idiots," PPB is still very much at the genius stage. The technique is not yet routinized to the point where it can be managed by persons of modest competence; in its present, pioneering stage, PPB calls for remarkable qualities of objectivity, thorough grounding in operations, and a creative intellect. It is clear that the federal government will have to set the pace simply because there are more intelligent executives in Washington than in most of the state and local agencies. In time, a diluted, vulgarized, simplified version of PPB will filter out through the federal establishment and down to state and local government.

Up to this point, our discussion has largely focused on the potential benefits of PPB. If we are honest, we must squarely face some of the inherent limitations of the technique, the dangers in its use, and the difficulties in converting it into a form suitable for wide consumption. The interesting and, on the whole, melancholy history of the abortive attempts to inject cost-benefit techniques developed for water-resource projects into such other government operations as urban renewal may be remembered. Other extremely attractive innovations have foundered on the rocks of inherent but not fully recognized rocks and shoals.

NEW REFORMS, OLD PROBLEMS

ZBB is new-style PPB, applied, it is said with much success, at Texas Instruments and in Jimmy Carter's Georgia state government. The new wave in government reform is ZBB. Zero Base Budgeting[5] provides a mechanism for compulsory review and evaluation of all existing programs through the analysis of discrete program decision packages. In contrast to current budgeting procedures which bear heavily on the incremental—this year plus 6 percent for next year—ZBB carries PPB a step further, purporting to start from ground zero by suspending a permanent guillotine over all programs. Each year, each program would be compelled to justify, not some modest increase, but all of its funding, its very existence. This hard-nose executive branch approach toward executive agency expenditures and operations was paralleled during the late 1970s by growing legislative interest in "Sunset" legislation aimed at automatically self-destructing government programs unless they could prove to the legislative branch that they deserved to be renewed.

THE TEMPORAL TEMPTATION: PLANNING FOR THE MILLENNIUM?

While it is impossible to identity all of the problems likely to be encountered in applying PPB and ZBB techniques at the various governmental levels, we can begin to delineate a few of the more outstanding obstacles. Experience suggests that many future problems cannot be anticipated, but even a brief analysis suggests that the approach will encounter a full quota of obstacles as it wends its painful way through the government agencies.

One of the specific reasons for the increasing enthusiasm for stretching public agencies on the PPB-ZBB rack is the difference of attitude toward the passage of time between most political leaders and many bureaucrats. The pat distinction—between statesmen (good) who allegedly plan for the next generation and politicians (bad) who are concerned exclusively with winning the next election—loses some of its meaning when it is recognized that, like the politician's, the statesman's career is a painstaking, step-by-step affair in which immediate problems must be overcome if one is to be permitted to work on grand designs with long-term impacts. It may be recalled that Abraham Lincoln numbered among his many gifts a remarkable ability to manipulate postmasterships and popular generals to win elections. The inherent incompatibility between long-term, comprehensive plans and the pragmatic "project" orientation of the politician has been discussed at some length by Alan A. Altshuler and Edward C. Banfield, among others.[6] PPB and ZBB have the benefit of isolating program elements for inspection, and hence escape some of the odium (and futility) attendant on large-scale, slow-moving, closely interwoven, comprehensive plans that tend to be pretty much ignored.

This preamble is by way of suggesting that one of the chief problems in arriving at reasonable goals and translating them into reality with the help of PPB or ZBB relates to different time scales. PPB is supposed to have required four years from design to fruitful results in the DOD. The politician and his upper-echelon appointed executives must think in terms of efforts that yield perceptible, publicly demonstrable progress within a year or two. This is not to say that they are opposed to programs aimed at achieving medium- and long-term objectives, but they are confronted with an unending series of crises calling for immediate action. As a rule, an elected official has relatively little time or attention to devote to those who plan vast operations that may or may not bear fruit in his successor's administrations but that obviously have only a marginal relevance to his current problems—not the least of which is his reelection.

This sense of political urgency is usually shared by the appointed executive at the highest level to almost the same degree as the elected official. At one conference, for example, a senior administrator remarked that a junior planner, disillusioned by the futility of long-range planning, had remarked that henceforth the planning profession should concentrate on short-range efforts. The young man subsequently explained that by "short range" he meant five years. The senior official suggested that this time span, while an improvement on some previous programs that moved at a glacial pace, was still far too extended for political utility. He argued, that from the viewpoints of the voting public, the president and Congress, and appointed supergrade executives like himself who are charged with implementing legislation, five years is a political lifetime; half a decade may embrace a change in control of the Senate, two congressional elections, and a turnover in the presidency. If there were no substantive payoff within two years, the planning operation was not likely to secure much support, he observed.

The matter of timing is crucial to any number of government programs ranging from the Supreme Court's variously interpreted "deliberate speed" for racial integration of school systems to the surfeit of hastily drawn program requirements and preposterous deadlines that have confounded the local poverty program administrator. Determining the point at which a digestion problem arises in assimilating new legislation, at which a transient political opportunity for reform must be exploited despite the risks of overloading a frail administrative structure, and the point at which cautious delay may fade into indefinite postponement calls for delicate exercises in judgment. Critics of the politicians' and reformers' penchant for haste may be reminded that passion more often than prudence makes the political world go round. Waiting for plans to be perfected is usually an exercise in theological patience rather than practical politics. Successful politics and administration are largely matters of seizing fleeting opportunities. PPB and ZBB will have to adjust to this built-in urgency if it is to have much significant impact on policy. This means that with or without new-style budgeting, program planners and administrators must be prepared to offer judgments and recommendations on the basis of incomplete information, half-finished matrices, and subjective hunches, because events refuse to wait until the last word in research and program evaluation has been spoken.

If it can be assumed, as a general rule, that more progress may be achieved by launching a leaky administrative vessel than by waiting for the waters to recede, PPB and ZBB do offer methods of testing for hidden holes below the waterline, both prior to and after embarkation. There would seem to be no reason why a preliminary PPB or ZBB (like cost-benefit) analysis should not be required as a prerequisite to justify proposed new endeavors as well as to test existing programs. The danger would seem to be in the misuse of half-baked budgeting systems as another handy method of formulating plausible rationalizations for shoddy programs. A false aura of scientific objectivity can be enlisted to sell more than patent medicines.

HOW MUCH COMMITMENT?

If there is one central problem in implementing reform legislation and injecting controversial new techniques, it is the combination of underlying resistance to change by vested interests and the minimal support at the crucial moment vouchsafed by those who had previously been lavish with friendly rhetoric. It takes a lot of pushing to penetrate the layers of inertia and hostility, and unless there is genuine muscle to back up the speeches, the result is frustration and disillusionment.

The phrase "lip service" is used to denote verbal commitment to an objective unaccompanied by any real efforts to achieve it. Accusations that those in power are freer with promises than with action are of ancient vintage; doubtless cave drawings will someday be discovered attacking the probity of some clan chieftain who solemnly promised happier hunting but failed to deliver on his pledged word. This gulf between words and deeds was perhaps a major key to the domestic credibility gap. It has been charged, for example, that the bold promises of clean rivers, pure air, and slumless cities can not be redeemed by minimal budgetary allocations. Administrations' budgetary requests and subsequent dehydrated congressional appropriations are not consonant with either the stirring rhetoric of the legislative preambles or eloquent presidential messages.

It should by no means be suggested that skimping on money is the only way of slowing progress on a program like PPB or ZBB that promises to upset many bureaucratic applecarts. Belief in good intentions may be severely tested. The administrative saboteur who wishes to give the appearance of cooperation and open-mindedness, or indeed the politician who is not committed to his platform beyond election day or is simply short of discretionary funds, has a wide choice of weapons. The PPB-ZBB movement may be slowed to a walk by solemn and protracted bickering on details and concentration on tangential or irrelevant issues. Defensive bureaucracies and powerful client groups can agree on selecting policy and implementing committees that offer a combination of incompatible views, clashing temperaments, and feeble administrative sense. One step beyond, artistic undercutting can be managed by relegating the program to unsympathetic, weak, and/or captive administrators certain to decelerate forward movement.

Even progress designed to achieve ostensibly noncontroversial goals is susceptible to blockage at the operating level. For example, community development programs aimed at the presumably consensual objective of improving the local economy are so much the rule that the city which openly opts for the economic status quo is a rarity. Yet, although all communities affirm their verbal adherence to efforts aimed at stimulating new economic growth, for various corporate or personal reasons, leaders in some communities have been fertile in devising techniques that halt every concrete step in this direction. When adherence to a common goal is barely skin deep, a cynic might suggest that opponents can think of a problem for every solution.

While it is not difficult to discover any number of instances in which practice is not consonant with ideals in the city hall or the state house, skepticism can be exaggerated to the point of paranoia. PPB and ZBB can play a significant role even in their early stages by examining and clarifying goals because goals possess a force of their own, even if long unachieved. The exposure of hypocrisy is often an effective method of squaring current reality with accepted objectives. As Gunnar Myrdal correctly predicted with respect to America's treatment of blacks, a moral commitment to a goal, even if long unfulfilled, can in time be a powerful weapon in securing passage of corrective measures.[7] By linking program achievement to goals, PPB and ZBB can be significant levers for social change. They can document, in detail, our modest progress in moving toward accepted goals. The new approach to budgeting may, as one of its by-products, provide copious ammunition for basic reforms.

Conflicting Goals and Priorities

At bottom, PPB and ZBB assume that meaningful goals exist against which programs can be tested and evaluated. This is quite an assumption. Certainly there is no shortage of goals and objectives, but there is considerable difficulty in assigning priorities between them.

The financial limitations placed on Great Society programs in fiscal 1967–68 point up two most serious problems. The first and most obvious involved finances. Escalation of the American involvement in Vietnam, a conflict that was assigned priority over domestic programs, had absorbed the financial reserves for the projected expansion of Great Society programs. Appropriations for the war on poverty, model cities, aid to education, and antipollution measures reflected this budgetary malnutrition. The rhetoric remained unchanged, but the money was not there, nor was it forthcoming within the next fiscal years. Widespread racial rioting during the summer of 1967 did not elevate priorities for the city slum population to the damn-the-deficit level that has historically been accorded only to overseas conflicts.

More strains on civilian programs can be anticipated in the late 1970s and beyond. The revolution of rising expectations may, in fact, result in an intensification of internecine struggles by warring interest groups, all of whom can reasonably claim that a budget reduction would jeopardize an important national goal. Such battles might pit rural and urban areas against each other and could stimulate conflicts between programs designed to aid the aged as against efforts to help dependent children and lead to demands that funds be allocated to public transportation against pleas for more highways. The struggle could easily spread to include civil wars among urban, ethnic, and racial groups, as well as choices between equally valid national and international goals. Perhaps the bitter struggles for funds among neighborhoods of some cities are ominous omens of coming disturbances. Paradoxically, limitations on funds may force the pace of moves to introduce PPB, ZBB, and other program soul searching by the federal agencies. It will not be the first time an ill wind has blown a little good.

For Motherhood or Flag?

It would be an error to suggest that goal setting for PPB can be translated into a simple matter of financial priorities. Were this in fact the case, a cutback in overseas commitments and subsequent release of a major share of the federal surplus could eliminate problems of choosing between alternative goals and priorities by permitting a massive advance on a broad program front; virtually all significant budget requests could be honored. But there is obviously much more involved in achieving goals than a doubling or redoubling of appropriations. There are implicit conflicts between various goals. To cite a specific example, massive intown highway construction to provide easy access for a dispersed population to their work places and other destinations (as perhaps desired by a voting majority) is in conflict with other urban goals such as neighborhood stability and efficient urban development patterns. An across-the-board green light that includes heavy allocations for more urban expressways is therefore likely to diminish the possibility of achieving other, equally accepted objectives.

There is a more significant problem: Experience has proved that larger appropriations may not yield commensurate results. In fact, it has been charged that appropriations may have precisely the opposite effect for which they were intended. To cite one example, Scott Greer charged that the net result of an expenditure of $3 billion in urban renewal funds was a net reduction in the number of housing units available to low-income families.[8] Others have pointed out that funds allocated to regulatory agencies may end up as a kind of supplemental budget for the industries supposedly being regulated. Furthermore, there is often a matter of outright wastefulness of various types, including some programs that have outlived their usefulness, others that make no visible impact on their clients, and still others that leap from one costly, abortive experiment to another. It is hardly necessary to point out that a weak or stubbornly foolish bureaucracy wedded to obsolete ideas and practices can dissipate very large sums without commensurate product.[9] The Middle Eastern sheikdoms are not the sole instances where funds have been squandered with little resulting public benefit. There are instances in which additional funds may make a bad situation worse. Allocating new money to the old men may perpetuate and reinforce rather than remove the problems that the input of funds was supposed to solve. On the other hand, a prime argument for PPB and ZBB is that very often much can be achieved with little in the way of new allocations. Within urban areas, for example, training and recruitment programs for the police, better selection and promotion policies for the schools, and more effective housing code enforcement may be undramatic, but a realistic PPB or ZBB may discover that modest improvements like these—aimed at doing better with what we have—may be of more lasting benefit than some massive, costly programs.

The idea that progress can be bought, that military victory and social progress can be achieved by more lavish spending, is not purely American, but it would be fair to say that Americans seem to be especially prone to suggestions that in larger budgetary allocations can be found the answers to intricate domestic and foreign problems. One reason for the surge of interest in PPB is that faith in this simple-minded approach may be waning; at least a limited awareness that less money and more hard thinking may provide part of the answer is slowly creeping through the federal establishment. Success in this endeavor may compensate for temporary, less than hoped for funding of domestic programs.

It is clear that one of the basic problems with the selection of goal and program priorities which must provide the basis for effective PPB or ZBB is that the nation seems firmly committed to just about everything good—slum-free communities with healthful, attractive environments, and moral uplift, high-paying jobs for the employable, and livable incomes for welfare recipients. It is entirely possible that within a generation or two, when the gross national product doubles and trebles, it will be feasible to provide the trillions of dollars needed to achieve these goals. Meanwhile, as has been suggested, choices must be made not only between the clearly vital programs and the obvious marginalia but between a number of efforts that are normally accorded high-priority status. If this were not sufficient complication, there is evidence that some goals may be in direct conflict with other, equally cherished objectives.

It may be useful to cite a case that caused much concern in the mid-1960s, the improvement of housing conditions for black slum dwellers. Each avenue selected or recommended to achieve this highly desirable goal seems to be in actual or potential conflict with other goals and values:

1. Fair housing programs to provide access to relatively affluent suburban communities for blacks able to afford such housing may seriously deplete the

thin leadership stratum in the ghetto. Open housing of this type may defeat the objective of strengthening stable black community leadership.

2. Programs aimed at large-scale dispersal of the ghetto to white areas through rent supplements, creating pockets of public housing, or other means may lead to early, violent conflict in previously orderly white working-class and lower-middle-class communities.[10] These strata of the population seem to be afflicted with disproportionate amounts of insecurity and bigotry that often take overt physical expression. Similar although less explosive opposition may be encountered in moving large numbers of low-income blacks into close proximity to middle- and upper-income groups. There may also be some resistance to the dispersal concept from advocates of black power who view the ghetto as a political base and see its dilution as reducing blacks to a permanent political minority status among white majorities.

3. Improving housing within the ghetto through construction of public housing and/or large-scale renovation and rehabilitation will tend to perpetuate housing and school segregation and the economic and social divisions that breed mutual fear and hostility. On the other hand, requiring public housing projects (or other housing under direct government control) to be fully integrated (particularly if a substantial number of welfare families are included) may alleviate the pervading pattern of segregation to only a limited extent because the net result is likely to be the creation of socially unstable islands in the midst of all-black areas.

4. Permanent improvement in housing conditions for slum residents will require a fundamental change in living habits of many disadvantaged families. There are no hard data on the proportion of low-income blacks in the ghetto who differ from the white and black middle class only in their lack of money, sharing similar values and aspirations. Many blacks are moving each year into the middle class, and it is apparent that more would do so if the path could be made easier. In contrast, a substantial, although undetermined proportion of blacks and whites apparently do not share middle-class and/or (even) working-class values, as, for example, a moderate respect for property and cleanliness. A minority of building residents who are not yet housebroken can reduce a new public housing structure or a private apartment building to a shambles in short order. Effecting a significant large-scale improvement in slum housing may therefore require isolating and possibly retraining hard-core vandals under close supervision and/or selecting and segregating slum residents who can be relied on not to wreck the building in which they live. However, this kind of supervision can easily be labeled a bigoted, callous move to create racial or low-income concentration camps.

This example may suggest some of the limitations of PPB-ZBB. The technique can indicate progress and program impact, but it cannot reconcile the irreconcilable. Perhaps it is wisest to agree with the conclusion that its principal usefulness is educational: It will force agencies to do some unaccustomed, rigorous, systematic thinking about their programs.[11]

This is not to suggest that PPB or ZBB will revolutionize the ways in which goals are formulated and implemented. The United States (and perhaps most nations) seems to develop goals through some mysterious organic process. A climate of opinion is gradually established in the press, in the articulate portion of the community, among business leaders, and among a few bellwether reformers in the Congress. Gradually, as this process of subliminal educational exposure percolates into the lairs of the Philistines, it becomes transformed into legislation and thence settles firmly into the political landscape.

A classic example of the osmotic process of goal formation is discernible in the field of public higher education. In the late 1950s and early 1960s, a decision seems to have been taken in a number of states to provide every qualified high-school graduate with an opportunity for a low-cost college education at a public institution located within commuting distance of his home. This frightening outline is now an accepted, unchallenged feature of the political environment. The same is discernible with respect to a variety of programs that have undergone the same process.

DESIGN FOR GENIUSES?

Perhaps none of the problems that surround the injection of PPB into the governmental bloodstream is more crucial than the supply of trained, or trainable, technically capable manpower. The belated realization that shortages of qualified manpower rather than shortages in funds are crucial obstacles to program implementation has already been reflected in evaluation programs, funded by the Departments of Labor, Housing and Urban Development (HUD), and Health, Education, and Welfare (HEW), among others. It is also reflected in legislation introduced by the U.S. Civil Service Commission (the Intergovernmental Personnel Act of 1967), by Senator Edmund S. Muskie, and by HUD and HEW to expand the supply of trained professionals. In addition, some federal agencies have begun to tap outside manpower to conduct critiques of major programs, a form of independent evaluation that was almost unthinkable only a few years before.

Whatever corrective measures are underway or foreseeable, the prospects are far from promising. The Joint Economic Committee looking into federal human resource programs found, for example, that although its queries did not call for "the extensive analytical effort, special studies, detailed program examinations, and financial tabulations" that are required by the Bureau of the Budget, the questions bearing on economic impact "referred to types of information which apparently were unfamiliar to some of the Government personnel who were called upon by their agency heads to prepare the replies."[12] Only a few agencies were able to prepare an effective response (that is, the Social Security Administration, the Office of Manpower Policy, Evaluation, and Research, and "several" units of the DOD). But the committee expressed its hope that such difficulties will "gradually be overcome by the disciplines of the formal PPBS which carries its own internal sanctions," but it "anticipated a transitional period of incomplete analyses and shallow analyses of costs and benefits." The Joint Economic Committee concluded on a grim but realistic note, calling attention to the immensity of the task:

> Either there is a scarcity of penetrating analysis in many program operating units or the assignment to prepare responses was often given to persons who were not familiar with program analyses. . . . Much work needs to be done in the clarification of objectives and concepts, the formulation of analytical techniques, the explanation of procedures to individuals called upon to produce the necessary studies, and the definition of criteria for the interpretation and evaluation of findings. This will require a continuous process of examination and instruction throughout the executive branch.[13]

In a direct sense this depressing rate of progress with PPB is responsible for the popularity of ZBB as a guaranteed method of holding agencies' feet to the fire and forcing them to plan rationally or face the risk of termination.

Douglass Cater has quoted a Brookings Institution study to the effect that the Congress has done little to strengthen the top level civil service. The top 3,000 or more career executives who head the various bureaus and divisions were found to be "predominantly inbred. . . . Many had started in government service at a lower level, had risen through the ranks by concentrating on specialties and are frequently indifferent to the larger problems of government."[14]

> Although the problems of the executive branch are essentially similar throughout the hierarchy, it is important to bear in mind that the mass of government workers—the *lumpenbureaucracy*—marches to a drumbeat that only it can hear, which (if it exists at all) is faint indeed. Higher levels of government, although presumably more responsive to broad social needs, generally find their choices so circumscribed by business-as-usual decisions further down the line that their theoretically available policy options become dissipated by the inertia of the machinery. . . . In practically every agency of government, at almost every level, there develop strong and seemingly almost irresistible pressures to maintain the *status quo.* . . . There are also powerful personal influences that affect the career civil servant—influences that are environmentally, in current bureaucratese, "counter-productive." As one observer has put it, the "paramount objective of the permanent bureaucracy is permanence." This contributes directly to the institutional resistance to change already noted. Agency employees tend to react self-protectively, and in so doing they protect their own institutions. . . . This problem is

> compounded by a frequent lack of clear policy direction from the upper levels of government to the lower. New policies may be found in new regulations and pronunciamentos which go religiously unread, or they trickle down by word-of-mouth through a number of communicants, each with his own built-in bias. This communications system serves as an efficient filter for any content which may fortuitously have crept into the public statements of the man or men on top. These problems should not be ascribed solely to bureaucratic malevolence. Their problem is essentially the same as that of the private citizen: they are not programmed to relate everyday decisions to any specific action of the government machinery.[15]

Has planning in federal agencies improved since the early 1970s? An evaluation of the Department of Justice is instructive, since this agency, representing the focal point of the law-and-order emphasis of the Nixon administration, spends over $2 billion annually. Secretary Elliot L. Richardson, in his farewell letter in late 1973, summarized the problem succinctly: DOJ exhorts but does not practice: "It is an unfortunate irony that the Department of Justice has for the past several years been preaching the merits of comprehensive planning to states and localities—without in any serious respect practicing what it preached."

Richard Stillman sees DOJ as a operating a nonsystem, its autonomous divisions concentrating on public relations and on bricks and mortar (that is, building more prisons) rather than prison reform. The federal Law Enforcement Assistance Administration (LEAA) has spent $5 billion in six years to fight crime only to see crime rates go up—while increasing dramatically the size and cost of state and local criminal justice planning bureaucracies. Immigration and Naturalization Services strategies have not stemmed the flow of aliens, 17 strike forces located in major cities have had no impact on criminal syndicates, and antitrust activities have had little effect slowing the trend toward oligopoly. Stillman sees the various divisions deliberately failing to clarify policy issues and goals, to measure program impacts, to develop predictive social indicators, and to develop program innovations involving allocation resources. "At the annual DOJ preparation the decisional basis is the smallest increments of line items. . . . Never is there reflection on the adequacy or relevance of the entire program base, or more fundamentally, the assumptions of the policy upon which the program was originally justified."[16]

Stillman's harsh characterization of DOJ as "a decaying bureaucracy" which only a social revolution could modernize can be applied with equal validity to a very large number of federal, state, and local agencies. So too can his conclusion that "policy science," such as PPB and ZBB, is utopian if it avoids the bureaucracy problem entailed in the current managerial class. He poses a fundamental question to which budgetary techniques, however sophisticated, provide no answer: What do we do about modernizing bureaucracies that have "deteriorated into something almost akin to a Merovingian form"?

Difficult as is internal budgetary reform within a single agency (particularly if it is a sprawling miscellany like DOJ or HEW), establishing goals, evaluations, and priorities among different agencies is an even more horrendous task, especially if surgery is indicated. Joseph Califano, a key member of Johnson's White House staff, concludes that "the investment of political capital is so great and the risk of loss so substantial that a president can at best achieve one or two major reorganizations during his years in office—if he sets his targets shrewdly."[17] On the other hand, Johnson's successful reorganizations, the creation of DOT and HUD, have not been universally acclaimed as great improvements in achieving goals of efficiency and responsiveness. Further, Califano underscores the problems posed by divided loyalties of agency heads who receive directives from the executive but who must, in the final analysis, please the committees in the legislative branch which control their funding. One tempting approach, creating special executive agencies (like the Office of Economic Opportunity) as a means of bypassing recalcitrant line agencies, provides considerable flexibility but risks offending Congress and the older agencies without building a compensatory base of supportive constituencies.

Califano's comments respecting the federal government also apply to the states and municipalities. Bureaucracy problems encountered at the federal level are in fact multiplied exponentially in most state and local governments. One can agree with George C. S. Benson that "in some states the personnel is superior to federal personnel,"[18] and still hold with Charles R. Adrian that, of the three levels of government, "the states have been slowest of all to professionalize and this has crippled the administrator at that level in his attempts to share in the decision-making process."[19] It is not surprising that in late 1969 Selma Mushkin reported some progress but even more problems in applying PPB to state and local government.[20] Seven years later the verdict is much the same. The ninth (1975) edition of Burns and Peltason's standard political science primer summarizes the situation for the novice: "After more than a decade of experience with PPBS . . . it has neither introduced a significantly higher level of rational choice-making nor given analytic or systems experts an advantage over the politicians either in congress or the administration."[21] One can add that the whip hand also remains with the stubbornly unreformed old-style agency bureaucrats.

Assuming that competent staff can somehow be located to operate PPB or ZBB in government agencies, questions arise as to the orientation and direction of this staff. Budgeting is not a neutral, value-free process. The measurement techniques selected can have a powerful influence on goals and priorities. The budget process cannot itself define benefits, nor can it determine what kinds of weight should be given to alternative results affecting different income groups and different, conflicting objectives.

It must be understood that while PPB and ZBB can be useful in reexamining old prejudices, sophisticated budgeting is no guarantee against new forms of snobbery. To cite a specific example, critical problems may arise because the program-design assignment is virtually certain to be relegated to holders of college degrees whose middle-class outlook will undoubtedly be reflected overtly or subtly in the performance standards and targets. In effect, technicians whose orientation reflects the status and aspirations of a particular social class are called on to set standards for programs affecting lower-income people with different living patterns and often with different aspirations. This is not a new situation. It may be recalled that standard intelligence tests have aroused considerable opposition on the ground that they are formulated in a middle-class framework, and hence the test scores discriminate against working-class children. In the mid-1960s, one of the basic questions was whether the poor or the redevelopment areas were or should be evaluated on the basis of their progress in effecting a transition into the national, middle-class mainstream.

Obviously some amount of class bias is inevitable in any program because a substantial amount of conformity to middle-class standards is usually a prerequisite for admission to the ranks of the goal setters and program designers. However, it is vital to recognize that either by calculation or simply because certain values are assumed as "givens" by the planners, unless great care is taken, PPB, ZBB, or indeed any system of performance evaluation reflects and measures a relatively narrow spectrum of activities closely linked to the background of the designers. This may suggest that impartial, independent opinion should be brought into the design phase. More than likely, in time there may be demands for "maximum, feasible participation" in designing goals and performance measures for welfare, education, housing, and other programs. This may entail equipping the various client groups with the technical assistance advocates needed to protect their interests in program design and performance measurement. From the viewpoint of dissenting client groups, whenever controversial matters are involved, no panel of savants and/or corporation presidents is likely to produce a satisfactory consensus in assigning program priorities or in deciding exactly what it is that should be measured.

This brings us, of course, to the inevitable question: Should programs be geared to the tastes, abilities, and aspirations of the majority, or should goal setters and administrators continue to assume a paternal responsibility for remolding the masses toward some desired end?

Much has been said on both sides of this issue of mass and class. In recent years, there has been considerable attention to the need for redressing the traditional, quasi-elitest thrust of government operations by according greater weight to the opinions and values of the public as a whole or of major and minor elements of the population. The evils of government-by-expert and government programs designed by small groups of relatively affluent and articulate persons imposing their standards on the inarticulate majority, on the unorganized, the politically inarticulate, the currently unpopular, and the minority groups have been given wide currency.

Unfortunately, because government rests on a foundation of successful communication and manipulation of expertise and money, there is no easy solution to this dilemma. One obvious response is to ensure that every group has its capable spokesmen to give its interests adequate representation, not only in the political arena, but also in technical disputes. This would entail that some planners, economists, and sociologists join the legal profession in preparing partisan briefs for clients, a development which in any event seems to be well on its way in some new fields, particularly city planning.[22] But it would be a mistake to limit attention to the organized or potentially organizable.

Provision must also be made to guarantee adequate protection for submerged segments of the population. The question is how to achieve this objective for groups (like children on welfare) who cannot communicate easily or perhaps at all. There is also the problem of securing representation for groups who are obviously able to make themselves heard but who cannot or will not devote sufficient attention to complex operations in the face of competing issues that demand their attention. It is often difficult to secure meaningful responses from interests like downtown businesses—organizations which one would believe wholly capable of participating fully in the process of setting goals and performance standards. Even the goals established for a discrete and manageable area like the Minneapolis Central Business District evoked little comment from the downtown businessmen whose interests were presumably most directly involved. In fact, the detailed planning subsequently undertaken to implement goals evoked little reaction in Minneapolis until the plans were subsequently simplified in highly specific terms that clearly indicated the potential impact on traffic, or parking patterns, or on individual business establishments.[23] If PPB's or ZBB's design is to avoid charges of backroom manipulation and dictatorship-by-technician, it will obviously be necessary to translate a highly technical process into bread-and-butter terms meaningful to potential clients.

The experience in Minneapolis suggests that preparation of generalized goals is a task congenial to politicians and civic and business leaders, but involving them in a continuing dialogue with professionals is likely to be frustrating. Few nonprofessionals can devote the time and effort necessary to master a technical subject, and most groups are unable to employ a capable protagonist, nor are they willing to empower a technician to commit the organization to significant planning proposals. Because few interests are in a position to employ qualified lobbyist representatives, the result is that it usually falls to the technician to seek out meaningful responses from many of his client groups, particularly those without the technical knowledge or funds to employ professionally trained spokesmen. This, of course, does not place an unusual amount of new responsibility on the professional but rather recognizes a situation that has always existed.

As John Dyckman observes, "Most social planners have at least a modified caretaker orientation."[24] Leonard J. Duhl sees the planner-forecaster as an agent of social change acting as a kind of ombudsman, "returning the franchise" to the people partly by serving as a communications link with the "invisible colleges" of intellectuals and partly through conscious efforts as a political manipulator.[25] It is incumbent on the technician involved to develop a concept of short-run and long-run client interests. If he is to engage in this perilous activity, he cannot attend the luxury of technically neutral detachment. As Dyckman suggests, he will not be handed a ready-made packet of goals in the form of a set of well-ordered preference functions, and the task of discerning "latent" goals will take great patience and much interpretation.

It should be made clear that the relatively restricted technically supportive role suggested for the new budget program staff is at variance with other views on the function of the program planner in government. A more exalted pivotal role is identified by John Friedmann, who underscores the potential of the researcher planner as an agent in effecting social change and, implicitly, in assuming a major responsibility in selection of goals and programs. In his articles on "innovative planning"[26] Friedmann differentiates between the cautious creatures engaged in sanctioned, gradualist planning with its emphasis on effective allocation of resources within a system of incremental change, and the innovative planner. The latter seems to be a cross between a swashbuckler and an *eminence grise* who has deliberately chosen to become an engineer of rapid change in performing a planning, advisory, and manipulative role, working closely with top-level executives.

The innovator seeks to legitimize new social objectives by concentrating on crucial points of leverage and, like a bold staff Saul Alinsky, he seeks to "organize dissatisfied creative minorities to translate general value propositions into new institutional arrangements." Concentrating his efforts on making maximum use of all available resources by focusing on areas likely to produce the greatest changes, he eschews comprehensive planning in favor of strategic actions based on what he interprets as demonstrable results. Because innovative planning is associated with periods of crisis and change, Friedmann feels that it was more prevalent in the 1960s than the conservative, allocative variety. This proved to be a transitory phenomenon. The advent of the Republican administration in 1968, two business recessions in the mid-1970s, the end of the Vietnam war, and a cooling-off of the campuses and ghettos resulted in a profound change in direction. By and large innovators left or became conservatized.

While it may be argued that in playing a free-wheeling semiconspiratorial role, the planner arrogates responsibilities which are, or should be, in the province of the elected official, it can be countered that he functions as the chosen instrument of the politician. If he operates under a loose rein, it may be presumed either that he possesses the full confidence of his boss and has the sense to check sensitive decisions with his elected superiors or that his tenure will be short-lived. Further, it may be assumed that this *modus operandi* has considerable attractions for the result-oriented politician, provided the planner stays out of too much hot water. Under varying job descriptions, most incumbents number practicing bureaucrat-planner-researchers among their trusted subordinates. These are people who can be relied on to get a job done without bothering their superiors and without making too many waves. They are usually prepared to serve as loyal expendables; if things go wrong, they deflect the blame from the man who appointed them whether or not the trouble arose from bad luck or faithful adherence to orders. In fact, because a considerable amount of friction from change-resisters is inevitable, the turnover among innovators may be substantial. For this reason a quick, thrusting, hit-and-run strategy is clearly in order rather than the incremental type of planning associated with planners who have hopes of retiring on the job.

Whether this description is accurate or indeed whether it is a role that planners and administrators should deliberately choose is open to question. Clearly, some have found this a congenial role, working as a trusted lieutenant to an imaginative executive. In any case, the innovator seems to be more suitable for the executive's personal staff than for the staff of technicians committed to long-term service with a permanent agency. Furthermore, he must recognize that his enlistment may be drastically curtailed unless he possesses remarkable personal gifts and a great deal of good luck. The planner who attempts to manipulate the facts, control the news, and engage in behind-the-scenes social engineering is likely to end up in a pot of hot water, particularly if he discusses his role openly with friendly reporters. It can probably be taken for granted that social planning will be an uneasy, hybrid mixture of open plans openly arrived at and the kind of high-minded conspiracies described by Friedmann.

Whatever the particular mix in a particular time and place, there are areas in which wholly objective tests can be developed as, for example, such indisputable yardsticks for health programs as the infant mortality rate or family income patterns, the occupational distribution of minority groups, and the proportion of college graduates in various communities and population groups. But there remains a wide latitude for bitter disputes on the type of performance standards to be employed in measuring progress on such basic issues as the status of the blacks in America or the quality of life in our cities. The fact is that such performance measures as exist in these and other areas are traditionally established in societies by a small group of cultural pacesetters. This returns us to the original dilemma: Do we set standards that satisfy the current tastes of the electorate or are there overriding professional standards? If purely mass standards were to serve as the criterion, the outlook for a host of subsidized activities ranging from parks and universities to operas and educational television would be bleak indeed. It would appear to the author, at any rate, that adoption of Philistinism in the guise of a modern-day slogan of *vox populi, vox Dei* represents an abdication of responsibility rather than, as some argue, a progressive step in the direction of democratic freedom.

The danger of bowing uncritically to popular sentiment shows up most clearly in relation to racial and religious issues. If local referenda were to be the guide, antiblack prejudice would be certain to bar progress on civil rights in many areas, North as well as South. While it is perfectly true that it is all too easy for middle- and upper-class residents (or program budget staff) to prescribe racial balance for working-class areas because their neighborhoods escape most of the potential hazards to life, schools, and property,[27] even if it is admitted that there is some rationale for white backlash, abject surrender to popular bigotry is hardly the answer.

To a degree this mass-class argument is, in every sense of the word, academic. Whatever the technique in vogue for measuring the popular will—elections, polling, or revolution—in the end, most decisions are made by elites. Decisions may be modified or influenced by systems that accord greater weight to wider strata of public opinion, but the number of persons actually involved in decision making is almost always very small. Nor is there any indication that mass education and mass communication have fundamentally enlarged the proportion of the population which has a significant influence on decisions. The civil rights movement, like the earlier successful efforts aimed at securing legal and political equality for labor unions and women, has enlarged the spectrum of clienteles who must be taken into account in formulating and administering public policy. As government and society grow more complex, the distance between technician, administrator, and politician can be bridged only in part by mass media, opinion polls, periodic elections, sporadic disorders, technical interpreters, advocates, and ombudsmen. Demonstrations are a method of calling attention to a cause, not a consistent approach to influencing day-to-day program operations. For this reason, the burden of representing much of the public will continue to fall in great measure to program designers and administrators. There must be an awareness of this extremely important responsibility.

The person at the upper echelons in government also has broader responsibilities. He must not be contented with programs and efforts good enough to satisfy his clients but short of what he knows is desirable and possible. Moreover, he is, or should be, an educator rather than either a bureaucratic calculating machine or a pliable professional survivor. He has a duty to the spirit and substance of his program rather than solely to generate laudatory comments in the legislature and the press. PPB or ZBB, if he uses it properly, can serve as an effective teaching aid. On the other hand, if he misuses it or promises too much from its use, the result is likely to be growing cynicism and suspicion on the part of client groups convinced that a new black art has been developed to justify unpopular decisions.

WHO KILLED COCK ROBIN?

Like military combat, the challenges entailed in mounting a genuine PPB or ZBB operation cannot be fully appreciated until one has actually been in the field. From its inception through its inescapable revision, the designer is called upon to render a series of judgments involving interpretations of legislative intent, community values, and professional standards.

One of the thorniest problems in measuring impacts is disentangling programs from their environmental context. It is necessary to identify the role of each layer of government, of each relevant program, and of other societal factors that may have an equally important influence on events. Moreover, since the sum is often greater than the total of the individual parts, the combined impact of various programs must also be examined.

In attempting to isolate the effects of any single government program in the field of health or employment, for example, it is extremely difficult to determine, with certainty: (1) which changes occurred as a direct result of a particular program; (2) which changes can best be classified as indirect or corollary impacts; and (3) which changes are attributable to exogenous factors. A manpower training operation, for instance, can exhibit a combination of all these: a group of trainees may be hired as a result of a good literacy campaign, because of an unanticipated increase in the gross national product, success in a local area development effort, or a modification of union rules or company policy. Thc inhcrcnt mcrits of program dcsign and cxccution may havc littlc relation to success in locating good jobs for the trainees.

Tracing the indirect impact of a program or its effects in combination with other programs is often a tricky affair. One example may be cited: the relationship between poverty programs, singly and in combination, and the violent disorders that erupted in the black ghettos during the summer of 1967. In the spring of 1966, officials in poverty agencies claimed that the constellation of programs financed and administered by the Office of Economic Opportunity (OEO) had been instrumental in taking the steam out of riots by providing hope, tangible accomplishments, and employment for potential agitators. During the summer outbreaks, critics subsequently suggested, with somewhat tenuous logic, that, on the contrary, racial disorders occurred in some measure because poverty programs had titillated but not satisfied the aspirations of the poor. In partial agreement with this stand, Sargent Shriver, the OEO chief, later pointed out that poverty funds represented only a fraction of the amounts requested by the riot cities, indicating that larger allocations might be more effective in muffling violent protests. From a slightly different perspective, other observers suggested that the modest improvements introduced by the poverty programs and related efforts by the mid-1960s had accentuated social disequilibrium by breaking through the thick crust of despairing passivity that had kept the slums passive under worse conditions (such as the 1930s depression).

Obviously identifying cause and effect is far from an easy task under these conditions. Programs do not operate in a vacuum, and it is not always possible to state with certainty that effect B was caused in part or in whole by program A.

There is a further problem in creating defensible yardsticks for evaluating programs: Assessing highway beautification, open space, historic preservation, the impact of placing utility lines in urban areas underground, of cultural development, and other programs in purely monetary terms is ridiculous. How is the quality of life to be measured, and who is to do the measuring? How can emotions like pain, grief, humiliation, anger, and happiness be converted into comparable dollar units? Costs and emotions are often related, but it is hard to enter them on the same balance sheet even after the linkage has become obvious. The decades of humiliation and despair that exploded in the 1967 racial disorders have had measurable consequences running into hundreds of millions in property damage. However, the anger and hatred that led to the arson and robbery are not quantifiable.

There is also an obvious temptation to expend many years and much money in assessing the probable, possible, and conceivable, and the immediate, middle-range, and long-term relationship between programs and consequences in both the so-called pure and applied categories. An affluent nation can pursue all kinds of research avenues that might be of value; it is feasible to feed the entire pack rather than run the risk of starving one of the hounds that might have caught the quarry. The difficulty is that much time and effort may be expended in belaboring the obvious. The ancient gibe that a sociologist is a scholar who spends $100,000 in research grants to locate a brothel has more than a glimmer of truth in it. On a more sophisticated level, there is the danger of overconcentration on one or a few enticing aspects of a problem to the exclusion of other, possibly more promising, research areas. The results may make a good deal of sense, but they may divert attention if the study fails to take account of the major dramas on the periphery. In short, while research is needed to identify the relationship between specific programs and their impact, it is just as hard to formulate useful research studies as it is to design effective programs.

In formulating program design for PPB or ZBB it must be recognized that the information received in the form of impressive print-outs and charts may, nevertheless, be superficial and misleading. Any number of key items may be missing, like, for example, confidential information on program impact in slum areas or sensitive data pointing to administrative lapses. There is also the question of how far to rely on self-justifying statistics furnished by separate agencies with similar or identical missions. Substantial knowledge is necessary to reach behind the budget and performance data when attempting to measure the relative effectiveness of different but overlapping programs, some of which may be twice or even six times more expensive per trainee but may also be six times more productive. In addition, there may be corollary, nonmonetary benefits (such as a fresh perspective for trainees) that compensate for the higher costs.

To summarize, PPB and its successor ZBB offer a number of extremely attractive prospects. They may shed new light on tired programs and demonstrate just how much we do not know about government and the society in which we live. On the other hand, overselling or overreliance on PPB or ZBB would be tempting fate. Quite probably the by-products of the intellectualization of government represented by the new budget approach will be a species of technical warfare between warring advocates, each of whom can point out the fallacies in assumptions, values, and techniques of his opponents, their programs, and their recommendations. In brief, budgeting may become a new arena for informed but nonetheless deadly conflict.

At the risk of appearing tiresome, it must be noted that one critical shortcoming appears glaringly obvious when we consider introducing new and intricate programs. PPB and ZBB call for outstanding intelligence in the design and evaluation phase and solid competence in operation. They cannot conceivably be made a foolproof, self-adjusting mechanism. Surely the technique is beyond the current capacities of many government agencies, particularly in state and local government. Ideally, the process should be delayed until there is assurance of adequate staffing, but government does not work in a simple, logical progression. Realistically, the best that one can probably hope for is that parallel, strenuous efforts will be made to enlarge the supply of trained staff as new-style budgeting is diffused through the governmental structure. After much preliminary floundering, people competent to handle the mechanics of the system will be available, and we can proceed to the next plateau. On these Plains of Abraham to be scaled in the late 1970s and 1980s will be waged interesting technical battles involving ideological and value issues that reach into the heart of government.

Based on the past experience of consistent failure at all levels of government in phasing out unwanted or allegedly unneeded programs, the results of both ZBB and Sunset reforms are likely to fall below promises and expectations. Some of the obstacles are familiar: Over time, programs develop strong and resistant legislative, interest-group, and public constituencies and are operated by tough, narrowly oriented bureaucracies highly resistant to fundamental reform. Since the process of performance evaluation is relatively new and its conclusions and assumptions highly debatable, we can confidently anticipate prolonged technical disputation between learned and eloquent proponents of abolition, reform, termination, expansion, and modification. On a five-year cycle, ZBB calls for the review of every agency once in five years. This goal would clearly generate a huge quantity of paperwork and a huge increase in jobs for program analysts, evaluators, and much in the way of other budget experts, but there is no assurance of results.

The author's firsthand experience with attempts at ZBB in settings where the financial wolf was at the door suggests that the dawning of a new age of technical warfare may be at hand. Clouds of alternatives, justifications, rationalizations, and mobilizations can be anticipated, rather than any weeding out of the unworthy. Quite likely is a replay of the municipal experience in New York, Detroit, and other hard-pressed cities: across-the-board cutbacks applied with some discretion toward vital services, followed by a slow erosion in program quality as middle-aged administrative and operational staff are retained and young people are either fired or never hired. In short, talking phase-outs may be good politics and good sense, but actually doing it is politically dangerous and may yield unintended and, on the whole, undesirable consequences.

The basic question remains: How do we institute fundamental innovative reforms in policy, management, and operations in the face of powerful interests —and people—working in an environment which is inevitably parochial and resistant to change? It is a system in which most executives either perpetuate the status quo with minor slow incremental alterations, or, if they persist in demands for sweeping, rapid reform, risk becoming the system's transitory, frustrated victims. Viewed in this perspective, imaginative management tools like PPB and ZBB are interesting and perhaps even useful, but they are instruments that can more easily be sabotaged than effectively used.

NOTES

1. U. S. Bureau of the Budget, *Bulletin No. 66-3, Planning-Programming-Budgeting* (Washington, D.C., 1965); and *Supplement to Bulletin No. 66-3* (Washington, D.C., 1966).

2. For an excellent, very short, but authoritative description of PPBS, see statement of Charles L. Schultze, Director, Bureau of the Budget, *Hearing Before the Subcommittee on Intergovernmental Relations,* "Creative Federalism," 90th Cong., 1st sess., pt. I, pp. 388–419.

3. See the comments of Professor Charles A. Reich, Hearings Before a Subcommittee of the Committee of Government Operations, House of Representatives, *The Computer and Invasion of Privacy* (Washington, D.C.: U.S. Government Printing Office, 1966), pp. 22–42.

4. Wilbur J. Cohen, "Education and Learning," *The Annals* 373 (issue entitled *Social Goals and Indicators*) (September 1967): 87–88.

5. See Peter A. Pyhrr, *Zero-Base Budgeting: A Practical Management Tool for Evaluating Expenses* (New York: Wiley Interscience, 1973).

6. See Alan A. Altshuler, *The City Planning Process: A Political Analysis* (Ithaca, N. Y.: Cornell University Press, 1965), chaps. 4–6. Also Edward C. Banfield, *Political Influence* (Glencoe, Ill.: The Free Press, 1961), chaps. 8, 9, and 12.

7. For opposing views on this critical matter, see C. Wright Mills, *The Power Elite* (New York: Oxford University Press, 1956); Floyd Hunter, *Community Power Structure* (Chapel Hill: University of North Carolina Press, 1953); and Edward M. Banfield, op. cit. Also Gunnar Myrdal, *An American Dilemma: The Negro Problem and American Democracy* (New York: Harper and Bros., 1946).

8. Scott Greer, *Urban Renewal and American Cities: The Dilemma of Democratic Intervention* (Indianapolis: Bobbs-Merrill, 1965), p. 3.

9. See Senator Edmund S. Muskie, "Manpower: The Achilles Heel of Creative Federalism," *Public Administration Review* 27, no. 2 (June 1967): 193–94.

10. See Herbert Gans, *The Levittowners* (New York: Pantheon Books, 1967), especially pp. 427–28.

11. See William Gorham, "Notes of a Practitioner," *The Public Interest* 8 (issue entitled *PPBS, Its Scope and Limits*) (Summer 1967): 408.

12. U.S. Joint Economic Committee, Subcommittee on Economic Progress, *Federal Programs for the Development of Human Resources,* 1 (Washington, D.C.: U.S. Government Printing Office, December 1966), p. 31.

13. Ibid., pp. 31, 92.

14. Douglass Cater, "The Fourth Branch," in *Power in Washington* (New York: Vintage Books, 1965), p. 244.

15. U.S., *Hearings Before the Subcommittee on Air and Water Pollution of the Committee on Public Works (Senate),* "Air Pollution—1970," 91st Cong., 2d sess., 1970.

16. Richard J. Stillman, "The Bureaucracy Problem at DOJ," *Public Administration Review,* no. 4 (July/August 1976): 429–39.

17. Joseph A. Califano, Jr., *A Presidential Nation* (New York: Norton, 1975), pp. 27–28.

18. George C. S. Benson, "Trends in Intergovernmental Relations," *The Annals* 359 (issue entitled *Intergovernmental Relations in the United States*) (May 1965):5.

19. Charles R. Adrian, "State and Local Government Participation in the Design and Administration of Intergovernmental Programs," *The Annals* 359 (May 1965): 36–37.

20. See *University Training in PPB for State and Local Officials,* synopsis of the Airlie House Institute on University Training, Selma J. Mushkin, Chairman (Washington, D.C.: The Urban Institute, August 1970).

21. James MacGregor Burns and J. W. Peltason, *Government by the People,* 9th ed. (Englewood Cliffs, N. J.: Prentice-Hall, 1975), p. 476.

22. Paul Davidoff, "Advocacy and Pluralism in Planning," *Journal of the American Institute of Planners* 31, no. 6 (November 1965): 331–38.

23. Altshuler, op. cit., pp. 235–90.

24. John Dyckman, "Social Planning, Social Planners, and Planned Societies," *Journal of the American Institute of Planners* 32 (March 1966): 70–71.

25. Leonard J. Duhl, "Planning and Predicting: Or What to Do When You Don't Know the Names of the Variables," in *Daedalus* (issue entitled *Toward the Year 2,000: Work in Progress*) 96, no. 3 (Summer 1967): 779–88.

26. John Friedmann, "Planning as Innovation: The Chilean Case," *Journal of the American Institute of Planners* 32, no. 4 (July 1966): 194–203.

27. William Lee Miller, *The Fifteenth Ward and the Great Society* (New York: Harper and Row, 1966), chap. 6, pp. 99–111.

CHAPTER

4

SOCIAL INDICATORS AND REVENUE SHARING

DO URBAN PROGRAMS HAVE A FUTURE?

A provocative, question-begging heading demands immediate clarification. Our dilemma is that we can pass a flood of new legislation, fund it generously, and then find to our dismay that it does not do the job it was supposed to do. Obviously, one reason for disenchantment is faulty conception. Spending in some cases was totally inadequate in relation to the size of the problems, and too many hopes were loaded on rather modest programs. In putting together the voting coalition to pass new housing, area development, and poverty legislation, it is fair to say that the Congress and the public were promised too much for too little. But excessive fervor and the kind of insulated millennalism prevalent in Washington during the first half of the 1960s were not the only reasons for the growing disillusion with government programs.

While many of the new programs were reasonably sound in design, we lacked the people to administer them properly. The desperately mistaken assumption of the early 1960s was that an enormous reserve supply of competent cadres of federal, state, and local administrators existed to staff the new, massive programs and successfully adapt them to local needs and changing circumstances. Typically, perhaps, the initial response to poor execution was not prompt action to increase the supply and quality of administrators but an attempt to develop increasingly sophisticated management techniques valuable in highly experienced hands but totally beyond the ken of the typical bureaucrat available for program operations. All this would not be so tragic and ludicrous if we had not had ample warning, albeit on a lesser scale, at least a decade earlier. To cite one example, the 1960s' attempt to infuse the government structure with advanced PPB techniques was far from dissimilar to the enthusiasm of the 1940s and early 1950s for cost-benefit analysis. Similarly,

Nixonian management by objectives in the late 1960s and early 1970s followed by ZBB in the late 1970s and a proposed Sunset approach are likely to face the same inadequacies in staff and methodology and the same political obstacles that frustrated earlier efforts.

COST-BENEFIT ANALYSIS: *DÉJA VU?*

Youthful enthusiasts for PPB, ZBB, and other systems and operations approaches are sometimes appalled by the cautious reserve of their elders toward promising innovations. It may be that some of this skepticism is attributable to past experience with such devices as cost-benefit analysis. Like PPB, the cost-benefit approach attempts to develop a systematic and orderly relationship between total investment inputs and total expected outputs. Ideally, the system produces a simplified statistical balance sheet listing all costs on one side and anticipated results on the other, with the relationship between the two reduced to a simple arithmetic ratio. A range of alternatives can be compared with ease and dispatch by the busy executive and politician and, *ceteris paribus,* the investments with the best ratios—the highest yields in relation to costs—are then given high priority.

Developed and systematized for use on water resource projects, cost benefit generated considerable scholarly interest in the 1940s and 1950s. As is the case with PPB and ZBB, there was much talk of applying the technique wholesale to transportation, housing, education, and other programs. And, if historical parallels may be pursued a step farther, as cost benefit was considered for such wider uses, probing questions began to be asked regarding its alleged triumphal progress in guiding dam-building and irrigation projects.

On closer examination, the technique was found to have serious disadvantages. For example, it was discovered that there is a tendency for decision makers to ignore textual addenda and prologues and explanatory footnotes, and, instead, reach their choices solely on the basis of grossly simplified, consolidated balance sheets—provided these were in agreement with political necessities. In the cost-benefit analyses prepared for water resource projects, it was found that "scientific" ratios and other data could be, and were, manipulated to secure desired results, and that, as always, political logrolling usually guided the decisions. Equally important, cost benefit provides a beguiling but misleading common denominator permitting inaccurate comparisons between actions that may differ tremendously in characteristics and impact. One study concluded that:

> comparisons of governmental programs in terms of expenditures is deceptively simple and can be misleading as a basis for public policy choices. This

> is not only because the figures, with their appearance of precision, gloss over numerous difficulties, discrepancies, and ambiguities that inevitably beset the compiler. That kind of shortcoming—a common attribute of analytical and accounting data—is serious enough. But the principal reason that expenditure comparisons are an inadequate basis for policy preferences is that they necessarily treat equal dollar expenditures as though they were equal contributions to the solution of various problems when, in fact, the problems may be quite dissimilar in quality, resources marshaled for different purposes may be quite varied, and the effects of equal expenditures may differ in intensity as well as kind.[1]

A variation of cost benefit is the cost-revenue study that enjoyed considerable popularity in the 1950s. In their crudest form, such studies elaborated on a rather obvious truism: Slums cost more in tax expenditures and yield less in tax revenues than other neighborhoods. This reasoning was used (and in fact is still used) in support of proposals for urban renewal and related programs on the dubious assumption that slum areas can be changed by improving the quality of the housing. More sophisticated studies in the mid-1950s were concerned with alternative tax returns and costs generated by decisions on various types of urban land development, expenditures for public services, and tax policies.[2]

The overriding problems with the cost-benefit technique are not only the tendency to slight unquantifiable essentials but the consistent failure, until recently, to evince much interest in obtaining critical social data bearing on program operations. In fact, it is only when cost benefit is broadened into PPB that we have come to realize just how little the scholars know and, surprisingly, the extent to which this ignorance is shared by the operating agencies.

Bertram M. Gross and Michael Springer suggest that "among the weakest links in benefit-cost-output analysis" is the lack of comparable, systematic, and periodically gathered social data. They maintain that "no conscientious budget-examiner could rely uncritically on the data presented on education, mental illness, crime, delinquency, transportation, and urban problems by scores of competing bureaus anxious to justify budget proposals."[3] Thus, not only is there not enough of the right kind of data but the statistics that are developed and presented for legislative action are often self-serving and suspect.

Extremely crude cost-benefit comparisons are freely offered to guide major expenditures of government funds. In the 1960s appropriations for the Job Corps were solicited, to cite one of many examples, on the basis of comparisons between per-trainee costs in Job Corps camps that ran as high as $12,000 annually for only a year or so as compared to the similar amount required to support and guard a prisoner for a longer period in a federal penal institution. In a burst of political hyperbole, President Johnson charged that opponents of the administration's urban reform and poverty programs were "helping to produce convicts." The president wondered "why some people are willing to sit idly by and are willing to take the more expensive route—the delinquency route, the jail route, the penitentiary route."[4]

A certain amount of simplification is inevitable in politics, but serious problems may develop when sweeping judgments are habitually used in justifying or, for that matter, in attacking particular programs and proposals. At the very least, when better information becomes available, attacker and defender can engage in bloody combat with more plausible weapons systems. Partly for this reason, a study on the human problems of technology has called for a system of social accounts to measure performance in achieving goals. A system of social accounts would be created to measure the social costs and net returns of innovation, to assess social ills, to create performance budgets in areas of defined social needs, and to develop indicators of economic opportunity and social mobility.[5]

As was suggested above, one reason for the failure of cost-benefit analysis as a planning tool is the difficulty in assigning adequate weight to unquantifiable factors. This point is underscored in James C. T. Mao's theoretical framework for measuring the costs and benefits to society derived from a residential slum clearance project.[6] While it is feasible to assign dollar values to changes in land values, to measure tax returns and savings in public programs, and to identify various project costs, assessing project impact on the community's social fabric, on esthetics, and on the strengthening or disruption of neighborhood coherence is an extremely hazardous undertaking. Boston's West End project, which was attacked at great length by Herbert Gans[7] is a net gain in some accounting systems. Gans and others like Jane Jacobs[8] have stressed the debit side of the ledger in this massive total clearance project in terms of human costs and the destruction of a stable Italo-American neighborhood that offered a satisfactory environment for its residents.

The cost-benefit equation becomes even more complicated when problems arise in allocating limited amounts of funds to alternative methods of meeting the same social need. For example, social planners and administrators have experienced much difficulty in assigning priorities to projects for: preschool children, teen-agers, family heads, neighborhood organizations, manpower training, health programs, or the aged.

Martin Rein and S. M. Miller point out that if one takes into consideration long-term, second- and third-stage benefits, this inevitably leads to a bias in favor of child-oriented programs as opposed to efforts aimed at assisting the elderly.[9] Unless other goals and values are taken into consideration, cost-benefit analysis is likely to reinforce the emphasis on child-centered and youth-centered expenditures observable in much of the poverty strategy. A workable system of cost-benefit analysis that would help to determine the proper weight to be given each component of the poverty program would be most welcome. Realistically, this goal is probably unattainable.[10]

On a practical level, it would not appear that cost benefit or any other technique is going to be of much use in a close race. Most of the underpinnings, the inputs, goals, values, and assumptions, are much too debatable to permit honest choices between the front runners.[11] Assumptions with respect to future interest rates, consumption patterns, occupational distributions, and income levels are particularly vulnerable to manipulation and attack, but even a factor as innocent and technically neutral as population projections rests on uncertain, hard-to-defend foundations. It is difficult to escape the conclusion that cost-benefit analysis can function as a quasi-administrative spectroscope ordering material into tidy, measurable components only so long as it remains unchallenged. By changing a few assumptions, the informed critics are able to revolve the lens again and again so that the instrument begins to function like a kaleidoscope, presenting patterns and results pleasing to the operator.

What cost benefit can be used for, aside from its invaluable assistance in injecting fresh perspectives into policy and operations, is to help rule out the worst projects, proposals that are patently outrageous. If this limited role is visualized as a principal contribution to government decision making, we may approach a situation in which a prestigious legitimizing technique is used by administrators to fend off proposals that unaided common sense indicates are ridiculous or to justify actions that the administrator is convinced are necessary. Perhaps an analogous situation occurs with respect to civil rights legislation that provided liberal-minded administrators with a handy excuse for taking action which they had wanted to take before the legislative enactment. In short, cost benefit, like PPB, ZBB, and other techniques, is helpful in aiding the administrator and legislator not only in arriving at decisions, but in the last analysis, in validating the subjective, informed, partly intuitive, and politically influenced judgment that has been and will remain the key to goals, priorities, and measurement.

SOCIAL INDICATORS: THE BIG PICTURE

One of the attractive possibilities opened up by PPB and cost-benefit analysis in the late 1960s was their use in formulating and operating a system of social indicators. The keystone of this approach is the creation of an observation post at the summit, a federal council of social advisers.

In 1967, Walter F. Mondale, then a senator from Minnesota, introduced legislation to establish a council of social advisers; paralleling the Council of Economic Advisers' report on the economic state of the nation, the new council would be assigned the responsibility of devising a system of social indicators to advise the president and to help in evaluating national social policy. The president would be required to submit to the Congress an annual social report, indicating progress, identifying future goals, and delineating policies for achieving these goals. The new council would construct yardsticks to measure the nation's progress toward social goals, and, implicitly, the impact of the various government programs in achieving that progress.

The Mondale proposal aimed at creating an agency whose function would closely parallel the functions of the present Council of Economic Advisers. For example, a third component of the legislation called for the creation of a joint committee of Congress to review the presidential report, just as the Joint Congressional Economic Committee exercises a similar responsibility over the president's report.

Social indicators, in effect, were to represent a kind of report card for the nation. On the "macro," national level they were to provide part of the framework for PPB—cost-benefit analyses for many of the individual agencies measuring overall progress in achieving social goals. The indicators were to be used by both the council and the agencies as a reference point for measuring overall progress and as a first step in evaluating the contribution of each agency toward achieving national goals. The proposal to extend the indicators on a subarea basis was designed to add a further dimension to the analysis as well as enormous headaches in program design. There is no reason why indicators could not be carried a step further; it would appear logical to develop indicators for social classes and ethnic groups. In a fairly crude way, this effort has been going on for some time with respect to distressed areas and blacks; in both instances, indices of family income and unemployment as well as of educational welfare and health have long been used to chart progress and to bolster proposals for various programs.

The historical origins of the nation's first attempts to create social indicators (Thomas Jefferson in the 1800 census) and the potential benefits and very difficult problems involved in their design and use are discussed at considerable length in the seminal volume edited by Raymond A. Bauer.[12] Including contributions from six outstanding authors and running to almost 350 pages, the reader is warned that this massive effort does not do much more than scratch the surface of what promises to be a lengthy and complex as well as rewarding task.

The authors point to literally scores of unanswered questions and complications entailed in the process. They include many of the problems that bedevil PPB and cost-benefit analysis: the lack of much useful data, the tendency to concentrate on quantifiable statistics to the neglect of other vital information, and the temptation to seize on measurable symptoms (such as poor housing) as a surrogate for more basic problems. There is also a pessimistic inflationary bias on the part of designers that may make the situation look much worse than it is. Furthermore, there is the possibility that the close investigation required to develop valid indicators may in itself actually change situations. The information uncovered in the process of examining social ills is often a political weapon. Some conservatives have long feared that the federal government would one day create a center of unrest and dissatisfaction under the aegis of research. A Council of Social Advisers could serve this function.

With the Nixon victory of 1968 the prospect of creating a Council of Social Advisers receded into the governmental mists. Not only was the social indicators movement relegated to the political deep freeze for the next eight years, but it barely surfaced during the candidate maneuvering for the 1976 nomination. The Democratic party's winner, Jimmy Carter, was a ZBB proponent on the basis of personal predilection and gubernatorial achievement with this approach during his term in Georgia.

On the assumption that an attractive commonsensical notion like a Council of Social Advisers will indeed be rescued from its cryogenic vault, we can predict that conservative fears of muckraking radicalism are much overstated. If the history of the economic advisers can be used as an analogue, a federal Council of Social Advisers would function as a semiautonomous body engaged in pioneering research, clarifying public policy issues (for example, improving the ghetto vs. dispersing the ghetto), and adding fresh perspectives on existing programs. It would probably not, as some of its proponents hope, revolutionize government operations by guaranteeing the injection of hitherto neglected social considerations and the social sciences into the decision-making process.[13] Instead, again based on the experience with the economic advisers, it would open up a new field of technical disputes in an area presently governed by all sorts of implicit assumptions and dominated by partly understood and/or inadequate data.

Following the trail blazed by the economic advisers, the social advisers would be one authoritative voice among many that claim equal or greater wisdom. The social science equivalents of the Federal Reserve Bank, the Brookings Institution, and university departments of economics and sociology will doubtless be available to challenge the findings and recommendations of a new council. Moreover, substantial overlapping in responsibilities, research, and program advice between the economic and social advisers is virtually certain to ensure disagreements on socioeconomic issues. Treading on unexplored, controversial areas, the new council will present an enticing target for congressional, journalistic, and professional criticism. In Albert D. Biderman's phraseology, there has been a demonstrated tendency for social indicators to develop from "social indicators" to "social vindicators" or "social indicters," depending on the orientation of the designer and consumer.[14] The dispute in the mid-1960s concerning the pace of black progress in urban areas offers only one example to suggest that the possibilities for argument on the basis of interarea, interclass, and international comparisons are endless.

A basic difficulty in the use of the indicators is that the central thrust of national policy seems to veer away from readily quantifiable indices like income, housing starts, or air pollution. Increasingly, problems seem to involve exploration into spongier areas involving community morale and environmental livability; the black problem has moved away from simple, measurable demands for equal housing opportunities, voting rights, and jobs onto psychological terrain involving motivation, alienation, and pleas for recognition of dignity and manhood. By all quantifiable standards, enormous progress in solving black problems has been made, but the figures can be deceiving; victory or even interracial tranquility has proved elusive.

As was suggested earlier, if there are separate councils of economic and social advisers, one of the difficulties in social indicators may be their separation from economic indicators. Are poverty and the lagging redevelopment area social problems or economic problems? Whose analysis and recommendations are to prevail? Which indicators are most significant? What makes good economic sense from the standpoint of efficiency may not have desirable social consequences. A given amount of investment in a flourishing metropolitan area will usually yield more than an equal amount allocated to a distressed area, which, like the underdeveloped nations, is often weak in capability, labor skills, and infrastructure. Despite special legislation aimed at providing special help for redevelopment areas, it is not surprising to find that, through the workings of normal economic and social processes, the thriving metropolitan areas receive more government aid per capita than most distressed areas.

An examination of available indicators raises some important issues concerning the nation's choice of values and goals. As an example of things to come, it may be useful to examine one economic indicator that borders on the social-per capita incomes. It can be assumed that one consistent objective in a sometimes conflicting pattern of national goals will be further action to diminish interarea disparities in incomes and living standards. It is not at all difficult to develop a broad series of indicators that can be used for measuring the qualities vital in area progress: community leadership, worker motivation, social frictions and factions. It is perhaps instructive that as we become more sophisticated and disillusioned with our accustomed indices of change, more and more of the informative research on the problems of the poor is coming from psychiatrists and social psychologists rather than economists. To cite one example in which quantifiable indices offered a mixed reading even to the sophisticated analyst, in early 1967, statistical "radar screens" failed to pick up advance warning of the forthcoming summer of ghetto riots, but instead turned up indications of slum-area unemployment and delinquency that differed not very much, if at all, from earlier, less turbulent years. As in the case of the larger redevelopment areas, social indicators in urban distressed areas provide masses of conflicting data on symptoms and progress. What the indicators can help us to do is to raise the level of ex post facto argument to an informed, technical, and possibly less heated level. Moreover, the technique inevitably leads to a searching self-examination on just what are the nation's goals and priorities. But it is also clear that hard, interpretive analysis which goes well beyond, or more accurately, behind, under, and around, the figures is crucial if the social indicators are to be satisfactory policy instruments. The consolidated tables themselves can or should be regarded only as the tip of the iceberg; one can only hope the other seven-eighths will receive the attention it deserves.

REVENUE SHARING, OR AN EXPOSÉ A DAY

Cost benefit, PPB, ZBB, and social indicators are attractive but complicated techniques. A chronic shortage of professionals even capable of asking the proper questions, let alone providing plausible answers, raises some doubts concerning their use in the federal establishment. One's skepticism multiplies geometrically if the burden of adaptation to the new world is to be placed on the frail shoulders of state and municipal staff.

A special facet of the problem of injecting sophisticated management techniques into state and local government is their lack of capacity not only to exploit new opportunities opened up by PPB and other approaches but even to muster sufficient expertise to handle their current operations satisfactorily. Access to quantities of free money is not the simple answer to structural incapacity. It is ironic that side by side with mounting evidence of their painfully slow progress in mastering complex advances in management, there are simultaneous efforts in progress to increase state responsibilities vastly.

Since the 1950s, there has been a recurring cycle of innovative government programs, followed, in diminishing time frames, by scathing criticism. Formerly most of the attacks were linked to financial scandal, but more recently they have been focused on inefficiencies and on the disappointing gap between promise and performance. The time period between high-level hearings, instant, laudatory press releases, and the first virulent exposés seems to be becoming increasingly truncated. For example, while the blasts against the urban renewal program required an elapsed time of five to ten years, the poverty program became a target for liberal as well as right-wing critics in less than a year. It may be possible to accelerate further this pattern of initial huzzas followed by bitter disenchantment as program control is transferred to state and local governments.

There was a growing tendency beginning in the mid-1960s to decry centralization in government. Proposals to turn over a share of unearmarked federal tax revenues to the states, suggestions for a more local federal-state partnership in urban development,[15] and recommendations for a stronger state and local role at the expense of a rigidified federal establishment[16] are only a few manifestations of a change in climate that may result in significant changes in the structure of federal-state relations. (This assumes that the end product will be more meaningful than the Eisenhower-era Kestnbaum Commission that labored in vain in efforts to transfer federal programs to the states.)[17] The parallel and conflicting demands that the cities, rather than the states, be given direct access to federal tax revenues for urban renewal and other programs may also meet with some response. Legally, cities are creatures of the states, and many city problems require action on a metropolitan or state level. Whether the main thrust is in city or state government, the outcome may be predictably dismal, at the very least passing through a difficult transitional period.

Given a working knowledge of the programs, the available alternatives, and the orientation and limitations of the cast of characters, it is possible to begin writing the first exposés before the shift in operational responsibility away from the federal level takes place. It required no power of clairvoyance to predict that one major controversy would involve racial issues. Although there are likely to be a number of surprises when some local governments take hold of programs currently under tight federal supervision, it can be anticipated that observers will conclude that most state and local governments are poorly equipped to do an adequate job. Whether flexible approaches can be developed that permit a wide variation in federal control depending on local capability is another question. Such arrangements do, in fact, exist on an administrative ad hoc basis, but it is doubtful if they can be codified into law without considerable wrangling from states and localities that have the will but lack the means to perform competently without close federal scrutiny.

One keen observer, Lawrence Houstoun, summarized the situation in 1971 in the lengthy subtitle of his brief article: "Simply Sending Money Down Will Worsen the Situation by Postponing Essential Reforms." He pointed out that rural dominance in state legislatures had been replaced by suburban dominance in programs and funding and that archaic state-local tax systems perpetuated by suburbs were leading directly toward the bankruptcy of many central cities. Houstoun called for heavy weighting in favor of disadvantaged cities by using federal leverage to compel the states to reform their fiscal inequities and to force the suburbs to eliminate exclusionary zoning practices so the territorial burden of poverty could be fragmented more equitably rather than concentrated in core cities.[18]

Houstoun was prescient on two counts. The state and local Fiscal Assistance Act of 1972, which allocated $5 billion a year to states and localities, did allocate proportionately more funds to the cities; but most of the money was used simply to stave off bankruptcy while suburbs with less revenue-sharing money but far fewer problems used the new allocations to expand services, including in some cases bridle paths and tennis courts.

The shift in management responsibility and funds to state and local government will most likely represent an exacerbation of rather than a departure from the pattern of program innovation at the conceptual level and fumbling at the operational level noted in federal agencies. Considering the well-documented weaknesses in federal executive agencies, we can anticipate early scathing attacks from liberal elements on the ineptitude, callousness, and impenetrable stupidity of many state and local governments. On the other hand, attacks from the conservative right may be delayed because of the importance of grass roots in the conservative political ideology. However, a substantial swing in the pendulum is likely; even conservatives will not be able to stomach the results of giving a green light and a full purse to utterly incompetent bureaucrats. In particular, conservatives are likely to declare open season on the blunderers appointed by the opposition party. Ammunition for the barrages will undoubtedly be supplied, in profuse quantities, by federal bureaucrats who have little faith in local competence and who deeply resent their loss of authority, by enterprising journalists, and by disgruntled elements on the local scene. In addition to maladministration, the possibility of substantial pilfering at the state and local level, a minor problem in the federal bureaucracy, cannot be discounted. All in all, lively times lie ahead.

REVENUE SHARING: SHREDDED WHEAT FOR BREAKFAST?

In mid-1970 a number of regular users of many breakfast cereals were appalled to learn that we had been feasting on filler containing all the nutritive value of toasted straw, a fact which may have accounted for our ravenous appetites by lunchtime. In their defense, Nabisco and its colleagues pointed out that their bulk materials were never served unaccompanied but were always surrounded by orange juice, milk, sugar, and vitamin pills. It is my contention that revenue sharing in its present form is analogous to some of the oversold, downrated food substitutes unless it is combined with the real McCoy: modernization and reform of state and local government, and binding productivity-oriented contracts with municipal unions.

In terms of sheer budgetary disaster, any jury would award first prize in the show-and-tell misery contest to New York. What other city can demonstrate such an enormous gap between revenues and expenditures? And with revenues rising by only 5 percent per year—only one-third of the 15 percent yearly rise in expenditures—who else is going downhill so fast on so large a scale? It is no wonder that New York pleaded for a massive no-strings-attached injection of federal money as a means of warding off a looming disaster, a disaster that finally arrived in 1975 as the city flirted with outright bankruptcy.

We are indulging in the wildest kind of optimism if we think that revenue sharing will make much of a difference. New York's federal funds—and indeed revenue-sharing money in other cities—were gone, vanished, absorbed, and liquefied in a huge swamp of insoluble problems. In short, as presently proposed, revenue sharing will have no discernible effect on the quality of life, not only in New York, but almost anywhere in the nation. Why so gloomy? Because the facts are depressing. To begin with, there are huge budget deficits.

The revenue sharing just about covered current shortfalls, leaving city finances in a precarious balance, waiting for the next year's fiscal hemorrhage.

Since New York is the subject under discussion, we can focus on that unhappy place, although we must never forget that New York's fiscal troubles are pandemic rather than local. New York's budgetary problems stem from four main sources:

1. An enormous backlog of accumulated problems in housing, transport, and other areas, and the city's willingness to tackle them, drawing heavily on its own resources, including the earnings of its posterity.
2. Powerful municipal unions which have shown no compunction in forcing the city to its knees to gain their objectives.
3. An out-of-control welfare budget and related programs linked to welfare pathologies, all due in part to the city's generosity.
4. A muscle-bound municipal bureaucracy and administrative structure.

Suppose we consider this last point first, if only because it never seemed to receive much attention in discussions of revenue sharing among either the blessed givers or the blessed receivers.

In fact items 2, 3, and 4 only began to receive the attention they deserved in 1975, when the city came to the very edge of default. Surely it is no secret by this time that many municipal and state agencies are havens for mediocrities. The problem of outright thievery by the new con men or by the old-style rapacious Neanderthals has probably been overstated. But while far more is lost by incompetence than by boodling, public enthusiasm for government tends to wane perceptibly with each new juicy scandal. But speaking of honest stupidity, a fair number of studies, including some by the Advisory Commission on Intergovernmental Relations, have shown that local and state government is less talented, less responsive, and less efficient than federal government. One observer has summarized the experience of the past few decades in two sentences:

> Every single new activity of state government in our state in quite a few years has been the direct consequence of federal grant programs. The result is that its people in Washington who are deciding in what direction our state government moves—but then, if the federal government didn't move us, we wouldn't be moving at all.[19]

One can argue that state and local agencies would do a better job if they could hire better people by paying higher salaries. The difficulty is that salaries have gone up without any commensurate improvement in performance. Too often the same old clowns are getting paid more for doing less. In many occupations, municipal and state salaries are higher than salaries in private enterprise, particularly if generous fringe benefits are taken into consideration. Take New York as our example: Can anyone detect any genuine improvement in the city's schools, police, or sanitation services after the last rounds of pay increases? We are familiar with the spastic performance of New York's poverty agency, its school system, and its urban renewal program. We can be quite current in surveying the disaster area: In January 1971, the New York *Times* reported that the city's model cities program, snarled in its own red tape for 19 months, would be able to spend only one-half of its $65 million federal grant.[20] A day later, the *Times* carried another gloomy item: "plagued by delays in starting school programs, New York City has lost $16 million in state funds meant to improve education in the slums."[21] Apparently the city gave a repeat performance; a year earlier most of $20 million in unused state education funds in this program reverted to the state treasury.

In its behalf, the city can rightfully plead the delays inherent in consultation and review with an often fragmented community, a requirement of model cities and other municipal programs. But community paranoia hardly accounts for the *Times* discovery that "it now takes 71 steps through 10 different agencies for the city to buy equipment such as a desk or a sanitation truck."[22]

The substandard performance of many local agencies is due to a combination of a substandard staff operating in jerrybuilt administrative structures. David Rogers' scathing description of a "sick bureaucracy" comes uncomfortably close to a panoramic photograph of a host of state and local agencies. He sees a major agency as typical of organizations

> whose operations subvert their stated missions and prevent any flexible accommodation to changing client demands. The system has the characteristics of all large bureaucratic organizations, but practices have been instituted and followed to such a degree that they no longer serve their original purpose. Overcentralization, fragmentation, the development of chauvinism and protectionist baronies within particular units, in-breeding, compulsive rule-following and role-enforcing, rebellion of field supervisors against headquarters directives, insulation from clients, and the tendency to make decisions in committees—making it difficult to pinpoint responsibility and delay in implementation of programs—are the institution's main pathologies.[23]

Rounding out this devastating portrait of the New York City school system, Rogers adds a negative attitude toward client groups, limited expertise, and poor relations with outside institutions. To those familiar with the airless, incestuous world of state and local agencies, Rogers' scathing observations are all too familiar.

The real question is this: Setting aside the simple faith that revenue sharing will release a burst of creative energy at the state and local level, on the basis of past performance, could we have confidently expected New York to make good use of revenue-sharing funds in 1972? Was the debacle of 1975 inevitable? And does New York City represent only one—and by no means the worst—of hundreds of examples of unwieldy, chaotic governmental operations at the state and local levels? Is there any rational reason for believing of a calcified bureaucracy that, in Winston Churchill's words, "Give them the tools and they can do the job"? Can they? Or are we likely to discover that state and local government machinery is so feeble, so incompetent, that with notable exceptions the result of revenue sharing will be momentarily happier agencies serving still dissatisfied constituencies? In view of the circumstances, the following (preenactment) ACIR colloquy on revenue sharing has a distinctly hollow ring:

> State-Local Modernization Should be a Condition
>
> Allegation: States and localities should be required to modernize their organizations and to restructure their politically fragmented metropolitan areas before they are given "no expenditure strings" aid.
>
> Response: There is no denying that much remains to be done to modernize State government and to restructure local government. Indeed, much of this Commission's time and effort has been devoted to pointing up the organizational and structural shortcomings of State and local government and to recommending policies for correcting them.
>
> The Commission is keenly aware that progress on this front is painfully slow. Some of the proposed reforms, such as the reduction in number of local units and the creation of metropolitan-type governments are highly controversial. Others suffer from the lack-luster appeal all too often associated with "good government" causes.
>
> It would be a disservice to the cause of balanced federalism to insist that every State put its structural house in perfect order before the principle of revenue sharing is enacted.[24]

The operative phrase is in the last sentence—"perfect order." Perfection is always an unreasonable expectation. Most of us would settle for demonstrated modest competence.

People calling for reform in the midst of crises are often accused of being cold-blooded nonparticipants who would demand a higher standard of efficiency on the part of the fire department before they would release the water to put out fires. In the view of the Advisory Council on Intergovernmental Relations, counsels of "perfection" for state and municipal government as prerequisites for receiving federal aid are uncalled for, yet, if basic reforms do not take place, there is every prospect that the new funds will vanish almost without a trace.

I. D. Robbins suggests a sweeping series of reforms which would strike at one of the chief sources of fiscal evaporation—the inordinately high cost of providing essential services through vast, swollen, and largely uncontrollable bureaucracies. Focusing on New York City, Robbins advocates privatization of key services like refuse collection, hospitals, building and housing inspection, and record keeping. Most important, he provides an alternative to the public employee unions, which seem to be fully capable of swallowing huge amounts of revenue sharing in one or two massive gulps.[25] As events proved, the unions could only be tamed by genuine, imminent bankruptcy.

To each his own disaster area. Matthew Dumont's domain is state government.[26] His uncharitable comments lend little support to the belief that an influx of new money can change life-styles among the old men. Between a legislature of "marvelous unaccountability" and a regressive civil service system, he posits as a first principle of state government: "Nothing works." The hot-shot reformist professional has little impact, since the long-term civil servants who administer the programs are motivated in other directions. Their ingenious sabotage, foot dragging, and last but not least, their sheer incompetence, constitute almost impenetrable barriers to reform.

Dumont also identifies another overlooked reason for delay. In enormous bureaucracies, simple acquiescence is not the way to receive attention, to build one's self-esteem. A complex system generates feedback to the naysayers. Persons who point out reasons for further prudent reflection, raise constitutional issues, and identify unforeseen but potentially calamitous consequences from precipitate action are accorded more attention than bureaucrats who do not impede the flow of paper from desk to desk.

Revenue sharing, Dumont suggests, is based on a fantasy if it assumes that providing more juice to lubricate the machinery will result in necessary reforms. Dumont does not directly discuss the delicate matter of unproductive absorption of larger amounts of federal funds (state employee unions are powerful and would be likely to clamor for raises), nor does he raise the private divestiture alternative as a realistic possibility. What is clear, however, is that unremitting federal pressure is needed to keep many moribund state and local agencies functioning with even a modicum of efficiency and equity, and removing the overseers in the hope that free cash will result in self-generated reform is more likely to perpetuate than to correct existing faults.

In one pessimistic view, revenue sharing, which is being marketed as the salvation of state and local government, will probably make things worse by making it unnecessary to exact needed improvements in governmental efficiency and equity:

> It is possible, if not probable, that simply transferring federal money to the states and through them to all local general purpose governments—or relieving them of the financial responsibility for all or most welfare costs—will worsen the situation in the long run by postponing essential reform. . . .
>
> States have taken to distributing their tax dollars, especially those for education, according to formulas that favor rural and suburban school districts over urban ones. In 1967 only six of the 36 largest cities received more aid per pupil than their suburbs, and only two received more aid on a per capita basis.

> The NAACP Legal Defense and Educational Fund found that the states even cheated schools in poverty neighborhoods out of federal funds intended only for the most deprived children.[27]

To a degree, the pessimists were proven right. Compared to categorical grant-in-aid programs which were often earmarked for use by the poor, revenue-sharing money allocated to the general fund was used to ease the burden on taxpayers, many of them middle-class homeowners. Some argued that this was disguised racism or at least a Nixon-Ford tactic aimed at consolidating a property-owning majority in the Republican camp.[28]

One of the most difficult problems in modern urban management relates to the demands of previously underpaid municipal employees. Now unionized and no longer fearful of injunctions and dismissals, each branch of city government jobholders has successively brought New York to its knees and has accomplished as much for other cities. If they have done this while municipalities are demonstrably broke, what will happen when there is real money around? In the same issue of the *Times* which had Mayor Lindsay foreseeing the possibility of a $1 billion shortfall between income and outgo, Police Commissioner Murphy announced his support of a $15,000 minimum salary for patrolmen.[29] This raised the alarming prospect that any substantial amount of funds received from revenue sharing would be quickly absorbed in raises for municipal employees. In truth, the New York City unions were extremely helpful in swallowing revenue-sharing funds by 1975.

There is no purpose in discussing New York City's welfare problems at any length. One-eighth of the city's population is on the welfare rolls, and the proportion is steadily rising. An excellent case can be made for the proposition that New York and other core cities are the fall guys for a major national problem, which should be supported and alleviated by the nation. A federal takeover of welfare programs, passage of some form of national minimum income plan or welfare equalization with federal aid is simple, belated justice. But before indulging in premature euphoria over the potential impact of removing this burden from the municipal budget, we should be aware of the fact that Boston is still financially strapped, despite the fact that the state assumed financial responsibility for all welfare programs in 1968. Furthermore, there is no guarantee that if the federal government does in fact iron out the disparities in welfare payments between New York and lagging areas that the present breed-your-own welfare population will diminish or that the corollary crime and housing problems will become any less complex or serious.

Finally, consider the problem of effecting a substantive improvement in the physical structure of the city. There are the subways which, in comparison with modern systems elsewhere, qualify as a transit slum. And there are the vast and growing slums throughout the city's infrastructure—the obsolete schools, the inadequate hospitals, the aging public housing developments, the ancient, crowded jails. Everything seems to cry out for more funds. This is equally true of the delivery of services. And New York is not alone: aside from a few lavishly supported operations such as highways and airports, the basic fiber of state and municipal government is frayed and tired from decades of patchwork improvements.

If one could be sure that money alone could do the job, by all means—let's shovel it in. But if we have learned nothing else from foreign and domestic aid programs in the past two decades, surely we know by this time that, in the absence of ability to use funds effectively, money simply disappears, some in graft but most in a morass of inefficiency.

We should draw the proper conclusions from history. First, past failure should offer no support for present callousness. People need help, cities and states need help, and they should get it. But two further observations (or perhaps more accurately, warnings) are in order. First, the proposed scale of revenue sharing is ridiculously small compared to the awesome dimensions of the need. An additional $5 billion for New York City alone out of the total of $50 billion for the nation's states and localities may be required. Second, if aid on this scale is not forthcoming by the late 1970s there is a clear alternative to massive revenue sharing in prospect: spreading local bankruptcy, with New York City leading the way, although Newark and at least a dozen other cities are strong contenders for second place. There is precedent for this forecast—many cities were in state receivership during the depression. Without a really huge revenue sharing, civil service unions and welfare recipients may very well find themselves arguing with trustees in bankruptcy by the end of the present decade.

Realistically, in all probability aid will be forthcoming to stave off outright collapse. Surely the cities are no less deserving of a federal bail-out than shaky private enterprises like Lockheed Aircraft and the Penn-Central Railroad. The question is whether revenue sharing will do more than solve the problem of meeting weekly payrolls. And over and above the difficult problem of municipal employees, if there is to be such an impact, there must be standards of performance not only to ensure that blacks or Latins are treated fairly but to guarantee that added funds make a significant dent in the problems.

Federally imposed minimum performance standards are desperately needed to keep state and local government up to the mark. In fact, despite all the complaining about federal snooping and meddling in the present categorical aid programs, federal supervision tends to be weak and slipshod, fearful of provoking open confrontations with states and localities. Remove even the present level of weak supervision and the results could be disastrous.

Some major problems with revenue sharing have already surfaced. Aside from the tendency to give increasingly lower priority to the poor and minorities, there are allegations of serious fraud. A 1976 report by the General Accounting Office charged that the $6 billion in revenue-sharing funds assigned to 39,000 state and local governments had not been properly audited. Many programs were initiated in haste and confusion with little or no provision for auditing expenditures or evaluating program results.[30] It seems clear that Pulitzer prizes await enterprising journalists who can trace and document the passage of revenue-sharing funds from the federal supply agency to the local co-optors.

The continuing confrontation with municipal unions poses another set of questions. While capitulation to striking municipal employees is not confined to New York City, the city's 40 percent expansion of the municipal payroll in just two years, 1969 and 1970, probably set some sort of track record. Meanwhile the quality of services has been deteriorating, and few can be optimistic about New York City's "one real hope . . . that it will be able to buy some worthwhile improvements with the new money (i.e., impending pay raises)."[31] The time has come to examine the use of collective bargaining in municipal government. What may be good for General Motors may not be so good for America.

Are there viable alternatives to the municipal trade unions? It may be possible to contract out public services to private enterprise, with clauses embodying cancellation for nonperformance. Perhaps the monopoly position of the unions will be weakened, but more likely the construction industry syndrome will prevail. Wages could continue to outpace productivity, since unions will probably be far stronger than their private employers. If this alternative should not work, one can foresee a new version of the "withering away of the state," a kind of continuation of post-1975 trends as despairing governments shrink their payrolls and implicitly encourage their citizens to purchase police protection, sanitation services, and other essentials from private corporations. Federally aided experiments like school chits for parents to place their children in private schools, if they desire, may become commonplace. Chits for garbage removal or private police protection are awkward but entirely feasible. Private arrangements for purchase of police and sanitation services are already in effect in commercial and office centers, and it does not take much imagination to foresee more of the same in more areas.

To return to the main point: Without the most intensive program auditing and evaluation based on rigorous standards and performance guidelines, revenue sharing on almost any conceivable scale will evaporate like the famous mists over San Clemente. As Selma J. Mushkin put it:

> There is no provision in the proposal restricting expenditures to the meeting of urban problems . . . it does not undertake to encourage any particular pattern of local government that would facilitate greater access of the people to government or improve efficiency in the use of public funds for effecting results.[32]

Henry S. Reuss suggested that unrestricted grants be awarded only if state and local government is thoroughly overhauled:

> In order to qualify, each governor would have to present a plan setting forth just what it proposed to do by way of modernizing local government. . . . Federal planning funds would finance the preparations of the Modern Governments Program. And the Advisory Commission on Intergovernmental Relations—that excellent organization of leaders from federal, state, and local levels—would have to approve the Modern Governments Program of each state as reflecting "sufficient creative State initiative so as to qualify that State for Federal block grants."
>
> Simply to give unrestricted block grants to the states, without requiring . . . that the state get on with the business of allowing local governments to modernize themselves, could well be simply to pour money down a rathole. With their fiscal problems eased, there would be a great temptation for states to be more lethargic than ever.[33]

These warnings were not heeded. As a result cities blew the wad on higher wages and any number of treadmill expenditures. It may sound harsh at a time when the cities and states are drowning in deficits, but revenue sharing will continue to be the fiscal equivalent of shredded wheat unless the intended recipients can be modernized and the municipal union problem can be licked. To a degree the latter problem has been confronted. Municipal worker layoffs became a fact of life in 1975 and 1976. But genuine modernization seems as far away as ever, partly because seniority clauses are turning municipal civil service into gerontocracies; it is the older incompetents who stay on, while there is a general erosion of service quality.

It is useful to examine the kinds of cutbacks in services adopted by municipalities as a result of increasing fiscal stringencies in 1975 and 1976. Cutbacks included closing half the galleries at Detroit's Institute of Fine Arts, terminating preventive maintenance at St. Louis hospitals, shortening school days in New York City and Detroit, and cutting Buffalo's street resurfacing program by almost half.[34] The overall impression is not one of selective cutbacks with a tighter, leaner staff, but one of decay and dissolution.

While the preceding discussion has focused on a broad panorama of state and local weaknesses, the picture, it must be emphasized, is a generalization. The pattern of incompetence not only varies from state to state, but, depending on circumstances, programs, and staff, from agency to agency and even from division to division of the same agency.

In one agency, a third-echelon federal official of modest abilities may be seen in action on the average of once each month, strutting past tiers of cringing, slow-witted executives who are terrified by the awesome shadow of federal power. Fifty feet away, on another floor, his status undergoes a radical change. He is the picture of humility in a sister bureau of the same agency that is headed by an intelligent, ruthless chief who has developed close ties to the Washington headquarters of his agency. Not only would Chief 2 not entertain the notion of catering to the whims of a lower-echelon federal errand boy, but he has used federal funds to hire the project staff he needs to strengthen his hand against the federal professionals. This Tale of Two Bureaus is illustrative: a few key appointments can change the pattern of agency competence almost overnight. It is not surprising that the pecking order in intergovernmental relationships is constantly changing and that consequently there is more than a ray of hope for the optimists.

Some political scientists are hopeful that increased responsibilities will improve state and local competence by attracting more able people into their bureaucracies. They begin by assuming more responsibility and offering higher salaries. Others, perhaps more prudent, demanded—in vain—that minimal federal program standards should be imposed before revenue-sharing cash was made available. One step of major significance should have been action to relieve the desperate staffing problem. Senator Muskie and President Johnson, among others, in the late 1960s recommended greatly enlarged federally assisted programs to train people for public service along with other incentives such as salary subsidies for highly skilled personnel serving in state and local government. But it must be recognized that this should have been done a decade or two earlier. This is a long-range or, at best, a middle-range solution for the problems that afflict states and municipalities. Even if large-scale programs are finally and belatedly put into operation by the late 1970s, an extended period of painful, sometimes scandalous, transition can be anticipated while we wait for state and local government to develop adequate capability.

The preceding discussion should not be construed as an indictment of either the humanitarian intentions or the capacity of even the most backward state to carry forward a few effective programs. If there is room for believing that a transition to broaden state responsibilities need not have horrendous consequences, it lies in the remarkable record of the majority of the states in such vital areas as public higher education.

However, it is apparent that if progress has been painful in the federal establishment despite a civil service equipped with reasonably[35] well-paid and well-trained executive cadres, the strain on bureaucracies in state and local government will assume awesome dimensions.

STATE AND LOCAL PROBLEMS

Clearly, any discussion of state problems runs the risk of generalizing the way sophomores do about men and women, or some people do about blacks,

Chinese, or other seemingly discrete groups or categories. Obviously, there are vast differences among the states, as between New York and Arkansas or California and West Virginia. Nevertheless, certain generalizations can be made. To begin with, unless many things change, it is certain that the states will not enjoy primacy or, indeed, even exercise a major role in policy formulation and implementation. The weaknesses are well documented in *The States and the Urban Crisis,* which asks the provocative question: "State Government: Fallen Arch?"[36] At this point, a brief summary of certain salient weaknesses will suffice. Most will agree that:

1. The states and municipalities are short of money. Furthermore, since federal agencies have most of the financial resources, the states and localities tend to develop certain program distortions; they either stop short at the limits of federal matching funds or design programs to reflect the availability of federal money, rather than local needs. State and local officials who anxiously looked forward to implementation of revenue-sharing proposals as a cure for their fiscal dilemmas found that $5 or $6 billion can disappear with barely a ripple in an era of rampant inflation. Most states would greatly appreciate a federal takeover of welfare programs, while cities would be happy if states assumed more (or all) responsibility for public-school costs. Unfortunately, the dimensions of state and municipal financial problems are such that these modest rescue efforts would make only a slight, almost imperceptible dent in the extent and progress of their fiscal predicament.

2. The states in many cases tend to have less power and influence than they would like over many significant aspects of urban affairs. Many states, reflecting the rural and small-town gerrymandering of the past, exhibit a continuing lack of responsiveness to urban problems.

3 Agency organization tends to be obsolescent, and major urban responsibilities fall between agency cracks.

4. Some troubles can be ascribed to the difficulties of working with federal agencies: year-to-year funding, which hampers consistent programming, and rigid program guidelines are only two of a number of problems which could be cited.

5. The states are confronted with equally severe weaknesses in local government, which hamper the delivery of services.

6. There is a serious talent shortage in state and local government. States are afflicted by a combination of the Peter Principle and two or three decades of talent starvation. The result is a general hostility to innovation, a tendency to exhibit a patter of government by exhausted, timid dullards who serve as objects in space rather than as serious actors. Too often, government is run by senior clerks elevated to executive status on the basis of seniority and longevity; they remained on the governmental escalator while their livelier, more employable colleagues departed in frustration and disgust. The general grayness tends

to be interspersed with a few of the genuinely competent along with colorful paranoids and intriguers, but the prevailing atmosphere is one of mediocrity. Although there is still a thin red line of talent holding off the threatening chaos, the good people tend to be spread extremely thin. Moreover, the supply of talent finds life increasingly difficult as they struggle to enlarge their working day to cope with the requirements of new, complex federal grant-in-aid programs and state responsibilities. It is extremely difficult to free the relatively scarce talent from day-to-day crises so they can undertake PPB or ZBB, when much of the bureaucracy is functioning as an employee welfare system. Paul Ylvisaker has called state government "a dark continent." Unfortunately, it deserves the insult, and most local government is even more in outer darkness.

In this context it is a ludicrous display of ideological blindness or outright naiveté to proclaim as a goal in the 1976 Republican party platform that "Washington programs must be made as cost-effective as those in the states and localities." If the statement were not made in all solemnity one could discern a trace of Swiftian satire or Kafkaesque dark humor.

Criticism of state capability does not always sit well when it comes from academics with no experience in operating responsibilities or from representatives who themselves have not always been models of coherence and efficiency. As has been discussed earlier, all levels of government are guilty of neglect, incompetence, and promising more than they can deliver in meeting urban problems. Some of this simmering hostility was pointed up in an exchange between Secretary of HUD George Romney and Seattle Mayor Wesley Uhlman at the United States Conference of Mayors held in Denver in June 1970. While Romney endeared himself to the mayors by acknowledging the need for more federal resources for the cities, he and other federal officials also sternly lectured the mayors on the urgent need for local government reforms to cope with the urban crisis. Mayor Uhlman in all likelihood expressed the feelings of many of his colleagues in state and local government when he charged that talk of the need for municipal reform "is a copout by those who don't really want to face up to the problems we have today. I would say to the Federal Government, 'Physician, heal thyself.' "[37]

STATE POTENTIALS

While we may be concerned about state weaknesses, it is still far too early for an execution. In the first place, the states have strong legal powers, and their current weaknesses are reversible, since they are primarily attributable to a failure of will and intelligence. We have witnessed a prolonged abdication, but constitutionally the states retain enormous latent strength. There is also a considerable spread of sophistication, which offers a friendly climate for reform and modernization. Events of the past decade have created much higher expectations among the citizenry (including a willingness to pay decent salaries); the bureaucrats and the legislators may be lagging behind the public rather than reflecting their enlarged horizons.

A few observations are in order concerning state planning agencies, which have customarily played a fairly marginal role in most types of urban development decisions. State planning agencies have not had a particularly significant influence on basic economic development trends, including the location of industries. They have not been strong factors in influencing decisions of the transportation agencies or the education and welfare agencies. Even the natural resource agencies have gone off on their own in planning and developing parks and other recreation areas, with little reference to the official state planning agencies. The planning agencies have produced a series of reports which make pleasant reading, a series of speeches which make pleasant listening, and not much more. In short, they have viewed with alarm and pointed with pride, but they have not been major factors in shaping government policy or private development. As one publication summarized the situation in the late 1960s:

> State planning agencies traditionally have been remote from the decision centers of government. Thus sheltered, they could produce plans freely, without fear that their results would imply policy commitments by decision makers. Remoteness from policy-making authority resulted from planning's location within operating agencies, and from boards which insulated the planning activity from the policy-making authority.[38]

Another area in which state planning agencies have found an excellent response is the field of technical assistance. Such aid not only can be useful for the communities but can also be an extremely good way of building support among potential constituencies for the planning agency. Many states, for example, have displayed outstanding qualities in responding to needs for public higher education, and some (including Florida, New Jersey, California, Vermont, and Hawaii) have demonstrated substantial innovative capacities in dealing with land use and environmental problems.[39]

There are, however, certain dangers confronting a state renaissance. As was suggested, one of the most obvious problems is federal centralization: the money and much of the talent is in Washington, and, despite all the talk about a vital role for the states, there is an obvious temptation to make policy, implement policy, and judge policy in Washington. Partly as a consequence, there is a continuing temptation to bypass the allegedly incompetent state agencies. This is not sheer discrimination or illogical behavior. The federal bureaucracy can make a good case for putting the money where the problems are, that is, in the cities. In short, the federal agencies can follow the federal-to-city government precedent of the initial years of the urban renewal and poverty programs (although, more recently, states have begun to be assigned more responsibility in federally sponsored programs). In this manner, federal executives can bypass state government, which many of them view as a noncontributory layer of deadness, a complication rather than a help in meeting urban problems.

Another newer form of potential federal bypass is neighborhood control. Money can go directly to neighborhood agencies concerned with poverty, redevelopment, employment, education, or other problems. In effect, this represents a way in which the federal government can treat neighborhoods somewhat like small suburban towns, funding community agencies closer to the people than the large and often unresponsive city bureaucracies. But perhaps the most interesting and enticing bypass mechanism is direct assistance from federal programs to the citizen. In this case, local and state government—and neighborhood agencies—may be written off as costly intermediaries between the individual and his friendly federal government. We have numerous precedents, like the G.I. Bill and Social Security, and federal family assistance is next if the trend continues. The net result might be a significant diminution in the power of state and local government, and, for this reason, strong resistance can be anticipated to moves in this direction.

It is true that some foresee a virtual dismantling of state and local welfare and education bureaucracies in favor of federally issued income programs or service chits. In theory, this approach would widen the range of consumer choice by stimulating the individual to purchase services from either government or private purveyors. The individual could buy his own housing, his own medical care, or anything else he required, without the necessity of processing and administration by either state or local agencies. It is assumed that private enterprise will be able to respond effectively to new consumer markets in free competition with the state and other governmental entities. Obviously, this involves the further assumption that most people have enough knowledge to exercise prudent choice—an assumption which may be debatable. But, at the same time, we have to recognize this alternative as a strong potential threat to enlarged state activities, to say nothing of local government, the chief function of which is the operation of school systems.

The withering away of state and local government operations may extend beyond welfare and education. Examples already exist of private concerns providing services which have been considered traditional government responsibilities. This includes, most notably, police protection for business and industry, as well as increasingly for private residential areas under contracts paid for by the company or the residents who feel public protection is inadequate. Private citizens are now also turning to the private sector to provide them with other services, such as garbage collection, because local government has failed to maintain satisfactory sanitary conditions. This trend might well extend into other areas—health and transportation—in which citizens directly contract with private businesses, bypassing the governmental structure, to obtain a standard of service necessary to maintain the quality of life desired in the urban environment.

To add another note of pessimism, there is the omnipresent threat of state government avoiding action by way of rhetoric, study commissions, advisers, coordinators, guide plans, and conferences. The states can limp along behind federal initiatives indefinitely. They may find themselves meeting in solemn conclave every year or two, discussing what went wrong, what they should be doing, and how best to adjust to the new federal guidelines. Again and again, there may be talk about an indispensable role for the states on the part of a federal establishment which has shown itself ready, able, and willing to explore, nurture, and develop effective alternatives to state government.

While recognizing the potential for closer ties to the universities, a word of warning is also in order. As noted in Chapter 1, professors come in all shapes and sizes and in all degrees of productivity and general usefulness. Too often states have not had the expertise to choose consultants wisely. The answer is not to write off the institutions of higher learning. Federal agencies have learned to make effective use of carefully selected stables of professorial consultants, and the states—and localities—can surely do the same. By doing so, the states will be happy to know that they not only help themselves, but aid the progress of the social sciences. As Charles Frankel sees it,

> there is also enough on the historical record of this and other societies to suggest that an intellectual or scholarly community will be seriously incapacitated in its understanding of public affairs if it contains no people who have had direct, practical experience in government and politics. It would be in the position of anthropologists discussing cultures in which none of them had ever been. At the best, such a community would be bookish. At the worst, it could be unconsciously sectarian or militantly self-righteous. The scholar-practitioner is probably as necessary to the development of social and political science as the clinician to psychology or the poet to the criticism of poetry.[40]

In theory, most of the framework for improvement in state government presently exists. In many states budget and finance agencies have the legal authority to coordinate and implement policy and program planning, but there is a gulf between theory and practice. The current pattern can perhaps best be classified as first generation, using the categories developed by Allen Schick.[41] The period roughly between 1920 and 1935, the first stage in modern budgeting, Schick suggests, was dominated by efforts aimed at developing an adequate system of expenditure control. From the mid-1930s to the early 1960s, the second or New Deal stage focused on the movement for performance budgeting. The emphasis was on improved management, work measurement programs, and the focusing of budget preparation on the work and activities of the agencies. The third and most recent stage has witnessed the mergence of PPB linked to modern information technology. This third generation is only beginning to have much of an impact even in the most advanced states. Most states seem barely to have crossed from stage one to stage two and are obviously a long distance from stage three. For this reason, one is forced to the conclusion that recommending or requiring that PPB, ZBB, and other highly sophisticated techniques be adopted by a typical administratively backward state (or local government) seems analogous to assigning open-heart operations to barber-surgeons who have only recently become aware of the limitations of leeches.

The task of mediating between, let alone coordinating, activities of two or more federal agencies along with their state counterparts is not a job for the faint-hearted. It requires talented staff, thoroughly conversant with a range of information well beyond the scope of the average bureaucrat. What is striking about the area of the vital information-processing function at the state level is not only the absence of this extraordinary level of skill, but the seeming inability to do a creditable day-to-day job on many agency programs.

A special facet of the serious staffing problem is the generational gap that separates the mature administrator, who knows his program but is relatively unfamiliar with modern electronic data processing from the young computer specialist with limited knowledge of governmental policy and program problems. Administrators who possess a rather sketchy knowledge of computers may be unable to detect misuse or to direct younger administrators with impressive expertise in the new technology but little program background. The introduction of PPB and ZBB exacerbated the hostility between enthusiastic young specialists and their irritated, uncomprehending seniors.

Given the pervading weaknesses in staff capability, it is hardly surprising to find serious deficiencies in the area of agency planning. Major problems in this area include the following: (1) few agencies have completed meaningful comprehensive plans; some agencies clearly regard comprehensive planning as a token exercise useful only in satisfying federal requirements for grants-in-aid; (2) in some fields, there are overlapping, unintegrated plans; (3) there is no central guidance or framework on which to base agency plans; in many states there are no consistent population or employment projections, to cite a glaring example.

In the absence of overall state guidelines, the agencies tend to operate and to plan in a policy vacuum. Although agency plans may satisfy the requirements of their federal funding agencies, plans, programs, and operations are not related to each other within an overall policy framework in which relative priorities are assigned and scheduled.

There is considerable variation in planning operations from agency to agency. Agencies whose federal counterparts place strong emphasis on planning prerequisites for funding tend to be committed to both long- and short-range planning activities. With some exceptions, agencies without federal counterparts or sponsoring federal agencies place much less emphasis on long-range planning. In this category are most of the authorities established by the state legislature that have no current access to federal funds or other connection with federal agencies. There is not much interest in comprehensive planning in other agencies as, for example, in public welfare, which is responsible for expenditure of large sums of money but which has limited functions in construction of capital improvements. In brief, although many agencies can wave thick documents about, duly certified in Washington as acceptable master plans, it would probably be accurate to conclude that no major area of state government can be characterized as operating in accordance with a well-conceived, comprehensive plan.

This rather gloomy picture of state government can be overdrawn. As was noted earlier, some states are on the whole well governed—Wisconsin, California, and Oregon are three often-cited examples—and most states can boast at least two or three areas in which they have demonstrated competence or even outstanding leadership. It is conceivable, although hardly probable, that laggard states will rise to the occasion and that the decades of abdication and irrelevance can be quickly ended when responsibility is thrust on them along with the cash to hire the staff they so badly need. Frankly, one is entitled to have serious doubts that this happy situation can or will occur. The defects of many states, their legislative resistance to modernization and change, and the backwardness of their entrenched bureaucracies will take much time and effort to correct. With hard work, the overall quality of state government has been improving, and perhaps in time most of the states will be able to assume the partnership role to which they aspire. But until they do a better job in meeting their present responsibilities, it seems reckless to entrust them with new areas to administer. In fact, it is quite possible that one of the by-products of moves to apply PPB or ZBB in the states will be to expose rather than to cure the profound weaknesses of state government. After examining a few of the problems that the federal agencies have already encountered with PPB, social indicators, and other assorted Chinese puzzles, one can hardly expect most of the states to rack up an impressive record.

NOTES

1. U.S., Joint Economic Committee, Subcommittee on Economic Progress, *Federal Programs for the Development of Human Resources,* I (Washington, D.C., December 1966), p. 28.

2. See Ralph M. Barnes and George M. Raymond, "The Fiscal Approach to Land Use Planning," *Journal of the American Institute of Planners,* Spring-Summer 1955; and William L. C. Wheaton and Morton J. Schussheim, *The Cost of Municipal Services in Residential Areas,* prepared for the Housing and Home Finance Agency (Washington, D.C., 1955).

3. Bertram M. Gross and Michael Springer, "A New Orientation in American Government," *The Annals* 1 (issue entitled *Social Goals and Indicators in American Society*) (May 1967): 10.

4. New York *Times*, June 22, 1967, p. 3.

5. U.S., National Commission on Technology, Automation and Economic Progress, *Technology and the American Economy* (Washington, D.C.: U.S. Government Printing Office, 1966).

6. James C. T. Mao, "Efficiency in Public Urban Renewal Expenditures Through Benefit-Cost Analysis," *Journal of the American Institute of Planners* 32 (March 1966): 95–106.

7. Herbert Gans, *The Urban Villagers: Group and Class in the Life of Italian-Americans* (Glencoe, Ill.: The Free Press, 1962).

8. Jane Jacobs, *The Death and Life of Great American Cities* (New York: Random House, 1961).

9. Martin Rein and S. M. Miller, "Poverty Programs and Policy Priorities," *Trans-Action* 4, no. 9 (September 1967): 60–71.

10. For penetrating analyses of some of the problems involved in calculating the net returns from health, education, and other programs, see U.S., Joint Economic Committee, *Federal Programs for the Development of Human Resources,* op. cit. See also Theodore W. Schultz, ed., "Investment in Human Beings," paper presented at a conference called by the National Bureau Committee for Economic Research in *The Journal of Political Economy* 70, no. 5 (October 1962), supp.; and Robert Dorfman, ed., *Measuring Benefits of Government Investments* (Washington D.C.: Brookings Institution, 1965).

11. See Aaron Wildavsky, "The Political Economy of Efficiency," *The Public Interest* 8 (Summer 1967): 30–48. Wildavsky makes a plea for examination of political costs and benefits in program planning.

12. Raymond A. Bauer, ed., *Social Indicators* (Cambridge, Mass.: M.I.T. Press, 1966).

13. See the editorial by Irving Louis Horowitz and Lee Rainwater, "Social Accounting for the Nation," *Trans-Action* 4, no. 6 (May 1967): 2–3.

14. See Albert D. Biderman, "Social Indicators and Goals," in Bauer, op. cit., p. 78.

15. See Norman Beckman, "For a New Perspective in Federal State Relations," *State Government* 39, no. 4 (Autumn 1966): 260–70. Beckman is fully aware of the current inadequacies of state government but in his article discerns many hopeful signs of reform.

16. See Richard N. Goodwin, "The Shape of American Politics," *Commentary* 43, no. 6 (June 1967): 25–40. See also James Q. Wilson, "The Bureaucracy Problem," *The Public Interest,* no. 6 (Winter 1967) pp. 3–9.

17. The Kestnbaum Commission (1955–59) and the Joint Federal-State Action Committee (1957–59) were created to reverse alleged overcentralization. The latter, after much huffing and puffing, in the end recommended transfer of two small programs involving 2 percent of total federal grants in 1957. Neither recommendation was accepted by the Congress. Morton Grodzins, "The Federal System," in *Democracy in the Fifty States,* ed. Charles Press and Oliver P. Williams (Chicago: Rand McNally, 1966); President's Commission on National Goals, *Goals for Americans* (Washington, D.C., 1960).

18. Lawrence O. Houstoun, Jr., "The Revenue Sharing Debate: Simply Sending Money Down Will Worsen the Situation by Postponing Essential Reforms," *City,* May-June 1971, pp. 15–18. The Advisory Commission on Intergovernmental Relations agreed, pointing out that in the absence of mandated reform, an unwanted effect of revenue sharing would be "to freeze the existing governmental structure and to prop it up without regard to its viability." Advisory Commission on Intergovernmental Relations, 14th Annual Report, *Striking a Better Balance: Federalism in 1972* (Washington, D.C.: U.S. Government Printing Office, 1972), p. 6.

19. James L. Sundquist and David W. Davis, *Making Federalism Work* (Washington, D.C.: The Brookings Institution, 1969).

20. New York *Times,* January 11, 1971, p. 1.

21. Ibid., January 24, 1971, p. 1.

22. Ibid., January 11, 1971, p. 36.

23. David Rogers, "New York City Schools: A Sick Bureaucracy," *Saturday Review of Literature,* July 20, 1968, pp. 47–49, 59–61.

24. U.S., Advisory Commission on Intergovernmental Relations, "Revenue Sharing—An Idea Whose Time Has Come" (Washington, D.C.: U.S. Government Printing Office, December 1970), p. 19.

25. I. D. Robbins, "Cutting City Government Costs," *Wall Street Journal,* May 19, 1971, p. 19.

26. Matthew P. Dumont, "Government as Dada," *Trans-Action* 8, no. 7 (May 1971): 6-8.

27. Lawrence O. Houstoun, Jr., "The Revenue Sharing Debate: Simply Sending Money Down Will Worsen the Situation by 'Postponing Essential Reforms,' " *City* 5, no. 3 (May/June 1971): 15–18.

28. Vernon E. Jordan, Jr., "Local Control Hurts Blacks," *Wall Street Journal,* September 19, 1973, p. 13.

29. New York *Times,* January 23, 1971, p. 1.

30. John L. Hess, "The Poverty Program's for Politicians, Too," New York *Times,* August 15, 1976, p. E5.

31. Ibid., January 24, 1971, sec. 4, p. E3.

32. Selma J. Mushkin, *National Policy on Urban Finance* (Washington, D.C.: The Urban Institute, January 1970), pp. 77–78.

33. Statement of Representative Henry S. Reuss, "Revenue Sharing and Its Alternatives," *Hearings Before the Subcommittee on Fiscal Policy of the Joint Economic Committee,* 90th Cong., 1st sess., 1967, p. 263.

34. Robert Dallis, "Wave of Service Cutbacks Hits Rich, Poor Communities," Trenton *Sunday Times Advertiser,* August 15, 1976, p. B14.

35. The word "reasonably" is used advisedly. See Douglass Cater's discussion of the federal bureaucracy, *Power in Washington* (New York: Vintage Books, 1965), chap. 6. Cater quotes a Brookings Institution study to the effect that the Congress has done little to strengthen the top-level civil service. The top 3,000 or more career executives who head the various bureaus and divisions were found to be "predominantly inbred." Many had started in government service at a lower level, had risen through the ranks by concentrating on specialties, and "are frequently indifferent to the larger problems of government."

36. Alan K. Campbell, ed., *The States and the Urban Crisis: The American Assembly* (Englewood Cliffs, N.J.: Prentice-Hall, 1970).

37. John Herbers, "Big-City Mayors Leave Conference Concerned by Shift of Power to the Suburbs," New York *Times,* June 13, 1970, p. 34.

38. The Council of State Governments, *State Planning and Federal Grants* (Chicago: Public Administration Service, 1969), p. 52.

39. M. R. Levin, J. G. Rose, and J. S. Slavet, *New Approaches to State Land-Use Policies* (Lexington, Mass.: Lexington Books, 1974).

40. Charles Frankel, "Being In and Being Out," *The Public Interest,* no. 17 (Fall 1969), p. 58.

41. Allen Schick, "The Road to PPBS: The Stages of Budget Reform," *Public Administration Review* 26, no. 4 (December 1966): 243–58.

CHAPTER

5

THE PERILS OF PROJECTIONS

INTRODUCTION: FORECASTING FOR FUN AND PROFIT

For many of the same reasons that astrology, palmistry, and gypsy tearooms retain their faithful followers, peering into the future with the help of modern planning techniques enjoys great popularity. An examination of some of the pitfalls in the projection business suggests that less time and effort should be devoted to this pastime. Such an approach implies lesser expenditures on fewer expensive and elaborate projections, and more humility entails less chance of erroneous clairvoyancy.

One of the more enjoyable aspects of the planning profession is the art and alleged science of preparing projections for municipalities, metropolitan areas, states, and large regions. Unlike the case in other professions, palpable and repeated errors are apparently no bar to a planner's advancement. Although his projections may seldom be even within close range of the target and occasionally are wildly inaccurate, the planner has mastered the indispensable skill of escaping the odium for mistaken forecasts. In fact, the exposure of past errors offers a useful opportunity for learned post mortems. These excuse the departure of predictions from subsequent reality by carefully pointing out that a variety of unpredicted (and hence unpredictable) events were responsible for greater-than-anticipated deviations. Further, it is made clear that truer prophets were either extraordinarily lucky or were culpable of similar inaccuracies which, fortunately for them, had a more beneficial impact on their overall projection.

Also, planners change jobs frequently, and the passage of time and substantial physical distance effaces the consequences of wrong forecasts. Like doctors, planners bury their mistakes, although they use file cabinets rather than coffins to inter the remains. More often than not, time is an ally of the blunderer because new problems of such magnitude emerge in the forecast period that such gaffes are obliterated as (to cite one notable example), a 50-million or 100-million person misestimate in national population projections.

As if all this were not sufficient to obscure one's errors, planning forecasts are, at best, nine day wonders. Most reports, along with the projections they contain, can be assumed either to go unread or to be quickly forgotten, a further invitation to sloppiness. Finally, certain professional standards tend to protect the luckless and incompetent. To return to the medical analogy, a mistake that has proved fatal to the patient is not necessarily harmful to the late patient's physician unless the doctor has covered his tracks so badly as to leave himself open to proof of malpractice. In the planning world, as in other professions, a colleague is always available to point out that planning is not a product but a process, involving many unforeseen variables and requiring highly trained talent to review and revise the rather numerous errors that time and new research have uncovered in last year's expensive plan. As in prolonged, losing wars, the battle cry after each debacle seems to be requests for more money, more staff, and more sophisticated weaponry. And there is irritation with unsophisticated laymen who remember past promises and fail to comprehend the subtle reasons for failure to achieve the expected results.

Since the preparation of advanced, modern planning projections is by no means an inexpensive undertaking, there is ample cause for disenchantment when, more often than not, the efforts and funds expended in developing planning projections for such programs as economic development, population growth, and transportation prove to be a poor guide to subsequent events. But expense is partly an illusion. Large federal subsidies are usually available to finance the projection business. Hence, it is not uncommon to find small communities spending a disproportionately large amount for projections of various sorts, even though the forecasts bear little relationship to any economic, financial, or social ventures or expenditures. At any level of government, there is often no discernible relationship between elaborate projections and decisions. Close inspection usually reveals that action is based on an intuitive judgment linked to a few rough calculations scribbled on a sheet of foolscap. Subsequent projection operations that may be conducted are more in the nature of ex post facto justification than guides for future action. In short, the vast sums expended on elaborate forecasts tend to serve as retroactive rationalizations for decisions that have already been made. Highway construction is an excellent case in point. The fancy and extraordinarily costly computer-based projections that were generated in the area of transportation studies in the 1960s have rarely served any purpose other than to secure the planner's imprimatur for the existing plans of the highway agencies.

Most of the massive capital improvement programs in cities, metropolitan areas, and states are based principally on immediately foreseeable departmental requirements and some rough measure of future needs. These simple-minded estimates of medium- and long-range needs have two advantages: they are unpretentious and inexpensive. The fact that departmental operations are not linked to the long-term planning projections is by no means surprising. There is an understandable suspicion that the costly projections are not much better than the horseback estimates prepared by an experienced administrator.

Projections do not necessarily have to be statistical. Dennis O'Harrow, former director of the American Society of Planning Officials, took just as gloomy a view of one type of projection, the regional land use plan. The land use forecast and development alternatives differ from the economic or population projection by being prepared with colored pencils and being presented on a map, or, more accurately, three to a dozen maps.

> A favorite indoor sport of metropolitan planning staffs is the preparation of comprehensive regional planning alternatives. Which means constructing from three to a dozen maps on which are shown ingenious—or ingenuous—arrangements of residential, commercial and industrial land patterns, parks, greenbelts, new towns, urban corridors, nuclei, all laced together by hypothetical rapid transit lines that will probably never be built.
>
> The alternatives are tested by picking great quantities of numbers off the maps and pushing them through a mysterious formula in a computer, and then further testing by exposing the maps to public scrutiny. . . .
>
> So long as planning for urban regions continues as it is now practiced, this fatuous exercise in public participation will continue.[1]

There seems to be no close correlation between the possibility of errors creeping into long-term as compared to shorter-term projections. However, it is noteworthy that demands for periodic revision and updating seem to have accelerated after disillusionment with the long-range forecasts prepared during the 1930s. During this first broad surge of interest in areawide planning in the 1930s and 1940s, preparation of a single forecast series for planning and programing periods covering 20 and even 30 years were not uncommon. The quickening pace of events in the 1940s seems to have shortened the time perspective in planning projections. Following World War II, in the late 1940s and early 1950s, the commonly accepted planning period for most area planning studies was a slightly more realistic 20 years, usually rounded off to the nearest five-year period for convenience.

Two further advances in projection technique became popular during the 1950s. In many planning projects, it became the practice to identify short-term and long-term planning goals rather than to select a single long-term goal, as had been the practice in the past. The use of alternatives also allows a little more room for maneuver as circumstances change. This technique was also useful in raising the important matter of priorities that had frequently been overlooked or neglected in long-range planning projects. High-priority items could be accorded some urgency by being grouped among short-term goals.

A second important innovation of the 1950s was the step projection. Using this technique, projections are made for a long-term period as in the past, but interim, shorter-period projections are also prepared as part of the study. These intervals help to establish priorities and also provide a basis for checking the progress of a plan or program and for gauging the accuracy of its forecasts.

The transportation studies that were conducted in the 1960s to satisfy the requirements of the Federal Aid Highway Act of 1962 incorporated another principle of long-range planning. There was an attempt to design data collection and analysis operations in order to facilitate updating in future years. In actual practice, these innovations were perhaps less useful than advertised. Step projections have been prepared on more than one occasion merely by taking the appropriate value from the long-term projection rather than by preparing genuine intermediate forecasts. Moreover, technicians often found that there were so many unknowns and assumptions piled on assumptions within a planning program that their projections were rendered almost meaningless. Thus, paradoxically, while it was believed perfectly feasible to make long-range projections, the intermediate step projections were in many cases considered less realistic than the projection that looked 20, 30, or 40 years ahead. Thus, the step-projection technique tended to underscore rather than eliminate the need for constant review and updating. As a result, in the 1960s, efforts were concentrated on study designs that would facilitate updating with a minimum of expense, on the premise that the projections would need a thorough overhauling almost as soon as they were published. One observer, Edward C. Banfield, suggested:

> Change occurs so rapidly in our society that it seldom makes sense to try to look ahead more than five years. The importance of technological change is obvious . . . but changes in consumer tastes and public opinion occur just as fast and may be even more important. (Who even five years ago predicted the civil rights revolution?) It is impossible to provide now for the future as people will want it 10, 20 or 30 years from now if we have no way of knowing what they will want.[2]

Subsequently, Banfield's observation has been borne out by any number of carefully prepared projections that proved wildly off the mark: A notable example was the admission that in 1970 the nation would produce more than twice as many doctoral degrees (27,000) than the 12,000 estimated by a study group in 1954.[3] The subsequent doctoral glut of the mid-1970s naturally gave rise to concern, particularly because projections of college enrollment suggested a further decline in the demand for Ph.D.'s. Some academic administrators were consoled, however, by the very inaccuracy of past forecasts. Having erred once on the side of optimism, might not the gloom be overdone and the surplus only temporary, as in the case of jobs in engineering in which pessimism had been proven wrong?

The long-range value of second-generation planning studies in terms of their money and time-saving potentials has yet to be assessed. They do represent a hopeful development in that they recognize that the process of periodic updating is superior to the attempt to prepare one-time projections, only to observe the predictions quickly overtaken and confounded by unforeseen events. On the other hand, they are damnably expensive.

The purpose of this chapter is to identify a few of the key issues and problems relating to planning projections. The laboratory area selected for this exercise is New England, with special focus on Massachusetts and metropolitan Boston. Two particular problems are discussed, both bearing on unpredictable elements in long-range forecasting. The first considers a major change that occurred over the past three decades. This is unpredicted transformation of metropolitan Boston, and indeed, much of southern New England, from a decadent, laggard area to a position of national leadership. The second is the problem of population forecasting in the Age of the Pill and increasingly costly child rearing.

In the past 30 years, there was a fundamental and totally unforeseen change in some of the Boston region's economic and social roles. In the 1950s, the region that had been a slow-growing backwater area became an attractive prototype area considered by other parts of the nation as a goal and a model —despite setbacks to the area's technologically oriented industries in the early 1970s. This change in role was not reflected in planning projections and in fact tended to escape notice until the transition was nearly completed. Looking ahead to developments at the turn of the century, it is important to recognize that there are many elements in population projections (as well as related land use and transportation forecasts) that cannot be accurately forecast. It is necessary and useful to prepare such projections, but as the discussion of a possible deceleration in the projected rate of population growth suggests, in the last analysis, scientific methods of prediction are based in large measure on variation in human behavior that may change over surprisingly brief time periods.

METROPOLITAN BOSTON: LAGGARD TO PROTOTYPE

In the alteration in statewide patterns and trends over the past years, it is useful to begin with a benchmark year. Fortunately, a point of comparison useful for planning purposes is available in the 1936 progress report of the

Massachusetts State Planning Board, a comprehensive document covering many aspects of state development.[4]

The distance that separates the 1936 report from 1976 is little more than a generation in time, but it encompasses great changes in almost every aspect of regional development. Unemployment has been reduced to about 8 percent —a figure which itself reflects the impact of the 1973–75 recession. New England's textile industry has nearly vanished and has been replaced by such industries as instruments and electronics, which were relatively insignificant or which barely existed in the mid-1930s; birth rates increased in the 1940s and 1950s but returned to depression levels by the late 1960s. Real incomes have skyrocketed; and motor vehicle ownership and suborganization have proceeded at a much faster pace than could possibly have been predicted. There are, however, some striking similarities between the description of planning progress prepared in the middle of the Great Depression and the situation in the 1970s. The similarities can be attributed in part to failures to solve long-standing problems. Identified as critical issues in 1936, water pollution, serious slum conditions, disproportionately high electric power rates, and traffic congestion persist as unfinished business a generation later. Other items discussed in the 1936 report also bear a close resemblance to conditions in 1976. One example is recreation. By 1936, recreation and tourism had developed to the point where it had allegedly become the state's second-largest industry. Another is the critical importance of education, especially higher education, to the state economy that had already become fully apparent in the 1930s. Finally, the state's rates of population growth and employment expansion were well below the national level, just as they are today.

In measuring the progress of the past four decades, it is essential to place particular stress on certain unquantifiable factors that had a major, unanticipated impact on economic and social development. The state's renowned private universities had been producing business and research leaders for the nation, but it was only in the 1940s and after that this function assumed a central role in stimulating area development. The extent to which this unique asset would have a direct economic spillover into the area economy only began to be apparent during World War II. Allied to these generators of scientific and business activity, there were certain long-standing assets, especially a high quality of local amenities, which created a desirable environment for management and scientific personnel.

In the 1930s and up to the late 1940s, New England, Massachusetts, and metropolitan Boston were regarded as economic museums allegedly populated by tired antiquarians and warring ethnic groups, offering excellent college educations and pleasant holidays, but unsuitable for either investments or careers. By the mid-1950s, this view had radically altered, and metropolitan Boston in particular emerged as a much envied and emulated prototype for aspiring areas throughout the nation.

In the late 1940s and early 1950s, the state experienced a basic alteration in both its inner and outer aspect: A lagging deviant became a leading prototype for the nation. The seeds of this change were already present, but as has been suggested, the forcing ground and dividing line between the two eras was World War II, with its emphasis on research and sophisticated weaponry. Although various dates can be selected for the subtle but basic alteration in role, the early 1950s, when electrical machinery employment in Massachusetts surpassed textile employment, represents an arbitrary but perhaps accurate point. Whatever the date, the effect has become obvious. It may be noted that in metropolitan Boston, which contains over half the state population, per-capita incomes relative to the U.S. average had declined by 28 points between 1929 and 1950, but between 1950 and 1962, the trend was reversed and the area rose by seven points.[5]

It is useful to recall the deepseated sentiments that colored the outsider's view of New England. A rigid social class structure, the absence of significant natural resources, and the decreasing number of enterprising immigrants were thought to have created an atmosphere unfavorable to economic expansion. The region, some said, consisted largely of dying family businesses hostile to new people and new ideas, and its economy was clearly lacking in resilience and potential. Novelists like J. P. Marquand and Edith Wharton[6] helped to fix in the public mind an image of an ingrown population living in an area located on a kind of obsolescent economic and cultural peninsula, outside the mainstream of the nation's social and economic development. Fiction spilled over into fact: The prospective industrialist and financier was often discouraged by certain real handicaps such as high electric power rates but even more repelled by old-fashioned ways of doing business and by the reputed overly conservative investment policies of New England banks. Most important, he was usually more impressed by the availability of excellent alternative locations in other regions. Perhaps even more significant was the fact that many wealthy New Englanders had written off their region, preferring to place their capital in more promising areas; in many cases, the more enterprising younger people chose other places for their lifetime careers.

The unfavorable view of the region dated well back into the nineteenth century, and it grew stronger with the passage of time and the opening of the West. During the first decade of the present century, a New England booster felt it necessary to examine and attempt to refute allegations of regional unprogressiveness and attitudes inimical to progress. This defense was illuminating:

> The New England temper has been loath to accept optimism for its guiding motive. There has been a certain grim liking for adverse conditions in the New England character. We are inclined to be persistently stubborn in our business methods. We do not like to experiment. . . . New Englanders went

> out into the nation and built it up. There has been a drain of New England energy and initiative. The wholesale and continued transfusion of her best blood to the veins of the newer states could only mean the weakening of her own constitution and the limiting of her own development.[7]

Despite this preamble, the booster and the report went on to suggest that the "decadence" of New England was a "fiction." Although the out-migration of talent and the abandonment of farms were admitted as realities, the authors contended that outside allegations regarding the region's loss of manufacturing —including textiles—were erroneous or exaggerated. (A decade later denials were no longer possible, and by the 1940s some New Englanders were taking comfort in the fact that in "exporting" textiles to the South, the region had also transferred the problems that seem to surround that industry like a nimbus, to the areas that had sent the Dixie raiders.)

Published in 1911, this Boston Chamber of Commerce report was prescient but premature by three or four decades in its assertion that "conservation and stagnation" were giving way to progress, thanks to the "high quality of the region's schools," the "abilities and industriousness" of its workmen, and even more, to such intangible factors as an "impulse toward progress" based on moral character, receptive attitudes, and a regional tradition of cooperative efforts toward improvement. However, the report's authors anticipated later scholars who have come to recognize the critical importance of technically trained cadres, favorable work attitudes, and an unquantifiable but vital spirit of receptivity to change. The region's problem was that these assets did not become marketable commodities again until World War II.

The study placed considerable emphasis on two other aspects of life in the region that have a distinctly modern flavor: New England's amenities for both year-round living and recreation, and its major cultural attractions. The comments regarding New England's "much maligned" weather as a beneficial component of its environment are also pertinent, particularly with the increasing popularity of winter sports. But the attempt to link the area's rigorous climate to a capacity for hard work and to the sterling character of the region's labor force would doubtless be considered debatable by Californians and others.

The authors quote a Chicagoan who summarized the view of Boston widely held about the turn of the century (and for some decades beyond). Boston is, he asserted, "a fine little city—historic associations, fine educational opportunities, delightful place to visit; but you must admit you are not in the same class with us when it comes to industrial energy and all that."[8]

In refuting the midwesterner's allegations, another modern note is struck: The outsider's misconception of Boston weakness is blamed on the U.S. Bureau of the Census reports that reflected a relative decline in population and economic activity in the central city. Because of Boston's long-standing inability to annex its suburbs, city figures exclude data for the area's growth communities. It was suggested then, as in later decades, that comparisons based on data for the "500-square mile" Boston region would have been fairer and far more flattering.

Among Boston's major assets half a century ago are many that remain valid today and will, it is hoped, continue to characterize the region. In the first decade of the century, Boston and vicinity had long been known as an area where residents enjoyed a better-than-average standard of living. Then, as now, Boston was concerned about the obsolescence of its port, and this resulted in great plans—and continued disappointment. The Boston area still remains the principal transportation and trade center of New England, and the city's downtown area was geared to great volumes of public transportation commuters.

One of the most up-to-date notes struck in the publication is the stress on the region's need for superior quality of production, on skilled people manufacturing high-value products from imported raw materials. Even some of the phraseology is up to date:

> What might be termed human resources, constitutes one of the most important industrial assets of Massachusetts. . . . They are the result of a century of industrial experience and the advantage of an early start. In the estimate of industrial resources, they must be reckoned of even more account than proximity to supplies of raw materials or markets. . . . The policy which will enable (us) to profit most fully from this advantage . . . to overcome the disadvantage of our geographical location and the dearth of mineral wealth, is one which will incorporate a very large amount of value in comparatively small bulk.[9]

In assessing the relative merits of suburban and central city location, the study describes the tendency of expanding manufacturing industry in need of sizable sites outside Boston, but it suggests, as others have done in recent decades, that the city was partly to blame for this industrial exodus because of its failure to develop adequate intown industrial sites. The report identified the Boston waterfront as an admirable place for new, large-scale industrial growth and the city proper as the host for a variety of smaller enterprises enjoying transportation advantages and access to large pools of labor. More recent publications have hardly improved on this prescription. Modern also is the description of the two Bostons, "the poor who remain in the city" and the more affluent who earn their living in Boston but who have moved to one of "two-score bedroom" communities. Suburbanization of the well-to-do is not a recent phenomenon associated with limited-access roads and FHA financing. The warning, too, is familiar: "Ultimately, unless the metropolitan district fuses into a single community, suburban selfishness is bound to be its own defeat, since the house is divided against itself."

The gloomy view of New England's prospects deepened during the Great Depression when one writer underscored New England's extreme pervading conservatism[10] while another suggested that New England, alas, "is a dying culture. . . . In years to come, America will probably see New England's main, because more lasting, achievement in the fact that its sons are chiefly responsible for the colonization of the South [*sic*] and the Middle West."[11]

Metropolitan Boston has traditionally lived by its wits. Daniel Boorstin devotes five chapters in the portion of his trilogy on the American experience aptly titled "The Versatiles" to New England's economic ingenuity. On closer inspection the leaders prove to have been mostly from the Boston area. In the eighteenth century its seafarers took up privateering against the British, exchanging ginseng and Canadian furs for Chinese tea, silks, and porcelain; nearby Salem led in the peppercorn trade. Later, in the early nineteenth century, prime exports were created out of two liabilities: the granite outcroppings that plagued the farmer and the rigorous winter climate that froze the ponds. Ice and granite became major exports. Fresh pond ice ended up as the basis of a worldwide ice cream industry, New Orleans to the Caribbean, Persia to India (marketing snowy mountains for skiers has an ancient lineage).

By the middle of the nineteenth century the emphasis had shifted to textile manufactures, particularly in nearby Waltham, Lowell, and Lawrence.[12] In short, Boston had developed a tradition of not only moving with the times but keeping ahead of them with resourceful innovations long before the phrase "research and development" made its formal entrance into the American vocabulary. Boston, in the phrase of one development specialist, had "jumped through the hoops" again and again, and its success in the 1950s and 1960s was another proof that age need not result in a crippling stodginess and loss of agility.

Between the ebullience of 1911 and the bright prospects of the 1950s and 1960s came the Great Depression, two world wars, and the postwar transformation of the late 1940s and early 1950s. To a greater extent than the period following World War I, the second major conflict was a turning point in the economy and social patterns of the region and the nation. It would be an error, however, to suggest that the change was unrelated to the past. In fact, traditional Boston values such as superior higher educational institutions and the intangible complex of attractive living conditions were discovered to be major local advantages in an era when many growth industries were freed from reliance on local raw materials and low-cost power and were oriented instead toward a combination of universities and amenities. New England and mainly the Boston area had educated a substantial share of the nation's business, scientific, and intellectual leadership, but as late as 1952, a careful research study could report a significant "brain drain," with large numbers of native New England science graduates relocating out of the region after graduation, partly because higher salaries and better opportunities were available elsewhere.[13] The region was weak in major industrial research laboratories and secured only a disproportionately small share of research and development contracts.[14] To a great extent, these observations also applied to the Boston region, which comprises roughly one-third of New England's total population.

Only a decade later, the situation had materially improved. For example, in the mid-1960s, a study by the National Aeronautics and Space Administration (NASA) justified selection of the Boston area as the site of the agency's new Electronic Research Center by pointing out the area's highly competitive standing not only in the awarding of large numbers of advanced scientific and engineering degrees but also in the number of scientists and engineers at work. In its study of location factors, NASA identified the proximity of "electronic research oriented graduate-level educational resources of proven high quality as being the most important criterion."[15] Boston's compactness was a significant factor in this performance rating. Although the Boston area ranked second to New York, the New York area's resources "are so scattered that it does not seem realistic to consider them as a single unit."[16]

NASA estimated that the proposed center would add 300 to 350 graduate-school student enrollments in nearby institutions and that many would be enrolled in doctorate-level courses in electrical engineering or physics. A demonstrated capacity to award five or six doctorates in electrical engineering and two or three doctorates in physics a year was a prerequisite for consideration.[17] (The Boston area averaged 29 doctorates per year in electrical engineering and 45 in physics in the period 1960–62).

Other criteria (in which all of Greater Boston ranked high) included attractive amenities, a major airport, and the presence of a substantial science and engineering community, including an array of professional personnel, industrial laboratories, and related firms. The total number of electronic research and development personnel identified by the U.S. Bureau of the Census for NASA in the Boston area in 1961 was 37,800. In 1960, the National Academy of Science included 14,700 area residents as industrial research and development personnel. Only two areas exceeded the Boston area on both counts—New York and Los Angeles.[18]

In 1963, in the Boston area, there were an estimated 1,500 doctorate holders and 4,700 holders of masters' degrees engaged in research and development work in industries. The critical numbers that played a significant role in justifying NASA's decision were clearly quite small in relation to the Boston area's labor force of over 1 million. The element of size is even more apparent in considering the number of scientists engaged in basic research in the area —only 1,609 in 1962.[19] It would have been foolhardy indeed to suggest in the 1930s that the presence of a few thousand engineers and scientists and the existence of universities, hospitals, banks, and other institutions that had become a customary part of the landscape would, within decades, be significant factors in reversing the area's economic trends.

One effect of the alteration in Massachusetts' role in the past generation has been to transform the state—paced by metropolitan Boston—into a major beneficiary of federal spending, particularly in the fields of defense, research, and urban renewal.

It had long been believed that because of a combination of high incomes and the effectiveness of southern and western legislators in securing federal aid for military installations, agriculture, and public works, Massachusetts was among the wealthy victims who contributed far more in taxes to the federal treasury than were returned in dollar benefits. This view is sharply contradicted by 1957–63 data which show that, far from being drained by federal taxation, Massachusetts has been the beneficiary of a relatively large and rising proportion of total federal spending.

A report published in mid-1966 indicated that, in 1963, Massachusetts received a total of $735 in per capita federal expenditures in the national income accounts, 20 percent above the $597 per capita for the nation and well above the levels of the Midwest, Southeast, Southwest, Plains, and Rocky Mountain regions. Only the Far West figure ($862 per capita) was higher.[20]

In 1963, federal expenditures amounted to 27.3 percent of total Massachusetts personal income versus 22.3 percent in 1957. This percentage was higher than the nation (25 percent), although somewhat lower than the South and Far West (29-32 percent). Massachusetts personal income is so much larger ($2,800 per capita in 1963 versus $1,800 in the Southwest) that a slightly smaller percentage represents a larger dollar amount than in poorer states. The data tend to refute the notion that federal government expenditures necessarily result in a reallocation of income from wealthy states to poor states.

The primary sources of Massachusetts federal expenditures were defense and welfare payments. In both respects—the share of the total provided by defense and federal transfer payments for welfare programs—Massachusetts is one of the national leaders.[21]

It might be noted that metropolitan Boston was a net exporter of population during this period. The birth rate began to head downward years before the national rate in the 1950s, and relatively smaller natural increase was accompanied by consistent net out-migration. In the 1960–70 decade, for example, metropolitan Boston grew by only 8 percent (versus 13 percent for the nation), and in the early 1970s population actually declined. To a considerable extent the area's relatively high per capita income and its moderate unemployment rate are due to this inherent tendency to adjust its population and labor force in accordance with available economic opportunities.

Within a few years the ebullience of the 1960s had given way to something like despair. The NASA center had folded, sharp reductions in defense and space contracts had brought unemployment to an estimated 10,000 of the region's engineers and scientists, and the universities were warned that they were turning out far too many specialists with advanced degrees. In the mid-

1970s another painful transition was underway. But there were important divergences from the grimmer problems of the 1930s. For one thing, the 1973–75 recession had left some important components of the economy unscathed. The medical complexes continued to flourish, the insurance and banking industry was thriving, and a host of manufacturing and service operations kept on growing. Boston, with an unemployment rate of under 8 percent, was far less hard hit than many areas where unemployment during the recession penetrated the 8 to 10 percent level. More significant perhaps is the region's basic strength in higher education and research, which virtually guarantees it a significant role along whatever new economic frontiers may be developing in the 1980s and beyond. To put Boston's case simply, it is far easier to adapt research- and development-oriented industries to changing needs than it is to turn around a mining industry or textile manufacturing. In short, the recession could be viewed as a marginal matter, creating serious hardship for part of the region but leaving its major assets as important as ever.

An attempt has been made to describe the transformation of the Greater Boston area during a period of rapid and largely unexpected changes. The question is, could these changes have been foreseen? Who, in the mid-1930s, could have predicted World War II and its aftermath and the opportunities presented by these events for the special assets offered by metropolitan Boston? Who, for example could have foretold that a single major laboratory established under MIT auspices to meet the government's wartime needs in electronics and other fields would, 20 years later, "spin off" over 60 research and development (R & D) firms and provide subcontracts for over 200 R & D firms? The magnetic attraction of the major educational institutions in Cambridge and Boston, allied to the complex of laboratory and research facilities in the area, generated a substantial new industry in two decades, with over 500 private firms employing 26,000 people.[22] It was clearly impossible to penetrate through the murky gloom of the Great Depression and look ahead to the mid-1960s. Perhaps an assessment of the shape of the 1960s was feasible by the early 1950s, but who foresaw the brutal blow to the Route 128 industries dealt by the recessions of the 1970s? Or the recovery and growth of such Boston-area stalwarts as Polaroid, Gillette, and Raytheon, as well as the area's large university and medical employers by the mid-1970s?

BOSTON, THE NORTHEAST, AND THE SUNBELT.

Metropolitan Boston's unexpected success in weathering the decay of the 1920s and the economic storms of the 1930s offers special lessons for those in the mid-1970s who see nothing but gloom ahead for the older areas of the Northeast and Midwest as the nation's population and economic expansion shift to the South and West, the balmy Sunbelt. Long the recipients of an inordinate share of military bases and other federal allocations, the Sunbelt, it was charged, has added a powerful surge of private investment as corporations allowed their northern plants to obsolesce and put their new capital equipment in southern and western states. Fears were voiced that the northeast quadrant of the nation would develop into a vast urban Appalachia as a result of prolonged neglect by both the public and private sectors.[23]

In many respects the cries of despair are not unlike those of New England, including metropolitan Boston in the 1940s and 1950s, when textiles were heading south and the large shoe industry was disappearing. At this time it is impossible to know whether we are witnessing an enlarged rerun of past history or whether this time the cries of wolf will be justified. Certain elements in the Boston experience are worth citing.

The first is that the prophets of gloom in the 1930s and 1940s were proved wrong. The second is the tendency to adjust population to the opportunities afforded by the economy. If the Sunbelt does grow faster, there is absolutely no reason why population should not flow out of the Northeast as an accepted and unlamented modern manifestation of the kind of ebb and flow of people and industry inseparable from a changing, dynamic nation.

The success of this realignment depends in part on whether the Northeast can follow Boston's example. In effect, metropolitan Boston upgraded its economy, losing low-wage textiles and shoes and picking up better-paying electronics and high-quality R & D industries. One ebullient Boston developer put the changeover succinctly, albeit crudely: "We lost the crap and we got the cream."

To summarize, metropolitan Boston's postwar transition suggests that slow growth or even modest declines in population are not incompatible with high living standards—provided the region maintains a healthy grip on education, research, and the advanced components of the economy.

The long-range planning studies of the 1930s are today curios rather than basic documents which through constant usage, revision, and updating have become working guides for continued planning and programing. The question that now arises is whether our current studies are designed for the library or the work table. Analysis indicates that in the short-term sense, two to five years, many of them will indeed be used. Highways, schools, and medical institutions will be constructed on the basis of master plans that embody a response to immediate needs in the perspective of some type of long-range projection. While there is no difficulty in identifying urgent and obvious requirements, it is in this latter area, the forecasts, that there are problems similar to those which confounded the false prophets of the 1930s.

The new planning studies in many cases do not really build upon either the studies or the lessons of the past. Instead, they refer, with a touch of humor, to their predecessors' efforts, noting the quaint ways in which they went astray. It now remains to be seen whether our current efforts are likely to be much more satisfactory. In essence, the question may be rephrased: Is it possible to discern coming events or trends in the foreground or on the horizon that can have as dislocating effects on present projections as World War II and associated developments had on the forecasts of the 1930s?

PROJECTIONS AND REVISIONS

The built-in uncertainties involved in preparing population projections suggest some of the difficulties in developing and using forecasts. In this connection, a 1966 U.S. Department of Labor projection on nationwide manpower needs for 1970 notes some significant problems in looking ahead only four years:

> The projections are dependent on assumptions about unemployment rates, growth in productivity, the mix of consumption, investment, government expenditures and other key economic variables. A crucial assumption underlying the projections is that the Vietnam situation will have been resolved by 1970 and that defense expenditures reduced to a more normal level.[24]

Of course, the department was dead wrong. The war lasted until 1973. This offers only one example of why, in view of such international, diplomatic, and military uncertainties, it is rightly considered extremely hazardous to make firm predictions even three or four years ahead. When projections are prepared for longer periods, the results have often been wildly out of line with subsequent events.

In contrast to the U.S. Bureau of the Census, which in the 1930s predicted that U.S. population would level off by 1960 or 1970, a census projection prepared in 1943 projected a national total of almost 200 million by the year 2000. The nation surpassed this level by the end of 1967.

A high point in the bureau's projections was reached in 1964. The U.S. year 2000 population was estimated at a low of 291 million to a high of 362 million. Two years later, the bureau had lowered its sights to 280 to 356 million by the year 2000.[25] Quite probably, further downward revisions can be anticipated. In 1975 the Statistical Abstract added a new low—245 million. The critical problem facing population specialists and the nation in the last third of the twentieth century is the huge potential for population growth created by the nation's present age distribution. It is difficult, if not impossible, to predict in advance the number of children families will desire in coming decades now that low-cost, effective contraceptive techniques render choice rather than accident a key factor in child bearing.

Population specialists point out that the U.S. birth rate declined from 55 per 1,000 in the early nineteenth century to 18 per 1,000 a century later, during the Great Depression, and to less than 15 per 1,000 in 1975. Meanwhile, in the same period, the death rate declined from 20 to 25 per 1,000 to 19 per 1,000 in 1975.

On the critical factor of family-size preference, there have been significant changes over the years. In the early nineteenth century, the number of children ever born to the typical, married, American female is believed to have been between eight and ten. By 1920, the number had declined to three, and in the midst of the depression, to two. It might be noted that to keep the population level stable, all that is necessary is that each adult couple have two children who live through childbearing age and whose offspring similarly survive and reproduce.

Population studies published in 1959 and 1966[26] comparing family-size preference in the past few decades indicate that the preferred two-child family of 1940 rose to a modal preference of three children by 1945, and to four children in 1955 and 1960. It is almost as if children were regarded as a luxury denied by the depression, and larger families had become an expression of postwar affluence.

Since maintaining population at a stable level requires only about two children per family, the current downward trend below a 2.0 level will, if it continues, probably result in a stabilized population before the middle of the next century. This is complicated by another factor—immigration. In the 1970s over 20 percent of U.S. population growth was attributable to legal immigration. Estimates of the number of illegal immigrants are obviously hazardous, but it has been suggested that the total number of illegals entering the U.S. each year—mainly Hispanic—is double the size of legal immigration.

Errors of great magnitude in population forecasting in past decades ranged from 1929 forecasts of continuing prosperity to warnings of a recurring depression issued during World War II. In Massachusetts in the 1930s and beyond, forecasts of future highway traffic, water demand, and the need for classroom facilities have proved to be gross underestimates. Throughout the nation in the 1960s, planners erred in predicting increases in central city populations only to have their forecasts shattered by the 1970 census.

In assessing the accuracy and usefulness of projections, a clear distinction must be made between prediction and control. There has been much criticism, for example, of forecasts that appear to rest on assumptions of some type of central control over growth rates and over the distribution of population density (for example, regional zoning) where such coordinative powers do not exist.

The possibility of making projections come true by fiat has probably been overestimated. Even totalitarian societies have found that there is wide scope for initiative outside the scope of the plan. One of the principal areas where personal preferences confound the planners even in dictatorships is in family size. Low birth rates have become a major issue in Hungary and East Germany. Conversely, India has adopted a variety of expedients including bonuses and mandatory sterilization of fathers with three or more children to reduce its rate of population growth.

It seems possible that population trends may have in store more surprises for American planners. Short of such events as a major military cataclysm or a severe economic depression, over the course of the next 10 to 30 years, a further steep decline in birth rates may be one of the principal factors in rendering current projections as ludicrous as those prepared in the 1930s. Slower population growth (or a leveling off of growth) would have a major impact on every aspect of national life, ranging from housing to food production, from jobs to needs for land and water. It would be difficult to overestimate the significance of a stable population that, after 350 years of continued expansion, had at last reached its upper limit.

Up to the mid-1960s, projections for the nation, state, and Boston region generally pointed to a continuation, with some modifications, of the growth rates of the 1950–60 decade. It has become increasingly apparent that these population projections may be on the high side.

The total number of live births in the nation began to turn downward in 1961. Massachusetts anticipated this trend by a full four years: in Massachusetts, the total number of births in 1965 had declined to a point well below the level of 1957, despite the fact that the state population had grown by 50 percent during the period. This decrease in births occurred in the face of a nationwide trend toward marriage at earlier ages and despite the "bulge" in teen-agers as a result of the sharply higher postwar birth rates during the middle and late 1940s. The relatively high birth rates of the late 1940s and 1950s seem, in fact, to represent transitory peaks similar to those which occurred in earlier periods. In 1950, for example, Massachusetts produced approximately the same number of births as it did in 1917, when the state's population was less than 4 million, 20 percent smaller than in 1950.

Wide publicity has been given to the change in the Roman Catholic church's policy and to the pill as prime elements in the downturn of the birth rate. In past decades, we managed without either. For example, in the 1930–40 depression decade, the national birth rate reached a point slightly lower than in 1966. The rate fell to just over 18 per 1,000 in 1933.[27] It may be useful to indicate the numbers involved in a declining population growth rate in Massachusetts, a state that has consistently tended to grow at a modest pace as compared to the nation. As is indicated by the following statistics, the population projection business is in a state of flux. In 1966, the Bureau of the Census forecast a rate of population expansion in Massachusetts between 1960 and 1980 at close to 0.9 percent annually, the 1950–60 annual growth rate. However, the bureau also indicated that the increase might be as high as 1.2 percent per year.[28]

In actuality, Massachusetts increased by only 1.9 percent from 1970 to 1974, an annual growth rate of less than 0.5 percent per year.[29]

The reason for a careful watch on birth rate trends is clear enough. A small revision in the natural increase rate resulting from a moderate shift in birth rates can have important implications. For example, given a total 1974 population of 5.8 million in the state, a decline of only 0.1 percent in the growth rate over a 25-year period can eliminate the need to construct perhaps 50,000 new homes, 2,000 classrooms, and 2,500 hospital beds. There would also be a similar decline in the consumption of open land, in requirements for other public facilities and services, and in the private sector of the economy. If there is a more sizable decline in the annual growth rate, perhaps down to the 0.3 percent level, the impact would be correspondingly greater.

Although birth rate trends are often considered more stable than economic and employment trends, the year-to-year fluctuations in birth rates in Massachusetts have been 10 or 20 times greater than 0.1 percent, and decade-to-decade changes in a 25-year period can be 50 to 100 times greater. The decline of the U.S. birth rate to 19.2 per 1,000 in 1965 and 14.9 per 1,000 population in 1975, well below the depression low point, has led some observers to predict further steep declines in birth rates leading to a population plateau by the year 2000 not only in the United States but in most advanced nations.[30] Another authority is reasonably optimistic concerning the prospects for a stabilized U.S. population.[31] If this view is accurate, population expansion in Massachusetts may level off completely within the next two or three decades, a development which would have staggering consequences for every aspect of the state.

To reiterate, a change in the birth rate is the critical factor. No significant alteration in the death rate is expected; reductions in the infant mortality rate and anticipated improvements in health conditions among disadvantaged segments of the population are likely to be offset by lower birth rates as incomes, living conditions, and expectations all rise.

CONCLUSION

The great variations in past birth rates, and especially the recent decline, suggest the adoption of a cautious attitude in assessing population projections. If we consider the impact of foreign immigration, legal and illegal, there is all the more reason for hedging one's bets. Preparation of population forecasts is necessary to guide operations of public agencies, but as the evidence of the past suggests, it behooves planners to exercise extreme care in preparing projections, in advancing claims for their accuracy, and in advocating the expenditure of large sums to prepare projections that are necessarily based on many uncertainties and shaky assumptions. The same observation is valid for economic projections. In the 1930s or even the 1940s, it would have taken divine guidance to foresee the shape of metropolitan Boston and Massachusetts in the mid-1970s. There is no reason to suppose that similar surprises may not be in store for the forecasters of the 1970s who are peering through the mists to the 1990s and beyond.

NOTES

1. Dennis O. Harrow, "A Broad Brush With A Sharp Edge," *American Society of Planning Officials Newsletter,* June 1967.
2. Edward C. Banfield, "The Uses and Limitations of Metropolitan Planning in Massachusetts," in *Taming Megalopolis,* ed. H. Wentworth Eldredge, vol. 2 (New York: Doubleday, 1967), p. 712.
3. Dale Wolfle, "Can Professional Manpower Trends Be Predicted?" *Seminar on Manpower Policy and Program,* U.S. Department of Labor, Manpower Administration (Washington, D.C., May 1967), p. 4. An error of much lesser magnitude (15 percent) was made on the projection on college graduates.
4. Commonwealth of Massachusetts, State Planning Board, *Progress Report,* "A Report Prepared by the Commonwealth of Massachusetts State Planning Board" (Boston, November 30, 1936).
5. U.S. Department of Commerce, *Survey of Current Business,* table 1 (Washington, D.C., May 1967).
6. J. P. Marquand's *H. M. Pulham, Esquire* and *The Late George Apley,* along with Edith Wharton's *Ethan Frome* exemplify the problems and quaintness of those who chose or were forced to remain, while Marquand's *Sincerely, Willis Wade* provides an excellent example of the upwardly mobile career man who severed his ties with the region, liquidating a local mill in the process. Edwin O'Connor's novels about Boston have probably been less influential in this respect because of their unique ethnic and political themes.
7. This section draws on a report prepared by a special committee of the Boston Chamber of Commerce, *New England, What It Is and What It Is to Be,* ed. George French (Cambridge, Mass.: University Printing Press, 1911). The quotation is on pp. 3–4.
8. Ibid., p. 208.
9. Ibid. This quotation and succeeding comments are in the chapter entitled "Boston: The Next Phase," pp. 221–32.
10. James Truslow Adams, "The Historical Background," in *New England's Prospect: 1933,* ed. J. T. Adams, H. S. Graves, et al. (Boston: Little, Brown, 1931), pp. 5–6.
11. Herman Keyserling, "Genius Locii," *Atlantic Monthly* 144 (September 1929): 304, quoted in Howard W. Odum and Harry Estill Moore, *American Regionalism* (New York: Henry Holt and Company, 1938).
12. Daniel J. Boorstin, *The Americans: The National Experience* (New York: Vintage, 1965).
13. Report by the Committee of New England of the National Planning Association, *The Economic State of New England* (New Haven: Yale University Press, 1954), pp. 566–70.
14. Ibid., pp. 560–66.
15. Report of the National Aeronautics and Space Administration, *Electronic Research Center* (Washington, D.C.: U.S. Government Printing Office, January 31, 1964), p. ix.
16. Ibid., p. xi.

17. Ibid., p. C. 6, table H. 1.

18. Ibid., table C. 3.

19. Ibid., Appendix H. Boston Area (c).

20. U.S., Committee on Government Operations, Subcommittee on Intergovernmental Relations, "Federal Expenditures to States and Regions," 89th Cong., 2nd sess., June 29, 1966, table C-10, p. 134.

21. Ibid., table A-10, p. 117.

22. Anne H. Cahn and Ashok Parthasarathi, *The Impact of a Government-Sponsored University Research Laboratory on the Local R & D Economy* (Cambridge, Mass.: M.I.T. Press, 1967), tables 3 and 4.

23. A series on this topic in the New York *Times* in February 1976 offered a variety of graphic heads "Sunbelt Region Leads Nation in Population Growth," "Houston Sets Pace in Sunbelt Boom," "Aging Process Catching Up with Cities of the North," "Federal Funds Pour into Sunbelt States," and so on. *Newsweek* and *Time* also featured major stories, and New York senatorial candidate Daniel Patrick Moynihan called for federal action to redress the balance.

24. U.S. Department of Labor, *Projections 1970, Interindustry Relationships, Potential Demand, Employment,* Bulletin No. 1536 (Washington, D.C.: U.S. Government Printing Office, 1966), p. 1.

25. Population Reference Bureau, "Boom Babies Come of Age: The American Family at the Crossroads," *Population Bulletin* 22, no. 3 (August 1966): 63–64.

26. Ronald Freedman, Pascal K. Whelpton, and Arthur A. Campbell, *Family Planning, Sterility and Population Growth* (New York: McGraw-Hill, 1959); and Pascal K. Whelpton, Arthur A. Campbell, and John E. Patterson, *Fertility and Family Planning in the United States* (Princeton, N.J.: Princeton University Press, 1966).

27. In 1967, the nation's birth rate declined to 17.9 per 1,000, the lowest in recorded history. As noted, the further decline to 17.5 in 1968 was followed by a rise to 17.7 in 1969, partly as a result of a scare affecting use of birth control pills. However, there is every reason to believe that the low point has not yet been reached. By the late 1970s, a rate of 14 per 1,000 was in sight.

28. U.S. Bureau of the Census, *Current Population Reports, Population Estimates,* "Illustrative Projections of the Population of States: 1960 to 1985," series P-25, no. 326, February 7, 1966.

29. *Statistical Abstract of the U. S.,* table 12, p. 13.

30. See Donald J. Bogue, "The End of the Population Explosion," *The Public Interest* 7 (Spring 1967): 11–20.

31. *Population Bulletin,* op. cit., p. 79.

CHAPTER

6

PLANNING FOR METROPOLITAN AREAS

Metropolitan areas present a planning paradox: opinion polls and voting patterns indicate that most of their residents seem satisfied with existing governmental structures, but a consensus of planning and administrative opinion calls for substantive changes. Before examining the reasons for this divergence in outlook and alternative futures for metropolitan areas, it is necessary to establish some of the key facts.

In August 1975 the Census Bureau delineated 272 metropolitan areas containing almost 150 million people; only 65 million Americans lived outside metropolitan areas in the mid-1970s. The figures compare to the bureau's 169 metropolitan areas as of 1950 with a combined population of only 85 million. The same growth pattern was evident with respect to metropolitan land area, which increased from 207,000 square miles in 1950 to just over 500,000 square miles in 1970. The proportion of the U.S. population in such areas rose from 56 percent of the total in 1950 to 73 percent in 1975.[1]

Although there has been some liberalization of qualifying criteria (for example, a central city need not have 50,000 population; 25,000 is sufficient if it is surrounded by high-density urban territory), most of the gain in metropolitan areas is attributable to the fact that this is where most of the population growth has been taking place. By 1973 the nation's metropolitan suburbs contained 79 million people.

A few more statistics provide one clue to the metropolitan problem: in 1970 64 million people lived in the 272 central cities, and many of these cities were in serious trouble. But problems in finding sufficient government resources are not confined to central cities. There are approximately 20,000 government jurisdictions—municipalities, counties, and special districts—in the nation's metropolitan areas. Many small government units in suburban areas lack the resources to undertake an adequate range of municipal functions. In the late 1960s, of the 20,000 incorporated municipalities within metropolitan areas, one-third had fewer than 1,000 residents and another third, fewer than 5,000. One-third of the public-school districts in metropolitan areas operated only a single school.[2]

This is not to suggest that progress in reducing fragmentation has not been made. Between 1942 and 1967, consolidations decreased the number of U.S. school districts from 109,000 to less than 22,000. These losses were offset to some extent by an increase of 13,000 in other types of special districts,[3] such as sewer, water, and parks. Moreover, based on present indications, there may well be another 10,000 new special districts created by the turn of the century.[4]

At this point we can depart from the statistics and proceed to an examination of local governments in metropolitan areas. A national business organization, the Committee for Economic Development, summarized them under six main headings:[5]

1. Many local governments are too small to provide effective and economical solutions to their problems.
2. Extensive overlapping layers of government cause confusion and waste the taxpayers' money.
3. Popular control over local government is ineffective because of the excessively long ballots and the confusion caused by the many-layered system of government.
4. Policy leadership is weak, if not nonexistent.
5. Archaic administrative organizations are totally inadequate to the functional demands made up on them.
6. The professional services of highly qualified personnel are typically not attracted to local government.

This list does not consider other major problems, including great disparities in government fiscal resources and the cumulative regional impact of fiscal and snob zoning to attract upper- and middle-class people and clean industries and to zone out the poor. There are special problems with special districts. Many of them are unresponsive, either because they are controlled by narrow interests or simply because they have evolved into autonomous self-perpetuating organizations beyond the reach of the voters. And there are recurrent problems in metropolitan planning involved in reconciling the divergent interests of different jurisdictions to locate major regional facilities (no one wants jails, public housing, airports, or incinerators).

HOW SERIOUS A PROBLEM?

The proposition that metropolitan areas require any fundamental change in governance is disputed by a small group of scholars and, on the basis of the record, by most residents of most metropolitan areas. It is argued, for example, that the ailments afflicting metropolitan areas, particularly municipal fragmentation into small units, are, properly considered, very real assets. Within the metropolitan complex we have numerous suburban governments, responsive to their electorates, but differing from community to community in outlook, services, or amenities. In effect, there is in existence all of the objectives eagerly advanced by proponents of decentralizing big-city neighborhoods—schools, police, and other services reduced to manageable, human scale without the intervening layers of semi-autonomous bureaucracies.

It is said that the diversity offers a range of choices; the prospective homeowner or renter can select from a cafeteria of communities, some offering low densities, others apartments, some combining high taxes and high-quality services, others skimping on both.

The problem with this free-choice model is that it takes a good deal of money to purchase tickets in this particular cafeteria. Although the average price of new housing is at the $50,000 level, most prospective new homeowners have less than $20,000 a year in annual income. Centers where suburban apartments are available usually find the going rate at $250 to $300 per month for a two-bedroom unit, requiring an annual income of at least $12,000. Low-cost two-bedroom condominiums, much smaller than detached single-family units, are in the $30,000 to $35,000 range, requiring a family income of at least $15,000 to pay principal, interest, taxes, and assorted upkeep expenses. For this reason most residents of metropolitan areas are subject to severe economic constraints: in practice, their housing and neighborhood options are sharply restricted.

The smallness argument is also open to some doubt. Smallness can indeed offer a reassuring degree of control over municipal affairs, but in the many instances where communities are extremely small the control may not mean much. If, for example, the land area is limited, careful local control over land use may be of no avail in preventing polluting industries from impinging on the borders. There is, in fact, a pronounced tendency for less desirable facilities like municipal dumps and sewage plants to be sited in isolated locations directly on some other community's boundary. Furthermore, very small services—schools, libraries, and police forces—may offer an equally small range of efficiency, quality, and choice.

Although this view seems to have lost most of its supporters in recent years, its proponents made a plausible case for a polycentric metropolitan decision-making process in which a multiplicity of governments function rationally and with reasonable efficiency. As necessary, these governments enter into intermunicipal compacts, arrange informal agreements, or create functional metropolitan entities for the provision and/or purchase of services. Using the Los Angeles area as a model, Ostrom, Tiebout, and Warren see major advantages to this approach, which in their opinion avoids the necessity for creating inappropriate, gargantuan, unresponsive metropolitan governmental units.[6] They would appear to be in agreement with Norton Long, who stated: "The metropolitan area is a kind of natural government ecology . . . a system of largely unintended cooperation through which things get done . . . existing metropolitan areas are going concerns." In Long's view, the prospects for radical reform are exceedingly dim because with all its faults and contradictions, the system works.[7]

As these observers see it, when large size is desirable it is usually for small communities to form regional compacts or to purchase services from some larger entity. Through the use of this technique, it is alleged, the virtues of miniaturization can be combined with the advantages of scale.

While there is much to be said for the notion that Americans cherish local autonomy but are sufficiently sensitive to practical needs to establish appropriate regional entities as needed, there is another, darker side to this picture. For one thing, regional special districts, as noted above, display a tendency to evolve into independent, unresponsive empires. The New York area's Port Authority is a well-known example, but there are hundreds of other "metropolitan giants" operating throughout the nation. The Port of New York Authority has engaged in lengthy battles with the city of New York over the division of rights and responsibilities in port development, has been fruitlessly attacked by New Jersey railroads as a major contributor to their woes, and has consistently avoided involvement in vital but money-losing ventures like subways in favor of such peripheral, controversial enterprises as the World Trade Center.[8]

A further problem is at least as serious. This is the cumulative impact of local autonomy on regional land use patterns. The lack of an adequate supply of suburban apartments, and of housing for low- and middle-income families in the suburbs of virtually all metropolitan areas attests to the fact that a mosaic of individual community land use decisions can add up to a pattern of regional discrimination. It is debatable whether court cases in state supreme courts and coercive action by the federal government to withhold federal funds from communities engaging in snob zoning or other restrictive practices can combine the best of both worlds: retain local autonomy but force communities to desist from engaging in discriminatory measures.

This leads to two final points concerning the status-quo hypothesis. The first is the need for referees and *force majeure* by higher levels of government. Disputes between localities and issues which clearly require regional action are resolved, as a matter of course, by state government and, less frequently, by the federal government. The timing and construction of major highways; the expansion, retention, or cessation of service by public transportation lines; and decisions on university construction and expansion, large recreational facilities, and airports involve state and often federal input. Localities react, and often object, but without the power of final disapproval. In the clinches, as many communities can testify, local autonomy is more myth than reality.

It is sometimes claimed that metropolitan fragmentation offers useful insulation from intercommunity conflict. Divisive social conflict, it is said, is more bitter in the direct head-to-head confrontations that take place within large cities than in the community-verses-community battles that occasionally erupt in metropolitan areas. Residents of an aggrieved central city are required, in a multiple jurisdictional system, to take to the courts (as in a number of suburban zoning cases), to enlist the central city government in court action, or to lobby in the state legislature, the Congress, or federal executive agencies.

Of all the arguments advanced in favor of the status quo this seems the weakest. The evidence indicates that conflict takes place with or without municipal fragmentation. There is, in fact, no evidence at all to suggest that experience in those metropolitan areas which have adopted one of the stronger forms of metropolitan government is any more bitter, divisive, or prolonged than in those areas which have made only modest moves in this direction. In any event, if conflict is to occur, it can as easily emerge at the state and federal level where the metropolitan kind of governmental fragmentation is absent. In this context, other arguments advanced in opposition to a metropolitan approach seem equally feeble. It is pointed out that long-range or even medium-range planning is extremely difficult in a society so beset by rapid change that long-range planning is a useless exercise. The answer to this objection is simple: All sorts of decisions, from purchase of homes with 25-year mortgages to highway construction, represent long-range commitments. Once again, if no metropolitan agency is available, some other level of government will do the long-range planning because difficult or not, the job is inescapable. Further, it has been indicated that a metropolitan area has no goals, no consensual public interest, and no knowledge of how to implement long-range social goals, if such were available. This is why, in Edward Banfield's opinion, "so many metropolitan planning bodies have confined themselves to collecting data, helping local planning bodies, and other such innocuous and futile tasks."[9]

Setting aside the harsh judgment concerning local technical assistance and research, it would appear that the reality to which Banfield refers, the weakness of many metropolitan agencies, does not mean that someone else is not going about the task of metropolitan planning and governing. If indeed most present metropolitan agencies are flabby, this simply means that the responsibility for such vital tasks as transportation and utility services planning remains in the hands of other agencies. As Banfield points out, the ultimate responsibility rests with the state government.

COGS: THIS WAY TO THE FORUM

Under federal pressure, during the late 1960s well over 100 Councils of Governments (COGs) were established in metropolitan areas ranging in size from 60,000 to 18 million. If a reluctant metropolitan area found itself in the position of having to establish some sort of harmless metropolitan organization, COGs were the answer. COGs were not a grassroots movement. From the mid-1960s to the mid-1970s the federal government made it increasingly clear that it was a case of no tickee no washee: no metropolitan agency, no federal approval of a variety of local applications for grants for sewage and water systems, housing projects, crime prevention funds, and so on.

The surge in the growth of COGs was phenomenal. The first agency was established in metropolitan Detroit in 1954, and there were only nine such agencies in 1964. Then came the deluge. Between 1965 and 1969, 91 COGs were created, with another 40 established by the early 1970s. All told, there were 140 COGs in existence in 1973.[10]

Unlike other forms of metropolitan government, COGs are federations of local governments with representation on a one-government, one-vote basis. Normally they meet once or twice a year, and the majority in each is composed of elected officials. In practice, most are controlled by a small executive committee and professional staff.

A series of federal actions since the mid-1960s has steadily broadened the responsibilities of the COGs. The 1966 Metropolitan Development and Demonstration Cities Act (even the nomenclature sounds quaint in the mid-1970s) provided that municipal applications for planning projects in metropolitan areas would have to be officially reviewed by a designated metropolitan agency. The 1968 Intergovernmental Cooperation Act provided that a majority of COG representatives would have to be elected officials. Also in 1968 came the Omnibus Crime Control and Safe Streets Act, which endowed the metropolitan agencies with the responsibility of reviewing local applications in this area. And in 1974 there was revised Budget Circular A-95, establishing a Project Review and Notification System (PRNS) to perform many planning functions. These included coordination of municipal projects, service as a metropolitan clearinghouse for exchange of useful information, and the review and validation of local applications for water and sewer projects, other physical programs, and increasingly applications for operating programs in crime prevention and other areas.

It is clear that far from representing a groundswell of public opinion in favor of metropolitan government, COGs reflect a simple, minimal response to federal prerequisites for securing funds. The verdict on their performance is indicative of the weakness of a confederation resembling the General Assembly of the United Nations, where large and small countries each have one vote: review and approval of member applications tends to be pro forma; controversial, potentially divisive social and economic issues are avoided; and consequently COGs tend to represent a kind of comforting pageantry, safely outside the mainstream of political action and policy determination.[11] Since the primary allegiance of COG members is to their local governments, and since the real political action is in the state house and in Washington, knowledgeable municipalities work through their elected representatives on a direct line to the states and the federal government. COGs are frequently asked for ex post facto validation after the deal has been made, particularly if the applicant is a large central city or an influential suburb. Perhaps the most telling evidence of their dependent status, however, is that lack of any independent revenue base: they must rely on municipal and other contributions and grants for sustenance.

Does this mean that COGs are solely a matter of outward display for the benefit of federal officials, minimal, symbolic, politically acceptable responses to well-meant but fundamentally unintelligent outside pressures? To a great extent they are. However, while they have no authority to make binding decisions and usually find it expedient to avoid grappling with touchy issues like race, poverty, and suburban zoning, they do serve as a forum where issues can be discussed if not resolved, a means of reducing tension and hostility, and a source of useful research on regional problems. This latter responsibility can be important. Some regional agencies have evolved into the one regionally acceptable source for population projections, housing studies, water and sewer studies, and so on. In areas where the courts or government bodies have mandated fair-share housing plans, COGs have devised allocations which, if not welcomed with enthusiasm, are perhaps less suspect than plans generated by localities or other jurisdictions. The final verdict therefore is mixed. If they play a much less important role than was hoped for by their federal sponsors and some local advocates, many have fulfilled moderately useful responsibilities in their respective areas. As implied by this statement, the pattern varies widely: some COGs are active and influential, while others are not much more than paper organizations shuffling letters and proposals and generating rhetoric and research studies in a routine and almost mindless fashion.

TWO-TIER FEDERATIONS

In the minds of many of their proponents, voluntary regional planning associations and weak planning organizations like COGs were to be an attractive introduction to regionalism: once they had sampled its benefits, metropolitan areas were certain to go on to the next step, a form of regional government with real powers. In fact, this is not the way matters progressed. Instead there are a handful of operational two-tier planning federations and a small number of consolidated city-county governments, with the ranks increasing at the rate of perhaps three or four per decade.

Among the two-tier federations, perhaps the best known are Minneapolis-St. Paul, established in 1967, Dade County-Miami (1957), and Toronto, Canada, created by action of the Province of Ontario in 1954.

Covering 3,000 square miles, 320 municipalities, and seven counties, the two-million population Twin Cities federation is an example of state legislative approval of a metropolitan government designed to preserve substantial autonomy for localities with a central review and operational authority. Important evidence of this power can be found in the Twin Cities federation's independent taxing authority and its significant specified functions. These include regional sewage, water, and solid waste disposal, highway planning, parks, mass transit, and pollution control. As if authority over these fundamental components of regional development were not sufficient, the federation has the responsibility of reviewing and, if it wishes, of delaying local zoning changes. Furthermore, it can disapprove—legally halt—special district projects and plans if these are deemed to be inconsistent with the metropolitan plan.

After a decade or so of experience, the Minneapolis-St. Paul federation has achieved an enviable reputation among other areas. Evidence of its organic roots is the fact that it has been given more taxing power and genuine responsibilities, a clear indication of its popularity with its two governmental constituencies, the state, and component municipalities and counties. In fact, critics are constrained to point to the Twin Cities' special advantages in explaining why their own areas cannot do likewise. It is indicated that Minnesota state government, the city of Minneapolis, and many suburban municipalities have enjoyed good government for many years. (St. Paul is a complicated, checkered story.) The area is homogeneous, with a relatively smaller proportion of blacks and Hispanics; the central cities are considered livable areas rather than pestilential places which people flee or avoid. And there are no extraordinary obstacles involving urban territory across another state line, an unstable declining economy, or headlong real estate development of the type that makes planning difficult in Florida.

The Miami-Dade County history is not considered quite in the same class, if only because of the bitter, albeit unsuccessful, attempts to commit fedricide; the chief instigators and abettors were local and county officials whose powers had been lost or curtailed by the creation of the federation. Aside from its inability to develop as powerful and unswerving a constituency as the Twin Cities, the clearest evidence of the inadequacy of the Miami-Dade County metropolitan approach can be found in the passage of state legislation to control land use and protect the endangered environment. State government apparently did not see the federation as capable of confronting and mastering the powerful interests involved in real estate development and construction. When a consensus developed that the job had to be done, the task was not entrusted to Miami or other Florida metropolitan areas but was instead reserved as a state responsibility.[12]

Before leaving the topic of U.S. two-tier federations, mention should be made of proposals to establish a complete two-level organization arrangement.

The 1970 study sponsored by the Committee on Economic Development, a liberal businessmen's organization, came close to this notion by proposing a combination of metropolitan government and small neighborhood governments created, in part, by decentralizing government structures in the central cities.[13] The CED report also recommended, wherever possible, making use of existing county governments. Based on experience, this prescription seems appropriate for states in the Midwest and South, but it is much less applicable to the Northeast, where county government is frequently no more than a vestigial anachronism. (To cite an extreme example, the state of Connecticut has totally eliminated county government.)

One of the best-known examples of federated metropolitan governments in North America—a term which Canadians use to refer to the United States and Canada, excluding the Latin nations between Mexico and Panama—is Toronto. Reflecting Canada's very different historic relationship between its provinces and municipal government, metropolitan Toronto was created entirely by Ontario government fiat, without a local or metropolitan vote or referendum. Among the formidable powers of the federation are responsibility for assessment and taxation of property, mass transit, parks, and major roads. Local governments retained responsibiltiy for fire, water, and sewer services, for local planning and zoning, and for local recreation and community services. One of the major achievements of the Toronto federation has been to eliminate the local fiscal disparities which are responsible in many areas for a wide gap between the quality of services between communities richly endowed with a tax base and those of slender means.[14]

As was the case with the Twin Cities, the excellent reputation of the Toronto metropolitan federation has been ascribed to the excellent quality of local and higher levels of government, to good leadership, and to the relative homogeneity and livability shared by central city and suburban communities. The homogeneity argument can be overdone; since the 1940s Toronto has changed from a quiet, Waspy, provincial city to a large cosmopolitan community. Nevertheless, the tradition of good government, tolerance, and livability has been successfully maintained. It is not surprising that other provincial governments have followed Ontario's lead and have established metropolitan governments in a number of other areas.

One final comment is necessary before leaving the subject of Toronto. The existence of a federated metropolitan government and the retention of component municipalities does not preclude the possibility of a loss of vital contact with the grass roots. The case in point is the Spadina Expressway, a proposed in-town arterial road which aroused substantial neighborhood opposition in the middle and late 1960s.[15] In this instance the metropolitan government continued to insist that the road was absolutely necessary only to be overruled by the provincial government using a "people—not roads" argument. By all accounts the decision, like similar actions in halting such expressways in a number of American cities including Boston, San Francisco, and New Orleans, has been well received by a public disenchanted with in-city highway construction.

SINGLE AREAWIDE GOVERNMENT

A step beyond the two-tier federation is the single areawide government, in this case meaning consolidation of city and county governments into a unified entity. There are three well-known examples, Nashville-Davidson County (Tennessee), where consolidation occurred in 1962; Jacksonville-Duval County (Florida), where consolidation dates back to 1967; and Indianapolis-Marion County (Indiana), where the consolidation date is 1969. Several points are immediately apparent: there are only a handful of instances; all are located in the Midwest or South; and none is of post-1970 vintage.

For one reason or another, these three governments have not generated as much scholarly interest as the two-tier metropolitan federations. It is known, however, that in the case of Nashville, consolidation was originally feared and resisted by some central-city blacks who felt that their needs would be better served by a municipal government in which blacks would constitute a very large proportion of the electorate, as compared to a metropolitan government in which black voting power would be diluted among a host of predominantly white suburbs. It may be noted that metropolitanization reduced total black population and voting strength in the Nashville, Jacksonville, and Indianapolis areas by 30 to 50 percent. Since blacks compose only 15 to 25 percent of the metropolitan electorate, the chances of a takeover are much diminished.

The hard core of the opposition of metropolitanization is usually found in suburban communities. Suburbs fear that their resources will be drained to bail out troubled central cities, that central city misgovernment will spill over into their bailiwicks, and that they will lose control over vital functions like public schools, the police, and control over land use.

Based on the Nashville experience, it would appear that fears on both sides are somewhat exaggerated, but that suburbanites can more than hold their own in protecting their interests. Nashville blacks were perturbed, for example, over actions of the metropolitan federation with respect to an urban renewal project and an expressway cutting through the black residential areas. On the other hand, the suburban communities have done well. Total suburban population is usually larger than in central cities, voter participation is much higher, and eloquent and sophisticated technical arguments can be generated to shortcut aid and counter central cities' pleas for special help.

Over the long haul, metropolitan governments in the South, far from exhibiting overt racial bias, have acted to further some types of integration. These include an increase in blacks employed in civil service jobs and substantial gains in school integration.[16] However, no progress was reported on perhaps the touchiest issue, residential desegregation.

Annexation

Obviously, the simplest solution to the problems posed by a multiplicity of governments in metropolitan areas is to continue the historical process of central city expansion and absorption of outlying territory. The fact that many central city boundaries were set in concrete two or three generations past creates this particular difficulty. In short, if cities could grow to include their suburbs we would be confronted with enlarged versions of municipal problems rather than the typical metropolitan problems of overlapping jurisdictions, tax disparities, and zoning and service differentials. True, neighborhoods within cities can differ as much as central cities and suburbs; but in theory, if not in practice, there is a focus of governmental responsibility and accountability: one mayor, one council.

Before proceeding with a lament for the vanished trend toward central city expansion, it is useful to examine the data. Scholars from the Northeast tend to overstate the rigidity of city boundaries: Boston, New York City, Philadelphia, and other old eastern cities have not grown at all for over 60 years. It is easy to fall into the trap set by parochialism. In point of fact, about a quarter of the cities with populations in excess of 50,000 have annexed significant amounts of territory since 1945. (A total of 40 cities with population of 100,000 or more added 40 square miles or more; there are 153 cities of this size.) Although one researcher maintains that cities which "continue to annex are relatively small"[17] (with the exception of Houston), a glance at Table 1 reveals growth in a substantial number of sizable municipalities.

Table 1 indicates that 19 large cities increased their size substantially in the 22-year period 1950–72. To place this figure in perspective, it should be noted that this represents a sizable proportion of the nation's 48 cities with a 1970 population in excess of 300,000. Clearly annexation is a far from negligible approach to the challenges of governmental fragmentation in metropolitan areas. However, it is clear that the annexation response is mainly a southern and western phenomenon; only four of the expanding cities were outside these two regions. Furthermore, none of these four areas was in the Northeast. Overall, however, annexation is far more widespread than either two-tier or city-county federations, the other serious attempts to confront metropolitan problems.

TABLE 1

Increase of At Least 40 Square Miles in Land Area Among Cities with Populations of 300,000 Or More

City	1970 Population (in thousands)	Land Area (square miles)		
		1950	1972	1950–72 Increase
Jacksonville, Florida	529	30.2	766.0	735.8[a]
Oklahoma City, Oklahoma	366	50.8	635.7	584.9
Nashville-Davidson, Tennessee	448	22.0	507.8	485.8[a]
Indianapolis, Indiana	745	55.2	379.4	324.2[a]
Houston, Texas	1,233	160.0	439.5	279.5
Phoenix, Arizona	582	17.1	257.0	239.9
Kansas City, Missouri	507	80.6	316.3	235.7
Dallas, Texas	844	112.0	266.1	154.1
San Diego, California	697	99.4	246.8	147.4
Tulsa, Oklahoma	332	26.7	171.9	145.2
Memphis, Tennessee	624	104.2	235.7	131.5[b]
Fort Worth, Texas	393	93.7	223.2	125.5
San Antonio, Texas	654	69.5	198.1	128.6
San Jose, California	446	17.0	142.0	125.0
Columbus, Ohio	540	39.4	147.1	107.7
El Paso, Texas	322	25.6	122.3	96.7
Atlanta, Georgia	497	36.9	131.5	94.6
Milwaukee, Wisconsin	717	50.0	95.0	45.0
Toledo, Ohio	384	38.3	81.2	42.9

[a]Most or all of the increase resulted from the consolidation of the city with a county.
[b]Includes an undetermined amount of water area.

Sources: John C. Bollen and Henry C. Schmandt, *The Metropolis: Its People, Politics and Economic Life*, 3d ed. (New York: Harper and Row, 1975), table 21. U.S. Bureau of the Census, *Land Area and Population of Incorporated Places of 2,500 or More: April 1, 1950*, Geographic Reports, ser. GEO no. 5, January 1953. Data were obtained from local officials by means of a mail survey. U.S. Bureau of the Census, *1972 Boundary and Annexation Survey* (Washington, D.C., 1973), and unpublished data from the Bureau's Geography Division. The published and unpublished survey data on city areas are estimates provided by local officials, not computations by the U.S. Bureau of the Census.

CONCLUSION

This brief survey of metropolitan problems leads to a number of conclusions.

First, there is a broad and sustained resistance toward metropolitan government. At the rate of progress of the past century with two-tier federations and consolidated city-county federations, it would require another century to make major inroads into the problem of metropolitan fragmentation.

Second, despite the seeming inability of some eastern scholars to discern reality, the most promising avenue for relief in much of the nation may well be outright annexation of surrounding territory by central cities.

Third, on the basis of a simple head count, the most popular approach to ameliorating metropolitan fragmentation is the Council of Governments. While COGs represent either modest progress or meaningless pageantry designed to qualify for federal funds, depending on one's point of view, the author is inclined to the latter viewpoint: at bottom COGs are more showy froth than solid substance.

Finally, it seems clear that despite federal prodding and pressure to develop uniform minimum standards, America is too large and too diverse for any one approach toward metropolitan problems. To sweep the board, consider the following facts: In some states, notably Rhode Island and Delaware, a single large metropolitan area contains most of the state population; rather than operate a parallel metropolitan governmental structure, in such cases, state government itself would seem to be the appropriate structure. Two states, Vermont and Wyoming, contain no metropolitan areas; in these states a combination of municipal, county, and state government seems appropriate. One in six—24 large metropolitan areas (population 250,000 plus)—cross state lines, with a few containing contiguous urban territory in three stages; government restructuring in such areas clearly calls for interstate treaties.

The hard core of metropolitan areas stubbornly resistant to significant government reorganization is located in the older cities of the Northeast. In such instances the choice seems to lie between toothless COGs or assumption of significant metropolitan governmental responsibilities by state governments. Whatever the shortcomings of these state governments, the latter seems to be the appropriate course of action. As noted elsewhere by the author:

> The temptation in most states is to adopt a policy combining drift and planning display, high-minded, long-winded conferences with acquiescence to developer initiatives. . . . Unfortunately, a passive governmental posture will lead to disaster. In less than a generation little . . . will remain habitable by any reasonable standard unless there is an effective state planning mechanism. If justification is needed for taking what appear to be dangerous political risks, one should consider the alternative, which is even more horrendous. Indeed, it is not inconceivable that after a decade or two we may witness a powerful trend toward abandonment of major parts of environmentally degraded states just as we have seen wholesale abandonment of sizable slum areas of central cities.[18]

In conclusion, the alternative seems clear: the decisions will be made without effective metropolitan entities, an unlikely prospect in most areas; the choice is between effective state input and continuation and exacerbation of existing trends.

NOTES

1. U.S. Department of Commerce, Bureau of the Census, *Statistical Abstract of the U.S.* (Washington, D.C.: U.S. Government Printing Office, 1975), pp. 884–85.

2. Allen D. Manvel, "Metropolitan Growth and Governmental Fragmentation," in *Governance and Population: the Governmental Implications of Population Change,* prepared by the Commission on Population Growth and the American Future (Washington: U.S. Government Printing Office, 1972), vol. 4, pp. 177–217.

3. Ibid., p. 182.

4. Ibid., p. 183.

5. Committee for Economic Development, *Modernizing Local Government* (New York, 1967).

6. Vincent Ostrom, Charles M. Tiebout, and Robert Warren, "The Organization of Government in Metropolitan Areas: A Theoretical Inquiry," in *Regional Development and Planning,* ed. J. F. Friedmann and W. Alonso (Cambridge: M.I.T. Press, 1964), pp. 542–53.

7. Norton E. Long, "Who Makes Decisions in Metropolitan Areas?," in *Metropolitan Politics: A Reader,* ed. Michael Danielson (Boston: Little, Brown, 1966), pp. 100–08.

8. See Robert C. Wood, *1400 Governments* (Cambridge, Mass.: Harvard University Press, 1961).

9. Edward C. Banfield, "The Uses and Limitations of Metropolitan Planning in Massachusetts," in *Taming Megalopolis,* ed. H. Wentworth Eldredge, vol. 2 (New York: Doubleday, 1967), pp. 710–18.

10. Alan Shank and Ralph W. Conant, *Urban Perspectives: Politics and Policies* (Boston: Holbrook, 1975).

11. See Charles W. Harris, "COGs, A Regional Response to Metro-Urban Problems," *Growth and Change* 6, no. 3 (July 1975).

12. Melvin R. Levin, Jerome G. Rose, and Joseph C. Slavet, *New Approaches to State Land-Use Policies* (Lexington, Mass.: Lexington Books, 1974).

13. Committee for Economic Development, *Reshaping Government in Metropolitan Areas,* New York, February 1970.

14. For a good analysis of the organization and conflicts within the federation in its formative years see Frank Smallwood, *Metro Toronto: A Decade Later* (Toronto: Bureau of Municipal Research, 1963).

15. The provincial premier hired Buckminister Fuller and Associates to develop an alternative plan for the cleared roadway site. Stories on the controversy appeared in the Toronto newspapers in October 1971.

16. John C. Bollens and Henry C. Schmandt, *The Metropolis: Its People, Politics and Economic Life,* 3d ed. (New York: Harper and Row, 1975). This volume is the best single work on this area.

17. Michael Danielson, "Differentiation, Segregation and Political Fragmentation in the American Metropolis," in *Governance and Population,* op. cit., p. 149.

18. Levin, Rose, and Slavet, op. cit., pp. ix–x.

CHAPTER

7

STUDIES IN HUMAN RESOURCES PLANNING

INTRODUCTION

By the mid-1970s persistent and well-publicized problems associated with the poverty program and Model Cities, among other government efforts, had led to widespread disenchantment with social planners. President Johnson expressed this view in a pungent complaint evoked by the ailing Model Cities agencies which, in his opinion, were in sad shape because of the "kooks and sociologists."[1] Despite this suspicion of claims, motives, and performance, planners have increasingly been called upon to provide guidance in translating judicial or legislative enactments into a reality embracing progress toward social goals. Moreover, there have also been requests—that is, contractual arrangements—for planners to evaluate traditional government line agencies in terms of their social impact.

The first part of this chapter considers two aspects of human resources planning. One is an analysis of remedies for exclusionary zoning, a lively topic in the mid-1970s. Second is an examination of transportation factors in relation to human resource regions. Third is an evaluation of recreation programs in a Model Cities area. Although parts two and three date back to the late 1960s and 1970, they remain extremely timely in their examination of the problems and opportunities associated with this kind of planning.

EXCLUSIONARY ZONING

During the Revolutionary War, New Jersey soldiers were famous for their extended and prolonged bouts of homesickness. Some historians have suggested that this malady was related to the Garden State's pattern of small yeoman farmers. Whatever the reason, New Jersey residents have long displayed a fierce attachment to their communities along with attenuated loyalties to their county and state.

It is possible that the bitter legal battles over local zoning practices now in progress in New Jersey are related to these deep community attachments. In addition, a combination of New Jersey's location in the path of expansion of the mammoth New York and Philadelphia metropolitan areas, and the advocacy efforts of the nearby Suburban Action Institute, have been critical factors in the eruption of large numbers of law suits instituted in New Jersey. Whatever the cause, it is apparent that a number of landmark land use cases have been launched in New Jersey. Names like *Mt. Laurel, Madison Township, Mahwah,* and *Middlesex County* have attracted national attention as a result of law suits seeking to overturn their zoning ordinances as discriminatory and exclusionary.

The author, along with colleagues, was a consultant in 1974–75 to four New Jersey communities directly or indirectly involved in exclusionary zoning suits. In the course of this maneuvering it became clear, to the author at any rate, that rather than be the subject of protracted costly litigation, most suburban communities are prepared to acknowledge the need for some sort of good-faith rezoning to permit apartments and moderate-income housing. It is also apparent, however, that there is a great distance to go before such housing is actually built in the suburbs, partly because of economic conditions and partly because a variety of delaying tactics is available in environmental legislation and legal obstacles.

To cite one simple ploy, a community can build an extensive file of resolutions, correspondence, and negotiations attesting to its willingness to construct new low- and moderate-income housing which proves that all its good intentions were blighted. Why? Because unfeeling developers refuse to construct housing with a system of rent control aimed at ensuring that rents would remain within the reach of the poor. Surely it was unfortunate to discover that tough rent controls to protect the poor seem to frighten off developers. And there are similar tactics which have been used, including exploring the outer limits of environmental impact statements. These can reflect a new-found sensitivity to the dangers from runoff, hazards to mud turtles, and the disturbance to avian nesting places liable to result from the construction of low-income housing. As Mary Brooks suggests, the litmus test for community environmental concern is to see if it preceded or followed proposed housing construction for poor families.[2]

To summarize, pressure from the courts has caused a number of communities in New Jersey and other states to enact inclusionary zoning ordinances. There is, however, an excellent likelihood that many communities will restrict their welcome to lower-income families to appropriate rhetoric and amassing paper proofs attesting to repeated failures to lure unaccountably reluctant developers. Meanwhile they are careful to remove any realistic prospect of actual construction through prolonged and sophisticated delaying action. The question then arises, Is it possible to minimize this community resistance movement? In the author's opinion it is possible to do so if three principles are observed:

1. that communities be assigned a housing goal which they perceive as fair
2. that most new housing be allocated to persons who live or work in the community
3. that virtually all new housing be allocated to moderate-income, not low-income persons

A fourth caveat: for some time to come in most suburbs it is unfortunately good advice to avoid reference to the largest contributor to low- and moderate-income housing in America—mobile homes.

In an excellent summary of the inclusionary zoning movement through the mid-1970s the authors examine the arguments for and against (yes, there are such), and outline federal policy and judicial rulings tending in this direction.[3] The volume includes a discussion of metropolitan fair-share housing plans in metropolitan Dayton, Ohio, the St. Paul, Minnesota, area, and metropolitan Washington, D.C.[4] This is only a sample of an enlarging universe. In addition to these three, areas and agencies which have implemented or proposed fair-share housing plans include the Delaware River Valley Regional Planning Commission, the Greater Hartford Process, the Commonwealth of Massachusetts, the Miami, Florida, metropolitan area (Dade County), metropolitan Sacramento and San Bernardino County, the Tri-State Regional Planning Commission, and the State of New Jersey.[5] With New Jersey apparently well represented in state and regional housing plans, a large-scale court case might appear redundant. But since previous plans clearly lacked implementing teeth, a prominent land use scholar recommended taking the case for regional housing to the courts.

Norman Williams recommended legal intervention, not on a town-by-town basis, but in a regional framework "sufficient to bring down an entire system of exclusionary controls in order to mandate an inclusionary policy."[6] Williams outlined criteria which resulted in a snugly fitted suit for one New Jersey county: a large swath of developable and rapidly developing territory and a range of restrictive devices to strike down.[7] In July 1974 such a suit was filed against 23 communities in Middlesex County, New Jersey, by the Urban League of Greater New Brunswick.[8] The decision in the case was delivered in May 1976.[9] Using Middlesex County's proportion of low- and moderate-income housing as a goal to be achieved by 1985, the court required 11 communities to rewrite their zoning ordinances. The remaining communities had already agreed to modify their zoning ordinances prior to the conclusion of the case.[10]

The author, as consultant to two of the Middlesex County communities, disagreed with the court's ruling on several counts, including the use of Middlesex County as a yardstick for a low- and middle-income housing, the stress on a separate goal for low-income housing, and the apparent recommendation for mobile homes.

Judge David Furman ruled that each of 11 municipalities deemed to have employed exclusionary zoning practices should attempt to construct or assist in construction of 1,333 low- and moderate-income housing units, that low- and moderate-income units should be divided 45 percent low and 55 percent moderate, and that a diversity of housing should include mobile homes at densities of five to eight units per acre.[11] Judge Furman called for affirmative action, not simply the removal of zoning barriers: making approvals of multifamily projects, and planned unit developments contingent on provision of mandatory minimums of low- and moderate-income housing. He also recommended pursuit of federal and state housing subsidy programs.[12]

Contrary to the decision to use Middlesex County as a unit (somewhat surprising in view of charges that the county as a whole had long engaged in exclusionary zoning practices), in the author's opinion it would seem less debatable and more acceptable to use New Jersey as a yardstick. The State of New Jersey remains the logical governmental unit for a number of reasons. It is inclusive, containing core cities, industrial towns, and developing suburbs. New Jersey state government possesses the power to act; communities, counties, and substate regions are in comparison feeble instrumentalities. Finally, the problem and disputes entailed by the allocation process are likely eventually to find their way for adjudication and implementation to the state level.

PROBLEMS IN ARRIVING AT REGIONAL ESTIMATES OF HOUSING NEED

A number of alternative methods have been evolved to estimate the numbers of housing units needed for low- and moderate-income families in various regions. Each method has certain advantages and disadvantages in terms of simplicity and persuasiveness. Some of the inherent limitations in the allocation process include:

Obsolescent Data. By default, the most comprehensive housing data available by census tract, community, county, and metropolitan area is the U.S. decennial census. In the late 1970s this means that we are constrained to use dated information. Practically speaking, in most communities there is insufficient information (other than housing starts and demolitions) on the changes that have taken place in the housing stock since 1970. To cite two examples, it is known that housing and neighborhood conditions have deteriorated in the core cities, the main reservoirs of housing need, but that many of the housing problems identified in the 1970s in many suburbs (such as overcrowding and structural deficiencies) have been corrected.

Inherent Weaknesses of Housing Census. While the 1970 census of housing represents a distinct improvement over previous decennial inventories, it still leaves much to be desired as an accurate barometer of housing need. There was encountered, for example, the perennial problem of population undercounting in the ghetto, a situation which leads to underestimating the extent of overcrowding. There was also the continuing problem of assessing housing conditions by a combination of direct questions and superficial inspection, a process which tends to rely on respondents' answers regarding plumbing facilities, courting the danger of overlooking serious but invisible structural flaws (for example, in foundations and walls). On the whole this inherent superficiality tends to minimize the seriousness of conditions in deteriorating core areas where structures may suffer from numerous unobserved deficiencies and to understate the extent of housing soundness in owner-occupied suburban housing and owner-supervised rental housing in stable suburban neighborhoods in which a reasonable quality of maintenance can normally be expected.

Furthermore, in assessing the quality of the urban environment, the quality of the neighborhood is at least as important as the soundness of individual residences. Indeed, it has been suggested that America's principal urban problem is not so much the shortage of good housing as it is the shortage of good neighborhoods. Numerous instances of good housing swiftly deteriorating in slum neighborhoods are cited as evidence. This observation leads to two conclusions: first, that once again the needs of hard-core slum areas are understated and those of suburban communities are very much overstated; and second, that viable neighborhoods and communities are precious, often fragile, and great care must be taken not to jeopardize their stability.

Impact of Prolonged Housing Recession: A New Era? Estimates of demand and projections of economic activity tend to be based on experience of the recent past. In the case of housing and employment volume the temptation is to reach back to the 1950s and 1960s (particularly the 1960s) and to downgrade the significance of post-1973 changes. This tendency to believe that the economic problems which unfolded with such startling impact in late 1973 are a passing phenomenon is extremely widespread. It is by no means confined to those who assert that housing allocations can be realistically predicated on a resurging and buoyant economy because all business recessions pass.

Some analyses of regional housing needs, particularly that aspect which focuses on possible population outmigration from core areas to suburban job opportunities, tend to be based on trends between 1950 and 1970 and to discount the possibility that 1973 may represent the beginning of a new era rather than a pause in a secular (long-term) trend. In practical terms, the proponents of opening up the suburbs tend to be optimists who want to ensure that the poor get in on the ground floor of the next suburban housing boom. Pessimists do not think there will be another big surge of suburban growth and, further, if there is a boomlet, they believe housing is likely to be too expensive for the poor and most moderate-income people, partly because they do not anticipate massive government subsidy programs to bridge the gap between family resources and rising housing costs.

Changing Demographics: Housing Concentration and Economic Dispersal. Some of the proponents of suburban dispersion of low- and moderate-income families find a good deal of hope in recent demographic trends and the reflection of these trends in the housing market. Specifically, the tendency toward no marriages, later marriages, childless marriages, and one- or two-child marriages has combined with rising housing costs and an increase in the proportion of women in the labor force to expand the market for apartments and townhouses at the expense of the traditional suburban free-standing dwelling. These demographic trends, particularly when added to inflationary pressures, have resulted in a major shift in the shelter industry in favor of smaller lots, less interior square footage, and a considerable urban coagulation in the suburbs in the form of garden apartments, townhouses, cluster zoning, and even high-rise apartments. This can result in reduced infrastructure costs and lower sales prices and rental levels.

Other demographic trends point to far less overall demand for low- and moderate-income housing than some proponents had earlier estimated. Lower birth rates, diminished state population growth, changing housing preferences, and the higher costs of suburban housing have altered regional population projections downward. In New Jersey, for example, Mercer County deflated the 1972 estimate of housing need for low- and moderate-income families prepared by the Delaware Valley Regional Planning Commission (DVRP). DVRP's upper-range estimate in 1972 was 80,000 new units needed between 1970 and the year 2000. Based in part on a sharp decline in building permits and subdivision activity between 1972 and 1976, the county planning board reduced the "need" total to less than 20,000 units.[13]

In combination, these diverse demographic trends and the higher-density suburban construction created to serve these new markets has led to the hope that public transportation could eliminate or at least diminish the long-term suburban dependence on automobile transportation. If this were indeed the case it might then be realistically feasible to conceive of a new suburban pattern, reducing the high costs of sprawl[14] and rendering feasible a substantial dispersion to the suburbs of the core-city poor and handicapped who do not have access to cars.

This assumption may be rendered inoperative by another fact: demographics and market factors leading to centripetal patterns of suburban residential construction have not been accompanied by a parallel move toward suburban concentration of industry, offices, services, shopping malls, and other nonresidential uses. One minor modification in the pattern—smaller, weaker shopping malls being squeezed out in favor of very large shopping aggregations —does not change the fact that the suburbs are likely to remain an aggregation of low- to moderate-density communities whence population scatters to dispersed destinations. Without access to an automobile it is extremely difficult to function, and 20 to 30 percent of New Jersey's population, mostly the poor, but also aged and handicapped persons, do not own or have use of an automobile.

Reversing the trend laid down in a generation of low-density suburbanization does not appear to be realistic. Certainly the numerous attempts to develop a new, workable system of public transportation in dispersed suburbs have proved unsuccessful. Short of a powerful system of direct controls over land use and the economy, which would heavily subsidize large-scale housing for the poor and, in effect, force suburbanization into a mold approaching that of the old central cities which combined home, workplace, shopping, and services within walking distance or at most within easy access by public transportation, the suburbs are likely to remain a zone for the upper class, the middle class, and the working class, not for the very poor. Indeed, one of the goals for the next quarter of a century might be to recapture for the blue-collar worker the possibilities for suburban residence which were available in the 1950s, the era of the Levittowns and the less heralded working-class subdivisions which developed in many suburban communities.

GUIDELINES FOR REGIONAL HOUSING ALLOCATION

It seems clear that 1970 data on suburban housing deterioration and suburban needs generally are too outdated and inaccurate to use as a basis for estimation. As noted elsewhere in this work, projection of future suburban population and employment gains (and losses) are extremely hazardous, subject to unpredictable cross-currents. Largely because of the growing gap between blue-collar earnings and housing costs, in the past decade a decreasing proportion of working-class families has been able to purchase suburban housing.

In the face of such uncertainties, an acceptable working model must be based on a reasonable estimate of present needs rather than conjectural future events. Moreover, a fair-share model should require every community in a region to provide a range of housing choices appropriate to its own and its region's population. There are three internal target groups in need of such housing in every community:

1. elderly and middle-aged "empty-nesters"
2. younger persons, married or single, who do not want, do not need, or cannot afford to purchase traditional, large-lot suburban dwellings
3. town employees who deserve the opportunity to live in the town which employs them

A "take care of one's own" approach falls short in failing to make adequate provision for housing for blue-collar workers employed in the community who form an indispensable component of its economic base. For this reason every regional community which benefits directly from tax ratables from local industries should be required to provide housing for workers employed in local firms.

However, even if a community does not have such industry it benefits indirectly from the production and labor of regional firms outside its boundaries. It should therefore be required to be responsive (that is, 5 percent of the housing stock) to the housing needs of those employees. Whatever model and allocations are agreed upon as viable, two points should be stressed: First, past history indicates that political and economic conditions change rapidly. For this reason any allocation must be subject to periodic review. Second, whatever model is adopted should be both simple and, if possible, acceptable to the target municipalities. As one authoritative study suggests:

> There is no way of demonstrating that the more complicated or more sophisticated the formula the more equitable or accurate the distribution. If the data upon which each formula is dependent were more precise, the preoccupation with sophisticated formulas might be justified. To date, however, almost without exception, the various housing allocation plans have had to undergo considerable amending to obtain appropriate data and criteria. Most plans are heavily dependent on U.S. Census data, with all its limitations. . . . The professional acceptability of such plans is not unimportant. Nonetheless, the public acceptance and understanding of plans is also critical.[15]

Whatever the fair-share plan, it should be understood that the objective is housing construction, not endless litigation. This is a primary reason for emphasizing the need for acceptability. Thus, one indispensable component of a housing allocation is the concept of balance. This implies that blue-collar communities which have already provided a major proportion of fair-share housing for low- and moderate-income families should not be penalized. It also implies that the allocations for exclusionary communities be limited in scope to provide a share rather than a preponderance of housing for low- and moderate-income families.

REGIONAL HOUSING ALLOCATION TARGETS

Assuming each community should be required to shoulder a fair share of housing for low- and moderate-income families, the next step is to establish a working model. In this respect a modified principle has been suggested: take care of one's own, plus persons employed in the community, plus some reasonable proportion of total regional need. The tentatively suggested percentages are as follows:

15 percent of total housing units to take care of internal needs: the aged and the empty-nesters, town employees, and young singles and couples
5 to 10 percent of total housing stock to house persons employed in the community: the amount depending on the amount of industrial-commercial tax base located in the community
5 percent of the total housing stock as the community's contribution to state fair-share needs

In summary, this means that each community would be required to have a minimum of 20 percent and a maximum of 30 percent of its housing stock in units geared to low- and moderate-income families. This maximum percentage is equal to the 1969 New Jersey proportion of low- and moderate-income families. New Jersey was selected as a model because, unlike suburban counties or regions, it is an inclusionary geographic unit containing a broad spectrum of income groups and housing types. Setting the upper limit at the state proportion implies that no community would be forced to carry more than a proportionate, fair share of the burden—housing for its own older people, its young people, its town employees, and a reasonable share of the needs of the state's low- and moderate-income population.

ALLOCATION RATIONALE

It may be noted that the allocation of the components of the 20 to 30 percent fair share is not arbitrary. Assuming that the state maximum proportion—30 percent—is accepted as a target for communities with very substantial amounts of industry, the next question is how best to divide the sum into proper elements. Clearly there should be some recognition of the net gains or lack of benefits from possessing or not possessing given amounts of tax base, particularly if such industry is staffed by sizable numbers of blue-collar workers. For this reason a sliding scale—20 to 30 percent—was recommended which can be calibrated, within this ten-point range, on the basis of the extent of the employment and tax base. In this connection, it may be noted that Woodbridge, a moderate-income, inclusionary, blue-collar community in Middlesex County, provided housing for 10,000 of the 37,000 persons employed in the township in 1975.[16] Assuming that the 1969 median wage of employed Woodbridge males reflects the wage levels of local industries, 40 percent of the 10,000 are in the low- to moderate-income bracket. It therefore seems probable that 3,500 to 4,000 housing units—40 percent of the 10,000 employees—are provided in that township for employees of local industries at low to moderate income levels.

Over and above local needs, some proportion—5 percent is suggested—must be set aside as part of a community's fair-share responsibility.

The remainder, 15 percent, can reasonably be allocated to the community's own needs for middle-aged and older persons, municipal employees, and young people. As a technique, the process of assembling 1970 census data on deficient housing in a given community and using this figure as a basis for estimating local need is totally unsatisfactory. In part this is because, as noted, 1970 census data are outdated and inaccurate. More important, setting local goals on the basis of defective local housing conditions condemns a poor community to a continued role as a center for low- and moderate-income housing and absolves the wealthy suburban community from doing much in the way of constructing new housing of this type. Part of the answer is fair-share allocation through a combination of a fixed quota and a sliding scale as suggested above, to ensure that no community can get away with not providing for its potential need by sloughing the burden off on other communities.

It is unfortunate that there is little guidance in planning studies to indicate how much demand or need there is in various types of communities for low- and moderate-income housing options. Fifteen percent is suggested as a working model or, more accurately, a hypothesis, on the assumption that (1) one-third of the persons over 55 in suburban communities—roughly 4 to 5 percent of the population—might be interested in this type of housing; and (2) two-thirds of a community's town employees (roughly 67 percent of the population), who with their families compose about 10 percent of a typical suburban community, might be interested in living within the community if given the opportunity;[17] and (3) a small number of youngsters might also be interested in remaining in their hometowns on a temporary or permanent basis. Obviously the proportions are as inexact as much else in the area of fair-share allocation, but this model seems to make more sense than most.

Some indication of the potential need for housing town employees can be ascertained by an examination of the relevant data for Woodbridge. In this blue-collar New Jersey community, 90 percent of the 1,700 low-paid (average 1975 salary $6,400) township employees live in the community. In contrast, only about half of the 1,400 higher-paid Board of Education employees (1975 salary range $9,000 to $19,000) lived in the community: the Center for Urban Policy Research found that in affluent Princeton most schoolteachers and other town employees preferred (or more accurately would have preferred) to live in the community. The exception was the police, who feared encroachment on their privacy and free time if they lived in town.[18] Thus, in Woodbridge —probably an extreme case in this respect—about 6 percent of the housing stock is occupied by low-to-moderate-income township employees and their families. This percentage reflects the fact that over two-thirds of these employees earn less than a moderate 1975 income level. One reason for terming Woodbridge an extreme case is that unlike many suburbs, Woodbridge provides a full range of municipal services, including a fire department and trash removal.

Obviously the precise mix and the size of the need or market depend on a number of variables, including the attractiveness of housing alternatives in other communities, whether or not there is a sizable institution of higher education in or near the community to serve as a magnet for young people, the availability of low-cost housing options (as, for example, low-rent single- or two-family housing), and ethnic and social factors.

ESTIMATING HOUSING NEEDS FOR THE AGED

An examination of housing demand patterns in West Orange, a moderate-income New Jersey suburban community, revealed that of the total of 6,000 persons over age 62, 500 had applied for subsidized housing units. In addition to such applicants, in most suburbs elderly persons prefer (and/or are able) to live in garden apartments, single- or two-family units. It may be noted in this connection that the minimum age for housing applicants in retirement communities like New Jersey's Rossmoor is 48. Given a reasonable range of low-cost housing options within their own community, a total proportion of 4 to 5 percent, including empty-nesters as well as the elderly, seems reasonable.

ESTIMATING HOUSING NEEDS FOR YOUNG PEOPLE

One of the most mobile population components of a community is its young adults, persons aged 18 to 34, single or married with up to two young children. If housing options are available, there seems to be a growing tendency for such persons to settle, probably on a temporary basis, in or near their home communities. This is particularly the case if garden apartments are available. Garden apartments have also been attracting an increasing share of the local elderly population.[19] As compared to residents in other types of housing, garden apartment residents are likely to be younger, of lower income, and of relatively lower educational attainments. There is a trend toward increases in the proportion of blue-collar workers and toward an expansion in the numbers of students and retired persons. Moreover, the percentage of residents moving into the apartment units from elsewhere in the same town doubled between 1963 and 1972–73.[20] Overall, garden apartments contain higher percentages of residents drawn from the locality than do other housing options. It seems probable that up to half such apartments might be occupied by young persons primarily drawn from the community.

MODERATE INCOME, NOT LOW INCOME

In most suburbs, it can be assumed that housing in the low-to-moderate income category will be heavily weighted toward upper-moderate income levels. A combination of inflationary land and construction costs and minimal federal or state assistance has virtually priced out of the suburbs families with annual incomes of less than $12,000 (apartments) and $15,000 to $20,000 (single-family housing). Average sales prices for single-family homes in New Jersey in the mid-1970s were in the $40,000 to $50,000 range. At best, within the foreseeable future it may be possible through density bonuses or other means available to communities to reduce the existing "entrance fee" for suburban apartments to annual incomes of perhaps $10,000 and for single-family housing to perhaps $12,000 to $15,000. In the event that substantial subsidy programs become available in the last few years of the 1970–80 decade it may become feasible to attempt to reach deeper into the blue-collar income levels.

It is unlikely that any significant in-migration to the suburbs of very low-income people is in the cards. Moreover, in view of the necessity of having access to automobiles and uncertainties concerning the availability of low-skill jobs and of services required by the very poor, it does not seem appropriate or realistic to attempt to generate major transfers of poor people from central cities or densely settled inner suburbs to low-density suburbs. As noted earlier, this cannot be effectively accomplished without an accompanying system of land use controls to reshape existing patterns of regional development into high-density urban nodes which offer easy access between residences, jobs, and services. In practice, the fact that there is likely to be a kind of income-screening process to include the regularly employed and exclude the very low-income groups with higher indices of social problems points the way to reducing community resistance to inclusionary land use and housing policies —once this fact is fully comprehended. Otherwise there is a very real risk that the primary result of all the legal huffing and puffing will be to generate inclusionary rhetoric without altering the realities of exclusionary zoning.

Finally, there is an additional consideration for blue-collar communities which are presently heavily weighted toward the lower end of the income spectrum. A "fair-share" housing strategy in such communities should logically point to an increase in the proportion of upper-income families in tandem with action which may be indicated to meet housing needs for low- and moderate-income families. Surely the concept of a balanced community might well embrace upper- as well as low-income strata in predominantly moderate- and low-income communities.

TRANSPORTATION AND HUMAN RESOURCE REGIONS

A period of roughly five years, beginning in the late 1950s and ending in the early 1960s, marked the start and finish of the great urban transportation crisis in the United States. In previous decades, attention in the cities had been focused on such topics as absorbing foreign immigration, municipal corruption, and substandard housing. Then came transportation. Before poverty, crime, and race problems moved up to center stage in the mid-1960s, highways and mass transit occupied what in retrospect appears to be an inordinate share of planning efforts and funds. Like all urban "crises," it grew out of publicity. In each so-called crisis, a spotlight is focused on what is alleged to be an urgent, unpostponable problem, the solution of which is a necessary prerequisite to the revival of our urban regions, if not to national survival. In point of fact, the entire transportation affair seems to have been related to the fact that in the late 1950s, a batch of commuter railroads decided that it was time to quit hauling local passengers. There was also a great deal of hullabaloo concerning the impact of interstate highways through densely settled urban neighborhoods. Equally important, for a few years, highway men and planners had reached a transient consensus on the notion that urban transportation systems planned in conjunction with land use development could be the key to a significant improvement in urban regions and that the time was ripe for large-scale, intergovernmental projects.

Now that other problems have moved into the spotlight, it would be tempting to say that it was all a mistake. Possibly, coexistence, or at best an uneasy détente, is the best we can hope for between such antipathetic interests as North and South, East and West, Turk and Greek, highway man and planner.

Looking back, it now seems that once a reasonably dependable system is in being, transportation is chiefly important in increasing the range of regional development alternatives. The thesis of this section is that transportation is not necessarily a determining factor in all aspects of regional development. Rather, a reasonably operable urban transportation system provides a broad framework within which a wide range of choices can be made, although, in highly specialized cases, transportation does represent a major determining element. In many programs, including the case studies in social planning examined here, the primary role of transportation as a major determinant disappears once the system is operating satisfactorily.

This leads to a corollary hypothesis: The tendency to inject impressive transportation data and graphics into decision-making processes in which transportation is not particularly significant serves either as a smokescreen concealing other basic factors or as a bit of marginalia, not much more important in many types of social planning than water or sewerage systems.

The areas in which transportation is a vital component are well known. New highways obviously have a major impact on structures and neighborhoods directly in their path and on adjacent areas. Transportation systems also have intrinsic values and development possibilities. At times, transportation projects can be deliberately designed to attack a social problem. For example, highways may be located to remove slum housing. Highway construction is relatively expensive and, until recently, resistance to the routes laid down by highway engineers was minimal. Situations like that portrayed in a science fiction novel in which a traffic engineer is employed by a hypothetical Latin American nation to prepare a highway plan that would blot out some of the urban-squatter hovels defacing the capital are not unknown in the United States.[21] The city of Fall River, Massachusetts, not only made use of an interstate expressway to cut a swath through some of its slums but also managed to eliminate its obsolescent city hall in the process. (There was a prior agreement to build a modern city hall on air rights over Route I-195 with the use of federal funds.)

There are other circumstances in which the crucial role of highways and public transportation systems is readily identifiable. Sometimes the impact occurs in cycles. The case of elevated transit lines in New York, Chicago, and Boston is a good example. Soon after they were constructed, property values along the elevated lines rose, only to fall as time, grime, and gloom took their toll. Subsequently, many of the old "Els" were removed and the values of contiguous property rose once again. As a rule, subway extensions in residential areas usually have been associated with the construction of high-density housing along the lines, with clusters of commercial development at the stations. In earlier decades, suburban commuter railroads were frequently associated with pockets of residential and business development surrounding the stations. In contrast, suburban highways were associated with low-density residential development, along with a new type of manufacturing center, the low-density suburban industrial park.

In each of these instances, there was clearly a close linkage between some type of change in land use and/or in property values associated with the construction or elimination of a key transportation component. However, the linkage between transportation and other aspects of the urban area and the region may be less significant, as indicated by the following two case histories. Both concern social planning conducted by Massachusetts state agencies. The first is drawn from a study prepared for the Massachusetts Board of Regional Community Colleges,[22] and the second, involving nursing homes, was prepared for a division of the State Department of Public Health.[23] Judging from these two examples, transportation is an important "given" rather than a determinant in the planning process.

PLANNING FOR COMMUNITY COLLEGES

The publicly controlled community college, a modern, broader version of the junior college, is one of the nation's fastest growing types of educational institution. In the period 1955–68, first-time student enrollment at the nation's two-year institutions nearly doubled, while the increase of first-year students at the four-year institutions doubled.[24]

The percentage increase in students enrolled at community colleges in Massachusetts has been far more rapid, partly because the program is relatively new. In 1958, the system was still in the discussion stage. Seven years later, nearly 6,000 students were enrolled in 9 colleges; by the fall of 1967, total enrollment (on a full-time equivalent basis) had increased to almost 14,000 at 13 community colleges.

The reasons for extraordinary growth are not hard to find. Regional community colleges offer two years of low-cost higher education within commuting distance, and tuition charges at many of the private institutions in Massachusetts are in the $3,000-$4,000 per year range. Moreover, many of the most respected colleges and universities have made the decision not to expand at the undergraduate level, or, in other cases, have decided to place an increasing emphasis on attracting out-of-state students. In consequence, public institutions of higher education have assumed a larger role in providing college training for Massachusetts youngsters, particularly since, in Massachusetts, as in other states, political leaders have apparently placed education at the top of the state's list of priorities.

A major function for community colleges will probably continue to be the education of transfer students. Freshmen and sophomores can complete their first two years of college at a fraction of the cost of attending a residential institution. However, the community colleges' currently rather small, adult, evening training program is likely to expand substantially as the demand for employee skills training grows and upgrading and periodic retraining of adult workers becomes virtually mandatory in many fast-changing parts of the economy. The one- or two-year, daytime, terminal training role forecast for community colleges, however, may not grow as rapidly as some had hoped. There are several reasons for this limited expansion. There is apparently less need for new technicians than was originally believed; a very large proportion of technicians are high-school graduates trained on the job or are four-year-college graduates; and finally, there are alternative methods of securing technician training, ranging from vocational high schools to public and private technical institutes and programs.

The primary objective of the *Planning Component Study* was to examine potential service areas for a partially developed community college system, particularly in the densely settled Boston area, where several colleges were planned. In theory, time-distance highway travel from existing and proposed community colleges was to be a major criterion. Final recommendations emanating from the master plan study, however, were based on more relevant issues. In a relatively small state, where travel demand is well served by highways, the time-distance factor is not a major determinant of institutional location.

Massachusetts is a state of less than 8,000 square miles, and its compactness is considerably enhanced by a good road network. Highway travel from downtown Boston to the ends of Massachusetts—Williamstown to the west and Provincetown on the tip of Cape Cod—is under three hours. Within metropolitan Boston, half an hour's driving distance will embrace a population of almost 2 million from the central city to circumferential Route 128. The time-distance relationship with respect to public transportation is far less satisfactory, but this is probably not a matter of critical importance. Even at colleges served by public transportation, most students arrive and depart by automobile. Whether Boston's public transit authority, the MBTA, can succeed in its objective of altering area transportation habits, particularly in severing the intimate relationship between the automobile and the adolescent male, is problematic.

The report that stimulated establishment of the Massachusetts regional community college system suggested the selection of locations within "20 miles or less commuting distance of the potential student body."[25] The subsequent master-plan study revised this to 30 miles, with a maximum driving time of 45 minutes from home to school.[26] However, most students will be in the 20- to 30-minute category. Any reasonable upper time limit in commuting is more likely a matter of local tradition; many residents of major metropolitan areas regularly commute for an hour to an hour and a half to work or school under conditions that would appall most of the nation. It was assumed, however, that one of the principal attractions of metropolitan Boston was the relative ease in moving from place to place. The highway system makes it feasible to serve the state effectively on the basis of substantial regions rather than a large number of small service areas.

As a general practice, the methodology used for estimating future enrollment in community colleges is based on a given population ratio. The community college is designed to provide adult education and adult vocational training, as well as freshman and sophomore college courses. Thus, use of the general population figure seems reasonable.

The rule-of-thumb ratio, which has proved accurate as a method of forecasting demand, is 75 to 100 full-time, day, community college students per 10,000 population.[27] Thus, in states where public higher education is dominant, community colleges are constructed in the expectation that enrollment will constitute about 1 percent of the total population. For a number of reasons, including the presence of fast-growing alternative public and private institutions, it would appear prudent to use the lower ratio in Massachusetts: 75:10,000, or .0075 percent of the population. A ratio of 75 community college students per 10,000 population would result in an enormous increase in student population, as noted above. One percent of the population yields an enrollment of almost 60,000.

Three statistical guidelines were developed by the Massachusetts Board of Regional Community Colleges to govern size and location decisions: (1) The acceptable optimum size for new colleges after ten years of operation was to be 2,000 students. On the basis of the 75:10,000 ratio, this suggests that a service area should have a population on the order of 250,000 persons. Most of the existing and proposed community college service areas are in the 200,000-500,000 range. (2) The maximum size for a community college outside the densely settled Boston core area, but within Route 128, was to be 5,000 students, a figure that suggests a maximum service area population of perhaps 700,000. This standard presents no special problem; aside from Massachusetts Bay Community College, none of the existing or proposed regional areas exceeds 550,000 in 1965 population. (3) The maximum size for a community college within the core area was not to exceed 7,500.

The board's decision to create a large number of community college districts in the state precludes the necessity for long-distance commuting except in rare instances. The 1963 Census of Transportation showed nationally that over 75 percent of the nation's total employees required less than 36 minutes to commute.[28] In the professional and managerial class, this figure rose to over 80 percent. Portal-to-portal commuting times to downtown Boston frequently approach and exceed an hour, because of long walking distances between downtown parking spaces and offices and also between rapid transit stations and offices. In the larger office buildings, time spent in walking through the buildings, waiting for elevators, and travel in elevators must also be considered as part of the total commuting time. Thus, a longer commutation to downtown destinations is to be expected.

Except for travel to the Boston Central Business District, however, a full hour commutation period is considered excessive in Massachusetts. A recent study made in a major manufacturing and research complex in a northwest suburban location shows average employee commuting time between 25 and 30 minutes, with few trips below the 15-minute mark, and few requiring more than 45 minutes. The portal-to-portal increment in these cases is small. Thus, for most community college regions, a 30-minute service area seems a reasonable standard.

In addition to pure travel considerations, other factors relating to community college planning were found to be of vital importance, including size, class, and race. The board's decision to place relatively low enrollment ceilings on the colleges had a number of extremely significant ramifications. The creation of one or more very large campuses in the central portion of Boston would have been entirely feasible from a commutation standpoint; perhaps two-thirds of the metropolitan area population can reach the downtown area in less than a half-hour. Moreover, all of the low-income areas in Boston, Cambridge, and other core communities are accessible via existing public transportation lines. Further, a decision to concentrate on one or two large campuses would have resulted in economies of scale, including the prospect of providing a greater variety of courses at less cost and closer physical proximity to the area's primary cultural and employment resources. It would also dictate a heightened degree of intermingling of classes and races which a system of suburban colleges would be likely to discourage.

There was one exception to the rule: Access to public transportation was considered important to Boston's low-income black population. The board selected a college site outside the central business district on the borderline between Boston's black district and the adjoining high-income town of Brookline. Because Brookline has a good school system, it is likely that most students from this community will enroll elsewhere, rather than attend a racially mixed college with much of the enrollment drawn from the Boston schools.

Several reasons were advanced for the decision to construct many smaller colleges rather than one or two major institutions. The first was an attachment to smallness. Amherst, Williams, Smith, and similar high-prestige colleges apparently provided the model that governed suburban enrollment ceilings. A student body of roughly 2,000 was believed to be the optimum number that would permit close ties among faculty, administration, and students. The enormous California-style community colleges of 10,000 to 15,000 students were believed to entail an unacceptable risk of alienation by all participants.

A second element in the size decision involved the goal accepted by many community college planners of a close identification between area and college. One tendency toward educational localism is based on the safety-in-the-streets and psychological arguments that are advanced in favor of the retention of neighborhood elementary schools. Community college orientation stresses the area service mission of an institution, designed to assist local industries as well as residents, adults as well as teen-agers.

One or two large Boston institutions serving 1 or 2 million people would obviously violate two canons of the community college creed. The institutions would be larger than thought desirable, and they would remove the possibility of creating area institutions to serve special local needs throughout the metropolitan area. There was also a vision in the minds of many community college administrators and board members of a quiet, tree-shaded, suburban campus rather than an urban skyscraper surrounded by concrete, traffic, and jarring neighbors. The decision to build on urban sites indicates that the board was not wholly bound by this image. The board took its responsibility for creating area service institutions quite seriously. Nevertheless, there seemed to be an obvious reluctance to place all of the college eggs in one or two large urban baskets, regardless of time-distance ratios and alleged social benefits. The area service function, as well as the possibility of a full outdoor athletic program, was advanced to justify the suburban schools, but undoubtedly a clear and strong mental picture of a grassy campus had some influence on the final decision. The obvious consequence of this decision was the creation of homogeneous suburban institutions mirroring the income and class characteristics of surrounding towns. Over time, it is likely that a hierarchy of colleges will emerge, each reflecting the special qualities of the area population. To a considerable extent, one or two larger colleges in Boston may serve as cross-cultural melting pots, but as suburban schools open, the overall income level from which the central-city community college population is drawn may decline. Moreover, given the central city location of most of the Boston area's black population, it is likely that the proposed community college system of small regions will reinforce racial and social segregation patterns. In fact, it does not seem that the racial segregation issue received much attention. It was apparently assumed that under an enrollment system with at least two community colleges located within easy access to both white and black neighborhoods, the chosen pattern of smaller area colleges would combine the advantages of modest scale and close relations with residents of the surrounding community.

Two other arguments were apparently involved in the little regions decisions. The first is the local economic advantage to be derived from a new college. Cities like Boston and Cambridge complain of land takings by institutions that create traffic problems and yield little in the way of taxes, but there can be little doubt that a substantial educational institution of higher learning offers significant benefits for the area economy. Older industrial communities in greater Boston are well aware of this fact, although precise measurement of this influence is difficult because of the nature of the components and variables involved, not all of which are quantifiable in any meaningful sense.

In one respect, the community college represents a vehicle for preventing economic losses rather than a new input to the area economy. Were it not for the community college, some hundreds of local residents would spend their freshman and sophomore years elsewhere. Others would either receive no educational or vocational training or would use alternative institutions. Neither of these possibilities creates the type of economic gain represented by institutions that attract substantial numbers of out-of-area students.

Based on a study of the economic impact of higher education, it is possible to develop a tentative estimate of this component of community colleges. Given an enrollment of 2,000 students and assuming that half, or 1,000, would otherwise have left the area for their schooling, the community college results in a retention of about $800 per capita or a total of $800,000 per year in student expenditures.[29] Much of these expenditures are apparent in retail stores, such as restaurants, drugstores, book and record stores, and gas stations. As compared to retail expenditures generated by manufacturing payrolls, the 1,000 "retained" students are the equivalent of perhaps 200 factory workers employed at an annual wage of $5,000 to $6,000.

Aside from these "retained" benefits, the community college is the source of two types of economic inputs identifiable as additional gains. First, at an average of $4,000 per student[30] in land, equipment, and building construction costs, there is the $8 million expended for construction of a 2,000-place college and the additional monies required for upkeep and maintenance. The employment stimulus of construction contracts is estimated at 223 man-hours per $1,000 of contract cost. An $8 million building is therefore estimated as the equivalent of a year's work for almost 1,000 persons. Approximately one-third of the total is on-site man-hours, with the remainder in various stages of manufacturing, mining, trade, and transportation.[31]

A second type of benefit is derived from the employment of faculty or administrative staff attracted from out of the area. One such person is employed for every 18 students, resulting in a payroll of about 100 for a 2,000-student college.

At an average salary of $10,000 per year, these 100 staff people represent the equivalent in payrolls generated of 150 factory workers paid $6,000 a year; an annual payroll on the order of almost $1 million can be anticipated. An additional 60 nonprofessional persons may be employed as clerical and maintenance workers. Based on 1969–70 data for the Massachusetts regional community college system (an average salary of $6,000 per year for clerical and custodial staff), the total payroll for this category is likely to be about $360,000 annually.

To summarize, the immediate cash benefits of a 2,000-student community college include: (1) $8 million in construction expenditures plus continued operating, maintenance, and renovation expenditures; (2) $800,000 a year in "retained" student expenditures; (3) an annual professional payroll estimated at $1 million; and (4) an annual nonprofessional payroll estimated at $360,000. Finally, over and above these ideological, educational, and economic considerations, apparently certain pragmatic advantages accrue from the creation of many smaller colleges; more colleges mean more college presidencies. There were some observers who argued that the decision to keep enrollment ceilings relatively low reflected a desire to maximize the number of presidential openings.

Finally, it is clear that a good highway system permitted a wide latitude for decisions governing the size and location of Massachusetts' burgeoning community colleges. Within the broad limits of half-an-hour's commuting time, the board established a pattern of class and race segregation or integration, depending on the set of values that it preferred. For the most part, location decisions were based on other than transportation considerations, despite the rather restrictive travel time standards adopted as a general guide.

NURSING HOMES AND AREA PLANNING

The typical nursing home resident in Massachusetts is an elderly woman on welfare whose stay lasts about two years, until her death.[32] Most of the nursing homes are small—under 50 beds—and are located in older, converted buildings. Almost one-third of the state's 730 nursing homes are over 50 years old, and only 1 in 7 was constructed within the last 20 years. For reasons that are largely obscure, a substantially higher proportion of Massachusetts' aged population is in nursing homes than in neighboring New York and Connecticut. In spite of the relative liberality of public welfare standards in these states compared to Massachusetts, families are apparently more reluctant to place their parents in nursing homes primarily catering to patients on public assistance.

Nursing home payments under public welfare in Massachusetts are generally considered inadequate: the $55 per week available for such patients in the mid-1960s was over one-third lower than the weekly payment in Connecticut. Thus, the fact that nursing homes are a highly profitable investment raised serious suspicions in many quarters regarding the treatment, feeding, and facilities accorded to residents. In Massachusetts, as elsewhere, nursing home operations have occasionally erupted into scandals ranging from nasty fires in converted wooden tinderboxes to outright neglect of patients and charges that underworld money was being attracted to this lucrative business.

Some improvements are clearly in evidence. Nursing homes built in the period 1955–65 average over 60 beds as compared to only about 30 beds in older homes. Facilities are newer, buildings are fire resistant, and staffing is not as minimal.

About 60 percent of the nursing homes in Massachusetts are privately operated for profit; only 1 bed in 10 is located in a nursing home run by nonprofit organizations. The dominant form of operation is the proprietary corporation, a pattern that prevails in the nation as a whole. In the past few years, hospitals have indicated increasing interest in sponsoring affiliated or directly operated nursing homes, partly as an adjunct to teaching and research functions.

For purposes of state hospital administration and planning, Massachusetts has been divided into 68 hospital service areas by the state Department of Health. Each of these service areas is centered around one or more general hospitals. In some instances, the hospital service areas are virtually identical with the Standard Metropolitan Statistical Areas (SMSAs) established by the U.S. Bureau of the Census. For the most part, however, there is a stronger degree of localization centering around communities too small (under 50,000) to qualify as central cities by census criteria. Until such time as a comprehensive medical services plan could be completed for the state, the study prepared for the Division of Adult Health recommended that existing hospital service areas be utilized as the basic unit in nursing home planning, rather than attempting to establish special nursing home service areas.

In 1965, the Division of Adult Health was confronted with a critical, pressing problem: the approval or disapproval of applications for the construction of new nursing homes containing approximately 6,000 nursing home beds. The U.S. Department of Health, Education, and Welfare has established a ratio of 3 beds per 1,000 population as a reasonable standard. This appears to be on the low side for Massachusetts, where the proportion of aged population is substantially higher than the national average (11.1 percent of the population versus 9.3 percent for the nation in 1960). The study prepared for the Division of Adult Health suggested that a more reasonable state ratio might be between 4 and 5 per 1,000, the proportion being somewhat lower in the Boston suburbs, where there are smaller proportions of older people, and with higher proportions in Cape Cod and other areas where the proportion of aged persons exceeds 12 percent of the total population. Furthermore, if the Medicare and Medicaid programs result in a permanent, substantial increase in the demand for nursing home beds, the ratio might well be increased to the 6 per 1,000 level.

Although the location of nursing home beds tends to correlate positively with population distribution, there are very substantial differences among various hospital service areas. Many of the state's hospital service areas were well above the federal 3 per 1,000 standard in 1965, but significant deficiencies appear to exist in a number of service areas, some of them located within the Boston SMSA.

If all the applications on file in 1965 were approved and the proposed nursing homes were placed into immediate operation, most of the state would be well above minimum federal levels; but in some areas, most of them in southeastern Massachusetts, the bed-to-population ratio would still be below the federal standard.

It should be borne in mind, in evaluating existing and future deficiencies, that these ratios were based on continued operation of all existing nursing home beds. In mid-1965, the Division of Adult Health recognized that approximately 50 small nursing homes housing 1,000 patients would not be able to meet proposed new standards being considered by the division. It appeared likely that an additional but undetermined number of beds would be ruled substandard on the basis of stricter federal minimum criteria developing out of the 1965 Social Security amendments. For example, it was estimated by state and federal officials that more than 75 percent of existing nursing home beds would not meet federal Medicare requirements, although it is probable that a substantial number could be successfully upgraded by expanding and improving medical and related services. Any significant reduction in the number of approved beds would create a need for construction of replacements. However, the possibility of releasing beds by restorative treatment of patients,[33] returning them to families or rest homes, or making other arrangements for their departure from nursing homes would substantially reduce the number of beds required by nursing home patients. However, the patient profile described above limits these possibilities.

In addition to population growth trends, program revaluation, and changes that will affect future bed requirements, other trends may exert an appreciable influence on future needs for nursing home beds. There is, for example, a reported tendency to transfer elderly, long-term patients from mental hospitals to nursing homes after age has made younger, unruly patients more docile. Depending on trends in psychiatric care and public policy, the mental hospitals can become a significant source of additional demand for nursing home beds. On the other hand, there are several factors that may depress future demand. These include increasing affluence, particularly higher pensions and improved medical insurance (which, among other results, will permit more elderly Massachusetts residents to migrate), and medical research and programs that will reduce the incidence of sickness among the elderly and hence decrease the need for costly care facilities. For example, incentive payments for families, relatives, or other persons may be effective, in conjunction with outpatient care, in reducing the number of older patients in nursing homes.

How Many Beds Needed?

At present, there are a number of imponderables whose future impact on nursing home needs cannot be accurately foretold. It is assumed that some factors tending to increase or decrease the need for nursing home beds will counterbalance each other and that further study will undoubtedly make it possible to estimate the effect of such factors with greater precision. It is clear, however, that a substantial increase in approved, high-quality nursing home beds is needed. Unless presently unforeseen factors intervene, by 1975 the state will require over 30,000 beds in nursing homes that offer a high quality of nursing care. The number depends on the impact of Medicare and Medicaid, realignments in patient care between nursing and rest homes, and the number of beds ruled substandard in terms of comprehensive nursing care criteria. For the purpose of this estimate, it is assumed that nursing homes with fewer than 30 beds can be assumed to be substandard. There are about 250 nursing homes caring for 6,000 patients in this category. All but two of these homes are located in converted frame buildings. Assuming a replacement need for 6,000 beds and a minimum of 1,500 beds to satisfy population expansion and medical needs among the elderly, up to 1,800 new, standard, quality beds a year might be required through the mid-1970s.

The projections of beds needed in Massachusetts may be compared to the estimates presented in New York. In its 1963–64 plan, the New York State Department of Health indicated that 4 out of 10 of the 786 nursing homes in the state were in nonfire-resistive structures. To receive federal aid, nursing homes that are adjuncts to general hospitals are required to have at least 30 beds. Nursing homes located apart from such a hospital must have a capacity of at least 60 beds and be affiliated with a general hospital. Under existing conditions in 1965, if this 60-bed criterion were adopted in Massachusetts, it would eliminate over 80 percent of the nursing homes and about two-thirds of the nursing home beds in the state.

Aside from the minimum size standard, the physical criteria of structures adjudged fire-resistive, physically safe, and therefore suitable for long-range planning resulted in classifying 40 percent of existing beds in New York (17,550 out of 42,100) as unsuitable.[34]

Patient Distribution

An analysis of patient origin and current location by community indicates that the service areas of nursing homes are relatively small. The figures show that between 70 and 80 percent of beds within most sizable communities are occupied by residents. For example, in Boston the percentage is 81 percent, and in other Massachusetts communities the figure is roughly the same. Where there are one or two smaller nursing homes in a small suburb of a large city, the percentage is much lower, but it rises rapidly if residents originating in adjoining communities are included.

Boston, the largest city in the commonwealth, does not show any substantially different pattern of patient origin than smaller centers in the state, such as Worcester and Springfield, or smaller metropolitan centers, such as Fitchburg and Lawrence. The same pattern of patient distribution is evident, with most of the patients originating from the central city and most of the remainder from abutting towns.

The relocation pattern of residents from metropolitan centers is similar to the flow-in pattern. There are very few patients who relocate outside their own towns to a nursing home. In the case of Boston, for example, only Brookline attracts any large number of patients, and a few other nearby suburbs attract smaller numbers. Accounting for the remaining patients, however, does demonstrate a wide scattering of patients throughout the entire state. It must be assumed that this wide distribution of a minority of patients is accounted for by personal preference, family situations, and other conditions that affect the selection of a nursing home.

The conclusion that can be drawn from this analysis is that the nursing home service areas are reasonably definable. By the same token, the relatively small potential service area of most new nursing homes can also be delineated with some precision. Thus, it becomes possible to evaluate a proposed nursing home on the basis of its potential service area and its current service level. This, of course, does not apply to a nursing home that serves a special category of patient, such as a religious institution, or to nursing homes designed to care for patients with particular types of disorders.

It would appear that the choice of the proper location and size of a nursing home within a particular community should be largely determined by local factors, such as the extent of the local market, land use, zoning, and street patterns. Relationship to the statewide network of highways or transportation facilities does not appear to be a significant element.

Staffing Needs

It was estimated that in 1965, the equivalent of 4,500 full-time staff were employed by nursing homes to care for 29,000 Massachusetts nursing home patients. In the future, higher standards of care, a restructuring of nursing home functions to weed out less seriously affected, restorable patients, combined with more comprehensive care, could result in a ratio of one employee for every three patients.

A standard that involves one staff employee for every three patients would require substantial increases in all categories of nursing home employees, ranging from janitors and orderlies to therapists, recreation workers, and physicians. Moreover, aside from the need for additional staff to provide comprehensive services, the need for staff would increase as the patients grew in numbers. Another factor that must be taken into account in calculating personnel needs is attrition: staff turnover, particularly among lower-echelon employees, is extremely high. For some occupations, it is reported to exceed 10 to 20 percent annually. Also, an estimate of the need for training must consider the necessity of upgrading managerial and other key staff now engaged in the operation of nursing homes. It is generally agreed that serious deficiencies exist in this area in Massachusetts as elsewhere in the nation. However, it must be recognized that a substantial proportion, perhaps two-thirds, of nursing home employees require little formal training. Janitors and maids, orderlies, laundry and restaurant workers, and yardsmen can be trained on the job. Other employees, including clerical personnel, therapists, nurses' aides, practical and registered nurses, administrators, and other specialized subprofessional and professional personnel require varying degrees of vocational training, ranging from high-school-level courses to professional degrees. It is assumed that other professional inputs will be provided (and in fact expanded) through close association with outside physicians and hospitals.

Relationship to Land Use and Zoning

Nursing homes have not been a subject for thoughtful consideration in land use planning. This neglect has apparently been general thoughout the nation. A report prepared by the American Society of Planning Officials (ASPO) was hard put to discover a significant number of zoning bylaws or studies reflecting special consideration of nursing home locations and community impact. Moreover, aside from problems created by parking, transportation access, and similar factors have apparently caused little concern in nursing home location. Since most existing nursing homes are converted older structures, many of them former single-family dwellings, most nursing home locations reflect the availability of deteriorating Victorian mansions.

The location of newly constructed nursing homes tends to differ from the location of older, converted structures. For the most part, new nursing homes are two-story brick buildings of undistinguished appearance, located on traffic arteries zoned for multifamily or commercial use. However, a number of suburban homes are found on comparatively isolated sites in districts zoned for single-family residences. Part of the reason for the scarcity of nursing homes in newer, single-family residential areas lies in the fact that most Massachusetts zoning bylaws and ordinances permit location of nursing homes in single-family districts only with approval of the local zoning board of appeals. Here again, access to public transportation or other transportation factors appears to be unimportant in location. Site availability is the major factor.

In 1964, ASPO devoted one of its special research studies to the topic of nursing homes, canvassing and analyzing planning and zoning practices related to nursing homes in a number of communities through the nation.[35]

Parking space standards varied considerably, ranging downward to one space for every six beds up to one parking space for every two beds. This relatively high ratio of one to two is currently required in Worcester, Massachusetts, Fort Lauderdale, Florida, and Ithaca, New York. The American Nursing Home Association recommends one parking space for every four beds, the same standard suggested by the Massachusetts Department of Public Health.

Various recommendations for outdoor recreation space, walks, shrubbery, and screening walls were included in the reports and ordinances analyzed by ASPO. Aside from prescribed setback and frontage provisions, however, recommendations for screening and outdoor recreation areas tended to be general, with requirements based on such subjective terms as "adequate," "sufficient," "ample," or "necessary."

The ASPO report bears out a major conclusion reached in the course of the analysis and inspection undertaken in the planning study for the Division of Adult Health: Old or new, nursing homes appear to have a minimal impact on the areas in which they are located. Currently found in all types of neighborhoods, nursing homes appear to be among the most inconspicuous types of development, often blending almost unnoticed into their surroundings. When a considerable amount of physical isolation on a suburban site exists, a nursing home tends to be even more of an "invisible neighbor" than is the case in settled urban areas. The general mediocrity of their design seems to have an advantage of assisting them to fade almost unnoticeably into their environment.

The ASPO report indicated that requirements for nursing homes have not been carefully considered in many communities. On the whole, the general public seems to expect that nursing homes should be located in high-density, multifamily, and commercial districts, but ASPO indicates a trend toward greater diffusion of nursing homes throughout residential areas. It is not clear how this trend accords with the reported desirability of locating nursing homes "near the center of community activities," as suggested by the U.S. Public Health Service.

The principal Public Health Service publication on nursing home problems and standards concentrates on medical care and service facilities, but it does include recommendations relating to site planning and location.[36] The report refers to the need to provide adequate space for outdoor recreation and to the need for screening this space for privacy. The principal locational recommendation of the Public Health Service was that nursing homes be placed at quiet sites within a reasonable distance of public transportation, and, as indicated above, "near the center of community activities."

Building and Site Standards

The Division of Adult Health of the Massachusetts Department of Health suggests that a gross-floor area of 180 square feet be provided for each bed. For a 100-bed nursing home, this would involve a total of 18,000 square feet of building space. Up to August 1965, the ground area covered by the structure could apparently vary between 1/2 an acre and 1/7 of an acre. The removal of the two-story maximum in 1965 reduced the building requirement to as little as 5,000 square feet, a postage-stamp size that the division believed to be consonant with high-quality land prices of intown areas.

The thrust toward improving the standards of nursing home care has had a direct impact on parking space requirements for more staff. On the basis of current estimates, the total staff required to provide adequate services for a 100-bed nursing home is about 25. An increase in standards to California levels, a development that can probably be anticipated in coming years, would increase the total staff to 35. Fewer than 25 to 35 parking spaces are needed for staff purposes, however, because employees work on three shifts.

In addition to employee parking, additional parking spaces must be provided for delivery trucks and other vehicles. Currently, one parking space for every four beds is considered adequate for this purpose. This ratio would involve the allocation of only 7,500 square feet of parking space for a 100-bed nursing home, using the commonly accepted ratio of 300 square feet per automobile.

Traffic Implications

One of the questions that has seriously concerned neighborhood residents is the burden which might be placed on local streets if a major traffic generator were located in their area. In general, a 100-bed nursing home does not constitute such a traffic generator. During the peak hours of the journey to work and return (7:30-9:30 A.M. and 4:00-6:00 P.M.), total traffic to and from such a nursing home would essentially be limited to 10 to 20 employees traveling in each direction, in addition to an occasional delivery truck or service vehicle. Most visitor traffic to a nursing home occurs during the evening hours and on weekends. Lesser amounts of visitor traffic may occur in off-peak weekday morning and afternoon hours. Finally, most deliveries and service vehicles arrive during off-peak hours. In summary, it would appear that as far as traffic is concerned, a nursing home probably generates less activity in the crucial peak hours than most other types of urban development.

Transportation

With a few exceptions, the nursing homes in the commonwealth are all within half an hour's driving time to a general hospital, although peak-hour driving time in congested areas may add 10 to 20 minutes to the total. The same half-hour time-distance relationship holds true for staff and visitors to most nursing homes. There are, however, a number of residents living in nursing homes at considerable distances from their home communities either as a matter of personal choice or by virtue of a family decision.

In cases where complex medical treatment is required that is not available in the locality, relocation from the home community is mandatory. Similarly, as the minimum economic size of nursing homes increases to 60, 80, or 100 beds, many residents of thinly populated communities will find relocation necessary. However, unless more than 20 to 30 miles are involved, relatives can visit them with little difficulty with half an hour of driving time.

One question that has concerned persons involved in establishing standards for nursing home location involves access to public transportation. The aged population is generally considered part of the captive market for mass transportation, and it has been thought desirable to situate nursing homes on bus and transit lines, to permit ambulatory residents freedom of movement and visits from aged friends. The proportion of nursing home residents reported to be fully ambulatory in the Boston College Study was 47 percent, while only 6 percent of the patients were fully bedridden.[37] However, while many patients can move freely within a protected environment, the percentage capable of using public transportation is probably extremely small. Since nursing home residents are by definition sick persons requiring custodial care, few are willing or able to travel via bus or subway. On the other hand, it is probable that rest homes which tend to house relatively well older people (as distinct from nursing homes) should be located on sites where such transportation is available.

Proximity to public transportation does appear to be significant in one respect. While professional staff and patients' relatives can be expected to own or have access to automobiles, this may not be true of the nonprofessional staff required by nursing homes. Hospitals and nursing homes located in suburban areas reportedly have encountered difficulty in filling nonprofessional positions because the principal labor market for this type of low-paid service occupation is found in core cities. With time, however, as automobile ownership becomes more diffused, some of these personnel recruitment problems may be alleviated, although they are unlikely to disappear.

Relationship to Hospitals and Medical Personnel

To a considerable extent, the reduction of travel time through expressway construction reduces the importance of immediate proximity to hospitals, medical facilities, and personnel. It would seem vital, however, to husband limited resources by locating patients requiring complex care that is available only in a few locations to the sources of care as is feasible; even the modest amount of time lost in travel by medical personnel can significantly diminish the time available for patients.

The Boston medical complex appears to be the major key to patient care in much of Massachusetts. An examination of the residences of physicians and other medical personnel and facilities indicates the premier role played by Boston as a regional, national, and international medical center.

Aside from the differential between the Boston area and other areas of Massachusetts, another type of geographic differential has caused some discussion. Like other middle- and upper-income persons, physicians and skilled nurses prefer to live in suburban communities, although much or most of their working lives is spent in core areas. If nursing homes are to be located near physicians and nurses, there is an obvious choice: They can be sited in proximity to medical workplaces (primarily hospitals, but also downtown medical offices), or they can be sited in the suburbs where most doctors and many nurses reside. At the present time, the core areas are clearly dominant in the nursing home field. For example, no fewer than 5,000 beds, over 1/6 of the state total, are in nursing homes in Boston. Overall, about 80 percent of nursing home beds are located in large communities in various parts of the state, with the remainder in suburban or, infrequently, in rural communities. Part of this central city orientation is attributable to the location of welfare patients. Over 70 percent of the commonwealth's welfare patients lived in core communities before entering a nursing home.

Up to the end of the 1960–70 decade, there appeared to be no pronounced tendency for the kind of core-to-suburb relocation of welfare patients or of urban poor families that has been characteristic of industrial plants, shopping centers, and business executives. In fact, the elderly poor are becoming more concentrated in central cities as financially better-off young families move to the suburbs. The growing stress on close ties to hospitals embodied in Medicare legislation may help to strengthen the existing central-area orientation of many of the aged.

It is obvious, however, that suburbanization is to have a significant if belated impact on the nursing home pattern. An examination of pending applications for almost 6,000 nursing home beds reveal that about 70 percent were to be located in suburban locations. Part of the reason for the increased emphasis on suburban locations can be found in population and income trends. Most nursing homes are operated by private entrepreneurs, and many hope to serve the $70 to $100-a-week suburban market and to keep the number of low-paying patients to a minimum.

There is also the site-cost factor to consider. In the late 1960s, well-located, intown sites cost $40,000 or more for the half-acre site required for a two-story nursing home with adequate off-street parking, and minimal set backs from property lines. In contrast, a suburban site usually cost no more than one-quarter to one-half that amount; one-acre sites could be secured for a maximum of perhaps $10,000 to $20,000. Thus, to some extent, the two-story limitation has tended to stimulate suburban nursing home location because of high intown site costs.

It is assumed that one of the principal goals of nursing home planning is to develop closer links with hospitals. The Medicare program, which makes explicit provision for close ties between hospitals and nursing homes, represents a clear statement of a hitherto largely unmet and obviously desirable objective. It is clear that a coordinated planning effort is required to bring together various types of regional and local medical facilities. Existing transportation systems permit a variety of medical care patterns. In short, as in the case of the community colleges, transportation provides a framework within which widely differing objectives can be sought. Nevertheless, other factors appear to be of greater significance.

RECREATION PLANNING IN A SLUM AREA

Three of the persisting dilemmas confronting planners revolve around the elitism issue, the need for criticizing, yet reforming, operations of old-style line agencies and the difficulty in drawing any clear line of demarcation between any specific problem and the needs and deficiencies of the larger environment. All of these problems emerged in a recreation study of the Model Cities area of Providence, Rhode Island.

Among its other functions, the Providence Model Cities agency serves as an outlet for the reactions and complaints of local residents. Some of these comments concern the recreation services and facilities available to the area. The Economic and Social Development Institute, Inc., a consulting organization which had previously been employed by the Model Cities agency in other aspects of its program, was employed to conduct a survey of the neighborhood residents' use of recreation facilities and to secure their comments and recommendations with respect to public recreation activities.[38]

The study of recreational services in the Model Cities area was designed to fulfill the following requirements:

1. Survey the demand for facilities and activities among the model neighborhood residents in terms of the following client groups: children (7-12), adolescents (13-19), adults (mothers), and senior citizens (65+).
2. Assess the use of, attitudes toward, and adequacy of existing recreational programs and facilities in terms of residents' stated and perceived needs.
3. Identify alternative program approaches.
4. Design a feasible action program consistent with client expressions of general need and design.

In the view of the city recreation agency there was no real problem in this predominantly black area of 20,000 people. The parks were in constant use, the basketball courts and swimming pools were full of active teen-agers, and the agency's 1969 annual report[39] was full of self-congratulation.

A review of the annual report reveals that the city provides a wide variety of recreational facilities for its residents. On the very cover of the report—which states that the department's motto is "serving youth"—the department indicates that it considers as its major responsibility services to the youth of the city. The list of the department's activities supports this conclusion, since it is clear that young people, particularly active teen-age boys, are most likely to use the recreational programs provided. Roughly 50 percent of the outdoor recreational facilities are allocated to basketball, baseball, football, or soccer. In some respects the recreation agency's programs clearly reflected the sports orientation of its staff, which was replete with ex-high-school athletes.

The department did not include in its program activities a really vigorous attempt to encourage local residents to participate in specific kinds of recreational activities. For example it did not provide incentives such as busing between homes and facilities to enable residents to participate; and it has not included extensive educational programs to encourage hard-to-reach residents who are unfamiliar with the opportunities available to them to learn how to take advantage of recreation facilities. Although total reported attendance figures are impressive—in the millions—it is difficult to determine precisely how these relate to the needs of the city's residents, particularly those in low-income neighborhoods. There is no explicit discussion of goals or of the nature and dimensions of the markets the department is attempting to serve. For example, the figures do not indicate coverage of the department's various programs with respect to target groups. In fact, survey data suggest that large attendance figures may reflect frequent usage by only a minority, perhaps a quarter, of the population. Neither is there any indication of the number of potential users for any given facility. Thus, when the report stated that 150,409 people attended the outdoor swimming pool that summer, it is impossible to know if that included all those people who could use the pool or reflects a high number of repeat users.

All the events on a list of special summer activities planned for 1970 were held outside the South Providence Model Cities area. The department made a special effort to reach inner-city youth, primarily those living in a large housing project, through special activities including field trips, arts and crafts, sewing, and outdoor games. Unfortunately, there is no indication of the quality of these programs or of any attempts on the part of the department to evaluate their effectiveness. Also, no attendance or participation statistics were provided for these inner-city programs.

Another project of the department for low-income youth involved transporting disadvantaged children to a state beach for swimming and subsequently to the city-owned Boys Camp on the shore for a hot dinner and supervised recreation. During 1967 there were an impressive 1,200 children participating in this program. But this number dropped to 50 during the summers of 1968 and 1969.

In summary, the Providence Recreation Department operates programs comparable to those of other cities and similar to programs operated in past years. As is the case elsewhere in the nation, however, the department has been charged with unresponsiveness to the needs of low-income residents, including general program irrelevance. These attacks do not represent perceptions of deterioration in the programs so much as a sensitization of client groups. This seems to consist of two factors—an unwillingness to accept traditional programs and facilities available to low-income areas, and black self-awareness.

The Model Cities agency and the local population were not in agreement with the department's self-portrait of a thriving recreation department operating a flourishing program. Model Cities in a sense was inherently suspicious of all old-line agencies, and among any slum population there is a festering grievance concerning alleged neglect and/or abuse by municipal government. In collaboration with the consultant[40] it was agreed that the only way to refute the assertions of the recreation department and to find out what the local population wanted in the way of improvements was through door-to-door sampling interviews.

A preliminary pilot study was conducted in July 1970, and the questionnaire was modified after further consultation with the Model Cities agency. Over a three-week period in August 1970, six local interviewers conducted 475 interviews on the basis of one interview for each thirtieth household. In all, the sample included over 2 percent of the approximately 20,000 people in the Model Cities area.

A large majority of the sample population contacted in the house-to-house survey was black, although blacks actually constitute about 50 percent of the Model Cities neighborhood population. This was due to a number of factors which reflect the attitude and opportunities of the white residents. A greater proportion of whites have jobs which take them out of the area during the day, and many whites who do not work make a special effort to leave the area during the day to visit friends or relatives living in other parts of the city. As a result, fewer whites were at home when interviewers called.

The polling approach for low-income areas adopted in the study is consistent with three major trends influencing the formulation and implementation of urban policy throughout the nation:

1. *The Delivery of Services.* Traditionally, the main reliance for reports on service effectiveness has been the operating agencies themselves. Welfare departments report on cases, fire departments on conflagrations, and park departments on teams and numbers of individuals participating in sponsored activities. In recent years there has been a growing realization that this type of reporting is incomplete and biased because not only does the operating agency have a vested interest in presenting a favorable image through optimistic reports, but the agency staff also clings to accustomed procedures and is resistant to any hint of criticism. Such criticisms tend to be particularly pronounced in low-income areas in which there are often widespread citizen feelings of neglect and second-class treatment.

As a result, there appears to be a special need in low-income areas to add an extra dimension to the traditional reports of agency activities by securing,

through household surveys, a cross-section of opinions regarding service coverage and quality among existing and potential consumers.

2. *Program Evaluation.*[41] Agencies, like people, are usually incapable of dispassionate self-evaluation. In recent years increasing efforts have been made to build an effective modification procedure into the governmental structure itself. One such method has been to employ outside, presumably objective evaluators who serve much the same function as the financial auditors who certify that agency finances are in order. In this case, however, an evaluation program had been mandated, and it was the evaluator's task to identify strengths and weaknesses for appropriate remedial action. This approach offers some hope that objective review of policies and performance can proceed in an orderly fashion.

3. *Planning with the Community.* It has long been assumed that despite the size of a municipality, the regular electoral process provides full opportunity for the accurate reflection of opinions and needs of all segments of the community. In recent years this view has been increasingly challenged on the grounds that the system has given a disproportionate weight to more affluent and more articulate neighborhoods while partially disfranchising the poorer, low-income groups. The burgeoning of organizations of welfare mothers and neighborhood organizations for education, fighting poverty, and urban development among a host of other community groups has drastically changed this situation. Under pressure from these and other forces, public agencies have increasingly admitted such groups into the decision-making process. "Planning with people" has taken on substantive reality only in areas where neighborhood organizations such as block clubs and neighborhood associations have become articulate.

One persistent problem with planning in the absence of community response is that large segments of the population tend to be slighted, as was the case with all but male teen-agers in the Providence Model Cities area. This is not, it may be stressed, the classic case of middle-class planners prescribing tennis and golf while central city residents want basketball and bocce.[42] On the contrary, the Providence program seems to reflect the working-class machismo of former high-school athletes. One study in Detroit found that inner-city blacks and other low-income residents rely more heavily on public play space than do suburban residents, but another report noted that there are few public play areas within walking distance in many low income areas. It is not surprising to find that proportionately ten times as many inner-city residents are dissatisfied with available public play space as are suburban dwellers.[43]

The inadequacy of legitimate recreation opportunities in inner cities emerged as a matter of concern in the 1960s, at the time when other central city problems began to receive substantial attention. By the mid-1970s a significant amount of research had been conducted in this area, most of it detailing deficiencies in planning, in the lack of citizen participation, and in the negative impacts created by fiscal austerity measures. A 1974 survey of inner-city parks in 25 cities revealed that "many urban parks and playgrounds are empty: inadequate maintenance, poor or uninspired leadership, and stifling summer heat exacerbated by unshaded macadam contribute to nonuse."[44]

The interviewing process in the Providence project contained several noteworthy features aside from the sample size. The division into age groups elicited specific responses from groups often overlooked in recreation planning, particularly very young children and housewives. Second, the open-ended nature of the questioning elicited a broad range of responses and complaints far beyond the purview of the municipal recreation program. Third, through photographs and program descriptions local residents were given a glimpse of a better model, in this case, pictures from the literature and the municipal recreation program conducted in Washington, D.C.[45] A proposed see-it-for-yourself bus tour of recommended recreation areas in Washington was rejected for budgetary reasons.

This is not to suggest that central cities are overflowing with prime models suitable for emulation. Seymour Gold in the early 1970s wrote that "few good examples of inner city playground development are evident except for some recent demonstration areas in St. Louis and New York City."[46] Moreover, he indicated that research in the recreation area reveals that only a fraction of the potential user population frequents neighborhood parks,[47] a finding that is consistent with the Providence study. Use levels rarely exceeded 10 percent of the potential market during peak periods and normally ran between 1 and 5 percent. The survey revealed wide-ranging complaints regarding a number of programs and facilities, many of which reflected a need for program revisions on the part of agencies other than the Recreation Department.

Complaints often expressed included: the lack of active sports and special facilities for girls of all ages; excessive distances between facilities and residences of younger children and older persons; rundown, unsafe condition of some facilities; fear of rampaging teen-agers. This reduced park use among the aged, young children, and some teen-agers (complaints of this nature regarding the local shopping center and the Drop-In Center were particularly pronounced); the lack of minority-group employment and black-oriented programs in various recreation programs; general charges that there was "nothing interesting to do" at existing facilities (this included outright hostility to offerings at school playgrounds and programs); and a series of complaints revolving around incompatibilities: little boys like to throw rocks, aged persons are afraid of rock throwers; smaller children complain of teen-age bullying at the swimming pool, teen-agers complain that little kids are always under foot.

The general impression is one of deprivation. One interviewer was told by a resident that there are many concerned people in the community who have been discouraged because it appears to them that "those who have get more and those who have not get less." (In the recreation area the one principal exception is the aggressive male teen-age basketball player. Even here, however, there are complaints concerning the substandard condition of the courts.) It may be argued that the complaint often expressed by young people that "there is nothing to do" is more a function of age and reflects a stage in development common to all youth regardless of available recreational opportunity. However, since this alienation is also displayed by the adults and senior citizens surveyed in the Model Cities area, it must result more from actual rather than imagined neglect. Among all groups there is a strong sense of alienation and simmering grievances. Plainly, much of the population in the Model Cities area harbors sentiments of helplessness, alienation, and anger based in part on their belief that they are accorded the status of neglected orphans. Much of the rest of the city may be convinced that an overly large share of federal, state, and municipal funds is being allocated to residents of the Model Cities area, but the residents themselves are convinced that the opposite is true.[48]

Conclusions

It is apparent that public recreation programs are especially important in low-income areas which lack the private alternatives available to middle- and upper-income families. The more affluent family may have a backyard full of play equipment, often enjoys access to private swimming pools and country clubs, and can provide music lessons, summer camps, boats, country vacations, and special attention for the recreation needs of the entire family. In addition, the middle- and upper-income family is well equipped to take full advantage of high-quality public programs by virtue of outlook as well as easy access to automobile transportation. Poor persons of whatever race or ethnic origins are constrained to depend much more heavily on public programs and facilities. For this reason, deficiencies in a municipal program or facility which may have a negligible effect on well-off families may result in serious deprivation for poorer families.

Agencies are often surprised to discover that their constituencies have no clear idea of the nature and limits of their responsibilities or of the finer points of the intergovernmental program system. Complaints concerning defects in welfare, police, health, or recreation programs may be combined with irritation over the behavior of young people and litter on the streets to create a general feeling of hostility to municipal, state, or federal elected officials and agencies. While this obviously represents a lack of understanding of the intricacies of operating government, in another sense it is an accurate reflection of reality. The citizen is less concerned over jurisdiction than service and is viscerally aware that police and parks, welfare and education, housing and poverty, jobs and shopping facilities are all part of a whole. No survey of citizen attitudes which stops at the boundaries of a single agency or performance of a single function can provide a valid portrait of neighborhood response.

The citizen is fully aware that private enterprise is responsible for the bulk of the available jobs and all of the stores and service establishment and is also knowledgeable concerning the differences between welfare caseworkers and recreation department personnel. But there is also a keen awareness of interrelationships that are sometimes obscure to the functional agency. In the Providence Model Cities area, shopping facilities were abysmal; a small retail complex was in the process of final extinction owing to low volume, poor management, and serious problems with crime and vandalism. Not only are eating out, drinking out, and going to beauty parlors and retail stores vital recreational alternatives, but such facilities are crucial to neighborhood vitality and identity. The lack of a broad range of private recreational alternatives such as shopping and restaurants for local residents of the kind that are available to middle-income families in other parts of the city is keenly felt. Residents are also fully aware of the relationship between the maintenance of public decorum and free use of public and private recreational and shopping facilities. For this reason, it was necessary that the survey include topics and elicit reactions which are not strictly speaking within the direct purview of recreational planning and programming.

A final issue raised by the Providence study concerns program evaluation. How should an agency program be judged, and who should do the judging? It seems clear that agency self-evaluation through formal annual reports reflecting image-building activity is not a satisfactory approach. In the case of a recreation agency the goal might well be service to the community at large —all segments of the community, including those persons who by reason of lack of income, age, infirmity, or other causes require a special effort to reach. Further, it is assumed that recreation programs are not only vital municipal functions per se but also serve broader community goals such as socialization and improving the general level of physical fitness. Moreover, although the desires of the community must be taken fully into account in program planning and implementation, it is also assumed that an effective municipal recreation agency should play an important educational role, as for example in persuading its clients of the critical importance of basic swimming skills. The leadership and educational role of the municipal recreation agency is particularly important in formulating programs for poorer persons whose experience tends to be limited. Yet the sophistication to exercise wise choices based on the most advanced tested models may often be almost as much of a problem with recreation agency staff as with their clientele. As with most institutional arrangements, the accustomed pattern is for a slow trickling down of newer concepts rather than for discarding obsolescent practices. Finally, it is desirable for as many agencies as possible to be tested by effectiveness measures. Indices for a municipal recreation agency include such yardsticks as performance on physical fitness tests for all community youngsters, possession of Red Cross swimming certificates, and evidence of active participation in one or more organized programs.

There must be a permanent, knowledgeable evaluation agency, outside the agency under review, to perform the review function. Unless these assessments are to degenerate into a farce, there must be a systematic follow-up to correct deficiencies on pain of truncated budgets, curtailed careers, or other real penalties. And before concluding with the topic of evaluation, it must be added that a balanced and objective evaluation agency should be empowered and encouraged to reward as well as penalize, to praise as well as admonish. If such is the case, in well-run agencies the review process, and the reviewers, may be regarded not as alien ogres, but as helpful allies securing support and understanding.

There is also the dilemma of limiting planning studies to a faithful reflection of the views and aspirations of clients and users or risking charges of elitism by performing a public education role. In this particular case, as in others when the client group is poor and has restricted experience with better models, they may be content with pitifully small improvements—mostly the absence of pain. For example, one of the respondents suggested that "it would be heaven" if the glass were swept up from around the swimming pool. Another asked only for "peace": if only the rowdies and rough kids would leave him alone he could really enjoy sitting in the park.

This kind of comment relative to improved housekeeping and maintenance of minimum standards of decorum obviously represents only a first step in broadening a client group's horizons to indicate the real range of options open to them. The photographs and program descriptions in this case were only a low-budget, crude approximation. As time and funds permit, tours, scale models, and films should be used extensively, particularly with client groups with limited educational and experiential horizons. Otherwise, the tendency is to restrict potential improvements sharply.

This educational function applies with equal force to the line staff of the target agency. The inherent resistance to innovation of such agencies has been discussed at length elsewhere in this volume. At this juncture it is only necessary to point out that the adversary relationship between slum populations and line agencies calls for unusually tactful behavior. The reform objective may be achieved if the line agency staff (whose horizons are often not much broader than their clients') is similarly offered an opportunity to see a successful model in operation. (Pioneering attempts with dullards are futile.) Further, the line agency staff must be convinced that people like themselves are fully capable of taking on the innovation, that it will generate favorable publicity and possibly increase appropriations, promotions, and so on. Innovation must be sold to the staff as an enticing prospect, an invitation rather than a threat, to employment or peace of mind.

In a provocative article forecasting a rather gloomy prospect for urban parks, Seymour Gold offers five critical questions as a guide in redesigning municipal recreation programs:

1. Have we made an attempt to really understand the recreation experience, why people come to public parks, where they go once there, what they do, their preferences and satisfactions, anxieties or disappointments?

2. If we understand the behavioral aspects of the recreation experience, have we made a sincere attempt to apply this knowledge in the planning and design of public parks?

3. If we have applied this knowledge in the planning and design of parks, have we complemented this with effective management practices and program leadership?

4. Have we seriously considered possible alternatives to public land acquisition, development, and program in measurable human terms that can be translated into public policy?

5. If we have done all of the above to the best of our professional ability, have we effectively communicated our efforts, needs, or hopes to others, namely the nonusers of public parks, taxpayers, and community decision makers?[49]

The response to these inquiries in most cities would be "No, we have not." And in a broader sense, the deficiencies in park planning are only part of a broader failure, a dinosaur persistence in pursuing outmoded techniques in the face of evidence that they no longer work. Gold terms urban parks "an endangered species" because of their increasing lack of relevance, as for example in "the liability and maintenance mentality" that has blocked introduction of "challenging and imaginative designs that parallel the creative and adventure play area concept."[50] Securing honest and effective answers to his illustrative questions would be a useful first step on the road back to relevance.

CONCLUSION

There are parts of the nation, mainly urban slums, in which transportation is critically deficient. To cite one problem that is receiving increasing attention, the absence of good access to suburban jobs may become a significant obstacle to achieving substantial reductions in ghetto unemployment. In this sense, adequate transportation—as long as it remains unavailable—is a key element in social planning.

The social planning cases discussed in this chapter are probably representative of a wide range of instances where transportation factors are not of great significance; transportation access does not present particular difficulties for most people in most areas. Consequently, once the system exists, it tends to assume the same taken-for-granted, backdrop role of public water or sewerage systems.

The key locational decisions governing the delineation of service areas for community colleges and nursing homes reflect differing concepts of client groups affected by these institutions. In the case of community colleges, the major factor was proximity to students. This general guideline did not in itself narrow the range of planning alternatives. The decision to limit the size of core area colleges and to opt instead for a number of small suburban colleges was not reached on the basis of transportation considerations but on the grounds of prevalent notions concerning the pragmatic and intangible benefits of smallness and close linkages between the colleges and their local service areas.

The case of the nursing homes presented a somewhat different picture. Until recently, the principal locational criterion was proximity to patients. In more recent years, the trend toward suburbanization that has affected the distribution of metropolitan area population and economic activity has exercised a growing influence on nursing home location. To a degree, this trend also reflects the predilections of upper-echelon staff, doctors, managers, and nurses, many of them car-owning residents of the suburbs. Two other counterbalancing trends are in evidence, however. The first is the need for tapping the low-skill labor market in the core areas. Orderlies, attendants, kitchen staff, and practical nurses seem to be more difficult to find and keep in the suburbs. In view of the heavy turnover in these occupations, location in or near the urban core on a site well served by public transportation may be indicated for many nursing homes, especially as they increase in size and staff.

Another locational trend is also exercising a growing influence on nursing home location. A stronger emphasis on providing a wide range of therapeutic services and on advanced medical care and research is associated in part with Medicare legislation. Medicare, however, is only one element in a heightened interest in gerontology linked quite probably to the expansion in numbers and impact of the nation's aged population. This tendency is likely to be reflected in a further accentuation of the trend toward locating nursing homes as adjuncts to hospitals. In this sense, the original location decision that prompted the choice of a hospital site leads to the concept of a medical complex including physicians' office buildings, housing for medical personnel, postconvalescent facilities, special research operations, and nursing homes. Medical facilities clearly display some of the same characteristics as other types of locational aggregation.

This discussion hardly suggests that transportation is no longer a significant element in social planning. It does indicate that transportation is only one of a number of factors bearing on locational decisions, although partly because of its susceptibility to quantification and colorful graphic presentation, it often tends to be overemphasized.

With the major exception of the poor and other elements in the population who require public transportation, most people in the metropolitan area rely on the automobile and a highway system that permits easy access to a large swath of territory. Under these circumstances, transportation systems, especially in sizable metropolitan areas, have become a foundation element in the decision-making equation, the chessboard on which a multitude of combinations can be worked out.

NOTES

1. Christopher C. DeMuth, "Deregulating the Cities," *The Public Interest,* no. 44 (Summer 1976), pp. 115–28.
2. See Mary E. Brooks, *Housing Equity and Environmental Protection: The Needless Conflict* (Washington, D.C.: American Institute of Planners, 1976).
3. H. M. Franklin, D. Falk, and A. J. Levin, *In-Zoning* (Washington, D.C.: Potomac Institute, December 1974).
4. Ibid., part 5, "The Regional Housing Allocation Plan."
5. David Listokin, "An Analysis of the Fair Share Approach to Housing," ms., Center for Urban Policy Research, Rutgers University.
6. Franklin, Falk, and Levin, op. cit., p. 44.
7. Norman Williams, Jr., *American Planning Law: Land Use and the Police Power* (Chicago: Callaghan, 1975), chaps. 4 and 7.
8. *Urban League of Greater New Brunswick v. Borough of Carteret,* no. CA 22-73 N.J. Sup. Ct., filed July 22, 1974.
9. Superior Court of New Jersey, Middlesex County, Chancery Division, *Urban League of Greater New Brunswick v. Borough of Carteret et al.,* decided May 4, 1976.
10. Ibid., p. 33.
11. Ibid., pp. 34–35.
12. Ibid., p. 37.
13. Melvin R. Levin and Harvey M. Moscowitz, "South Plainfield: An Industrial Core City in a Region: A Fair Share Analysis of Housing," analysis prepared for litigation in *Urban League of Greater New Brunswick v. Borough of Carteret,* May 1976.
14. Ibid., p. 9.
15. Franklin, Falk, and Levin, op. cit., p. 161.
16. Levin and Moscowitz, op. cit., p. 21.
17. Ibid., p. 23.
18. George S. Sternlieb et al., *The Affluent Suburb: Princeton* (New Brunswick, N.J.: Transaction Books, 1971), pp. 175–205.
19. Levin and Moscowitz, op. cit., p. 26.
20. Ibid., p. 24.
21. John Brunner, *Squares of the City* (New York: Ballantine Books, 1965).
22. Melvin R. Levin, Project Director, *Planning Component Study,* prepared as part of *Master Plan Study* (Commonwealth of Massachusetts: Massachusetts Board of Regional Community Colleges, March 1966).

23. Melvin R. Levin, Project Director, *Toward A State Plan for Nursing Homes,* prepared for the Division of Adult Health (Boston, October 1966).

24. U.S. Bureau of the Census, *Statistical Abstract of the U.S.,* 1970, tables 190 and 191, pp. 126–27.

25. Commonwealth of Massachusetts, Special Commission on Audit of State Needs, *Needs in Massachusetts Higher Education* (Boston, March 1958), p. 10.

26. Massachusetts, Board of Regional Community Colleges, *Access to Quality Community College Opportunity: A Master Plan for Massachusetts Community Colleges Through 1975,* A Summary Report (Boston, May 1967).

27. In contrast, the state of Rhode Island has used 36 to 50 per 10,000 population as the low and high range in estimating future community college enrollment. In view of the fact that several community colleges in Massachusetts have already passed or are approaching the 40:10,000 ratio, 75:10,000 appears to be a more reasonable working figure for Massachusetts.

28. U.S. Department of Commerce, *1963 Census of Transportation,* "Home-to-Work Travel" (Washington, D.C.: U.S. Government Printing Office, 1963), TC63 (A)-P5.

29. Francis S. Doody, *The Immediate Economic Impact of Higher Education in New England,* Education Studies no. 1 (Boston: Bureau of Business Research, College of Business Administration, Boston University, 1961), pp. 34–37. Data have been updated to reflect changes in the cost-of-living index.

30. Data supplied by Donald Deyo, Director, *Master Plan Study,* Massachusetts Board of Regional Community Colleges.

31. Claiborne M. Ball, "Employment Effects of Construction Expenditures," *Monthly Labor Review* 88 (February 1965):154–55.

32. Data characteristics of nursing homes and nursing home patients are derived from Boston College, *Fact Finding Survey of Nursing Homes* (Boston, 1963), and from information supplied by the Division of Adult Health, Massachusetts Department of Public Health.

33. In a 1964 study in Maine, physician interviewers estimated that 21 percent of nursing home patients possessed rehabilitation potential. An estimated 9 percent could be rehabilitated to the point where the patient could function with limited supervision or feeding and lodging. Maine, Office of Health Education, Department of Health, Education, and Welfare, *Nursing Home Patient Care* (Augusta, January 20, 1965), table 37, p. 41.

34. New York State Department of Health, Division of Hospital Review and Planning, *Priorities for Federal Grants-in-aid for Construction of Nursing Home Facilities* (Albany: State of New York, July 1, 1963).

35. American Society of Planning Officials, *Nursing Homes,* Information Report no. 185, April 1964.

36. U.S. Department of Health, Education, and Welfare, Public Health Service, *Nursing Home Standards Guide,* publication no. 827 (Washington, D.C., June 1961, reprinted April 1963).

37. *Fact Finding Survey of Nursing Homes,* op. cit., p. 28.

38. This report was funded by 701 funds under the State-Wide Land Use and Transportation Program.

39. Rhode Island, Providence Recreation Department, *1969 Annual Report.*

40. Melvin R. Levin, "Recreational Needs in the Providence Model City Area," a report prepared for the Providence Model City Agency by the Economic and Social Development Institute, Washington, D.C., May 1971.

41. For a good analysis of recreation effectiveness indices, see Harry P. Hatry and Diana R. Dunn, "Measuring the Effectiveness of Local Government Services: Recreation" (Washington, D.C.: The Urban Institute, 1971).

42. See J. B. Lansingaud and Gary Hendricks, *Living Patterns in the Detroit Region* (Detroit, Mich.: Detroit Regional and Transportation Land Use Study, 1967).

43. See S. M. Gold, "Nonuse of Neighborhood Parks," *Journal of the American Institute of Planners* 38, no. 6 (November 1972): 369–78.

44. National Recreation and Park Association, *Open Space and Recreation Opportunity in America's Inner Cities,* prepared for Department of Housing and Urban Development, July 1974 (distributed by NTIS), p. 12.

45. Melvin R. Levin, "Recreational Needs in the Providence Model Cities," op. cit.

46. Seymour M. Gold, *Urban Recreation Planning* (Philadelphia: Lea and Febiger, 1973), p. 94.

47. Ibid., pp. 101–02.

48. Since the mid-1960s an increasing number of law suits have dealt with alleged inequality in the provision of municipal public services (including recreation services) in slum areas as compared to more affluent areas. An analysis of municipal parks in Washington, D.C., resulted in a verdict of "not proven" with regard to discrimination in recreation services. See Donald M. Fisk and Cynthia A. Lancer, *Equality of Distribution of Recreation Services: A Case Study of Washington, D.C.* (Washington, D.C.: The Urban Institute, July 1974).

49. Seymour Gold, "Recreation and Leisure in the Future," presented at AIP/ASPO National Planning Conference, Washington, D.C., March 22, 1976, p. 11.

50. Ibid., p. 16.

CHAPTER

8

ASPECTS OF THE DISTRESSED AREA PROBLEM

It is difficult to conceive of any nation in which economic development has not proceeded unevenly, with one or more areas lagging behind the national averages and others well out in front. As a rule the divisions are north-south: The American South and southern Europe generally are poorer than more northerly areas. There are, of course, exceptions, particularly in far northern nations and England—north Scandinavia and Scotland are relatively poor—and also in the southern hemisphere: northeastern Brazil is one of the world's largest and poorest regions.

One of the outstanding characteristics of most distressed areas is their durability. Far from disappearing by a natural or government-aided process of migration to more salubrious regions, they hang on for decades, even generations. While they are indeed the source of heavy migration, the population loss never seems to be large enough to bring the labor force into alignment with job opportunities. In various parts of the world there are the equivalents of America's western ghost towns, mining villages that self-depopulated when the ore and the jobs gave out; but the deserted village tends to be a rhetorical and literary device rather than a realistic expectation. When the jobs decline, people tend to remain.

This persistent geographic imbalance in levels of living has given rise in many nations both to soul searching and attempts at remedial action. It is believed unfair and inequitable that substantial numbers of people are condemned to live in poor areas. And this leads to the next issue. Granting that distressed area residents are shortchanged, how is the deficiency to be made up? Specifically, should distressed area populations be encouraged, induced, or forced to move to economically flourishing areas? Or should it be government policy to encourage, induce, or force public and private industry to relocate to such areas? Bring the people to the jobs or bring the jobs to the people?

Distressed area advocates often develop elaborate proofs concerning the long-term nature of their exploitation and oppression. Their populations are shown as prey to a combination of powerful outside interests working in close collaboration with indigenous henchmen—politicians, judges, police, businessmen, and the local media. When it is suggested that their case is proven, that these conditions are indeed intolerable, and that it is fortunate that distressed area residents have the option of relocating, without hindrance, to other places, spokesmen for distressed areas are not eager to seize the migration option. Their response is rhetorical and cultural. Why should people who dearly love their ancestral homes, their neighbors, and their way of life be forced to tear up their roots? Why should there be no alternative to melting into the metropolitan mainstream, losing one's unique attributes, and quite possibly one's soul in the process? The fact that 50 million foreign immigrants and tens of millions of Americans have relocated, risking precisely this danger, does not seem to constitute impressive evidence for such spokesmen that a viable alternative exists. In a sense the advocates may be speaking for the nonrelocating hard core, people who, like many slum residents, are fearful of outsiders, of new, unfamiliar settings, and do not believe they can cope with the world outside their cultural ghettos.

By and large the official response to distressed area problems is the second alternative. Government installations, reforestation programs, housing construction, bonuses for relocating industry, subsidies to local firms, training grants for local workers, and vast quantities of research studies have been initiated to stimulate job formation in distressed areas, usually with limited results. The lack of great success is not a signal for cessation but for demands for more of the same: more plants, more subsidies, more economic development expenditures.

Why is there this persistent bias in favor of programs which offer little prima facie evidence of achievement? The answer lies outside economics: distressed area programs, as distinct from problems, are primarily political. The arguments employed to secure national government intervention lay heavy stress on the theme of neglected orphans, on the unique attachment of residents to their homes and their culture, and the ethnocentricity and cultural genocide implicit in depopulation. There is often much play on the theme of family breakup, generations of weeping parents bidding farewell to offspring for whom no local jobs were available. And there is a warning—help us or pay the price. This may be the penalty of absorbing unruly migrants in growth areas, swelling their crime, prisons, and welfare rolls. Or it may take the form of political revenge, revolt in Brazil's backlands, political manipulation in the direction of higher tariffs, or simply third-rate, venal congressmen come to the capital to wheel and steal. More rarely, revenge may take the form of seizure of control over a unique resource, as Scotland in the mid-1970s was trying to do with North Sea oil, or as some in Appalachia talked of doing with coal.

It is true that sometimes there is a thin economic veneer on the bedrock of political advocacy. The claim is made that distressed areas have a costly urban infrastructure of roads, housing, schools, and other public and private facilities which would cost billions of dollars to duplicate elsewhere if their population were forced to abandon their homes. The fact that much of this infrastructure is obsolete is rarely mentioned. Similarly, it is alleged that the choice is between gainful local jobs or wasteful local welfare, because distressed area people refuse to migrate—a claim which is sharply contradicted by population statistics. And it is said that many distressed areas possess unique natural assets—coal, soils, harbors, and so on—which make them a special natural resource which cannot be neglected. This argument overlooks the fact that there are usually perfectly valid economic reasons why private capital has assiduously avoided particular areas; regional economic hypotheses based on the supposed persistent blindness of profit-oriented businesses are generally unconvincing.

Some of the vexations involved in placating distressed areas are apparent almost everywhere. For a time they may be soothed with study commissions, tokenism, and pledges, but eventually they want substantial programs. Unfortunately, these often generate little substantive improvement. Allocating money to these areas runs the risk that much of the investment will be wasted, either because of a lack of local entrepreneurial and technical base or because the best jobs and most of the profits will be scooped up by a small local elite, outside investors, and a handful of outside managers and technicians. Equally important, the growth areas that have, over time, demonstrated their ability to make good use of new investments may also begin to feel slighted. And in terms of national economic growth goals, it usually makes more sense to invest in proven winners than dubious losers. In multiethnic nations this investment policy can be highly controversial. Slovenia, Croatia, and Catalonia, the most advanced areas of Yugoslavia and Spain, have long complained about national investment policies that lay strong emphasis on industrially backward areas, at their expense.

In the United States there was never really powerful resistance to the notion of providing special funds for distressed areas. The advanced regions were too secure in their relative wealth and position to complain very much if additional federal help was given to distressed mining areas like Appalachia, cutover forest areas, depressed rural regions, or the old New England textile centers. Noblesse oblige. But this situation seemed due for a change by the 1960s. The reason was simple. It was perfectly acceptable policy to locate army camps and missile facilities and to channel government funds to distressed regions when the Northeast perceived itself as far more affluent than its impoverished neighbors. By the mid-1970s, however, the increasing obsolescence of industrial plant and urban areas in the northeast quadrant of the nation disturbed many residents of that vast region. They were particularly concerned because the ingrained pattern of channeling military spending and other government allocations to the South showed no signs of alteration despite the growing prosperity of much of the South. What appeared to be in prospect was the kind of controversial battle over sectional favoritism not seen in the United States for several generations.

DISTRESSED AREAS AS A NATIONAL CONCERN

The awareness that some areas were lagging well behind others in economic development is older than the nation. Even in colonial days travelers, politicians, and citizens were constantly comparing relative degrees of progress and poverty, partly as a matter of pride but also as a test of differing approaches to government and social relations. One critical area of comparison involved the relative economic merits of southern plantation (later urban) slavery as compared with northern wage labor. Sectional economics, specifically the feeling on the part of the South that their region was being exploited by Yankee manufacturers through tariffs and banking practices, and the fear of northern workers and farmers that slavery would spread and undercut hired labor, were major causes of the Civil War. Subsequently, the impoverished South was recognized, up to the present, as the nation's largest distressed area.

The modern delineation of distressed areas awaited the New Deal 1930s.[1] Appalachia, the Ozark region, the rural coastal South, the Wisconsin-Michigan-Minnesota cutover forest region, and the New England textile areas were all identified as especially impoverished regions even in a time of general poverty. Not much beyond research occurred in the 1930s, but during World War II, as a sheer matter of necessity during a period of severe manpower shortages, war plants were located in distressed areas to take advantage of their pools of unutilized labor.[2] After the war, for a time there was virtual silence on this issue, at least at the national level, but by the mid-1950s the first stirrings of a new interventionist attitude toward distressed areas began to emerge.

During his 1954 election campaign, Senator Paul Douglas, the author of the Area Redevelopment Act, was confronted with the economic ailments of southern Illinois in much the same way that President Kennedy encountered similar problems in West Virginia six years later. Southern Illinois, an area known as "Egypt," containing picturesquely named communities such as Cairo and Karnak, had long been battered by declines in the dominant soft-coal industry that had been superimposed on a marginal agricultural economy.[3]

Better by far, the senator reasoned, to use costly existing social overhead capital (schools, streets, and other public facilities) in depressed areas than to have to replace it elsewhere if people from southern Illinois were forced to migrate for jobs. The senator recognized, moreover, that much of the manpower in labor surplus areas, particularly the older workers, was immobile. The best answer, the senator concluded, was to bring jobs to labor surplus areas.

Initially, Senator Douglas suggested that the way to achieve this objective was a combination of more public works, a modest-sized federal industrial credit corporation, federal technical assistance, and an extension of unemployment insurance to workers willing to undertake retraining.

By 1965, he had broadened his proposal. On the theory that one of the key problems was the lack of venture capital, the senator proposed the establishment of a $100 million revolving fund to permit new or expanded industries in depressed areas to borrow money at low interest rates. Further, in view of the unsatisfactory condition of many of the existing access roads and water and sewerage systems, the senator also proposed another $100 million revolving fund to help construct and renovate such local public facilities. In addition, the new bill included an extension of unemployment insurance for retraining and two new provisions—rapid tax write-offs for firms locating in depressed areas and area priority for federal purchases of supplies and services.

Based on the low unemployment rates prevailing in the mid-1950s, assistance was to be limited to urban areas that had experienced an unemployment rate of at least 6 percent for three years, or at least 9 percent for 18 months.

In 1956, extensive hearings on the proposed depressed area legislation marked out the battlefield for the coming five-year struggle. Conservatives displayed implacable hostility and suggested that the program was both useless and harmful. Any enterprising community, they asserted, could solve local problems without federal help. They warned that the Douglas legislation would sap local initiative, weaken moral fiber, and distort the healthy and natural processes of industrial location. Proponents of the depressed area legislation, however, argued for an even bigger bill with more benefits. They cited as evidence experience in Pennsylvania and elsewhere which seemed to suggest that a limited input of local venture capital ranging from a few hundred dollars to a few thousand dollars per worker could create permanent jobs in a depressed area. Ironically, identical case histories of local- and state-aided successes in stimulating economic growth had been used by the opposition as proof that local initiative could do the job without federal assistance.

A major impetus for broadening the coverage of the act came from southern legislators, many of whom are customarily suspicious of new nonmilitary federal programs, particularly those which call for large-scale expenditures in other regions. To secure needed southern support in the face of strong Republican opposition, the legislation was altered to include aid to low-income rural areas. In effect, this encompassed the entire rural South. The fateful decision to grapple with the intractable problems of the marginal farm counties created major difficulties after the legislation was finally enacted. It also helped to precipitate a battle to ensure that southerners would not use the program to accelerate industrialization in their region by raiding northern industrial centers. To placate the Northeast, a special protective provision was added prohibiting "pirating"—relocation with assistance from the Area Redevelopment Administration (ARA).

Another of the many ironies involved in this legislation was that its passage was helped considerably by nationwide recessions in 1957–58 and again in 1960–61. Sentiment for federal aid increased when unemployment reached the spectacular rates of 10 to 20 percent in some urban depressed areas. Although the rural unemployed and underemployed, camouflaged on subsistence farms, tend to be overlooked in jobless statistics, their suffering did not go unrecognized by their congressmen.

It is partly because of the total impossibility of devising purely rural solutions to meet the needs of redundant farm labor that the economic development districts were created. Since farm families were already accustomed to driving considerable distances for shopping, schools, sale of farm products, and recreation, the rationale could be carried one step farther: given federal stimuli, it was reasoned an adequate number of jobs could be generated in nearby urban centers to permit rural labor, miners, and loggers to remain in their homes while they commuted to work with no more discomfort than that experienced by an affluent suburban executive.

This was the original conceptual framework for America's postwar distressed areas programs. Unfortunately, in practice the reality proved disappointing.

PROBLEMS IN DESIGN AND IMPLEMENTATION

Sar Levitan[4] is at pains to underscore certain weaknesses in the act that he believes contributed to its disappointing impact on distressed area problems. Briefly, his assessment is that a new and untried agency was given inadequate tools to do too big a job under unfavorable conditions.

It has been suggested that tougher standards designed by the U.S. Department of Labor would have been helpful in limiting eligible applicants to a more manageable number, but it can be argued that the legislation might not have passed unless a large number of areas could expect to benefit. Because of this need to gain wide support, programs as finally enacted often fall far short of an administrator's ideal.

One basic problem was related to the fragmentation of responsibility. As in most parts of the nation, physical, economic, and human resources planning in redevelopment areas is fragmented among agencies, between central cities and suburbs, and among various levels of government. This splitting of jurisdictions and programs creates problems of varying degrees of severity in a flourishing economy, but in a long distressed area, it can create havoc. There, the backlog of needs is greater, the gap with the constantly improving major metropolitan areas is wider, local expertise is in short supply, and local financial resources are usually less than adequate. The obvious solution is to hire professional staff and compensate for local deficiencies by launching large-scale, federally aided programs. Unfortunately, the amount of money specifically earmarked for distressed areas is extremely limited when compared with funds available to all areas from the major grant-in-aid programs. The distressed areas often found it impossible to marshal the expertise, unity, and civic leadership needed to secure a proportionate share of federal allocations, let alone compensate for accumulated neglect. In short, the distressed area has more need but less capability to secure aid and less know-how in operating complex federally assisted programs.

The Economic Development District, a key feature of the 1965 legislation, provided one way to escape this dilemma. The provision for federal financial aid for professional staff—75 percent of the total cost—and the requirement that a meaningful development plan be presented as a prerequisite of receiving aid for development projects raised interesting possibilities. With this combination of incentives and painless funding, the objective was to have the distressed areas design and establish a single mechanism to formulate and implement comprehensive development plans.

While there was evidence that the Area Redevelopment Act of 1961 had achieved some positive results, most observers agreed that fundamental changes in area development legislation were in order. The Public Works and Economic Development Act of 1965 reflected some of the modifications suggested both by domestic empirical experience and European models. Following the Appalachian precedent, the legislation contained provisions for the creation of large-scale regional commissions. Second, reacting to criticisms concerning the tendency to dilute the impact of development programs by designating too many redevelopment areas, the states were required to delineate larger and presumably fewer economic development districts, each of which was to contain one or two designated growth centers to provide an attractive focus for economic expansion. It was recognized that not every depressed community and rural area could induce economic growth; the growth centers, it was hoped, would provide new jobs within easy commuting range, that is, within 20 to 30 miles, thereby permitting residents of distressed areas to remain in their present residences if they so desired.

It had been noted that in the midst of decades of surrounding social and economic gloom, Appalachian metropolitan areas and urban centers had displayed substantial growth during the 1950s.[5] This Appalachian, quasi-rural theme dominated development district and growth center legislation.

The new legislation also reflected thinking in Western Europe, especially in France, which has made strenuous efforts to counter overcentralization in the Paris area by stimulating growth in satellite regional centers.

Lessons From Abroad

It is worth briefly examining this French pattern, because it appears to be directly relevant to the future of area development in the United States. Despite recent efforts to reverse the pattern much of the growth in France continues to take place in the Paris region—if not in the immediate area of the city and its environs, then in an extended territory within an 80- to 100-mile radius.[6]

This drift toward the capital under the impetus of generations of past decisions and a wealth of internal and external stimuli is equally characteristic of other European metropolises such as London, Stockholm, Budapest, and Vienna. More recently, similar efforts have been launched by the Hungarian and Polish governments, fearful that unchecked expansion in the capital would result in the creation of mammoth goiters draining vitality and talent from the provinces.[7] To a limited degree, the same observation applies to Washington, New York, and other U.S. regional capitals such as Los Angeles, San Francisco, Chicago, Boston, Atlanta, Denver, Houston, and Minneapolis-St. Paul.

At home and abroad, complaints have been registered over the generations concerning the tendency of small-town talent to migrate to the big cities, a trend that is closely associated with limited employment possibilities and the social backwardness and cultural deprivation of rural areas and small towns; the depressing effect of these conditions on sensitive, sophisticated urban spirits has been a recurrent theme in international fiction.

French regional development plans place great stress on modernization of community facilities and commercial and small manufacturing plants, and expansion of government offices and universities. Within the nation's geographical framework, the objective is to foster a better population and labor force distribution as a function of natural resources and economic activities. However, as was true in the United States, the French efforts were discovered to be spread too thinly among too many areas, so that later attention was increasingly focused on a few key areas in Brittany, the west, and the southwest. This policy of concentrating the geographic focus of the development program contrasts with earlier decisions (in the 1950s) to include portions of northern and northeastern France among the "critical zones" requiring major government aid.

The final verdict on some foreign distressed area programs remains in doubt. One English study concluded, for example, that the number of jobs created by Board of Trade incentives and regulations in British distressed areas was 200,000,[8] roughly double the number that ARA claimed it helped to generate in the U.S. redevelopment areas in 1961–65. However, even this gain was not sufficient in England to halt the long-term drift of population to the southeast, away from redevelopment areas.

One reason for the failure is that in Britain, as in the United States, the growth of government jobs, trades, and services has provided a major share of employment expansion; the continued postwar drift to the southeast was partly due to the lack of control over the location of public and private white-collar employment and office construction in greater London. Not until the mid-1960s did stringent regulations on office construction, combined with mounting shortages of labor and incentives to locate elsewhere in Britain, succeed in bringing the "notorious surge of people from the impoverished provinces to the lush metropolis to an abrupt end."[9] Second, the authors question the role of out-migration in bringing about the balance between available labor and available jobs in distressed areas. In Britain, most migrants are in the skilled occupation groups, and their departure does not necessarily create job openings for the unskilled, hard-core unemployed. Moreover, to date, the total volume of out-migration from British redevelopment areas has been small, amounting to only one-sixth of the average number of unemployed.

PUBLIC ENTREPRENEURSHIP IN DISTRESSED AREAS

In much of the discussion preceding the enactment of the 1961 Area Development Act and its successor, the Public Works and Economic Development Act of 1965, there seemed to be an implicit assumption that there was a direct parallel to beleaguered England in 1940. "Give us the tools," Winston Churchill assured America, "and we will finish the job." In actual fact, the full resources of two great allies were needed for victory, in addition to Churchill's remarkable talents. Appealing political rhetoric has its limitations; it is apparent that Britain's power was inadequate for the task.

The same Churchillian claim was advanced repeatedly in the hearings preceding the passage of federal distressed area legislation. Based on experience in selected industrial areas, it was suggested that a sizable input of federal funds would generate sufficient private investment to create first- and second-round jobs for a large proportion of the unemployed in redevelopment areas. The ability to make effective use of these funds was taken for granted, perhaps because the mayors and governors testifying in favor of the legislation were so articulate and persuasive.[10] In practice, however, the experience has been closer to that of wartime Britain. The problems of the redevelopment areas are being met and to some extent, mastered, largely with the help of powerful outside forces. At this point, however, the parallel lines diverge: many of the redevelopment areas are short of Churchills; they lack inspired leaders.

The leadership factor is critical because solutions to the problems of unemployment—and, specifically, the uses to which inputs of outside resources to assist redevelopment areas can be put—take many different forms and can have very different consequences. Progress in tackling redevelopment problems is hampered and in some cases jeopardized by the fact that the quality of redevelopment area political and business leadership is unequal to the task of internal change, upgrading, and renovation. The net result is the widening rather than the narrowing of the gap that separates the redevelopment areas from the flourishing areas. They can easily become—or in some cases, remain—Caliban territory, suitable only as sources of low-grade labor and low-grade enterprise with social and political outlooks to match.

Many of these areas are sadly deficient in the critical elements of redevelopment area programs that cannot be imported from Washington—vigorous, inspiring, and effective political and business leadership, backed up by significant technical expertise to implement local programs. The immediate need for jobs is being met through a combination of out-migration and creation of low-wage, local employment opportunities. Abject poverty is met by direct federal aid to needy persons, but without the combination of better public and private local leadership to improve school systems, housing, physical facilities, and public services to lay the groundwork for higher types of private business and industrial development, many distressed areas will be reduced to a marginal social and economic role. They will provide a pool of undereducated migrant labor for low-wage jobs located in metropolitan areas and attractive sites for poorly paid, labor-intensive industry. They will also tend to choose legislators to serve in Congress and in state legislatures, as well as mayors and city councilors, from among the supply of residual talent attuned to an environment consonant with substandard intellectual quality.

The explicit assumption in this gloomy forecast is that a combination of outstanding political and business leadership and technical expertise is required to reduce the accumulated social and economic problems that distinguish the distressed areas from flourishing areas. It is also assumed that area initiative may yield fruitful results under almost any general economic conditions, but area progress can be rapid and lasting in a period of national prosperity, particularly when there is a strong federal commitment to assisting needy areas and needy people.

As a rule, each of the essential elements in the leadership-technical-expert pattern tend to be relatively weak in distressed areas. The political leadership is often inbred, weak, and factionalized to the point of near paralysis. A dearth of alternative opportunities combined with decades of selective out-migration have removed young, dedicated, well-educated, and well-motivated men and women whose views extend beyond limited local horizons. In job-hungry redevelopment areas, there is a parallel to underdeveloped nations. In both situations, most personal advancement is feasible only through inheritance, a rich marriage, or securing a niche on the political ladder. Setting aside a possible military career as a means of upward mobility, poor boys in either society tend to engage in fierce competition for the few lucrative local political openings available and to indulge in extensive private use of political office. As a result, local politics tends to revolve around personal cliques and petty scandals rather than public issues.

The business leadership in redevelopment areas has been diluted over the years by the dissolution or relocation of stronger local firms that, whatever their faults in "milking" their business and community, nevertheless retained strong local ties and supplied civic direction at critical junctures. The business newcomers tend either to be branch plant managers whose brief tenure permits little but noncontroversial, charitable activities, or marginal operators, often of an alien, suspect background, in a backwater economy. The latter group depends heavily on the favor of local politicians and tends to remain aloof from political controversy. Excluded from the area's inner social circles, the newcomers often strive to retain their ties to other areas. Like the branch managers, they are more often found in useful but essentially bland civic ventures rather than in reform politics.

Technicians employed by redevelopment areas are often underpaid, substandard professionals more akin in quality and outlook to local civil servants than to professional staff found in metropolitan communities. The occasional capable elected official finds himself seriously handicapped by the absence of technicians qualified to seek out federal and private outside capital and to design and implement effective programs. When a well-qualified technician is hired, he is usually a bird of passage whose term of service is brief; he is often repelled by local living conditions, especially by pay scales geared to poverty-level local standards rather than to inducement "combat pay" for services rendered under unfavorable conditions.

THE LOST GOLDEN AGE

Before proceeding to examine the indices of defective leadership, it may be worthwhile to sketch some of the history that preceded and helped to create the problem.

Redevelopment areas have been subjected to decades of economics travail so that, not unexpectedly, many residents have developed a special outlook. The struggle over 30 or 40 years to preserve their economic base has caused some residents to feel that history has put them through the wringer. Although past records indicate that, even in their heyday, mill towns offered grim living conditions for most of the residents, jobs were nonetheless plentiful. Thus, while their inequality with large metropolitan areas was established virtually from their inception, a persistent nostalgia prevails among older redevelopment area residents, including most of the 50- to 60-year-old leadership group, based on the supposition that conditions were far better in some bygone, almost mythical golden age. Against this glowing tapestry, present successes may appear hollow and trivial.

A persistent sense of having been bypassed by events has important implications. Residents in redevelopment areas and their elected officials tend to view themselves as the neglected orphans of the state and federal government. Often they nourish grievances that provide fertile soil for conflict. From the viewpoint of out-of-area officials, redevelopment area leaders seem exclusively preoccupied with continually demanding more local aid for ad hoc projects to the detriment of overall program planning. However, what to an outsider may appear to be merely local overreaction to outside proposals for reform or allocation is often traceable to the deep-rooted suspicion of state and federal governments growing out of local interpretations of past history. If redevelopment area officials display the "startle reflex" of a Maine jumper, lashing about in all directions to an unexpected tap on the shoulder, they have good cause. History for such areas has consisted of a series of plant closings and other nasty surprises, disasters that seemed to have grown up overnight from brief announcements on the back pages to banner headlines edged in black.

In addition to the myth of the lost golden age, one frequently encounters a remarkable amount of backbiting. There are many legends in distressed areas concerning the large manufacturing plant (often a branch of the Ford Motor Company) that was discouraged from locating by a key local firm which wanted to keep labor cheap and docile. There is also alleged to be an enormous amount of grafting among local officials, although on closer inspection, these venomous stories usually involve such piddling sums as to seem more closely related in scale if not reprehensiveness to robbing the poor box. On occasion, local businessmen are free with comments illustrative of the backwardness and laziness of the local labor supply that is alleged to prefer leisure and low pay to hard work at good wages. Beneath this underbrush of scurrility is a kind of chronic despair and a feeling of impotence in the face of the insoluble. To a great extent, the prevailing attitude is not that of the mainstream of our society; in fact, it is closer to what Americans have come to regard as the alien passivity that once seemed to characterize most underdeveloped nations in Asia, Latin America, and Africa.

The delusion which contrasts a happy, distant past with a difficult present and which tends to regard state and federal governments as insensitive to local needs makes it difficult to develop a reasonable, long-term strategy. Immediate problems seem so overwhelming that most areas tend to proceed from one fragmented effort to another, responding to transient local circumstances and to federal and state initiatives. There is continued frustration and a partly concealed conviction that local efforts are doomed by overwhelming historic forces, and that, consequently, current and future action will prove no more effective in reducing persistent problems to a tolerable condition than did the exhausting campaigns of the past. The result is a widespread feeling of running full speed on a treadmill. In addition, there tends to be mounting antipathy to perpetual mobilization for economic and/or industrial development: Many residents and their leaders are tired of never-ending contributions, speech making, publicity, meetings, and committees. Wearied by years of campaigning, at the first sign of a swallow (for example, a drop in unemployment rates), they are often only too ready to proclaim the advent of summer and to terminate further economic development operations.

New Bedford, one of Massachusetts' three larger (population 125,000) redevelopment areas, in the 1928–38 decade, provides a good example of the magnitude, character, and unrealized hopes that were generated by past economic development programs.[11] In 1928, an Industrial Development Division was established in the city's Board of Commerce to seek out new industry and to assist existing firms. The spring of 1929 saw the inauguration of a "Help New Bedford Plan" involving a public exposition of local products. This was followed in 1930 by the "New Bedford Forward" movement, also initiated by the Board of Commerce to bring together suggestions on attracting specific industries.

In 1938, the mayor created a new organization, the Industrial Development Legion. Following the example of the AEF (or the Salvation Army), he designated himself commander in chief, issued a declaration of war against unemployment, and appointed a chief of staff and a number of colonels. These field-grade officers were in turn empowered to appoint captains and lieutenants. A two-year enlistment term was established, corps designations were assigned, military reviews conducted, and distinguished community service medals awarded.

Most of the new plants induced to settle in the city in response to this offensive were low-investment, low-wage, light industries. The city offered the manufacturer 10 million square feet of vacant textile mill space at 10 to 12 cents per square foot. One firm was provided with free heat, free repairs, and a nightwatchman; free boiler facilities were offered to another; and the city sold a $750,000 mill to a third for $500. In another instance, workers employed by a failing cotton textile plant agreed to take a voluntary 10 percent cut from their weekly wages to pay the company's creditors: Four months later, the mill closed. Textile employees also contributed part of their slender earnings in vain attempts to save two other mills. The American Legion paid most of the moving costs for another manufacturing plant. Yet, despite these valiant efforts, by 1938, New Bedford's nontextile industries had provided employment for only one-fifth as many workers as had been displaced by the employment losses in the city's cotton textile industry over the previous decade.

New Bedford's experience was shared by other cities. The Committee on the New England Textile Industry appointed by the New England governors concluded, as recently as 1952, that it was "imperative" to maintain the textile industry in New England. The committee's study of seven textile towns "showed what happens when a mill closes or migrates. Community depression tends to persist even in years of national prosperity: tax rates rise; skills are lost; and the new industries that come into the depressed town are usually lower wage industries."[12] The committee reported that all seven communities tried vigorously to find substitute employment, offering subsidies such as free space, financial aid, and tax favors. Another study noted that Fall River, another textile city, granted major tax concessions in an attempt to retain remaining textile firms. Not only was there an adverse immediate fiscal impact, but the attempt was a failure: in 1950, textiles, which provided 44 percent of total manufacturing jobs in Fall River, contributed only 5 percent of the city's property taxes.[13]

At the time, Fall River's major industry "appeared to be reasonably well stabilized" in the committee's view. However, an earlier research study included a pessimistic but more accurate prognostication: "It seems unlikely that a period of [postwar] readjustment would pass without further reduction in the city's textile capacity."[14] And so it was. Like the fruitless efforts to save jobs in the coal industry and in marginal agriculture in other distressed areas, time, energy, and money were sacrificed with little measurable result aside from fiscal disaster and a residue of suspicion, civic exhaustion, and pessimism.

The result of decades of only partially rewarding struggles is, in some cases, a weakening of resilience and apathetic acquiescence rather than an eager response to outside stimuli and opportunity. Moreover, there is a growing belief that solutions, if these are to be forthcoming, will emerge from new federal programs rather than from local initiative. To a considerable extent, this supposition is well grounded in the fiscal facts of life. A number of areas clearly cannot afford to pay for many of the public improvements they obviously need. But surrender to passivity is also based upon a misconception of the nature of state and federal programs. Although it is true that most of the new investment funds pouring into the areas may be federal (or, less commonly, state) in origin, both their magnitude and their use depend largely upon the locality and its initiative. As a result, enormous interarea differences occur in the size, nature, and impact achieved by urban renewal, public works, manpower training, and antipoverty programs. The funds may be largely external in origin, but local use thereof and the impact created are largely determined by the sophistication and vigor of local leadership.

Local action is particularly vital. The practice of central government channeling large-scale economic development to redevelopment areas that is operative in parts of Europe is not now and is not likely ever to be adopted by the United States. In the United States, general grant-in-aid programs which are also available to and usually more heavily utilized by flourishing areas, far overshadow special programs to aid distressed areas. Area development, therefore, involves the task of sharpening area and community skills in securing and implementing aid from the federal and state governments, a technique that can be described as "public entrepreneurship."

It has been suggested that the major problems of distressed areas are their inability, or sometimes unwillingness, to invest in high-quality education, and their participation in proportion to their needs in federal programs.

> A region which is economically anemic is likely to underinvest in education; not necessarily in relation to its resources, but in relation to social return and the private return to the clientele. Moreover the institutional fabric is such that one cannot assume that it will upon its own initiative take full advantage of generalized programs of assistance, especially if they require local financial participation.[15]

URBAN RENEWAL EXPENDITURES: A MEASURE OF PUBLIC ENTREPRENEURSHIP

Assuming that the problems are roughly uniform and that all large communities are theoretically capable of conducting programs to deal with their physical and social deficiencies, one would expect that there would be no major disparity in the scale of their problem-solving, federally aided operations. However, this is not the case: On a per capita basis, Boston is by far the leader in urban renewal funding in Massachusetts. Why is this pattern so lopsided? Smaller communities receive their proportionate share of public assistance and unemployment compensation, funds allocated by the government directly to the individual recipient. But funds for renewal and poverty are forthcoming only on a community basis to municipalities that can pass a number of tests of skill and endurance. Desperate need is not enough. The community must have an effective organization, must be capable of satisfying complex and rapidly changing federal criteria, and must be able to compete for funds against rival claimants in regional and federal offices and in the state house. Moreover, if it wishes to receive further allocations, it must exhibit some evidence of performance. In short, the community must be able to operate like a large, efficient corporation with substantial government contracts.

As in the case of business corporations, perhaps there is a critical-size factor involved in attracting federal money. Smaller Massachusetts cities do not carry the political weight of Boston, nor do they have Boston's special potential for expansion, as shown in the development of a major Government Center, a Prudential Insurance Center, or a medical complex. Even allowing for their smaller size, they lack a proportional potential for expansion in government, finance, business services, medicine, and higher education, all of which are among the nation's key growth industries. But other compensating factors work in favor of the smaller communities in securing government aid. Federal and state agencies are normally reluctant to concentrate disproportionate amounts of their funds in a few large cities. Agency survival and expansion require a broad base of political support and this, in turn, depends upon practical demonstrations of their concern for districts that contain no metropolises. For this reason, federal and state agencies are often more than eager to channel some of their largesse into the needy smaller cities. But they cannot respond without an effective local stimulus, and many smaller cities are unable to generate approvable applications for funds. Thus, whatever the federal hesitations, an undeniable tendency exists to continue pouring large amounts of money into the same handful of cities. It is partially the result of momentum; once begun, programs cannot be choked off in midstream. Furthermore, as the large city increases its technical abilities, it is able to keep abreast of rapidly changing, extraordinarily complicated criteria for new types of programs.

To get down to first causes, however, the comparative grant-in-aid starvation of the small and medium-sized city in redevelopment areas is primarily a consequence of a deficiency in the combination of expertise and leadership.[16] There is apparently a shortage of specialized skills—those needed to qualify for funds in programs requiring substantial public entrepreneurship. Yet, some small cities have shown that size is not an insuperable handicap. New Haven, with a population of about 150,000 and in receipt of per capita federal renewal and antipoverty funding greater than Boston's, is one nearby example. There is an obvious correlation between New Haven and Boston. It is Edward Logue, the head of the Boston Redevelopment Authority in the 1960s, who had made his reputation in New Haven.

The example selected for purposes of comparison, the urban renewal program, is only a sample of a wide range of government assistance available to the active city. In passing, in view of the harsh criticisms leveled at urban renewal and other programs, it may be in order to remind ourselves that these are voluntary programs; the community has to exert considerable effort to participate at all. The undeniable hardships that were perpetrated in the 1950s when poor families were displaced as a result of badly conceived renewal projects represent, one would hope, both a deficiency in the state of the art of redevelopment planning and an inability of the disadvantaged to swing much political weight. The grant-in-aid program is an instrument: the community, in its wisdom or lack thereof, and through its political leadership, can use it well, or badly, or leave it alone.

There is no conclusive evidence to explain why the smaller Massachusetts cities, particularly central cities in redevelopment areas, have been less successful in securing federal and state grants-in-aid than Boston. But three hypotheses can be offered.

1. Redevelopment areas tend to be provincial. In an era of instant communication via mass media, it seems ridiculous to suggest that municipal officials can be unaware of the ground rules of applying for, receiving, and implementing federal aid; yet this is the case. The new programs are complicated, and a mayor's two-year term can slip by before he has found the time to comprehend the paper-work involved in these new programs. Moreover,

there are sometimes lingering pockets of hostility to federal aid reminiscent of the 1930s, residual attitudes to big government that predate the era of relatively amicable coexistence that began with the Eisenhower years.

2. Local bureaucracies are often weak. Mayors would find life easier if they could rely on a cadre of vigorous, flexible, and imaginative civil servants. Too often, they inherit instead an aging bureaucracy, barely capable of coping with routine operations and sometimes unable to select reputable consultants. Cities in redevelopment areas are simply not attracting their share of the available young talent, for, by and large, they offer neither inspiring nor remunerative employment for ambitious youth. The occasional, outstanding civil-servant-in-residence is often lured away by talent scouts from the federal agencies, larger cities, or private enterprise.

3. "Little league" criteria are used as the basis of self-evaluation. Too many redevelopment areas seem willing, even anxious, to settle for less in achievement, in salaries, and in aspirations. The local leadership is often inordinately proud of what exists, and it tends to be fearful of urging innovation lest calls for reform be construed as denigration of friends and neighbors. Thus, the smallness in scale and the closeness of personal ties tend to mute needed criticism and mitigate the dissatisfaction that must precede progress. To cite a specific example, salary levels for planning and redevelopment directors are often pegged to the level of that of the mayor despite the facts that the mayor is considered a part-time functionary who usually has a supplementary income from a business or law firm, and redevelopment areas that possess few instrinsic nonmonetary attractions for professional staff (such as major universities) must offer more rather than less cash to lure scarce talent.

The case is not entirely hopeless, however. It would not be accurate to imply that Masschusetts redevelopment areas have not managed to secure substantial inputs of federal and state capital. Each of the commonwealth redevelopment areas benefited from the federal-state highway program, each had antipoverty operations in progress, each has urban renewal projects in various stages of execution, and all contain, are within easy commuting distance of, or were scheduled to receive regional vocational schools, community colleges, state teachers colleges, and medical care institutions.

However, as the data on urban renewal expenditures suggest, the amounts received are not proportional to the population of the redevelopment areas, and they are even less commensurate with their relatively greater physical and human resource problems. Most have experienced frustrating difficulties in the application and implementation stage of these programs. For this reason, it is proper to identify public entrepreneurship as a distinct problem in redevelopment planning.

It seems clear that the city that is willing and able to act can secure a proportionate share of federal aid. On the whole, however, it appears unlikely that the imbalance can be corrected solely through local efforts. The cycle of inadequate skills and outlooks that traps poor families in poverty seems to apply equally to distressed cities and others not as destitute. What is apparently needed is a combination of outside technical assistance from state and federal sources and a greater local willingness to play by "big league" rules and standards.

Unless both are forthcoming—and soon—the skill gap between "haves" and "have nots" will grow wider. Just as the ill-trained poor find it increasingly difficult to advance in an education-oriented career structure, so will the poorly staffed city find it harder to qualify for the large amounts of federal and state aid that are available only to the sophisticated public entrepreneur.[17]

James L. Sundquist and David W. Davis put the problem succinctly:

> When the federal government is ready to extend financial assistance, the local communities must be ready to receive it. For that purpose, the federal government requires a network of expert grantsmen at the community level no less than the communities themselves require it.[18]

The difficulty is that the network is incomplete: real experts in this field are scarce, and they tend to shy away from most smaller cities and the distressed areas.

Dennis O'Harrow, the former executive director of the American Society of Planning Officials, summarized the trend toward complexity in government programs:

> In the beginning [back in 1954] you got your workable program accepted merely by professing good intentions. . . . Now a dozen years later, you have to deliver on your promises, or the purse out of which urban renewal grants are paid is closed to you. . . . Thc next step beyond urban renewal . . . is called the comprehensive city demonstration program. . . . The rules will be proof of financial ability, proper administration . . . modern building code[s] . . . will be some of the prerequisites. . . . Some day the federal coordinator will say you get no money for urban renewal until you clear up the pollution in your river, until you stop pouring guck into the air, until you set up a decent education system, until you build adequate medical facilities . . . we can be sure that he who pays the piper is readying up some new tunes to call.[19]

The chief difficulty appears to lie in the political and business sphere. As we have noted, good leadership is hard to come by in such areas. There are, however, a few hopeful signs. With the passage of time, the older leaders who still bear the scars of past failures are leaving the scene. In their place is emerging a new, more hopeful breed of better-educated, more widely traveled leaders whose horizons and aspirations are more comparable to those of flourishing areas.

A second source of optimism is the potential technical expertise that can be tapped in the universities and colleges located in redevelopment areas. Growing community colleges, state colleges, and technical institutes can be found in or near many redevelopment areas. In addition to the possibility of using regular faculty, it may be possible to attract and retain competent technicians who might otherwise prove unreceptive, particularly if close linkages can be forged with major out-of-area universities. Here again, local initiative is essential: Federal funds are available to assist small colleges in developing and maintaining quality standards through working arrangements with universities, but securing such funds requires aggressiveness and sophistication. The promise of a college environment—insulation from the political hurly-burly and faculty status—can be powerful lures for the professional who might otherwise be repelled by the prospect of a career in a redevelopment area. If the redevelopment area is not to evolve into a fully employed but low-wage area, providing resident strong backs and migrant strong minds for the nation, it must attempt to convert its specialized role into a more balanced replica of the great metropolis.

What of the communities in which leadership was, is, and will probably remain incompetent, corrupt, or simply inadequate? The question arises as to the degree that the unfortunate citizenry, especially nonvoting children, should be penalized by a geographic accident. In such cases, the only answer seems to be an increased reliance on direct federal-government-to-individual and federal-government-to-family programs that do not have to filter through the local government structure. Scholarships, welfare allowances, and medical grants may provide the prototype family allowances; relocation grants and other district forms of aid unrelated to the quality of local government may help to compensate for some of the disparity in public entrepreneurship.

An important objective in formulating area development programs should be the improvement of the environment and the quality of human resources, including the strengthening of local pools of talent that should be the sources of political leadership. Under the American political system, the local political candidate is usually a long-term area resident. A look at the congressional and senatorial pattern often discloses a reasonably close relationship between a backward economy and a retarded political outlook on the part of elected representatives, even to the point of being a retrogressive influence in national legislation. Politics in a long-distressed area often revolve around bread-and-butter patronage topped with emotional rhetoric that capitalizes on local sentiments, reflecting estrangement from national patterns. It is in the national interest, therefore, that strenuous efforts be made to augment the intellectual resources of the redevelopment area. A flourishing metropolis, as the host of a steady stream of distressed area migrants, therefore has a strong interest in the educational and medical backgrounds of these people as well as in their willingness and ability to perform as productive citizens.

MIGRANT TYPES AND MIGRANT PROBLEMS

In the past three centuries, the United States has been the recipient of millions of foreign immigrants. Between 1820 and 1976, over 50 million immigrants, primarily from Europe and for the most part unskilled or poorly skilled, came to settle throughout the nation. Most tended to concentrate in urban areas in the nation's northeastern quadrant.

While this process is well known, the process of internal migration has —at least until recently—been the subject of much less attention. One type of internal migrant has become an object of concern; over 4 million blacks moved out of the South between 1940 and 1976 or, similarly, legal and illegal relocation and immigration of Latin Americans, by some estimates in the 10 million range, has become a serious issue. Increasingly, as these disadvantaged groups become urban residents, the migration involves movement from city to city, a trend which tends to diminish some of the culture shock attendant on relocation from farms to urban slums. For the most part, the great historic migrant stream of white migrants from the rural areas and small towns to the city has been welcomed. The farm boy, with little education but alert and eager, who rises rapidly in the world, is a major theme in American legend. The problems of rural migrants only began to cause major concern when the movers were black, brown, or bleached Appalachian.

A third type of migrant, the relocatee from urban redevelopment areas, is the subject of this chapter. Usually Caucasian and fairly well educated, this type of migrant is warmly welcomed by employers in large metropolitan receiving areas. Unfortunately, he also represents a serious loss to his home area.

The American metropolis is the meeting place of these distinctive types of migrants. In order to understand the role of the urban relocatees, it is desirable to examine briefly the role of the immigrant from abroad, the migrant black, and the rural small-town migrants attracted to the big cities.

Migration Trends in Redevelopment Areas

Certain parts of the nation have long served as breeding grounds for the production of workers for larger industrial centers because a sizable segment of the population continues to reside in economic backwaters, unable to provide enough jobs for their labor force. As long as this pattern persists (and it will, unless there is a totally unforeseen reallocation of economic development), there will remain definable and identifiable areas where outmigration can be expected to be a way of life.

Outmigration tends to be one of the more sensitive issues among community leaders in redevelopment areas. Some meet the problem by refusing to discuss it; others deny that it exists at all or suggest that the very next census will see an upturn in population; still others call for major federal efforts to reverse the tide by stimulating the growth of the local economy to the point where it can provide jobs for its young people. It would be fair to say that few have faced the prospect with candor and realism. Many distressed areas have been particularly remiss in failing to prepare the majority of their young people to be fully competitive in out-of-area labor markets; they tend to be recruits for the lower end of the employment spectrum, not management trainees. In part, this failure in education is due to a consistent pattern of investment choices in distressed areas that favors allocations for construction over investments in human capital as the major strategy for area renewal. The redevelopment area leadership tends to opt for physical investments that generate visible campaign material, construction contracts, and jobs, and that promise the area future economic growth. On the other hand, investments in human resources, as experience demonstrates, involve sizable allocations to highly portable assets. Poor areas see no reason to beggar themselves in educating their children only to have their graduates pick up and leave; the harvest of investment in human resources may be reaped by other areas in the form of migrating skilled workers. There was also the tendency in past years to regard undereducated, low-wage labor as a major asset in attracting new industry, and it was believed by some that too much education spoiled a docile, hard-working (and inexpensive) labor force. It is only relatively recently that the need for first-rate schools and well-educated workers has been recognized by local development organizations which discovered that an adequate school system was a prerequisite for advanced types of industry. In earlier years, all the stress was on the eagerness and trainability of a willing, energetic labor force, grateful for any regular job at improved wages.

There are, however, a number of more basic reasons for resistance at facing the prospect of continued outmigration and of designing programs associated with the process. Many redevelopment area leaders sincerely believe that their people are better off at home, low wages or no. There are numerous studies (some of them vividly portrayed in fiction and nonfiction) devoted to the plight of the newly arrived migrant. The easily fleeced rubes, greenhorns, and yokels caught in the snares and ground to dust by the callous environment of the big town are still a topic of concern in fact as well as fiction. Clearly, the wrenching apart of family ties, the loss of an accustomed place in a stable social order, the exposure to debilitating slums, and the sometimes disastrous effects of the health of those relocating in the big cities can be very real threats to the well-being of the migrant.

Much time, effort, and money will be allocated to the problems created by the adjustment of the migrant in the next generation; the hardships encountered by earlier generations of migrants in the city slums are also still very much with us. As far as urban distressed areas are concerned, however, the adjustment problems caused by immigration are relatively minor. The social and economic strains on the big city or on the migrant himself are very much reduced when the migrant from the "sending" distressed area is white, has an urban background, and has completed two or more years of high school. Certainly any problems that may arise in the "receiving" area are susceptible to relatively simple solutions as compared to the complexities involved in facilitating a smooth integration of a rural, racially different, or non-English-speaking population.

SKIMMING OFF THE CREAM

In a highly mobile society like the United States, where one person in five changes his residence each year, the decision to pull up stakes often is far from a matter fraught with trauma or drama. Migration is a matter of fact, concomitant with a variety of high-status occupations. This generalization concerning the ease of migration is by no means applicable to a very large portion of the population. While restlessness affects the young, there is a strong homing instinct at work that makes for powerful attachments to one's home area. Furthermore, many parents regard rapid modern communications as no substitute for close physical proximity to their children and grandchildren.

This chapter is concerned not with the personal strains and hardships linked to migration of the young, but with its long-term effects on the future and on urban distressed areas. Migration from distressed areas may lead to deterioration of leadership, leaving such communities "abandoned to their own incompetence."[20] Moreover, the process may in time be almost irreversible if the labor force loses most of its attraction for new investments. If the migrant is young, well trained, and currently employed, as a large proportion of them are, the "sending" area's economic potential may thereby be diminished. A loss of skilled and enterprising persons may render an area less capable of reviving itself than before the migration took place.[21]

A research study on distressed area problems in Western Europe concluded that

> as virtually all studies show, voluntary migration is selective and greatly reduces the quality of the labor force remaining in redevelopment areas. With its age distribution becoming progressively poorer, the labor force degenerates into a pool of obsolete skills. . . . Full employment by itself cannot solve these problems [of the redevelopment areas]; indeed, it may well aggravate them by the progressive deterioration resulting from selective mobility.[22]

These observations are also fully applicable to urban redevelopment areas in the United States. For example, research studies show that in 12 chronically depressed areas in Pennsylvania, migration in the 1950s was concentrated in the prime working years, ages 25 to 44.[23]

On the basis of past performance, it can be expected that many youths will leave redevelopment areas after completing 6 to 12 years of public education. One report concluded that "the more a depressed region aids in the education of an individual, the greater the probability that the particular individual will leave the region of his education."[24] Since public and private family costs involved in nurturing and training children are quite heavy, the strain on family and local government finances in redevelopment areas is a major argument for increased contribution from outside sources to assist in child rearing. The plea for outside aid for child development seems particularly appropriate because many of these children represent part of the future labor force for more wealthy, economically expanding areas.

A disproportionate number of migrants from most distressed areas are young people—family heads under age 35 and college graduates. Only a small proportion of the family heads in redevelopment area cities were under 35 as compared to their counterparts in the suburbs, and slightly over 1 in 4 adults in the nation has had some college training compared to only 1 in 7 in U.S. redevelopment areas.

Lingering Impact of Migration

One result of migration is the creation of an "hourglass effect" in the age distribution pyramid. This means that fewer working-age people are available to support a relatively large proportion of dependent children and older people.[25]

Of the two types of dependents, it is the elderly who seem to be dominant in the outlook of urban redevelopment areas. The heavy outmigration of the younger, restless, ambitious, and articulate population leaves the social and political orientation to reflect the conservative patterns associated with a pessimistic older generation whose outlook is conditioned by generations of failure.

The impact of this selective migration on smaller communities is reflected in the inability of local and state governments to keep up with the times:

> The cream of small-town creativity has soured as small-town vitality has diminished. . . . By the end of World War II, these places consisted mainly of those who did not want to try to advance under the new rules . . . state government is suffering from an overdose of the small-town political ideology. . . . A querulousness about government "frills" is almost all that remains of the once-proud doctrine of small-town individualism. . . . Small-town morality finds no place for suspected academic or intellectual dreamers. . . . The trained specialist is regarded as a "fuzzy-minded" idealist, an overeducated fool.[26]

There are other more mundane side effects of the swelling numbers of aging population. As the number of older persons increases, public welfare costs rise, and the pressure on limited family income grows more burdensome.

Family incomes in redevelopment areas also feel the impact of demands from another quarter. The redevelopment area is a nursery as well as an old-folks home; the base of the age pyramid is relatively larger in relation to working-age population. The costs of educating and rearing the young can be ill afforded by areas in which wage levels are low and the tax base grows slowly, if at all.

Migration and Unemployment Rates

It would be unreasonable to dwell wholly on the unfavorable impact of migration. Of all the alternative manpower strategies open to distressed areas, the most disastrous is to encourage a deceleration in migration if enough jobs cannot be provided for their labor force. The obvious consequences of such a policy are rapidly mounting unemployment and welfare rates, and social unrest.

There is a long-standing tradition for ambitious young people in stagnant areas to pull up stakes for greener pastures. Tocqueville indicated that

> in 1830 thirty-six of the members of Congress were born in the little state of Connecticut. The population of Connecticut, which constitutes only one forty-third part of that of the United States, thus furnished one eighth of the whole body of representatives. The state of Connecticut of itself, however, sends only five delegates to Congress; and the thirty-one others sit for the new Western states. If these thirty-one individuals had remained in Connecticut, it is probable that, instead of becoming rich landowners, they would have remained humble laborers, that they would have lived in obscurity, without being able to rise into public life, and that, far from becoming useful legislators, they might have been unruly citizens.[27]

In contrast to potential negative, long-term effects, there can be a positive, short-run impact from outmigration of the working-age population. In the case of the city of New Bedford, a back-up in the migration stream during the Great Depression had disastrous effects on local unemployment rates.[28] In 1937, unemployment reached 32.3 percent for the "gainful workers" in the city, as compared to 18 percent in the state and 16 percent in the nation. In February 1939, approximately one-quarter of the city's population was dependent on public assistance.[29]

If the migrant is one of the long-term unemployed for whom local job prospects are poor, the area—and the nation—clearly benefits from his leaving if he can find work elsewhere or if his children can eventually find work of a quality that is simply not available in the distressed area. Some retailers and landlords may suffer, congressmen may complain about the loss of seats when the population diminishes, and many canons of American "growthmanship" may be violated, but most will agree that productive employment is preferable to stagnating idleness. In the absence of a very heavy, continuing outmigration from rural areas with high birth rates, the "sending" areas would be faced with extremely serious social and economic problems. The scale is much larger than may appear on the surface: One study found that in Alabama, a movement of 465,000 people from agriculture in the course of a decade reduced the farm labor force by only 127,000. The reason: In the same period, 338,000 new farm workers entered the labor force.[30]

There is a direct parallel between the relocation from domestic urban redevelopment areas and the "brain drain" in the United States and Western Europe that was the subject of much complaint among the drainees before the tide was reversed in the recessions of the 1970s. Unlike migration of unskilled or semiskilled labor, brain drains are often based on courtship rather than accident. In addition to their domestic recruiting programs, American firms have assiduously advertised in European newspapers for technical manpower. A British observer wrote in the mid-1960s:

> The Americans do not look for our selling or marketing men . . . it is our Ph.D and M.Sc. rather than B.Sc. men, that the Americans want—and get. . . . Our most sophisticated technological skills are drawn to the super-civilization, with California at the heart of the brain drain area . . . almost as many of our physicists go into American industry as into our own.[31]

By the 1970s the emphasis had shifted to medicine; many big-city hospitals were staffed by foreign-born, foreign-trained doctors in proportions ranging from 10 to 30 percent.

Commutation a Solution?

There is another method of attacking unemployment problems without depending either on local growth or outmigration—namely, commutation from redevelopment areas. Redevelopment areas located near flourishing metropolitan areas can make use of the larger metropolis as a cultural magnet to help in hiring and retaining professional and managerial talent. It is conceivable that through intensified, carefully designed education and training programs, which would improve the competitive characteristics of the labor force of these areas, and with the help of modern highways, a larger proportion of the distressed area's labor pool may be able to commute to job centers within relatively easy driving distance. While expanded commutation will not help much to alleviate local tax-base problems, commuting is probably preferable (from a redevelopment area standpoint) to outright migration and is clearly more desirable than a slowdown or back-up in migration that might increase area unemployment and public welfare rates such as occurred during the Great Depression.

There is another overlooked benefit from commutation. Well-educated executives and professionals employed in larger, nearby metropolitan areas have purchased homes in distressed area fringe suburbs. While they retain their occupational ties to their place of employment, in time the executives (and their wives) become increasingly involved in local affairs. To date, their influence has been most in evidence in community rather than area concerns, particularly in the improvement of the public schools. This influx of resident-commuter talent can have a significant impact on area standards and programs. It is particularly difficult to involve outcommuting suburban residents in the severe problems of central cities in which they have not visible ties. A commitment to area civic and development programs can serve as a useful substitute and possibly as an entree into the more vexations problems of the core neighborhoods.

The lower educational levels in redevelopment areas raise certain questions regarding more than the welcome that many migrants are likely to receive in the competitive labor markets of larger areas. Much remains to be done in providing children in all areas of the nation with a solid educational foundation.

Jobs for Low-Skill Migrants?

The trend toward increasing formal education and training for many occupations has led some to believe that while earlier immigrant groups could easily be absorbed in unskilled jobs, the current crop of migrants from distressed areas are difficult to integrate into the economy.

There is one distinction that must be clarified. Despite the evidence that migrants from redevelopment areas tend to be young, well motivated, and fairly well educated,[32] there is a considerable body of public and professional opinion that seems to confuse these relocatees with ill-prepared, rural migrants. Much of the public apparently believes that most migrants are more interested in access to welfare payments than in available jobs. This dim view of the migrant stream has ancient roots; each ethnic group has been scorned by its predecessors, who, forgetful of their chilly initial reception, maintain that the newcomers represent the dregs of humanity. This is not solely a matter of lay opinion. Some serious students of migration suggest that many migrants represent an inferior labor force component and hence make only a marginal contribution to the economy to which they relocate.[33] The result, they maintain, is a decline in per capita income and other adverse consequences in the receiving area. There are those, including the author, who see redevelopment area migration as a help to receiving areas but a diminution of attractions and talent to the redevelopment areas. On the other hand, some have adopted a rosier viewpoint, suggesting that such migration benefits both sending and host areas.

Perhaps the cautious answer is that the impact depends on circumstances —that, depending on employment conditions and prospects in the redevelopment areas, migration may be a help or hindrance to sending areas, to receiving areas, and to migrants themselves. At the present time, for example, there can be little reason to suggest that migrants from any type of area who will accept previously unfilled, low-wage service jobs are a drag on the area's economy. The difficulty is that migration is associated with the relocation of a demoralized rural population rather than the sober, industrious, and thereby virtually invisible migrants who staff a sizable proportion of the jobs in growing areas in the 1970s.

Earlier generations of migrants were welcomed as a source of casual labor in mills and service industries to perform a variety of tasks calling for muscle power rather than schooling. It is pointed out that while previous generations picked up most of their training on the job, this is no longer the case. Over two-thirds of the nation's workers aged 55 to 64 did not receive formal vocational training, while almost the reverse was true of persons in the 22 to 24 age bracket.[34]

This is a matter of direct concern to redevelopment areas as well as to receiving areas. Is a significant amount of formal schooling and occupational training really required to qualify local labor for available jobs within redevelopment areas or as migrants to other areas? If a high-school education and several years of formal training are actually prerequisites for all occupations, the chances of reducing distressed area unemployment would be substantially decreased, and receiving areas would have some justification for the jaundiced view they sometimes adopt toward immigrants. Fortunately, the problem seems to be overstated. Good motivation combined with modest basic schooling and good health is still the key to employment. Many white-collar as well as blue-collar occupations require only a limited amount of formal education in combination with on-the-job training or short-term vocational courses.

There are many examples of migrants with modest education but good motivation who have made a highly successful adjustment to modern urban conditions. It would appear that, despite the gloom over the disappearance of jobs for unskilled laborers and domestics, there is an adequate quantity of low-paying job openings each year. If the migrant is steadily employed, is respectful of home and property, and sends his children to school, he is quickly assimilated into metropolitan areas and is nobody's problem. This description applies to most of the present migrant stream from redevelopment areas and to a large and overlooked proportion of black migrants from rural areas.[35]

Surveys among large employers lend further support to the belief that lack of occupational training or formal vocational training is not a major obstacle to hiring. Many prefer to hire well-motivated individuals and to train them in company techniques and methods. Efficient, short-term training programs in these companies have produced better results than have been obtainable through less-concentrated and less-tailored manpower programs conducted with state and federal assistance.

This tendency to bypass formal occupational training is apparently confirmed by the U.S. Department of Labor, which shows that the majority of workers in most nonprofessional occupations either learned their trade on the job or picked it up through "casual" means. In 1950, the data indicate that three-fourths of the nation's labor force had received less that six months of training for their present jobs,[36] a pattern which did not change materially in later years. This accounts, in part, for the success of a number of public and employer short-term (less than 12-month) manpower training courses. In most instances, there has been no difficulty in locating employment for graduates of short-term courses designed to meet manpower needs in growth sectors of the economy.

Furthermore, it has been suggested that the possibilities of using poorly educated labor have not yet been fully explored. Aside from the development of "new careers for the poor" as subprofessional aides, there is the possibility of expanding a variety of public services to create hundreds of thousands or even millions of jobs in periods of recession. Twice-a-day mail deliveries, day nurseries for working mothers, the development of home health aid programs, foster grandparent programs, conservation and beautification programs could absorb large quantities of such labor. The recommendation that government assume the role of "employer of last resort" for the jobless could be adopted in an era of increasing public revenues and rising demand for an improved environment and better public services.

In recent years, there has been much criticism of vocational training programs[37] and job-locating services for the poor, particularly minority groups. Charges that past employment efforts were excessively concentrated on "dead-end," low-wage, low-status occupations have led to demands for programs aimed at providing job opportunities within the mainstream of the labor force. It has been urged that jobs and training for the disadvantaged be restructured to offer the possibility of upgrading and advancement based on merit, training, and application.

Substantial resistance to employment in low-paying, menial jobs in the underside of the economy is a new phenomenon. Black and white teen-agers who choose unemployment or streetcorner hustling in preference to employment as hospital attendants, kitchen help, stockroom workers, and carwashers stigmatize such jobs as slave labor, unacceptable for modern youth. This represents a significant change from immigrant generations who shouldered pick and shovel, shoved pushcarts and wheelbarrows, and generally, willingly or not, took whatever jobs were available. The new-careers approach is based in part on questionable premises regarding occupational trends, but it accurately reflects a widespread, overt distaste for jobs that carry neither prestige, money, nor hope for the future. Moves to develop career continuums are not only desirable but may be inescapable if the streetcorner youth is to be attracted into the mainstream of society. Experience may suggest, however, that the new-careers approach benefits those who would have done fairly well in its absence, among them the migrants from urban distressed areas.

EMPLOYMENT BARRIERS AND MIGRATION

One reason for resistance to inmigration of poorly educated labor is empirical evidence that more schooling is a characteristic of the persons employed in an increasing number of occupations. However, it is often not recognized that this trend is largely a function of generally rising levels of education rather than the imposition of stiffer educational prerequisites by employers or unions.

Inflated educational prerequisites may range from requiring high-school graduation to advanced degrees. Close examination would reveal no rational need for such levels of education in a wide variety of occupations that now require the symbolic parchment. Remedial action to remove or at least reduce job discrimination practices along with the fraudulent inflation of job prerequisites would appear to deserve high priority. They not only contribute to making life more difficult for the less-educated migrants from redevelopment areas but also create unnecessary trouble in providing adequate jobs for all types of disadvantaged workers, including rural migrants.

AUTOMATION AND FUTURE MANPOWER NEEDS

An issue that has generated considerable discussion is the impact of automation on future demand for poorly educated workers of the type available in large numbers in distressed areas and in slum areas of large cities.[38] During the 1950s and early 1960s, some scholars predicted that many industries would follow the lead of mining and agriculture (that is, manufacturing output would increase with a smaller work force as a consequence of heavy capital investments in labor-saving machinery).

Some of the popular publications in the 1960s suggested that the new jobs opened up by an increasingly complex technology would tend to be restricted to holders of college degrees or at least to persons with substantial post-high-school training. However, experience seems to indicate that, while in its early, pioneering stages, a new process requires highly trained staff, in time, routinization leads to job simplification, opening up the field to less well-educated and less expensive personnel. To take one striking example, computer programing was at first restricted to college graduates and included many Ph.D. mathematicians, but by the mid-1960s, high-school graduation followed by short-term specialist training was an acceptable background for a new programer.

Without delving into the detailed reasoning underlying these persuasive, conflicting scholarly works, it may be noted that if the gloomier predictions had proved accurate, the market for distressed area labor in the 1960s would be considerably smaller than it actually was, and fewer migrants could anticipate successful relocation. To date, however, automation has not had this type of impact. This does not mean that automation may not have a depressing effect on future demands for labor, especially in some areas that may experience severe employment cuts without compensating job gains. Dozens of dying mining communities testify to the fact that automation can have a crippling impact on a vulnerable local economy. However, up to the present time and perhaps over the next decade, automation seems not to have dehydrated overall manpower demand in large metropolitan areas, nor has it eroded the number of jobs for which modest skills are enough for entry. There is, in fact, no reason to believe that automation was in any way responsible for the increase in unemployment which occurred in the mid-1970s.

NOTES FOR A GOVERNMENT POLICY

From the viewpoint of governmental policy, there are at least two ways of looking at the problems of distressed areas. The first is to decide that their problems are largely beyond their control and that what is needed is federal policy. This approach would aim at allocating regional investment in order to maximize national economic growth and only secondarily to maintain "a certain interregional balance in levels of living, at least sufficient to preserve political stability in support of the drive to national growth."[39] Under this policy, the role of distressed areas would be extremely circumscribed; they could engage in "adaptive" planning of a "limited kind to exert a modest influence on improving their economy and their environment."[40]

A second approach to area development is implicit in federal distressed area legislation and allied federal programs. It assumes that national patterns and trends offer considerable room for local initiative, particularly because deliberate federal policy to write off the distressed areas in favor of flourishing metropolitan areas is not politically realistic.

These positions are obviously simplified. The polarity that has been indicated is actually more of a continuum, because few specialists hold extreme views. Nevertheless, the difference in approach is a crucial one, as one or the other basic assumption colors entire sets of policies and investment patterns.

On the whole, it may be concluded that the redevelopment area can do a great deal to influence its environment and its economic future. I hasten to explain that this by no means suggests that there is no need for national policies. Redevelopment areas lack both money and talent, and unless there is federal aid to help fill these deficiencies, they are not equipped to do very much to improve their social and cultural base and will continue to do an inadequate job of preparing many of their future migrants.

Some of the programs related to a national policy for redevelopment areas were mentioned earlier. The Economic Development Districts created under the 1965 Public Works and Economic Development Act, with their provisions for selecting and stimulating growth centers, have helped to a limited extent in creating more attractions for bright, well-educated people. Federal aid programs for institutions of higher learning have helped to strengthen cultural facilities. Assistance for public-school systems, urban renewal, manpower training, health services, industrial parks, and other aspects of urban life are all available, often on preferential terms for redevelopment areas, and these, too, have been helpful in modernizing areas with weak financial resources. At present, however, the nation does not yet have either a policy or a comprehensive program for interarea migration. In this final section, I will discuss some of the elements that might be included in a national approach toward this problem.

It is often easier to visualize and to market a product if one like it has already been successful. In the case of relocation programs, one of the most desirable products seems to be manufactured in Sweden. That country may offer the United States useful clues on how families of semiskilled and unskilled workers can be assisted to relocate with minimal hardship. Broadening the population stream relocating from distressed areas could be a useful contribution to their future development; a planned relocation program would help more marginal workers to leave.

Long recognized as being far in advance of the United States in many social welfare programs, Sweden has had notable success in its efforts to help poorly educated migrant families relocate under a comprehensive program dating back to the mid-1950s. The program includes medical examinations, aptitude tests, vocational guidance, training, family allowances, and payment of transportation and moving costs.[41] The cost per family may run as high as

$2,000, but officials feel that these are one-time expenses and that the large initial sum may prevent far costlier, long-term social problems.

It is clear that it is much easier to effectuate this type of program in Sweden than in the United States. The nation's small size, the homogeneity of its population, and the government's experience in national planning are significant and perhaps unique advantages. Furthermore, the Swedish program is part of a long-range national planning effort designed both to correct temporary imbalances in the labor market and, more important, to follow a well-defined and clearly directed path toward flexibility in restructuring the economy as the needs of the nation seem to dictate. This is one of the critical differences: The task of moving a tenant farmer and his family to the city, finding him a home, giving him training and a job can all be accomplished entirely within the context of labor market demands. What Sweden is attempting is far more significant. By ensuring that the working man is not adversely affected to any significant extent by structural changes in the economy, Sweden may be able to counter worker resistance to progress. There are fewer anguished cries of dismay on the part of a work force that is guaranteed that its livelihood is not threatened. Such pressures in the United States have been one factor in generating powerful protectionist pressures to shield and subsidize inefficient industries—and to decelerate entry of minority groups into skilled jobs. Unless some method is found to remove labor's fears, the nation may well be faced with an unending series of political obstacles to the process of economic rationalization. Surely there are enough barriers to progress without adding to them unnecessarily.

The Swedish experience suggests two prerequisites for maximum effectiveness in relocation programs: nationwide coverage and a broad national policy in which relocation is only one important component.

This obviously suggests that relocation programs should be operated by the federal government or at the very least be designed, coordinated, and evaluated within a controlling national framework. Action on the part of individual redevelopment areas, the states, or even large regional commissions such as New England and Appalachia would be most effective when linked closely to other areas. Financing and integration would clearly have to be a federal responsibility.

Would a relocation program be horrendously expensive? On the basis of cost-benefit analysis, probably not. Total expenditures for poverty and welfare programs in the United States can be reduced appreciably by a workable relocation program. Subsidized relocation is undoubtedly less costly than supporting idled, redundant workers and their dependants. If the balance sheet were longer (that is, if long-term national goals or intangible social benefits were included), the results are even likely to be conclusively in favor of a major federal relocation program. Unfortunately, neither the Swedish nor other Europeans nor Americans have developed adequate data on the process. One

United Nations report on the relocation of rural manpower to industry indicated:

> There is practically no information available concerning the costs and benefits of the adjustment process. Some concepts and tools have been developed to tackle the problem of the costs involved in migration, but as a recent publication states "provide only a sketchy framework for further empirical study of labor movement. Measures of the psychic cost of migration, for example, are hard to come by." The most essential conclusion, however, in this context is that "the relation between private and social costs of, and returns to, migration at best depends on market structure, resources, mobility in general, and revenue policies of state and local governments."[42]

In the United States, we have witnessed the consequences of a mélange of inconsistent development and manpower programs. But it would be more accurate to recognize that most relocation takes place with little reference to government policy. Government has not taken special action relating to manpower requirements. Changes in agricultural technology, distasteful environmental conditions, and a hope of betterment in the cities have sent millions of blacks and whites to large urban areas. Their past experience has poorly prepared rural migrants for new challenges, and they have experienced enormous difficulties in adjusting to urban conditions. On the other hand, to their detriment, migration from urban redevelopment areas has been heavily concentrated among the relatively well educated.

As we suggested, a rational national policy should aim at broadening the base of migration from redevelopment areas. It is likely that encouraging greater numbers of the less-educated workers and their families to relocate would doubtless require better communication linkages with the low-income population. As we know from recent experience with the urban ghettos, neither physical proximity nor exposure to the mass media is any guarantee that the poor will be drawn into the mainstream of the labor market or the available network of social services. However, because the distressed area population tends to be better educated and motivated than are the hard-core unemployed in the large city ghettos, the task is not likely to be as difficult or frustrating.

BROADENING THE TALENT BASE

Broadening the migrant stream attacks only half the problem of selective migration from distressed areas. What is also needed is an incentive system to enlarge the shallow pools of local talent. This suggests a need for a policy that might include, among its other components, relocation allowances "to move *into* the redevelopment area the labor force ingredients in terms of skill and age, necessary to maximize its usefulness."[43] This suggestion, which has been recommended for the relatively small Benelux countries, applies with even greater force in the United States. In a sense, public and private incentives are already available in the form of job opportunities, enticing promotion of recreational facilities, and company relocation allowances. But it would appear that this is not enough. It would be helpful if incentive pay and career opportunities could be offered as the Russians do in attracting migrants to Siberia, as the Israelis do in luring migrants to the desert, and as American construction firms offer in recruiting skilled labor for overseas hardship posts. A federal system of executive relocation allowances or bonuses could conceivably be part of a national relocation policy.

The problem of talent migration may involve even more sweeping federal action, including some controls over the distribution of economic growth. The brain-drain dilemma raises a number of fundamental questions involving national policies that are barely embryonic. For example, medical concentration in major metropolitan areas has resulted in physician-to-population ratios two to three times higher than the ratios in underdeveloped areas.[44]

Should the federal government take action to strengthen the talent base in redevelopment areas? If the answer to this question is yes, this raises a series of subsidiary issues. How far are we to go in this direction? How much federal incentive should there be to locate advanced types of development in such areas to provide jobs for college graduates? Would interference with the traditional flow of talent to large metropolitan areas, the "Class A League," eventually be harmful to national interests? Is there danger of parochialism and inbreeding if large-scale movement of talent is diminished?

Clearly, more than the future of a redevelopment area or even a metropolis is at stake. Can the nation afford to permit a continuing, possibly widening gulf between a relative handful of large metropolitan areas and the remainder of the nation? What would be the long-term consequences of such divergence in terms of leadership, culture, politics, and national progress? These are basic questions that need more than hasty answers. At present, we would be wise to limit ourselves to indicating the existence of a talent migration problem and probably remain content with modest measures to reduce its impact. But the problem is not temporally finite: it must be regarded as permanent, and thus it requires long-term policies and programs built into the governmental fabric.

It may be noted that this is not solely an American problem. For a number of years, a growing concern with overconcentration of talent in capital cities had led many European nations to adopt active policies aimed at devolution (building up provincial centers and restricting growth in the capital). French data for 1962 revealed that the Paris region contained a seventh of that nation's population, a quarter of its government employment, a third of its college and graduate students, two-thirds of its artists and writers, and almost two-thirds of its corporate headquarters. The government aims at creating a new balance through an environment plan that visualizes equipping cities in large "provincial urban complexes [so that they] can be real economic and social leaders in their regional spheres of influence and can in general be free from complete dependency on Paris."[45] It was estimated that by 1985, eight urban complexes with populations ranging from 360,000 to 1.5 million would be ready to play this autonomous role.[46] European successes and failures can be helpful in developing a sound policy suited to the American landscape.

WHERE DO WE GO FROM HERE?

It is hard to escape the conclusion that much of the programmatic concern with distressed areas represents a genuine response to political realities but an ineffectual tinkering with broad and powerful economic forces. This is far from a parochial view: experience in Britain, which has operated an extensive development areas program since the 1930s, suggests that it was a combination of prewar armament contracts, wartime manpower shortages, and postwar prosperity that contributed most to the upturn of the economy in south Wales, Scotland, and the other distressed areas. This leads to the first and most fundamental conclusion regarding distressed areas policy.

Most important is national prosperity. It is no accident that distressed areas often claim that a minor illness in the national economy is frequently a local disaster. ("A cold for you is pneumonia for us.") The other side of the coin is a buoyant national economy with plentiful jobs for out-migrants, a spillover of industry to engulf local pools of underused labor, and substantial federal help for modernizing the infrastructure and helping shaky local governments to finance adequate public services, particularly schools. In a serious depression, depressed areas can expect studies, not jobs or investments.

Growth centers offer some hope. The economic development legislation of the mid-1960s, based in part on initiatives adopted in France, represented a useful step forward in distressed area policy. For the first time it was explicitly recognized that only limited portions of distressed areas possessed significant growth potential. This emphasis on selective urban growth nodes is strongly supported by such authorities as Niles Hansen, who commented:

> Regional policy in the United States has been formulated and implemented on the assumption that it is possible to attract sufficient industry to lagging . . . regions . . . to give residents of these regions economic opportunities comparable to those enjoyed by other Americans . . . Experience of other countries which have been trying for longer than the United States to stimulate the growth of large lagging regions indicates that such force-feeding has generally be unsuccessful. . . . The most efficient use of public funds would be to encourage the growth of medium-sized cities, especially those that have already given some real evidence of possessing growth characteristics.[47]

Government-assisted relocation is essential. Foreign and domestic experience with voluntary and assisted relocation suggests that migration is a crucial element of a sound distressed areas strategy. The components of such a program include federal aid to localities to improve the education and health of relocatees, a good, informative system of advertising available job openings—television and the computer can be extremely useful—and a loan-and-grant program to finance the moves. A network of public and private social services to help relocatees get settled would also be a substantial contribution to successful movement.

Political marketing of government-assisted relocation might be feasible if two points were made clear. The first is that tides of economic development ebb and flow, so that considerable areal variation in migration trends can be expected over time. Second, and most important, relocation subsidies should be available to poor people wherever they live, big-city slum, rural poverty area, depressed mining or recreation area, Indian reservation. Once a national relocation network is established it can be of great service to a substantial proportion of the population, far more than those who live in distressed areas.

A CONCLUDING NOTE: A PLEA FOR DIVERSITY

The reader has probably concluded that despite the potentially unfavorable impact on both receiving and sending areas, the author tends to favor a policy of assisted migration which would include efforts to ease the strains of relocation. This policy should obviously be combined with a strategy of assisting the development of distressed area growth centers—in the full recognition that this implies substantial internal migration within distressed areas toward these growth poles coupled with migration, via relocation, to out-of-area growth centers.

At this concluding point the author would like to modify what appears to be a clear policy favoring rapid change with a plea for government recognition of the need to preserve regional cultural diversity. If historic preservation is now generally accepted as a valid government goal, then there seems to be no good reason why preservation of the special culture of distressed areas as an endangered species cannot be identified as another reasonable objective. We have come a long way from the days of General Philip Sheridan, who saw salvation for the American Indian only if he could be taught to "walk the white man's way." Cultural homogenization is no longer a national objective complete with measures aimed at stamping out public use of foreign languages by "hyphenated Americans" along with Navajo and other Indian languages. The time is past when the regional culture of the South and Appalachia could be casually dismissed as a repellent blend of poverty, bigotry, pellagra, and violence. The recognition by the rest of the nation that there are certain virtues in the traditional South, to cite one example, has been late in coming. As David Potter sees it, by the antebellum era

> [s]outherners placed a premium on the values of loyalty, courtesy and physical courage—these being the accustomed virtues of simple agricultural societies with primitive technology in which intelligence and skills are not important to the economy. By contrast the North and West . . . had begun to respond to the dynamic forces of industrialization, mass transportation and modern technology and to anticipate the mobile fluid, equalitarian, highly organized and impersonal culture of cities and machines. Their values of enterprise, adaptability and capacity to excel in competition were not the values of the South.[48]

Luigi Barzini sketches a similar north-south cultural differential in Italy, the southerners more intense, human, clannish, closer to nature, and violent, the northerners bourgeois, systematic—and economically successful.[49] Barzini stresses another point directly transferable to American experience: in proportion to population, southerners may not rise to the top in engineering or science, but they are superb politicians and produce a larger-than-proportionate share of writers.

None of this is meant to suggest that the virtues of courtesy, courage, and loyalty would disappear if unemployment in distressed areas vanished with an influx of modern industry; nor is it meant to suggest that the nation's sense of extended family and historic roots would be gravely weakened if all the distressed areas were depopulated. Neither is this meant to be a call for subsidized "paleface reservations" (a phrase Harry Caudill has used to describe contemporary Appalachia) providing picturesque native crafts and festivals for tourists. And most of all, it emphatically is not a proposal for the location and subsidization of uneconomic industries as a means of preserving native culture. On a fairly small scale, this kind of distortion may pose no danger; but the prospect that a sizable part of the urban Northeast may be headed for serious economic obsolescence in the 1980s and beyond raises nightmarish visions of enormous subsidy programs, protective tariffs, and other efforts aimed at keeping this vast area afloat.

The object of this final note is much more modest. It is a plea for the recognition of the uses of diversity, for tempering modernization with a due respect for tradition. Surely there is enough flexibility, adaptiveness, toleration, and innovation in the nation to permit custom-tailoring the new so that it harmonizes with, rather than destroys, the old. The model, to return to an earlier analogy, is historic preservation. Here it has been amply shown that full plumbing facilities can comfortably coexist with authentic façades, air conditioning with original fireplaces, and old beams with modern kitchens. Given some thought, perhaps we can do as well with distressed area programs.

NOTES

1. See National Resources Planning Board, *Security Work, and Relief Policies* (Washington, D.C.: U.S. Government Printing Office, 1942).

2. For example, a government ordnance plant in southern Illinois, a distressed area with a 1940 population of 350,000, employed 6,000 persons. See Melvin R. Levin, "The Depressed Area: A Study of Southern Illinois" (Ph.D. dissertation, Division of Social Sciences, University of Chicago, 1956).

3. The material in this section is derived in part from the author's review of Sar Levitan's *Federal Aid to Depressed Areas: An Evaluation of the Area Redevelopment Administration* (Baltimore: Johns Hopkins Press, 1964). The review appeared in the *Journal of the American Institute of Planners* 31, no. 2 (February 1965): 71–73.

4. Sar Levitan, op. cit.

5. David A. Grossman and Melvin R. Levin, "The Appalachian Region: A National Problem Area," *Land Economics* 37, no. 2 (May 1961): 133–41.

6. This discussion is based in part on a review article by Lawrence D. Mann and George J. Pillorge, "French Regional Planning," *Journal of the American Institute of Planners* 30, no. 2 (May 1964): 64–74; and U.S., Area Redevelopment Administration, *Area Redevelopment Policies in Britain and the Countries of the Common Market* (Washington, D.C.: U.S. Government Printing Office, January 1965). See especially preface and introduction, Frederick Meyers and Pierre Bouchet, "Regional Development Policies in France," pp. 111–28.

7. Stanislaw Chelstowski, "Deglomeration," *Polish Perspectives, Monthly Review* [in English], Warsaw, November 1966.

8. L. Needleman and B. Scott, "Regional Problems and Location of Industry Policy in Britain," *Urban Studies,* Glasgow, 1, no. 2 (November 1964): 153–69. For a discussion of British distressed-area policy, see also Benjamin Chinitz, "Regional Economic Policy in Great Britain," *Urban Affairs Quarterly* 1, no. 2 (December 1965) and 2, no. 3 (March 1966).

9. "Back-Into-Balance Britain," London *Sunday Times,* November 5, 1967, p. 34.

10. See, for example, U.S., Senate, Area Redevelopment Act, Subcommittee of the Committee on Banking and Currency, *Hearings,* 86th Cong., 1st sess., pt. 1, February 25–27, 1959.

11. Information on New Bedford's depression-era economic development efforts is taken from Seymour Wolfbein, *Decline of a Cotton Textile City: A Study of New Bedford* (New York: Columbia University Press, 1944).

12. Committee Appointed by the Conference of New England Governors, Seymour Harris, Chairman, *Report on the New England Textile Industry* (Boston: New England Governors Council, 1952), p. 4. Four of the seven textile communities were in Massachusetts—Lowell, Lawrence, Fall River, and New Bedford.

13. Thomas Russell Smith, *The Cotton Textile Industry of Fall River, Massachusetts* (New York: Kings Crown Press, 1944), p. 162.

14. Ibid., p. 163.

15. Benjamin Chinitz, "Appropriate Goals for Regional Economic Policy," *Urban Studies,* Glasgow, 3, no. 1 (February 1966): 5.

16. For an insightful analysis of the role of leading public entrepreneurs in large-scale, community, urban renewal programs, see Jewel Bellush and Murray Hausknecht, "Entrepreneurs and Urban Renewal," *Journal of the American Institute of Planners* 32 (September 1966): 289–97.

17. Since there are almost 300 federal programs dealing with education, environment, and community development, involving more than 100 departmental subdivisions in 18 different federal agencies, a major manufacturer of business machines has established a subscriber-information service on federal programs. Their first directory, *Directory of Federal Programs for Schools and Communities* (Washington, D.C.: Xerox Corporation, Education Division, 1966), covering programs for schools and communities, is over 600 pages.

18. James L. Sundquist and David W. Davis, *Making Federalism Work* (Washington, D.C.: The Brookings Institution, 1969), p. 222.

19. Dennis O'Harrow, "A New Tune for the Piper," *American Society of Planning Officials Newsletter* 32, no. 3 (March 1966): 21–22.

20. John Friedmann and William Alonso, eds., *Regional Development and Planning* (Cambridge, Mass: M.I.T. Press, 1964), p. 11.

21. See John B. Parr, "Outmigration and the Depressed Area Problem," *Land Economics* 42, no. 2 (May 1966): 158–67.

22. U.S. Area Redevelopment Administration, *Area Redevelopment Policies in Britain and the Countries of the Common Market* (Washington, D.C.: U.S. Government Printing Office, January 1965), p. 6.

23. J.J. Kaufman, "Labor Mobility, Training, and Retraining," *Studies in Unemployment,* U.S. Senate Special Committee on Unemployment Problems (Washington, D.C.: U.S. Government Printing Office, 1960), pp. 343–65.

24. University of Wisconsin, Industrial Relations Research Institute, *Retraining and Migration as Factors in Regional Economic Development* (Madison: University of Wisconsin, 1966), p. 2.

25. U.S. Area Redevelopment Administration, *Population, Labor Force and Unemployment in Chronically Depressed Areas* (Washington, D.C.: U.S. Government Printing Office, October 1964), pp. 12–13.

26. Charles Press and Charles R. Adrian, "Why Our State Governments Are Sick," *The Antioch Review,* Summer 1964, pp. 156–57.

27. Alexis de Tocqueville, *Democracy in America,* vol. 1 (New York: Vintage Books, 1954), p. 304.

28. This is not to suggest that during the 1930s there was a deliberate policy in New Bedford aimed at discouraging outmigration. There was, however, a series of futile attempts to resuscitate dying textile mills which nourished illusions of an imminent economic revival. A frank recognition that the situation was hopeless might have led to an "Okie"-style abandonment, a difficult transitional period for the migrants followed by successful integration into the more resilient economy of another area.

29. Wolfbein, op. cit., pp. 34–35, 37.

30. In underdeveloped countries where this scale of farm migration to productive urban jobs is not feasible, conditions approach the catastrophic.

31. "Careers 67," London *Times,* August 27, 1967.

32. Unlike other groups, this is not the case with respect to Puerto Rican immigrants, a fact which may account for the impression fostered by news media centered in New York City, the primary receiving area for Puerto Rican migration. Stanley L. Friedlander, *Labor Migration and Economic Growth: A Case Study of Puerto Rico* (Cambridge, Mass.: M.I.T. Press, 1965).

33. See Bernard Okun, "Regional Income Inequality and Internal Population Migration," *Economic Development and Cultural Change,* January 1961, pp. 128–43; and Stefan Robock, "Strategies for Regional Economic Development," *Regional Science Association Papers,* 17 (1966): 129–42.

34. Formal vocational training refers to training provided through school, apprenticeship, or the armed forces. The data obtained are from "Statistical Tables on Manpower," a reprint from U.S. Department of Labor, *Manpower Report of the President* (Washington, D.C.: U.S. Government Printing Office, March 1964), table F-8.

35. See the perceptive comments in Irving Kristol, "The Negro Today Is the Immigrant of Yesterday," The *New York Times Magazine,* September 11, 1966, pp. 50–51. See also Charles Tilly, "Race and Migration to the American City," in *The Metropolitan Enigma: Inquiries into the Nature and Dimensions of America's "Urban Crisis,"* vol. 2 (Washington, D.C.: Chamber of Commerce of the United States, 1967), pp. 144–69.

36. R.S. Eckaus, "Investment in Human Capital," *Journal of Political Economy* 71 (October 1963): 501–04.

37. A major shift in the MDTA program which had hitherto concentrated on training the readily employable occurred in fiscal 1967. A fourth of the trainees were to be disadvantaged young people and another two-fifths, disadvantaged adults. U.S. Department of Labor, *Manpower Report of the President* (Washington, D.C.: U.S. Government Printing Office, March 1966), pp. 3, 69–74.

38. Edward K. Kalachek, "Automation and Full Employment," *Trans-Action* 4, no. 4 (March 1967): 24–29. The threat and promise of automation have occasioned considerable research and controversy: *Automation,* American Academy of Political and Social Science, March 1962; Report from the President's Advisory Committee on Labor Management Policy, *The Benefits and Problems Incidental to Automation and Other Technological Advances* (Washington, D.C.: U.S. Government Printing Office, January 1962); U.S. Department of Labor, *Manpower Implications of Automation,* 1964 ; U.S. Senate, Committee on Labor and Public Welfare, 1964, 1965, *Selected Readings in Employment and Manpower,* 6 vols.; and *Technology and the American Economy,* Report of the National Commission on Technology, Automation and Economic Progress, vol. 1 (Washington, D.C.: U.S. Government Printing Office, February 1966).

39. Friedmann and Alonso, op. cit., p. 5.

40. Ibid.

41. "How Sweden Keeps Them Working," *Business Week,* July 15, 1967, pp. 100–02.

42. G. Beijer, *National Rural Manpower: Adjustment to Industry* (Paris: OECD, 1965); quotation from L.A. Sjaastad, "The Costs and Returns of Human Migration," *Journal of Political Economy* 70, no. 5 (1962): 80–93.

43. U.S. Area Redevelopment Administration, *Area Redevelopment Policies in Britain,* op. cit., p. 7

44. Accurate figures from the domestic brain drain are unavailable, but there are many data on international migration of talent. It is known that in 1966, immigrant scientific manpower added nearly 10 percent to the supply of newly graduated engineers and 26 percent of its new physicians (New York *Times,* August 27, 1967, p. 12). Of U.S. scientists, engineers, and physicians, 5 to 10 percent "are apparently of foreign origin in the sense of foreign birth and training." Thomas J. Mills, "Scientific Personnel and the Professions," *The Annals* 367 (issued entitled *The New Immigration*) (September 1966): 33–42.

45. *France, Town and Country Environment Planning* (New York: Service de Presse d'Information, December 1965).

46. Ibid.

47. Niles M. Hansen, *Rural Poverty and the Urban Crisis* (Bloomington: Indiana University Press, 1971), pp. 299–300. However, Hansen's emphasis on medium-sized cities (200,000 to 750,000 population) is disputed by John A. Kuehn and Lloyd D. Bender in "A Dissent: Migration, Growth Centers and the Ozarks," *Growth and Change* 6, no. 2 (April 1975). The authors analyzed 1960-70 census data and point out that so far as the Ozark Region is concerned, the fastest-growning urban centers are much smaller. The authors also indicate that nationwide, in the 1960-70 decade, the fastest-growing communities were in the 2,500 to 25,000 size category and that growth in nonmetropolitan areas far exceeded growth in metropolitan areas.

48. David M. Potter, *The Impending Crisis 1848-1861* (New York: Harper and Row, 1976), p. 30.

49. Luigi Barzini, *The Italians* (New York: Bantam, 1964), pp. 244–61.

CHAPTER 9
THE BIG REGIONS

THE BIG REGIONS AND AMERICA'S FUTURE

By the mid-1970s, Americans took for granted a new level of government —a region that covers several states or includes portions of several. In some instances, these will be traditional or "natural" regions; in most, their boundaries will follow relatively predictable lines based on unifying socioeconomic factors operating in a plausible geographic area.

These so-called big regions may assume some importance in the lives of the people of the United States during the last quarter of the twentieth century. Created as a "new dimension of federalism," an entity to operate between the states and the federal government, they have begun to develop identities based on their special problems and interests.

The new regionalism is one side of a developmental coin that, when turned over, reveals community development legislation. Both are aimed at helping to relieve intolerable social headaches—the persistence of gnawing poverty, stubbornly high unemployment rates, inadequate education and skills, racial and ethnic tensions, shabby housing, serious transportation needs, and, in general, wretched misuse of human and natural resource potential. Both stress the role of planning and impatience with existing governmental inadequacies; both stress massive, planned investment and new types of social and economic accounting.

Yet, clearly the new regionalism departs from the analogy in at least one major respect: it does not focus primarily on poverty. Rather, the states involved—some of which are relatively affluent—are engaged in an experiment in a new federalism as an expression of a new posture of cooperation. They have been using their political strength within the federal government to solve the problems of backward areas within their states which reach across boundaries to neighboring states. But there will be more emphasis on working with their neighbor states to secure the federal help needed to solve problems which are beyond the unaided capacities of even the wealthiest states.

This chapter, therefore, explores the status of the newly evolving regional commissions and speculates on their future possibilities.

The New Dimension

From 1965 through 1967, six massive new regional commissions were formally created under federal legislation, embracing approximately 40 million people. These include Appalachia, with 15.3 million; New England, 10.5 million; Ozarks, 2.5 million; Upper Great Lakes, 2.7 million; Four Corners, 1.8 million; and Atlantic Coastal Plains, 4.5 million. Almost a quarter of the nation's land area and nearly a fifth of its population were within these new regions.

The primary vehicle for the establishment of the new regional agencies was the Public Works and Economic Development Act of 1965, passed in late August, although Appalachia, the forerunner and model for PL 89-136, had been established some months earlier in separate legislation.[1]

In some respects, the new regions are direct descendants of the regionalism theory of the 1930s as outlined in studies by the National Resources Planning Board (NRPB)[2] and continue the strong emphasis of the NRPB programs dealing with resource depletion, misuse, and economic development. However, there is less attention to another, later type of regionalism, the urban regions; a child of the 1950s, it represents an attempt, mostly unsuccessful but still in progress, to deal with metropolitan problems.

Raising echoes of the New Deal, the new regions ostensibly are an economic response to area poverty. In fact, however, they are becoming organizations with far broader interests and concerns. In a sense, they are political regions; most owe their establishment to a quid pro quo for the support of their congressional delegations in the designation of Appalachia. They are also political in another respect: Their predecessors, operating in a climate of opinion in which violent hostility to government intervention and planning was commonplace, laid heavy stress on attempts to develop plausible proof of their profitability. In contrast, the new regions have departed both from the cost-benefit analysis of the river-basin variety and the seed money, investment-job generation formulas used in securing passage of area redevelopment legislation in the early 1960s. The new political and environmental dimensions reflect adjustments to an affluent, more sophisticated society, as evidenced by the regions' substantial attention to human resources and to physical environment.

This redirection is not totally divorced from sound investment principles; it can be and has been explained as belated pragmatism, as an attempt to modernize their defective infrastructure to compete for sound economic development. In the poor regions, social overhead facilities and services tend to be neglected and rundown, although they have been found to be indispensable prerequisites for modern economic growth.

There is clearly another assumption involved in the inclusion of public schools and public health in regional development programs that once riveted their energy on industrial parks or flood problems. The people who live in distressed regions, like other disadvantaged segments of the society, are no longer satisfied merely with basic shelter and steady, low-wage jobs in territorial or racial enclaves. The cries for redress of grievances for the underdogs of society—the poor, the minority groups, and the backward areas—can no longer be stilled by providing unskilled jobs or freedom from periodic flooding. Their aspirations are now much more ambitious and involve rapid movement into the mainstream of society.

While past approaches were by no means as simple-minded as some critics have charged, they are dwarfed by the new, broader focus that has cut loose from the familiar landmarks of cost-benefit irrigation projects and economic development promotion linked to public bonds for industrial parks. It is also noteworthy that it is no longer necessary to display the beggar's sores. The underdog argument has lost much of its force compared to political considerations when applied to areas such as New England, where incomes have been higher and living conditions have been more favorable than in most parts of the nation. In short, although some of the rhetoric of the 1930s has been disinterred, the examples of Appalachia and New England suggest that in the past few years, large-scale regional development programs in the United States have been profoundly altered in character and concept.

HISTORIC ROOTS

There is no clear agreement on what constitutes regional planning and development either as a field of study or as a field of operations. To a considerable extent, John Friedmann's caustic observation to the effect that regional planning has usually involved much research but little implementation in a "rather ill-defined combination of physical, economic, human resource and natural resource concerns" is clearly correct.[3] But the field is so amorphous that it defies even the loosest parameters. Even Friedmann's extremely wide definition for regional planning as the "ordering of human activities in supra-urban space"[4] seems too narrow to encompass all of the operations of the new regions, particularly the administrative, lobbying, investment, and organizational issues that occupy so much time and effort. The new regions are political entities with responsibilities that include but far transcend the economists' and planners' tasks of developing a technical framework and priorities for intraregional choices and allocations determined at the federal level.

Another major problem in developing a suitable definition is pinning down the slippery term "region." There is, for example, a great variation in size. The entire Southeast of the United States has been defined as a region in some studies, while minuscule "regions" with populations of less than 10,000 have been organized, recognized, and subsequently funded with federal assistance. Until recently, smallness seemed to be winning out; the "urban regions" of the 1950s were in most cases roughly equivalent to standard metropolitan areas, and most were geographically small, with populations well under a million. The redevelopment areas of the early 1960s were even smaller; a number of designated rural and resort areas had populations of only a few thousand. This was in distinct contrast to the practice of the 1930s, and 1940s, when regional activity was focused on vast river basins like the Tennessee,[5] the Missouri, and the Columbia. These watersheds of the depression decade were sizable in territory if not always large in population. Similarly, the identification of the economically and physically distressed Appalachian, Ozark, and Cutover areas in the 1930s also involved boundaries encompassing parts of a number of states. However, the total population involved was smaller than in the nation's leading states.

By the end of World War II, the always loosely defined term "region" had lost almost all relevance except as a convenient geographic expression. The one experiment that seemed to point hopefully to the future (and perhaps the point is that it was a generation before its time) was the brave new world of the Tennessee Valley Authority (TVA). In original concept, this was to be the source of a great transformation for millions of America's poorest people. A central argument for support of TVA by taxpayers from Bangor to San Diego was that the growth of a market in the Tennessee Valley would benefit everybody; the rising tide of prosperity along the Tennessee would help to lift all American boats.

This has been a salient point made by proponents of aid to depressed regions (and poor people) ever since—that they were simply bad business for a prosperous society. And certainly the economic development of northern Alabama and southern Tennessee provided testimony to the significance of the pioneering experiment in that region. But the danger with the river basin approach is its unsuitability for an urbanized nation. Water resources do not appear to be useful for organizational and program orientation in the present era. It seems questionable that a region created on the basis of its natural resource needs and problems can readjust its main thrust to focus adequately on urban problems. An organization's initial orientation, supporters, and staff place a permanent stamp on its subsequent conduct.

TVA also ran into another basic problem. The realities of political survival in the 1930s and 1940s dictated an agency emphasis narrowed to the simple production of electric power, with only limited side activities including flood control and recreation development. In the climate of state and local hostility to planning that existed in the 1930s and 1940s, TVA found itself forced to operate within these parentheses, largely as a matter of realistic accomodation with the land-grant colleges and their clientele, area businessmen, and other components of the local establishment. As compared to the programs in Appalachia and those in Title V regions, for example, TVA's direct involvement with human resource development will seem rather minimal. Had it been otherwise, TVA might well have succumbed to its enemies and might exist now only as a brave wraith, extinguished in a premature, losing battle for the tenant farmer and the poor.

Although the new regions more closely resemble the districts of the 1930s in size, they have clearly been influenced by the experience of the 1940s and 1950s. Two divergent trends were apparent in the 1950s. The first involved the transformation of the 1930s state research and planning agencies into industrial and tourist promotion organizations, usually with limited state planning responsibilities. The second was the previously mentioned focus on urban regions, reflecting the philosophies and policies of the U.S. Housing and Home Finance Agency (now the Department of Housing and Urban Development). Since these metropolitan areas were generally smaller in both territory and population, as compared to the mammoth regions of the previous two decades, the new EDA regions represent a return to the scale of the 1930s.

With the exception of weak, privately sponsored regional advisory agencies and public river basin commissions that have only a tenuous hold on political loyalties and power, the new multistate regions operate in a tabula rasa situation: The regional territory has not been as thoroughly staked out by strong rivals. It is likely that their confrontations and dissensions will result from internal fractionalism among governors, senators, and clientele groups rather than from head-to-head battles among regional contenders with overlapping spheres of activity.

APPALACHIAN ANALOGUE

Predicting the long-term evolution for large EDA regions is a difficult task because the enabling legislation is so broad that it offers adequate authority for an enormous variety of programs. Consider, for example, the research and advisory functions enumerated in section 503 of the 1965 legislation based on its predecessor, the Appalachian Act. The Title V regions are empowered to assist regional development by undertaking research, initiating and coordinating long-range development plans, promoting increased private investment, preparing legislative recommendations, and conducting research on resources. Given this broad mandate, the limitations are so vague as to be almost nonexistent.

While they are kissing cousins with respect to research, there is one vital difference between Appalachia and the Title V regions. From an organizational standpoint, Appalachia is a relatively robust relative. From its inception, Appalachia has received federal assistance for conducting programs as well as for research and advisory activities. Thus, it has had real muscle to ensure that recommendations were carried out. Under Title II of the 1965 legislation, the Appalachian region was allocated over $1 billion. This included $840 million for a development highway system, $69 million for demonstration health facilities, $63 million for various natural resource programs, $16 million for vocational education facilities, and $90 million to increase the normal federal matching share for a broad range of federal grant-in-aid programs. In combination, these funds gave the Appalachian organization substantial and sustained political leverage. Evidence of its strength was the passage in 1967 of a congressional appropriation for the region virtually identical with the president's requests. This was somewhat unusual, coming at a time when appropriations for other Great Society programs like Model Cities were subjected to major cutbacks. The fact that Appalachia has program funds of its own to distribute helps the region to achieve budgetary immunity, reflecting substantial grass-roots support.

The new regions followed Appalachia's lead and are not content to remain restricted to research and advisory roles. Before much time had passed, the multistate regions attempted to emulate Appalachian autonomy and move toward separate funding, independent of EDA control. However, EDA was not and is not entirely prepared to let its children go without a struggle. In early 1968, a presidential executive order designated the secretary of commerce to provide effective liaison between the federal government and the regional commissions (Appalachia excluded), assisted by an advisory committee composed of representatives of other agencies.[6] This role as compulsory intermediary—the Department of Commerce is EDA's parent agency—may tend to circumscribe the autonomy of the new regions, but the thrust toward autonomy was inevitable, particularly because of the availability of funds from other federal agencies. In fiscal 1969 EDA provided almost $4 million in planning funds and $12.5 million in supplemental grant funds for five regions; Appalachia received its own appropriation. So far as can be determined, some of the decision makers in the regions who had been initially wary of overidentifying with EDA, which has the reputation of being heavily political and ranking low on the Washington totem pole, saw no harm in securing a maximum of EDA funds, as long as it was made clear that they were not exclusively under the EDA umbrella. Moreover, in practice, DOT and other agencies have provided sizable amounts for the regions so that EDA does not have a total monopoly on regional sponsorship.

It is striking that both of the nation's large, autonomous regions to have been established were located in southern or border state territory. Despite violent attacks on TVA as a dangerous venture into socialism, the Tennessee Valley Authority has been fervently embraced by area politicians, many of whom tend to be highly conservative on other domestic matters. Often, elected officials in the South reserve ideological warfare for communism and the race issue and are otherwise supremely effective pragmatists (lobbyists for their constituents). TVA may have looked like creeping socialism to northern conservatives, but in much of the pragmatic South it has been considered an effective vehicle for pumping federal investment and payrolls into the area—an asset similar to the costly military installations and federal public works projects that freckle the Southland. By and large, it has been the North and Midwest that rejected, on ideological grounds, proposals to create similar regional river basin authorities on the Missouri and other rivers.

By the time the Appalachian region was created, much of the political controversy over TVA had dissipated, despite an occasional nostalgic flicker of hostility from private power companies. Even more important, perhaps, the Appalachian Commission, from its birth, was in reality the "establishment" creature that critics of TVA claimed it had become by the late 1930s—an administrative vehicle closely tied to the local power structure.[7] This stance has certain political advantages. Largely controlled and operated by state governments, the new regions do not provide a vulnerable target to a conservative opposition that has proclaimed itself the champion of states rights. Furthermore, within the states, the new regions are creatures of the governors; they in no way resemble the community action organizations that the U.S. Office of Economic Opportunity has financed to mobilize the poor and forsaken to do battle with city hall.

Perhaps the dichotomy between the establishment and the poor is not entirely meaningful. Governors are popularly elected, and the programs that help them to achieve and retain power are directed toward securing support from all segments of the electorate, including the poor. With some exceptions, mainly in the South, the poor are making greater use of their franchise, and the difference in program orientation between underdogs, many of whom are moving out of poverty, and larger middle-class electorates has become increasingly blurred. The Appalachian precedents suggest, setting aside the continuing commitment to highway construction, that the regions' gradual shift toward emphasis on human resource programs has resulted in a focus which on paper is probably reasonably close to that likely to be demanded by spokesmen for the disadvantaged. This is not to say that there is complete harmony between the middle class, the "interests," and the poor in Appalachia. The administration of these programs and their efficacy in meeting the needs of the poor became the subject of bitter controversy. Subsequent events—some disenchantment with the bricks-and-mortar approach and the availability of large amounts of other program funds—resulted in revisions in administration, program content, and outlook.

Human Resource Programs

The 1960 research study upon which much of subsequent Appalachian action was based recommended more emphasis on "portable investments" such as education and manpower training and less stress on costly highways and headwater dams.[8] The study also suggested that primary efforts be concentrated on developing urban areas of demonstrated growth potential. In part, the approach was based on this author's conclusions from research in southern Illinois, an area of marginal farming, declining employment in the coal industry, and shabby mining hamlets similar in many respects to Appalachia.[9]

Neither concept met with the complete approval of the governors assembled at the 1960 Governor's Conference on Appalachia. Some of the governors argued that acceptance of these human resource recommendations would be tantamount to adopting a policy of accelerating depopulation for much of the region; they were not receptive to programs that called for expending much of Appalachia's limited resources on education and training activities which amounted to a subsidy of the well-off regions receiving Appalachian migrants. Moreover, they were not enthralled with the idea of plowing most of their scarce development and promotion money into a few obviously thriving urban areas at the risk of alienating most of the dying small towns.

An idea that found greater favor was the development highway. A mountain region that possessed little but coal and timber to attract outside investors, Appalachia had been bypassed by the main thrust of national economic growth, partly because of its isolation. The governors suggested that new roads would open the region to the mainstream of the nation's economic expansion. However, they recognized that these new highways would never be built unless new criteria for road construction were created; they were to be "development highways" to generate future traffic. Current criteria for highway construction are grounded primarily on an extrapolation of present traffic volumes, a premise that usually discriminates against the underdeveloped region. The governors complained that the extensive federal interstate highway system and the ABC system[10] would link the region's major urban centers with first-class routes, but they were obviously not going to penetrate into many mountain areas.

The Appalachian Governors' orientation was fully reflected both in the 1964 report of the president's Appalachian study commission[11] and in the three annual budgetary allocations of the Appalachian Regional Commission (ARC) through fiscal 1968. For fiscal 1966 and 1967, total appropriations amounted to $282 million for a start on 2,350 miles of development highways and $18 million for local access roads.[12]

The commission has continued its stress on highway construction, which it regards as a vital prerequisite for development. Despite the care that had gone into program design, some of Appalachia's other original programs did not live up to advance billing. Two notable examples are the timberland and pasture operations. There had been much needless worry on the part of western cattle interests fearful of grassy, eastern valleys swarming with near-to-market beef, but for a variety of reasons, neither effort produced the type of early payoff that some had anticipated. In contrast, one of Appalachia's significant successes was financial matching to help impoverished areas take advantage of federal grant-in-aid programs. These supplementary grants-in-aid constituted a powerful weapon in helping the commission develop a strong, local power base and enabling it to attack a variety of problems along a broad front. To cite one example, progress is being made on the desperate problem of substandard rural housing. The commission found that it could make good use of technical assistance funds in helping farm areas complete complicated application forms required to qualify for grants and low-interest loans available from other federal agencies.

In passing, it may be noted that TVA also claimed that its free technical assistance helped to invigorate local communities.[13] While this is undoubtedly accurate, it has its ironic aspects. Roughly two-thirds of the TVA area is included in the Appalachian region, and its commission staff allege that many of the TVA communities are a mess. The TVA, it is suggested, has remained a hydrology-oriented agency rather than having evolved into a comprehensive planning operation, and Appalachia has inherited some of the consequences of TVA's failure to broaden its horizons. Over time the Appalachian Regional Commission too was attacked for not dealing effectively with the poverty problem. It is likely that the assault was partly concerned with the nature of the commission's program mix as well as the organization's inability to secure larger amounts of federal money for poverty-oriented activities.[14]

Unmistakable signs of a change in program emphasis—if not monetary allocations—quickly became apparent as the commission went into action. A preliminary report, financed by the U.S. Office of Regional Economic Development, the EDA branch responsible for regional programs, took account of the contribution of human resource development to the growth of the economy as an "implicit" factor in the economic analysis. In accordance with the terms of the research contract, which called for a delineation of subregions, the report placed much stress on the urban growth center concept.[15] A year later, in 1966, the commission reported that it was moving "toward comprehensive programs for helping develop the Region's manpower . . . a detailed assessment of the educational needs and potentials of the region,"[16] and toward a new-towns policy to regroup the dispersed population living in central Appalachia.[17] Most supplemental grant funds—82 percent of $13.7 million—were approved for higher education and hospital facilities, nursing homes, mental health centers, and libraries. In early 1967, the executive director reported that the commission had approved over 400 school and hospital projects, community colleges, and graduate research facilities, and that plans were being completed for a series of comprehensive health service facilities in several parts of the region.[18] The commission quickly discovered, however, that the more serious problem was not providing bricks and mortar, but the shortage of trained people. Commission programs in the health field, for example, were subsequently modified to reflect the need for augmenting the supply of qualified staff. Nevertheless, the commission program yielded most of its benefits to the relatively affluent, and much less was generated for the poor, particularly those in the mining and marginal agriculture heartland.

One of the central themes that runs through the Appalachian commission's study, as indeed through the hearings conducted on the 1965 EDA legislation, is the concept of social disadvantage as reflected in indices comparing the region to the nation. The Appalachian commission reports included data showing that the infant mortality rate in Appalachia was double the national average, that the region had a 50 percent deficiency in long-term health care facilities compared to the nation, that the region's per capita ratio of physicians and nurses was much lower, that the proportion of high-school and college graduates in the population was considerably smaller, and that housing conditions were relatively worse.

To the surprise of many observers, in view of their impressive political clout, the future of Appalachia and the other big regions was threatened by President Nixon's executive agency reorganization plan. Support for abolition was furnished by economists who evaluated the accomplishments of the ARC over the period 1965–69. The deputy director of the agency assessed the results as mixed, partly because of the severity of the problem.

> "They were at the bottom of the barrell and it's difficult to turn that around," says Howard Bray, deputy director of the agency, which is committed to improving the income, health and transportation of the 18 million people isolated in the 13-stage area.
>
> Mr. Bray notes the development of the "hardware of new roads, hospitals, schools and sanitation facilities."
>
> "But these have been damn small, damn modest," he says.[19]

The commission has pointed to the development of new roads, schools, hospitals, and sanitation facilities, but admitted that the strategy of public investment aimed at the goal of a self-sustaining economy has not been met.

The strong bipartisan political support for the commission was reflected in the fact that President Nixon left the Johnson ARC budget untrimmed, while the Congress increased it substantially.

Almost a year later the future began to look increasingly gloomy. The executive director of the commission was quoted to the effect that

> "any evaluation must begin with humility."
>
> "There are still millions of people in Appalachia who do not have access to a good education, or to decent health, or to an adequate job, and who still live below a level of acceptable income," he said. "From their point of view, not very much has been accomplished to date."[20]

The director suggested that there were in reality two Appalachias. One included the "suburban" fringe areas in states like New York and Georgia which were not seriously depressed and which benefited significantly from Appalachian aid programs. The second, the hard core "hillbilly ghetto" in the highlands, is still badly off. A major problem he indicated was the dilution of effort dictated by the generous drawing of boundaries: as a consequence, $7 billion in aid in ten years amounted to less than $400 per capita.

One reason for the continued trouble in the region was a one-third reduction in the out-migration rate in the 1960s, as compared to the 1950–60 decade. Heavy out-migration rates resulted in a 1.4 million decline in the region's population, with the largest losses concentrated in the Appalachian mining territory in Pennsylvania, West Virginia, Kentucky, and Virginia. Nevertheless, unemployment rates remain high, ranging from 20 percent to more than double the U.S. average. High-school graduates are still migrating in large numbers—90,000 a year, perhaps 1 million between 1970 and 1980.

Despite considerable progress in redirecting the program, the central thrust remains on construction of roads and other public facilities. The North Carolina ARC coordinator was quoted as stating that "unfortunately, it's a brick-and-mortar program rather than a people program."[21] One reason for this focus was the creation of the antipoverty program: OEO rather than the commission was assigned the human resources program. This cleavage has had unfortunate consequences.

> The two agencies have scrapped bitterly since then. Many believe that these disputes have weakened the ARC by disclosing that its constituents here in many cases are the same small town "Main Streeters"—merchants, bankers, coal industry leaders and civic boosters—from whom the OEO's antipoverty war has encouraged the poor to demand a better treatment. Some OEO activists here see the Appalachian program as chiefly a boon for the rich and for entrenched political interests.[22]

The New York *Times* story concluded on a hopeful note, suggesting that, despite its acknowledged failures, the ARC has become the most universally acclaimed organ of government since the New Deal. President Nixon was reported as considering applying the ARC concept to other regions. But by January all this had changed: The Ash Council report, blueprinting the reorganization of the federal executive agencies, called for the abolition of all of the big regions through a cessation of federal funding in favor of aid channeled through a 50-state revenue-sharing pool for rural community development.[23] The recommendation was received with consternation by the Appalachian Regional Commission and the other regional commissions, which were reported to be mustering their strength in the Congress for a showdown battle. However, the chilly reception accorded to the Nixon reorganization plan was an omen: their survival powers proved to be greater than that of the Nixon administration itself. The facts that a majority (28) of the nation's 50 states were included in one or two big regions, that all of Alaska has been designated as distressed, and that every state has at least one EDA distressed area are important considerations in shaping the future of distressed area policy.

It is not surprising that by mid-February 1971, the White House told congressional Democrats that it had reconsidered its proposal to liquidate the Appalachian Regional Commission.[24]

PROGRESS IN THE REGIONS

The decade since the creation of the Appalachian Regional Commission and the seven or eight years since the establishment of the Title V commissions has generally been one of progress for the nation, stimulated in Appalachia by a special factor—the boom in coal. In 1973, unemployment in the ARC as a whole was lower than the U.S. average, although rates in some parts of the region were substantially higher.[25] The ARC's population living in poverty declined from 31 percent of the total in 1960 to 18 percent in 1973. Moreover, the long-term population hemorrhage seems to have been stemmed: In the early 1970s, Appalachia gained almost 80,000 persons per year through net immigration as compared to net losses in the 100,000-a-year range in the previous 20 years. Between 1965 and 1972, Appalachia gained almost 750,000 jobs, a dramatic reversal in long-term employment trends.

In many respects the situation in the Title V regions was similar to Appalachia. To cite one example, the Ozark region began gaining population after two decades of net population losses. Nevertheless, there remain wide disparities between most of the big regions and the nation as a whole. In the Ozarks, Four Corners, Coastal Plains, and Upper Great Lakes, per capita 1973 personal incomes were $500 to $1,000 below the U.S. average, a differential of 10 to 20 percent.[26]

THE TITLE V REGIONAL COMMISSIONS IN THE MID-1970s

By mid-1975, the Title V regional commissions included 54 million people residing in 30 states in seven different regions. Four of these states also participate in the Appalachian Regional Commission. (The ARC is by far the largest region; with a population of 18 million in the mid-1970s, it contains a third of the total population residing in Title V regions.) Since a total of 40 states participate in the Title V organizations, 80 out of 100 U.S. senators represent states which have a vested interest in the continuation and funding of multistate regional commissions.

Public Works Subcommittee hearings on the future of the Title V commissions in June 1975 revealed that the substantial support which had seen the commissions through the Nixon administration was still very much alive. Strong expressions in favor of funding reflect solid backing from two dozen state governors and other officials. Many of these statements outlined unfinished business of the 1970s on the regional agenda, notably transportation, energy, and the environment.[27] Regional representatives laid less stress on issues of the 1960s such as poverty and substandard housing, and one issue omitted in the 1960s continued to be bypassed: racial problems are nowhere specifically mentioned with respect to blacks, Hispanics, or Indians in the western regions.

Among other features, the hearings on S. 1189 concerned a Ford administration proposal ostensibly aimed at coordination. A Commerce Department secretarial officer was to be assigned coordinative responsibilities, apparently superseding the federal co-chairmen and the EDA in all regions except Appalachia. In conjunction with other proposals which were regarded as similarly restrictive, this move was regarded with suspicion. Predictably, the governors and other officials were strongly opposed, interpreting the proposal as a diminution of regional autonomy in sharp contrast to the independence accorded to the Appalachian Commission. Typical responses to the Commerce Department included:

> If organizational changes are to be made, they should be to strengthen the position and role of the Commissions, rather than to hobble them.
>
> I understand the administration's proposal that the Appalachian Commission be extended four years, while the Title V commissions are only projected for one year. . . . Although the Title V commissions have a highly commendable and successful record it is logical that maximum efficiency and effectiveness is inhibited by legislation which restricts them to a year-to-year existence.
>
> The centralization focus of your amendments would dilute the effectiveness of the commissions by making them subject to the jurisdiction of a governmental agency, rather than the President. . . . Existing institutional arrange-

ments have permitted a joint state-federal-regional presence and enabled us to set our own priorities in the development and execution of Title V programs.

Your proposal would result in subordinating the Commission's major decisions to a Commerce Department official. This is not a full state-federal partnership. It would dampen the spirits of this region's Governors in dealing with our mutual economic problems. . . . Title V Regional Commissions provide a meeting place for the development of ideas, the expression of priorities and the execution of plans and programs that cross state boundaries.[28]

This summary points to several conclusions. First, it is clear that Peter Hall was right when he suggested that earmarking aid for particular areas—Appalachia and the Title V commissions—"represented a conscious attempt to break away from the bad American tradition of spreading help thinly among all states and all areas."[29] In reality, however, when a program covers almost a third of the nation's population, assistance is diffused rather than concentrated. Good or bad, there is reason to believe that the traditional logrolling, Christmas tree approach to allocating funds is very much in operation. In this important respect, the new regions are not a departure from past tradition but a continuation of it. The trend is almost always in the direction of spreading good things around rather than permitting one or two—or seven—areas to monopolize them.

Second, it seems apparent that the Title V regions, to an even greater extent perhaps than the Appalachian region, are being taken on faith. While there have been occasional press criticisms of their performance, there is none of the serious evaluation and breastbeating that in time helped to reshape the thrust of the Appalachian program. The Title V commissions seem to represent a convenient vehicle for securing entrée to federal funds that would otherwise be unavailable and would otherwise be exclusively channeled to other regions with the initiative to carve up a big multistate region. Beyond the fact that the participating states believe that they perform a useful function, it may be assumed that a search analysis would reveal that they conduct a mixed bag of research studies and programs. The question is, In whose interest is it to mount such an evaluation? By the mid-1970s the big regions had become a formidable political reality vulnerable perhaps to minor tinkering but quite probably no longer susceptible to major surgery.

AN EXTENSION FOR THE APPALACHIAN REGION

In a Senate hearing in June 1975, Senator Jennings Randolph of West Virginia reminded his listeners that in the first vote on the Appalachian region in the House of Representatives in 1965 there were 257 votes for and 165 against. Ten years later, in 1975, the vote to extend the Appalachian region was 399 to 88.[30] First on the scene, Appalachia stepped out in front in the search for federal funds. In fiscal 1973 the total combined appropriation for the Title V commissions amounted to 74 cents per capita, while appropriations for the Appalachian Regional Commission amounted to over $34 per capita.[31] The plain fact is that as money raisers, the Title V commissions are not in the same class as the Appalachian region. It might be argued that some of these other regions, like New England and the Pacific Northwest, were not as poor and hence did not need as much money; but this argument falls apart if one considers the grinding poverty of the Coastal Plains region or the Ozarks. In view of the huge sums that have been allocated to Appalachia, Governor Philip Noel's comment relative to converting Rhode Island's abandoned Quonset Naval Air Base to civilian use is instructive: the cost of upgrading the sewerage system, $5.5 million, "would utilize the entire annual allocation to the New England Regional Commission."[32]

Much of the tremendous imbalance between Appalachia and the other regions is due to a major influx of federal funds for capital development, particularly highways. Peter Hall points out that no less than $470 million of the total of $679 million in ARC funds was allocated to highway construction in the period 1965–69. In his opinion, this represented "a real distortion of investment. . . . The benefit passed mainly to outside business interests rather than to the hard-pressed people of the region."[33]

Niles Hansen suggested in 1970 that

> despite a relative shift in emphasis on the part of the Appalachian Regional Commission toward human resource programs, there is still widespread reluctance among local political leaders in the region to give up their attachment to public works projects. In part this relates to the migration issue. Public works projects of the highway type receive relatively high priority because (1) they are very tangible (2) they represent a means by which, it is hoped, economic activity may be attracted *to* lagging regions; and (3) they cannot be moved to other regions as can investments embodied in human beings.[34]

While Hansen quotes various ARC publications to the effect that one of the commission's objectives is to assist people to acquire the health and skills they need wherever they may choose to live, he indicates that the commission has not been encouraging surplus population to relocate. As noted elsewhere in this work, a direct, formal confrontation with the need for out-migration is definitely not part of the American political tradition. It is not surprising that the ARC has bypassed a head-on collision with local politicians and businessmen who equate net out-migration with western ghost towns, the many abandoned mining villages that represent an extreme response to a shortage of job opportunities.

A summary report on the activities of the Appalachian Regional Commission reveals a perfect political compromise, a continuation of heavy expenditures on the highway system augmented by substantial spending for human resources and other programs. The cumulative program summary of seven functional areas through February 1975 lists the following allocations:

1. Health and Child Development	1,339 projects
	$351 million ARC
	673 million Other
	$1,024 million Total eligible cost
2. Vocational and Other Education	1,235 projects
	$318 million ARC
	644 million Other
	$962 million Total eligible cost
3. Community Facilities	689 projects
	$117 million ARC
	495 million Other
	$612 million Total eligible cost
4. Housing	143 projects
	$8 million ARC
5. Natural Resources	$67 million ARC
	22 million Other
6. Development Highways	2,685 miles eligible for construction
	1,345 (50%) construction completed or underway
	$1,264 million ARC
	1,026 million Other
	$2,290 million Total eligible cost
7. Access Roads	263 projects approved
	705 miles
	$86 million ARC
	56 million Other
	$142 million Total eligible cost[35]

The ARC report makes no apology for the strong and continuing focus on highways. The region's new highways were credited with a major influence on location of new manufacturing industry, and the report indicated that over 60 percent of the 1,149 plants located in the region since 1965 were sited within 20 minutes travel of the region's new highways.[36] The report also stressed the improved commutation access provided by the new roads for the region's rural population commuting to regional urban centers and traveling to the large urban centers outside the region.

In contrast to its major role in highways, the ARC has had a much lower profile in education and housing. Education is seen as an area in which the ARC plays a catalytic and supplementary role, leaving the main thrust to the states and localities. The report indicates that during the first decade of its existence, "ARC investments represented less than 1 per cent of the total education expenditures within the region."[37] Similarly, in housing, through December 31, 1974, the commission had approved loan applications for only 12,534 housing units. Here again the states and localities, working with private developers, are seen as having the prime responsibility, and ARC is viewed as a catalyst and supplement.

An examination of the report and other materials in the hearings reveals ARC's awesome ability to attract federal funds. Certainly the Title V commissions have every right to be envious at the size of the ARC's "other" category —over and above the very large direct ARC allocations.

In pressing for extension of the Appalachian Regional Development Act it was necessary for proponents to draw a fine distinction between past progress and the need for future progress. Senator Howard Baker of Tennessee, while lauding the ARC's contribution to the infrastructure of roads, community facilities, and human resource programs, straddled the issue with considerable finesse:

> Considering the past success of the Appalachian program and the region's new relationship to the Nation, I know that to abandon this program now would be to leave a very important task unfinished. It would mean to leave a very necessary task unfinished. It would mean, moreover, failure to address the new challenges to a struggling regional economy.[38]

The commission made a similar point with respect to unemployment rates which, in the mid-1970s, looked suspiciously similar to national averages. The ARC stressed that hidden unemployment must be taken into consideration. If this is done, it is claimed that unemployment rates in Appalachia remain 3 or 4 points higher than the U.S. average.

Senator Baker introduced several new themes in his statement, reflecting the ARC's response to the improvement in the economy generated by the post-1973 coal boom and the change in population patterns in some parts of the region from a net exporter to a net importer of population: new trends equal new challenges. If losing people creates problems, so does gaining people:

> The influx of new residents and the growing tourism and recreation appeal of the region place added burdens on local and state planning and development institutions. Strong efforts must be continued to organize and guide new development in a way that protects our environment and avoids chaotic growth. The simple fact is that Appalachia, although well on the way to achieving its original goals, finds itself faced with a new set of problems.[39]

To confront these problems, the ARC laid out a program which combines a continued emphasis on highways (the "cornerstone" of the regional strategy in Senator Baker's view) with a broadened emphasis on human resources, a new focus on energy, and more subregional decentralization. In part, this latter restructuring was in response to critics. Over the years the ARC had been criticized for its role as a creature of the establishment—poverty program people and environmentalists led the attack—and for its tendency to operate from a narrow base of decision makers. A move toward decentralization would at the very least enlarge the number of actors.

The ARC indicated that investments will continue to be heavily directed toward provision of essential public services, particularly health care, and that new attention will be given to rural areas. In addition it was promised that more attention would be given to encouraging private entrepreneurship and to the potential for lasting development of using the region's vast coal resources to meet the nation's energy needs.[40]

Senator Baker elaborated on these themes: improved rural transportation and health care systems, more adult, career, and skills education, improved community services (particularly sewer and water systems), and more focus on energy resources. And Senator Baker called for alterations in the decision-making process, with greater powers assigned to the local development districts and multicounty planning agencies. The commission, in his phraseology, would "continue to serve as advocate and honest broker for the region."[41]

DEBITS AND CREDITS

Despite the passage of ten years, it is still too soon to reach a definite verdict on the Appalachian Regional Commission. Clearly the claims of its proponents must be taken with a considerable dosage of salt, particularly since they do not make any serious attempt to distinguish between what happened because of the ARC and what would have occurred in any event. By any standards, however, the ARC has been a superb lobbying organization. Certainly, in terms of sheer dollar volume, it has chalked up notable successes. The wistful envy of the Title V commissions is well deserved.

Whatever the responsibility assigned to the ARC in stimulating major improvements in the region's environment and living standards, the region has made substantial progress during the decade. As the ARC has indicated, past gains can provide a foundation for substantial future achievements. To a great extent, future progress depends on ensuring that the post-1973 coal boom leaves drastically different residuals than earlier eras of resource-oriented prosperity with timber and, subsequently, the coal industry. Harry Caudill and others have described these earlier periods of exploitation as tantamount to regional rape.[42]

One crucial question is whether the ARC will use its powers to attempt to impose some form of post-boom assessment on the coal corporations, along with tough environmental controls. Based on past performance, this is not a likely possibility. The ARC has avoided, almost by instinct, the kind of bruising, controversial battles that might be entailed by issues involving race, class, or direct confrontation with pillars of the regional economy. The ARC has indeed, in Senator Baker's words, been an effective advocate and broker. The region's future seems to depend on a different role for some level of government —combat with a powerful industry that has ravaged the region with the connivance rather than the opposition of the region's governmental bodies. In the past there has been neither a strong public environmental consciousness nor an ARC. It remains to be seen whether the combination of the two will tame the coal boom of the 1970s.

On the whole, one would predict that the ARC, like the Title V multistate regions, is simply not equipped for warfare. It may well be that the ARC and the Title V Regional Commissions will be able to continue to avoid serious controvery by shunting issues that arouse serious political passions to other levels of government, particularly Washington. The state legislatures may assume a larger, tougher role in environmental and resource industry taxation, but the principal arena for such activities as regulation of strip mining is likely to be the Congress and the executive. It is not so much a matter of federal control within the big regions where, as Joseph Califano comments, the president's executive branch speaks with the "authority of a senior partner" because it provides the funding.[43] Whatever the "senior partner" may desire—and it is not likely to be confrontations—the dynamics of political survival probably call for the junior partners to sidestep bitter struggles with powerful industries. For this reason, the control of resource exploitation involving head-on collisions with the corporations will be a task for the federal and perhaps state governments, not the big regions.

CONCLUSION: NEW REGIONS EQUAL NEW ARENAS

It is possible to discern the faint outlines of a national regional policy since the late 1960s, partly with the help of the Appalachian and Title V regional bellwethers. Under the prodding of the U.S. Bureau of the Budget, we can, eventually, anticipate embarrassing, intensive, and useful efforts in developing performance standards to measure the efficacy of various regional programs. A sophisticated form of technical warfare will probably develop as planners, economists, sociologists, and other professionals are mobilized to present, defend, or attack alternative plans and programs.

Unlike most of the COGs, metropolitan regions that remain federally sponsored clients with weak political roots, the new regions were politicized from their inception; they have developed into active political arenas, creating an interesting fourth dimension in the present federal-state-local system. However, there are several foreseeable problems in playing this role effectively. The first involves organization. Three southern states, the Carolinas and Georgia, are members of two regions, Appalachia and the Coastal Plains. Other states with varied territory and characteristics are likely to be confronted by the same challenge. It is extremely difficult to allocate limited staff resources and gubernatorial attention to two or more regional organizations, aside from the work entailed in dealing with metropolitan areas, economic development districts, and other units. Whatever the violence to economic logic, whole-state membership in a single region may be highly desirable.

A second problem concerns the level of public interest in regional problems and the activities of an interstate organization. Both of the burning issues of the latter third of this century, violence at home and abroad, come under the jurisdiction of the federal government, while cities are on the firing line of domestic disorder.

Similarly, other critical problems—like taxes, schools, and employment—are in the federal and local domain although the state role is being enlarged. Regional organizations are left with significant functions in such matters as air and water pollution and open space issues that apparently arouse little sustained public interest, secondary roles in research, and roles as political intermediaries and financial conduits in human resource and transportation development.

As research, lobbying, and troubleshooting organizations, the big regions have had more than enough to keep them occupied for their first few years. Subsequently, the regional commissions may find themselves grappling with some of the basic, unresolved issues in our society.

One such issue involves "overdevelopment," the point at which a national policy decision must be made between permitting population, economic, and other types of growth to continue to flow to one or two major centers as compared to deliberate policies of redirecting the stream of growth to other, smaller centers and new towns.[44] Many European nations have adopted this second alternative even at the risk of running counter to broad, deep, and historic trends toward centralization. The time may not be far off when the United States will no longer be able to avoid a similar confrontation between powerful, natural forces moving toward a continuing concentration and demands for effective action to stimulate decentralization. Beginning with research and policy recommendations and following through to attempts to influence national policy on resource allocation and development incentives, the big regions will surely be closely involved in this controversial issue.

In the long run, the efficacy of the new regional agencies will depend to a great extent on the quality of their staffs. A well-balanced, well-led research team, trusted by the states and federal agencies, can play an important part in broadening the focus of government operations and making programs more meaningful. The ability to perform sound, broad-gauge, action-oriented research rapidly can be a great strength. Conversely, a feebly led technical staff is not likely to have much impact.

There will obviously be a wide gulf between a high-powered regional research team, the states and localities that tend to lack impressive planning and research capacity, and the public whose attention is focused elsewhere and has insufficient understanding of the issues and complexities. Commissions can assist the states and municipalities to improve their capabilities and help to educate the public concerning their activities and decisions.

Finally, one can hazard the prophecy that interregional clashes are likely to provide additional stimulus for national planning. The new regions can conceivably play a significant role in recapturing some of the ground lost under the ideological onslaughts of the 1930s and early 1940s which killed the National Resources Planning Board.

On the whole, however, the regional commissions opened up new roles and new challenges for the existing cast of characters rather than bringing in "new faces of the 1970s." Existing state and federal agencies assumed new tasks, and governors and senators responded to new opportunities for achievement and maneuver. Finally, the road ahead is likely to be rocky: There seems to be a rule of governmental, academic, and military bureaucracy that each new coordinative mechanism further complicates the difficulties of coordination. It has been wisely said that a coordinator is a man who sits between two expediters. A remarkable combination of managerial and planning talent will be required to measure up to the challenges generated by the new regionalism. Despite Appalachia's reputation as a habitat for political sharks, the Appalachian Regional Commission has been ably commanded and staffed. There are disquieting signs of trouble in some of the EDA regions, which seem to be much weaker in terms of leadership and technical personnel. It appears that some key positions have been used to repay minor political debts and are occupied by amiable and personable lightweights lacking in both background and educability. Regionalism is an intriguing and attractive approach, but it is as susceptible as any other undertaking to incompetence and stupidity. As has been noted at frequent intervals in this volume, government accomplishment depends more on talented staff than on formal organizational structure.

NOTES

1. U.S., Congress, Public Law 89–4, "Appalachian Regional Development Act of 1965," 89th Cong., 1st sess., March 9, 1965.

2. See National Resources Planning Board, *Security, Work and Relief Policies,* a report of the Committee on Long-Range Work and Relief Policies (Washington, D.C.: U.S. Government Printing Office, 1942). The Cutover region (Upper Great Lakes) boundaries are similar to those

delineated in the NRPB research, but the Appalachian and other EDA regions are substantially different.

3. See John Friedmann, "Regional Planning as a Field of Study," *Journal of the American Institute of Planners,* 29, no. 3 (August 1963): 168–75; and idem, "The Concept of a Planning Region—The Evolution of an Idea in the United States," *Land Economics,* 32, no. 3 (February 1956): 213–27. See also Howard W. Odum and Harry Estill Moore, *American Regionalism* (New York: Henry Holt, 1938).

4. Friedmann, op. cit., p. 63.

5. The example of the Tennessee Valley was frequently cited in the Senate and House hearings on 1965 EDA legislation. See *Hearings* before the Committee on Public Works (Senate) and Committee on Public Works (House of Representatives), "Public Works and Economic Development Act of 1965," 89th Cong., 1st sess., 1965.

6. U.S. Economic Development Administration, *Economic Development* (Washington, D.C.: U.S. Government Printing Office, February 1968), p. 3.

7. Philip Selznick, *TVA and the Grass Roots* (Berkeley: University of California Press, 1949).

8. David A. Grossman and Melvin R. Levin, "The Appalachian Region: A National Problem Area," *Land Economics* 37, no. 2 (May 1961): 133–41.

9. Melvin R. Levin, *The Depressed Area: A Study of Southern Illinois* (Ph.D. dissertation, Division of Social Sciences, University of Chicago, 1956).

10. The ABC system refers to highways financed on a 50-50 basis by the federal and state governments. The smaller, generally higher-quality, interstate system is 90 percent financed by the federal government.

11. U.S., A Report by the President's Appalachian Regional Commission, *Appalachia* (Washington, D.C.: U.S. Government Printing Office, 1964).

12. The Appalachian Regional Development Commission, *Executive Director's Semi-Annual Report,* Table, "Status of Program Funds Through Fiscal Year 1967," Washington, July 1–December 31, 1966.

13. Charles McKinley, "The Valley Authority and Its Alternatives," *American Political Science Review,* September 1950, included as chap. 28 in John Friedmann and William Alonso, *Regional Development and Planning: A Reader* (Cambridge, Mass.: M.I.T. Press, 1964).

14. An opening salvo in this campaign was fired by Senator Robert F. Kennedy. See Ben A. Franklin, "Kennedy Calls Antipoverty Program a Failure," New York *Times,* February 15, 1968, p. 1.

15. Litton Industries, *Preliminary Analysis for Economic Development Plan for the Appalachian Region,* Prepared for the Area Redevelopment Administration (Washington, D. C.: Appalachian Regional Commission, 1965), pp. 259–60.

16. A proposal for creating new towns in eastern Kentucky had been recommended in 1960. See University of Kentucky, Department of Architecture, "A Case Study Located in Eastern Kentucky," *New Towns: A Proposal for the Appalachian Region* (Lexington: University of Kentucky, 1960). The proposal was stimulated by Grady Clay, editor of *Landscape Architecture,* who served on the advisory committee.

17. *Executive Director's Semi-Annual Report,* op. cit., letter of transmittal, Ralph R. Widner, Executive Director.

18. *Hearings on the Public Works and Economic Development Act;* op. cit., statements of Dr. John Peterson, University of Arkansas, pp. 226–27.

19. New York *Times,* January 10, 1970, p. 23.

20. Ben A. Franklin, "In Appalachia: Vast Aid, Scant Relief," ibid., November 29, 1970, p. 1.

21. Ibid.

22. Ibid.

23. *Congressional Quarterly Weekly Report,* 29, no. 8 (February 19, 1971): 435.

24. Ibid.

25. *Statistical Abstract of the United States 1975,* table no. 666, p. 406.

26. U.S. Congress, Senate, Committee on Public Works, Subcommittee on Economic Development, *Title V Regional Commissions, Hearing,* 94th Cong, 1st session, June 4, 1975, statement of Senator Dale Bumpers, pp. 22–23.

27. Ibid.

28. Ibid., pp. 75–85.

29. Peter Hall, *Urban and Regional Planning* (New York: John Wiley, 1974), p. 251.

30. Statement of Senator Jennings Randolph, Subcommittee on Economic Development, op. cit., p. 21.

31. Ibid., p. 23.

32. Statement of Philip H. Noel, Governor of Rhode Island, ibid., p. 35.

33. Hall, op. cit., p. 251.

34. Niles M. Hansen, op. cit., p. 76.

35. U.S. Congress, Senate, Committee on Public Works, Subcommittee on Economic Development, *Extension of the Appalachian Regional Development Act, Hearings,* March 10, 11, 12, and June 3, 1975, part. 1, Report of Appalachian Regional Commission, pp. 139–40.

36. Ibid., p. 146.

37. Ibid., p. 210.

38. Senator Howard H. Baker, *Congressional Record,* March 7, 1975, p. 8.

39. Ibid., p. 8.

40. Ibid., pp. 91–92.

41. Ibid., p. 9.

42. Harry Caudill, *Night Comes to the Cumberlands* (Boston: Little, Brown, 1962).

43. Joseph Califano, *A Presidential Nation* (New York: Norton, 1975), p. 91.

44. See Myles Wright, "Regional Development: Problems and Lines of Advance in Europe," reprinted in H. Wentworth Eldredge, ed., *Taming Megalopolis,* vol. 2 (New York: Doubleday, 1967), pp. 1119–42.

CHAPTER

10

SUMMING UP: ONE SMALL CANDLE?

BACKGROUND INFORMATION

The preceding chapters have constituted a guided tour around some of the perimeters of the urban nation. As the discussion of policies and programs has suggested, there has been no shortage of new ideas to deal with old problems. The trouble is that bold, imaginative concepts call for remarkable people to translate dreams into reality, and this is precisely where cutting edges of the new federalism have become dulled and chipped. PPB, urban planning, metropolitan governances, and the big regions not only require first-quality staff at the top but also competent staff in the middle and lower echelons. While not many additionally trained people are required in global terms—perhaps only five to ten thousand—we simply do not have them. This may be neither the first nor the last time in history that noble concepts and imaginative plans were degraded by faulty execution, but there is something rather odd in the spectacle of major programs in a major nation faltering for want of a few thousand trained professionals.

There are other difficulties beyond the people shortage: Events have moved so fast in the 1960s and 1970s that ideas and assumptions could become obsolete in a matter of a few years. On the whole, our programs tend to be mood pieces reflecting a transient consensus. They may crystallize years of awakening and discussion, but the actual legislation is essentially a response geared to handle a current crisis. Consequently, one senses less of an air of finality about government programs in the mid-1970s. Modesty and humility are less uncommon virtues than in past eras of self-righteous moralizing and dogmatic certainty.

This chastened outlook is due to a variety of exogenous forces, not the least of which is a forceful, albeit unsystematic, battering from Congress and the press. But internal pressures are also at work in this direction. PPB and ZBB, delightful concepts to progressive administrators, reveal in a systematic fashion that many programs rest on brittle, terra cotta foundations, partly because of the persisting talent shortage but also because we have discovered that, despite all our research, we know little about many basic aspects of our society. Government agencies are being exposed to a pitiless analysis that shows just how deep is our ignorance about the processes of economic development, manpower training, education and health programs, and, indeed, in what ways our various efforts affect client groups and the larger society. We are equally feeble in the vital field of projections; planning ahead is often an exercise in poor judgment. Even that basic building block for long-range plans, population forecasting, has repeatedly been shown to be a most inexact science.

New approaches like PPB and ZBB are not likely to eliminate uncertainty over ends, means, goals, and consequences. In fact, it is much more probable that they will be as vulnerable as cost benefit to charges that their basic assumptions are mostly unproved, that they can work only by screening out most of the real world, and that they can easily be manipulated to yield any desired result.

In a way, the series of chapters in this book functions as a dual Rorschach test and reveals as much about the outlook of the commentator as about the programs he studies and dissects. The author pleads guilty to having begun with a mild skepticism that has been strengthened by his research. It appears to him that bureaucracies find it difficult to reshape their policies without an externally originated galvanic shock and that their perceptions seem limited to the acquisition of sanctioned, generally favorable information which reaches headquarters through approved channels.

Insulated Agencies

This unwillingness or perhaps incapacity to assimilate embarrassing facts pointing to program weaknesses probably accounts for agency slowness in responding to criticisms of urban renewal programs and other domestic endeavors. Bureaucracy's capacity for self-delusion in domestic programs seems limitless and, unfortunately, is far from unknown in other, more dangerous areas. The second-ranking embassy official in South Vietnam in the early 1960s wrote:

> The root of the problem was the fact that much of what the newsmen took to be lies was exactly what the U.S. Mission genuinely believed, and was reporting to Washington. Events were to prove that the Mission itself was unaware of how badly the war was going, operating in a world of illusion. Our feud with the newsmen was an angry symptom of bureaucratic sickness.[1]

It is not surprising to find that opening the secret archives, as in the case of the Pentagon papers, usually reveals that government officials are as misinformed and wrong-headed in closed sessions as they are in public pronouncements. Intelligence is not concealed behind a smokescreen of simple-minded bombast. Public idiocy is usually a faithful reflection of private stupidity.

The inability of the bureaucracies to assess the impact of their programs and to make appropriate, timely adjustments related in part to an obvious unwillingness to hear bad news. This deficiency is closely related to a built-in tendency to exaggerate successes—each bureaucrat passes reports upward that cast his operation in a rosy light. Even a shaky program, crumbling around the edges, is bathed in radiance by the time the successive layers of bureaucracy have done their work, partly as a justification for personal survival, and partly to justify enlarged appropriations. Often there is also a professional reluctance to expose dirty linen to public view. Further, there is a tendency for programs to be captured by educators, generals, highway engineers, physicians, welfare workers, and other specialists. This leads to situations in which criticisms from laymen (that is, nonmembers) are usually resented as ignorant meddling, events are interpreted, problems are screened, and solutions are circumscribed by the narrow scope of professional ideology and practice.

Smith Simpson, in his trenchant examination of the ills of the Department of State, lays much of the blame on the inertness and incapacity of the "pyramidal mass" and on the built-in resistance to even the best-intentioned criticism. During most of the career officer's working life:

> He has been excessively bothered by suggestions of better policies and performance, and has joined with his colleagues in attributing criticism from without to obtuseness and general myopia and criticism from within to unspeakable treachery. So keenly resented has criticism been over the years that its points have been rarely deemed worthy of serious consideration and its factual validity has been generally dismissed disdainfully without examination.[2]

The failure to receive accurate information exacerbates inherent tendencies toward insulating top officials from the outside world. Deeply involved in day-to-day activities and minor crises, living in a closed, two-dimensional world of internal operations and interagency relations, the upper-echelon executive is barraged by huge, undigestible amounts of conflicting information; consequently, his span of attention to assimilate unwanted, upsetting criticism tends to be extremely short. In his view there are enough troubles around without looking for more. The world, however, is not hermetically sealed, and client and legislative feedback often exercises a salutary influence in penetrating this airless, abstract environment. But outbursts by Congress and the pickets and the press are symptoms of the disease rather than a remedy.

Anthony Downs[3] discusses a distortion arising from "noise" and semiautonomous, hierarchical screening processes inherent in bureaucracies as large quantities of program information are received, condensed, and transmitted up the hierarchy. He recommends a number of antidistortion methods that may be used by top executives to arrive at an accurate assessment of the situation, including deliberate injection of counterbiases, reduction in the number of middlemen filters, introduction of intra-agency competition to provide overlapping information, and use of out-of-agency information sources.

The fact is that the programs have grown so vast and so complex as to defy the casual investigation, the sporadic outbreak, and the one-shot committee grilling. The trend toward comprehensiveness in planning, toward creation of Byzantine interagency arrangements, and toward proliferation of agency guidelines and regulations has led to a situation in which many programs have grown harder to comprehend, much less to control. There are masses of data and piles of reports, but basic questions involving the effectiveness of enormous, expensive programs go unanswered. Moreover, over and above internal agency problems, any serious attempts at program evaluation run the danger of falling afoul of the interstices between agency responsibilities. It has become terribly difficult to assign blame and credit to particular agencies and agency components when responsibilities are fragmented, causes and effects are imperfectly understood, and values and goals are conflicting and/or poorly articulated. Surely this is why Jimmy Carter's 1976 campaign struck a responsive chord in calling for comprehensible, responsive, and efficient government agencies.

Arthur Schlesinger's "permanent government" is another term for Simpson's "pyramidal mass." In Schlesinger's opinion, it represents an awesome barrier to executive control over a mammoth establishment. Presidents Kennedy's and Nixon's methods of manipulating this leviathan included not only the customary appointment of trusted executives to key agencies, but a practice of shaking up the departments through presidential staff skilled at direct, out-of-channels contact with lower echelons. The bureaucracy does not take kindly to winds of change. As Schlesinger describes it in the early 1960s:

> Though a valuable reservoir of intelligence and experience as well as a valuable guarantee against presidential government's going off the tracks, the permanent government remained in bulk a force against innovation with an inexhaustible capacity to dilute, delay and obstruct presidential purpose. Only so many fights were possible with the permanent government. The fighters—one saw this happen to Richard Goodwin when he went over to the State Department—were gradually weakened, cut off, surrounded and shot down, as if from ambush, by the bureaucracy and its anti-New Frontier allies in Congress and the press. At the start we had all felt free to "meddle" when we thought that we had a good idea or someone else a poor one. But, as the ice began to form again over the government, free-wheeling became increasingly difficult and dangerous.[4]

Some help for the chief executive with the stumbling agency may be available if continuing, in-house program analysis can be successfully institutionalized. PPB, ZBB, and related techniques hold considerable promise, at long last, that basic questions will be asked about program objectives, inputs, and consequences. Getting defensible answers is, of course, another matter. At the end of the road, questioning and research may lead, not to the solution of basic problems, but simply to their being better understood. Moreover, because goals are elusive and the measurement techniques are primitive, PPB and ZBB also raise less attractive possibilities. They may generate endless turmoil or bitter technical disputes over the value judgments and techniques that provide yardsticks for performance measurements. There is much room for argument between agency staff, legislative investigators, and advocate technicians to plead their respective causes in assigning priorities and formulating criteria for measuring program impact.

The fact that an increasing number of clever people inside and outside the agencies will be embroiled in technical guerrilla warfare in disputes over means and ends is by no means an alarming prospect. A little violence is needed to break through the hardened surface that seals off agencies from the sulfurous but bracing atmosphere of the outside world. Perhaps, at some later stage, much of the new look can be made routine and packaged in standard manuals suitable for technicians of modest abilities. This is not the case at present, either at the federal level or in the states and localities.

The Prime Prerequisite: Staff Capability

One primary thrust in this work has been to underscore the need for qualified staff at all levels of government, but especially in the states and localities. The analogy between state and municipal government and underdeveloped foreign nations, not properly equipped to run their own affairs efficiently nor to absorb outside assistance, is perhaps harsh. It will certainly be disputed by those fortunate persons whose experience has brought them into contact with the minority of progressive states and cities in the United States.

There are, of course, compensating benefits that offset administrative deficiencies at the state and local levels. Granting the weaknesses of extreme decentralization during the 1830s, Alexis de Tocqueville maintained that Americans derive political advantages from localism, from smallish governments organized on a human scale. Many will argue that a little anarchy has its benefits and that stimulating local initiative at the cost of some corruption, some unfairness to minorities, and substantial inefficiency is a price worth paying. The tendency to develop an abundance of private associations and to rely on the powers of the ordinary citizen, alone and in combination, has accounted for much of the strength, growth, character, and stability of the nation. Tocqueville's comments on the consequences of centralization could well be taken as a text by those who wish to see the states and localities stronger, more capable of asserting rights and assuming responsibilities:

> The partisans of centralization in Europe are wont to maintain that the government can administer the affairs of each locality better than the citizens can do it for themselves. This may be true when the central power is enlightened and the local authorities are ignorant; when it is alert and they are slow; when it is accustomed to act and they to obey. Indeed, it is evident that this double tendency must augment with the increase of centralization, and that the readiness of the one and the incapacity of the others must become more and more prominent. . . . However enlightened and skillful a central power may be, it cannot of itself embrace all the details of the life of a great nation. Such vigilance exceeds the powers of man. And when it attempts unaided to create and set in motion so many complicated springs, it must submit to a very imperfect result or exhaust itself in bootless efforts.[5]

Tocqueville's mistrust of powerful central government may have had its origins in royal and imperial France, but in the early 1970s one sensed a growing body of opinion in the United States that had tasted the fruit of the federal tree and found it bitter. Interestingly enough, the critics included many liberals who had become disenchanted with the cyclical pattern characterisitc of a number of promising programs—innovation degenerating into suspended animation. Daniel Moynihan's gloomy chronology of the Johnson era portrays this sentiment vividly:

> The pattern persists: the bright new idea, the new agency, the White House swearing in of the first agency head followed by a shaky beginning, the departure eighteen months later of the first head to be replaced by his deputy, the gradual slipping out of sight, a Budget Bureau reorganization, name change, a new head, this time from the civil service, and slow obscurity covers all.[6]

Some social scientists, despairing of efforts to improve sprawling bureaucracies, suggest that the answer may lie in dismantling the complex apparatus and shifting the primary emphasis to government-to-people programs like social security. Their recommendations include guaranteed annual incomes and health service chits, rather than welfare, health, poverty, or housing programs, and family tuition allowances to permit parents to send their children to schools of their choice. There are also increasing numbers of suggestions aimed at turning over to private enterprise the operation of some government functions and responsibilities in attacking unsolved social problems. This can be achieved in a number of ways, including subcontracts to private corporations, and through government guarantees and incentives, as with the quasi-private corporations being formed to undertake new housing and economic development programs. If federal funds were available to supplement family income, some of the elaborate bureaucratic apparatus of poverty, urban, and welfare programs would be eliminated and replaced by government checks for the poor, covering the difference between their present income and some desirable income level. The assault on the federal bureaucracy also includes a final weapon—block grants to local governments—because it is argued, Tocqueville style, that if government must do the job, it is preferable to assign the task to localities and possibly to states.

In some ways, it is strange that so much recent criticism has focused on relatively better-manned federal bureaucracies rather than on states and cities, despite the latter's well-documented weaknesses. This is evidenced in revenue sharing, the growing tendency for the federal government to distribute no-strings-attached grants to replace the complex federal grant-in-aid programs to state and local governments.

While it is difficult to quarrel with the concept of individual and family allowances or with a wider use of corporate skills and organization, the trouble with block grants to lower-echelon governments as a method of curing the ills of the large federal bureaucracies is that state and local bureaucracies may be smaller, but they are also much more feeble. One not only finds at least a similar fog of confusion in program impacts and conflicting ends and means in state and city government but also much less in the way of average competence in dealing with the confusion. The dismal situation was succinctly stated by Senator Edmund S. Muskie, who concluded in the mid-1960s that:

> The primary need of state and local governments is to attract and retain quality personnel. . . . Unfavorable working environments and inadequate personnel systems discourage both prospective employees and careerists. Too often, administrative personnel are given assignments without clear objectives, are frustrated by complicated intergovernmental structures, and find that the public holds them in low esteem. Compensation is substantially below industry standards. Career development programs, including opportunities for job mobility, in-service training and promotions are minimal except in some of the larger jurisdictions. Lack of effective merit systems permits the loading of agencies with incompetent, uninspiring and often indifferent personnel. Responsible administrators are often frustrated by inflexible rules and regulations dictating whom they may hire; whom, when, and how they shall promote; and whether, if at all, they may discipline or fire the incompetent or insubordinate.[7]

Few would deny that substantive improvements in state and local governments were effected in the subsequent decade. The record is spotty, however, and there remain huge sectors in which the level of performance can be classified as fair to poor to abysmal.

Admittedly, the talent problem is not confined to state and local agencies. As one observer indicates with respect to the federal government during the first wave of disenchantment with President Johnson's Great Society programs:

> The supply of able, experienced executives is not increasing as fast as the number of problems being addressed by public policy. . . . Everywhere, except in government, it seems the scarcity of talent is accepted as a fact of life. . . . The government—at least publicly—seems to act as if the supply of able executives were infinitely elastic, though people setting up new agencies will often admit privately that they are so frustrated and appalled by the shortage of talent that the only wonder is why disaster is so long in coming. . . . "Talent is scarcer than money" should be the motto of the Budget Bureau.[8]

Unfortunately, one saw only painfully slow progress even at the federal level in enlarging the supply of talent through the mid-1970s. And so far as most state and local governments are concerned, unless their currently limited attractions for professionals can somehow be augmented, there seems to be little hope of achieving a more effective federalism. All their responsiveness and closeness to the voter, all their potential for experimentation and innovation will be of little use unless these governments can be ably staffed. Intelligent application of such techniques as ZBB, to cite one example, calls for extraordinary talents, not only in program analysis, but in sensitivity to bureaucratic and political nuances.

By default, we probably can look forward to a decade of uncertain federal leadership, accompanied by a few outstanding states and municipalities, with other governments limping along in the rear, responding as well as they can to federal initiatives and incentives. The handful of states and localities that have demonstrated significant capabilities will continue to complain of confinement to program straitjackets apparently designed for potentially dangerous criminals and cretins. Short of a near revolution in staffing patterns, however, it is hard to see how program guidelines can be made sufficiently flexible to combine discretionary block grants for Wisconsin with tightly supervised grants-in-aid for Mississippi.

To summarize, a working system of federalism requires a realistic ability to diffuse power. At present, most states and localities, because of their lack of competent staff, are having more than enough trouble in keeping abreast of existing programs, let alone taking on new responsibilities. To some extent, the problem can be bypassed by placing increasing emphasis on personal choice through direct cash grants to individuals. The extent to which a combination of federal money transmitted through government-to-people programs and massive injections of private enterprise in helping to attack urban problems can be combined to deflate and bypass unresponsive government bureaucracy has yet to be fully tested. Nevertheless this concept seems to be winning a surprising number of followers all across the political spectrum. If, however, it is conceded that this approach has its unspecified but definite limits, we are still left with the problem of weak states and weak localities.

What may be needed is some method of injecting more intelligence into state and local government on a nationwide, continuing basis, through infusions of new staff and consulting capabilities. The method should include, if possible, a means of upgrading the cultural and physical environment and of establishing higher standards of excellence. There should be direct economic gains for the local economy and at least the possibility of generating additional economic growth. No great increase in the size of government bureaucracy should be required, and there should be considerable room for experimentation and innovation.

Obviously, this is a tall order, and perhaps the best we can do is to meet most, if not all, of the criteria. The answer, so far as one is available, seems to lie in exploiting the latent possibilities of the vast network of public and private universities, colleges, and community colleges that presently exist in state capitals and in many other localities.

THE UNIVERSITIES AND THE FUTURE OF FEDERALISM

It is almost a cliché to remark that the university is assuming a pivotal position in economic development. The growing emphasis on resource allocation and priorities now primarily involves human resources; concentrations of scientific ability and the migration of professional and technical personnel have in recent years deservedly received more attention than proximity to coal or iron ore as key economic determinants. One of the major roles of the university is this direct and indirect spillover of economic vitality into its surrounding area. This role involves assemblage of a creditable, sizable faculty, close relations with the corporate and government worlds through off-campus research activities, and training of bright young people. In this manner, dozens of colleges and universities have blossomed into major components of their area economies.

This potential economic role is one reason for the recommended expansion of higher educational facilities in state capitals, in distressed areas, and, for that matter, in the small and medium-sized cities throughout much of the nation.

The nation's major metropolitan areas doubtless will continue to skim off the cream of the backwoods talent, although, doubtless, a national manpower and migration policy to encourage more bright people to locate in small cities and distressed areas would be helpful. One way of attacking the problem is to concentrate on developing the capabilities of local universities and colleges as a critical point in strengthening economic and cultural development and the injection of nationally recognized professional standards in lagging areas. Unless action of this type is pursued, what we seem to be headed for is an era of cultural and economic polarization, in which a relatively few metropolitan areas, particularly in the North and in Sunbelt states, wind up with brain-oriented activities, and the remainder of the nation is relegated to routine, colonial-type operations, supervised by a thin layer of imported, transient executives.

State and local governments can profitably be viewed as underdeveloped territories that lack the technical capacities and continuing, institutional structures to keep abreast of advanced areas. The problem of standards is crucial because the talent drain has reinforced tendencies toward parochialism. It may be suggested that many of the small institutions could be adopted by or otherwise integrated within a high-quality state system or, alternatively, could simply develop symbiotic relations with first-rank, out-of-area institutions. This might well embrace arrangements for exchange of faculty, student transfers, and graduate study. In particular, this technique might help in augmenting the leadership stratum in redevelopment areas; many of them have seen generation after generation of their bright young men depart in search of economic opportunity and wider horizons.

The university can also play a useful role in improving the general quality of its environment in several ways. Normally, a higher educational institution of any size represents a significant environmental factor. It creates an oasis attractive to outside talent; professors and their wives become involved in local schools, planning boards, ecological programs, and other civic endeavors. There is also a bread-and-butter contribution to the local economy that is of special interest to redevelopment areas. The university is a substantial source of jobs, retail and service sales, and construction activity. Moreover, there is always the prospect that professorial research and related attractions will bloom into smaller-scale versions of the Cambridge-Route 128 complex associated with M.I.T. and other Boston area institutions. In short, a growing university can make depressed areas reasonably attractive to outside talent. This is extremely important because only to a degree does the yawning gulf in bureaucratic quality between the federal establishment and most state and local agencies relate to differential agency pay scales, recruitment policies, and career opportunities.

Environmental factors tend to be overlooked in discussions of remedial measures. With some remarkable exceptions like Madison, Wisconsin, Boston, and Minneapolis, state capitals and many cities are grim, intellectually barren places, without major universities or other attractions that would render them habitable to high-quality professional staff. The same observation is even more applicable to redevelopment areas. A national policy aimed at strengthening state and local government must include some attention to upgrading their qualitative social and cultural aspects because of the increasingly migratory propensity of talent. A good professional can shop around for a community that offers much more than simply a paying job. Obviously, his preferences pose difficult problems because not much can be done to moderate the magnetic attractions of the larger metropolitan areas on the nation's periphery. Fortunately, much can be achieved in enhancing the attractiveness of the enormous number of territories that are being consistently bypassed by first-quality people. A key role in this endeavor clearly belongs to the local colleges and universities. For example, one of their special and thus far largely unexploited potentials is the luring of otherwise unapproachable public officials by offering them part-time faculty appointments. This can be an extremely powerful incentive; American professional men seem to be divided into two broad categories, the professors and the remainder, who apparently yearn for faculty status.

The foregoing is not to suggest that the university no longer retains a primary role as an educational institution. Here, too, there is a special potential that is only beginning to be realized, namely, training large numbers of practitioners for service with state and local government and other area organizations. Provided the danger of inbreeding can be avoided, the natural ties of the student to his university environment can help an area meet its needs for trained professionals. It need hardly be said, however, that supply must be matched by demand. As has been indicated at some length, the townie-run states and localities have not been overly hospitable to university intellectuals in past years. Unless this situation changes and the states and localities become more attractive, there is reason to suppose that, as in past years, a diploma from a local university for ambitious youth will continue to serve as a passport for migration to a more promising area.

The same observation is equally valid for the professors. Professors have traditionally played a number of roles in government. They are a potential source of new bureaucratic appointments, adornments for administrations anxious to show off to the intelligentsia, and a problem-solving lifeline for the permanent staff that must devote virtually all of its time to wrestling with routine agency functions. The university can play significant roles as a repository of consulting talent in helping to solve urgent problems and in continuing basic inquiries into governmental maladies. If the academicians are not employed by state and local governments in applied and basic research and advisory capacities, the outstanding professorial talent will continue to commute temporarily (or migrate) to Washington. Under these circumstances, the gap between the federal establishment and neglected lower echelons of government will not only remain, but may widen.

THE UNIVERSITIES AND THE EVALUATION OF GOVERNMENT PROGRAMS

As has been suggested, one of the more depressing patterns of the past few decades is the recurrence of troublesome situations in which skilled newspapermen know much more about the impact of government programs than do the bureaucrats who run them. Time and again, there have been foreign and domestic debacles in which the failure of an agency's hierarchical structure to transmit accurate, trustworthy information to the decision makers was a significant factor. If this distortion is an inherent defect of bureaucracy, as it appears to be, the question arises as to possible methods of securing valid intelligence. A third role for the university might be found in this area.

Given available research funds and the capacities and orientation of most academicians, it is probable that this latter function—hired men for the agency—will continue to be the principal relationship between government and the professors. This is a useful role, but if the government agency's weak evaluative potential and its early warning radar screen are to be strengthened, it is fairly clear that something more is required.

Robert Wood classified two principal types of professorial approaches to urban problems as a debate among "Cassandras and the Urban Standpatters—between those who see the city as beyond redemption and those who feel it needs none."[9] The Rorschach factor is very much in evidence among observers of the urban scene. One can be rather cheery about a society that has made enormous progress in providing most of its citizens with a remarkable standard of affluence and culture, in which a rough but effective system of political and economic priorities operates to offer most of the citizenry comfortable, pleasant lives. Or one can just as easily take the opposite tack and concentrate on unsolved and perhaps insoluble problems of the slums, the blacks, Appalachian poor, Indians, Hispano-Americans, and foreign affairs, to conclude that the nation is gravely and perhaps fatally afflicted.

What Wood failed to mention is that although each school of intellectuals may be bitterly opposed on substantive issues, they are united in blasting government agencies. Whether hawkish or dovish on matters of policy, they are united in agreement that current programs are faulty in conception, weak in administration, and barren of favorable consequences. Much of the growing body of political science literature concerns deficiencies in government programs, and many of the studies tend to be scathing denunciations. The impact of these publications on government agencies can be likened to a blowtorch that burns off the outer layers of insulated bureaucratic complacency. Because the government agency often resembles the legendary army mule whose attention could not be gained until he was whacked with a baseball bat, past experience indicates that there is a role for forceful academicians who awaken agency interest in an irritating and usually unappreciated manner.

This is, however, a brutal, costly, ex post facto way of going about the business of program evaluation and revision. What seems to be needed is preventive medicine. One approach is the pilot study run by highly motivated professionals that tests a program on a small scale before it becomes national policy. This technique has its advantages, although small, carefully planned pilots have a strange propensity to fly while their larger and more expensive successors, run by mediocrities, remain earthbound. Regardless of whether this trial balloon method is used, there appears to be a place for friendly academics, or more accurately, constructive professorial evaluators. Outside academicians can be employed by central headquarters, by foundations, or by publishers, to examine agency programs. The question is: Can the agencies act on information that is not wrapped around a baseball bat? The answer must necessarily be tentative, although some agencies have certainly arrived at the state of maturity and competence where friendly critics are welcomed instead of lacerated. The intelligent agency can help to establish a continuing, institutionalized critique, a mechanism that draws on the academic community to act as a combined, distant, early warning system, an evaluative laboratory, and an idea factory. Some federal agencies have already made some progress in this direction. Whether state and local governments can follow suit is another matter, but even there the ground has been broken by a few of the more sophisticated agencies.

It should be made clear that state and local governments are not wholly responsible for neglecting near-at-hand academic resources; the available institutions are not presently organized to provide substantial, usable assistance. There are several ways in which this deficiency can be corrected. The universities can probably enlarge their role as agency critics through improved consultation arrangements, particularly by encouraging academic departments to crossbreed with government officials. The "in-and-outer," as Richard Neustadt terms him, the academic who from time to time serves in government and the executive who occasionally serves on the university faculty, is fairly common at the upper echelon of the federal establishment. What is needed is a lot more of this mutual pollenation at other government levels.

This central focus can be developed under a variety of titles. The important ingredient is a concentration of productive, pragmatic talent in the university that shares a common outlook and retains a noble and unshakable faith in the improvement of government, whatever the current irrefutable evidence to the contrary.

In summary, the university comes about as close as any existing institution to meeting the critical needs of underdeveloped states and localities. The reshaping of the physical environment, narrowing of the cultural gap, training administrators and technical staff, and providing a continuing, local professional consulting resource will become a major responsibility for the universities and colleges, or the outlook for creative federalism is likely to be dim.

NOTES

1. John Mecklin, *Mission in Torment* (New York: Doubleday, 1965), pp. 100–01.

2. Smith Simpson, *Anatomy of the State Department* (Boston: Houghton Mifflin, 1967), p. 9.

3. Anthony Downs, *Inside Bureaucracy* (Boston: Little, Brown, 1967); see his "Communications Bureaus," pp. 112–31 and "The Fragmentalized Perception of Large Organizations," pp. 188–99.

4. Arthur Schlesinger, *A Thousand Days: John F. Kennedy in the White House* (Boston: Houghton Mifflin, 1965), p. 683.

5. Alexis de Tocqueville, *Democracy in America,* vol. 1 (New York: Vintage, 1954), pp. 93–94.

6. Daniel P. Moynihan, "You Can't Run the Nation from Washington," Boston *Globe,* October 28, 1967, p. 43.

7. Senator Edmund S. Muskie, "The Challenge of Creative Federalism," *Congressional Record,* March 25, 1966. See also: Committee for Economic Development, *Modernizing State Government* (New York: Committee for Economic Development, July 1967); and Terry Sanford, *Storm Over the States* (New York: McGraw-Hill, 1967). Governor Sanford points to danger from another quarter: overprofessionalization in which health, welfare, education, and other departments become closed agencies run by and for professional cliques and shielded from "the hand and eye of the public."

8. James Q. Wilson, "The Bureaucracy Problem," *The Public Interest,* no. 6 (Winter 1967): 3–9.

9. Robert Wood, "Government and the Intellectual: The Necessary Alliance for Effective Action to Meet Urban Needs," *Governing Urban Society: New Scientific Approaches* (Monograph 7 in a series sponsored by the American Academy of Political and Social Science), pp. 3–14.

SELECTED BIBLIOGRAPHY

BOOKS

Abrams, Richard M. *Conservatism in a Progressive Era: Massachusetts Politics, 1900–1912.* Cambridge, Mass.: Harvard University Press, 1964.

Adams, James Truslow. "The Historical Background." In *New England's Prospect: 1933,* edited by J. T. Adams *et al.* New York: Little, Brown, 1931.

Adrian, Charles R. "Metropology and the Planner." In *Planning 1962.* Chicago: American Society of Planning Officials, 1962.

Altshuler, Alan A. *The City Planning Process: A Political Analysis.* Ithaca, N.Y.: Cornell University Press, 1965.

Banfield, Edward C. *Political Influence.* Glencoe, Ill.: The Free Press, 1961.

———, and Wilson, James Q. *City Politics.* Cambridge, Mass.: Harvard University Press and M.I.T. Press, 1963.

Barzini, Luigi. *The Italians.* New York: Bantam, 1964.

Bauer, Raymond A., ed. *Social Indicators.* Cambridge, Mass: M.I.T. Press, 1966.

Bollens, John C., and Schmandt, Henry C. *The Metropolis, Its People, Politics and Economic Life.* 3d edition. New York: Harper and Row, 1975.

Boorstin, Daniel J. *The Americans: The National Experience.* New York: Vintage Books, 1965.

Boston Chamber of Commerce. *New England, What It Is and What It Is To Be.* Edited by George French. Cambridge, Mass.: University Printing Press, 1911.

Brooks, Mary E. *Housing Equity and Environmental Protection: The Needless Conflict.* Washington D.C.: American Institute of Planners, 1976.

Brunner, John. *Squares of the City.* New York: Ballantine Books, 1965.

Burns, James MacGregor, and Peltason, J. W. *Government by the People.* 9th edition. Englewood Cliffs, N.J.: Prentice-Hall, 1975.

Cahn, Anne H., and Parthasarathi, Ashok. *The Impact of a Government-Sponsored University Research Laboratory on the Local R & D Economy.* Cambridge, Mass.: M.I.T. Press, 1967.

Califano, Joseph A., Jr. *A Presidential Nation.* New York: Norton, 1975.

Campbell, Alan K., ed. *The States and the Urban Crisis.* Englewood Cliffs, N.J.: Prentice-Hall, 1970.

Cater, Douglass. "The Fourth Branch." In *Power in Washington.* New York: Vintage Books, 1965.

Chase, Edward T. "The Trouble with the New York Port Authority." In *Urban Government,* edited by Edward C. Banfield. Glencoe, Ill.: The Free Press, 1961.

Clark, Kenneth. *Dark Ghetto: Dilemmas of Social Power.* New York: Harper and Row, 1965.

Comay, Eli. "How Metropolitan Toronto Government Works." In *Planning 1965.* Chicago: American Society of Planning Officials, 1965.

Committee for Economic Development. *Modernizing Local Government.* New York: Committee for Economic Development, 1967.

______. *Reshaping Government in Metropolitan Areas.* New York: Committee for Economic Development, 1970.

Committee of New England of the National Planning Association. *The Economic State of New England.* New Haven: Yale University Press, 1954.

Council of State Governments. *Planning Services for State Governments.* Chicago: Council of State Governments, 1956.

______. *State Planning and Federal Grants.* Chicago: Public Administration Service, 1969.

Croly, Herbert. *Progressive Democracy.* New York: Macmillan, 1914.

______. *The Promise of American Life.* Edited by Arthur M. Schlesinger, Jr. Cambridge, Mass.: The Belknap Press of the Harvard University Press, 1965.

Dimock, Marshall E. "Expanding Jurisdictions: A Case Study in Bureaucratic Conflict." In *Reader in Bureaucracy,* edited by Robert K. Merton *et al.* Glencoe, Ill.: The Free Press, 1951.

Downs, Anthony. *Inside Bureaucracy.* Boston: Little, Brown, 1967.

Drucker, Peter F. *The Age of Discontinuity: Guidelines to Our Changing Society.* New York: Harper and Row, 1968.

Elazar, Daniel. *American Federalism: A View from the States.* New York: Crowell, 1966.

Eldredge, H. Wentworth, ed. *Taming Megalopolis.* Volume 2. New York: Doubleday, 1967.

Fisk, Donald M., and Lancer, Cynthia A. *Equality of Distribution of Recreation Services: A Case Study of Washington, D.C.* Washington, D.C.: The Urban Institute, July 1974.

Forrester, Jay W. *Urban Dynamics.* Cambridge, Mass.: M.I.T. Press, 1969.

France, Town and Country Environment Planning. New York: Service de Presse d'Information, 1965.

Freedman, Ronald; Whelpton, Pascal K.; and Campbell, Arthur A. *Family Planning, Sterility and Population Growth.* New York: McGraw-Hill, 1959.

Friedlander, Stanley L. *Labor Migration and Economic Growth: A Case Study of Puerto Rico.* Cambridge, Mass.: M.I.T. Press, 1965.

Friedmann, John, and Alonso, William, eds. *Regional Development and Planning.* Cambridge, Mass.: M.I.T. Press, 1964.

Galbraith, John K. *American Capitalism.* Boston: Houghton Mifflin, 1952.

Gans, Herbert. *The Levittowners.* New York: Pantheon Books, 1967.

______. *The Urban Villagers: Group and Class in the Life of Italian-Americans.* Glencoe, Ill.: The Free Press, 1962.

Gaus, John M.; White, Leonard D.; and Dimock, Marshall E. *The Frontiers of Public Administration.* Chicago: The University of Chicago Press, 1936.

Gold, Seymour M. *Urban Recreation Planning.* Philadelphia: Lea and Febiger, 1973.

Gottman, Jean. "The Rising Demand for Urban Amenities." In *Planning for a Nation of Cities,* edited by Sam Bass Warner. Cambridge, Mass.: M.I.T. Press, 1966.

Greer, Scott. *Urban Renewal and American Cities: The Dilemma of Democratic Intervention.* Indianapolis: Bobbs-Merrill, 1965.

Grodzins, Morton. "The Federal System." In *Democracy in the Fifty States,* edited by Charles Press and Oliver P. Williams. Chicago: Rand McNally, 1966.

Gross, Bertram M. *Organizations and Their Managing.* New York: The Free Press, 1968.

Hall, Peter. *Urban and Regional Planning.* New York: John Wiley, 1974.

Hansen, Niles M. *Rural Poverty and the Urban Crisis.* Bloomington: Indiana University Press, 1971.

Hayek, Friedrich. *The Road to Serfdom.* Chicago: University of Chicago Press, 1944.

Hofstadter, Richard. *Anti-Intellectualism in American Life.* New York: Vintage Press, 1963.

Hunter, Floyd. *Community Power Structure.* Chapel Hill, N.C.: University of North Carolina Press, 1953.

Jacobs, Jane. *The Death and Life of Great American Cities.* New York: Random House, 1961.

Klotsche, J. Martin. *The Urban University and the Future of Our Cities.* New York: Harper and Row, 1966.

Levin, Melvin R.; Rose, Jerome G.; and Slavet, Joseph C. *New Approaches to State Land-Use Policies.* Lexington, Mass.: Lexington Books, 1974.

Levitan, Sar A. *Antipoverty Work and Training Efforts: Goals and Reality.* Washington, D.C.: Institute of Labor and Industrial Relations and the National Manpower Policy Task Force, 1967.

______. *Federal Aid to Depressed Areas: An Evaluation of the ARA.* Baltimore: The Johns Hopkins Press, 1964.

Lewis, Hylan. *Poverty's Children.* Washington, D.C.: Cross-Tell (Communicating Research on the Urban Poor), Health and Welfare Council, National Capital Area, 1966.

Long, Norton E. "Who Makes Decisions in Metropolitan Areas?" In *Metropolitan Politics: A Reader,* edited by Michael Danielson. Boston: Little, Brown, 1966.

Markfield, Wallace. *To An Early Grave.* New York: Pocket Books, 1965.

Marris, Peter, and Rein, Martin. *Dilemmas of Social Reform.* Institute of Community Studies. London: Routledge and Kegan Paul, 1967.

Martin, Roscoe C. *The Cities and the Federal System.* New York: Atherton Press, 1965.

Mecklin, John. *Mission in Torment.* New York: Doubleday, 1965.

Miller, Herman P. "The Dimensions of Poverty." In *Poverty as a Public Issue,* edited by Ben B. Seligman. Glencoe, Ill.: The Free Press, 1965.

Miller, William Lee. *The Fifteenth Ward and the Great Society.* New York: Harper and Row, 1966.

Mills, C. Wright. *The Power Elite.* New York: Oxford University Press, 1956.

Monsen, R. Joseph, Jr., and Cannon, Mark W. *The Makers of Public Policy.* New York: McGraw-Hill, 1965.

Morris, Robert, and Binstock, Robert H. *Feasible Planning for Social Change.* New York: Columbia University Press, 1966.

Mowitz, Robert, and Wright, Deil S. *Profile of a Metropolis, A Case Book.* Detroit: Wayne State University Press, 1962.

Moynihan, Daniel P. *Maximum Feasible Misunderstanding.* New York: Harper and Row, 1969.

______. "Poverty in Cities." In *The Metropolitan Enigma: Inquiries into the Nature and Dimensions of America's "Urban Crisis."* Volume II. Washington, D.C.: Chamber of Commerce of the United States, 1967.

______, ed. *Toward a National Urban Policy.* New York: Basic Books, 1970.

Myrdal, Gunnar. *An American Dilemma: The Negro Problem and American Democracy.* New York: Harper and Bros., 1946.

National Resources Planning Board, *Security Work, and Relief Policies.* Washington, D.C.: U.S. Government Printing Office, 1942.

Odum, Howard W., and Moore, Harry Estill. *American Regionalism.* New York: Henry Holt, 1938.

Organski, A. F. K. *The Stages of Political Development.* New York: Knopf, 1966.

Polenberg, Richard. *Reorganizing Roosevelt's Government.* Cambridge, Mass.: Harvard University Press, 1966.

Potter, David M. *The Impending Crisis 1848–1861.* New York: Harper and Row, 1976.

Pyhrr, Peter A. *Zero-Base Budgeting: A Practical Management Tool for Evaluating Expenses.* New York: Wiley Interscience, 1973.

Rainwater, Lee, and Yancey, William. *The Moynihan Report and the Politics of Controversy.* Cambridge, Mass.: M.I.T. Press, 1967.

Sanford, Terry. *Storm Over the States.* New York: McGraw-Hill, 1967.

Schlesinger, Arthur. *A Thousand Days: John F. Kennedy in the White House.* Boston: Houghton Mifflin Co., 1965.

Selznick, Philip. *TVA and the Grass Roots.* Berkeley: University of California Press, 1949.

Shank, Alan, and Conant, Ralph W. *Urban Perspectives: Politics and Policies.* Boston: Holbrook, 1975.

Simpson, Smith. *Anatomy of the State Department.* Boston: Houghton Mifflin Co., 1967.

Sternlieb, George, *et al. The Affluent Suburb: Princeton.* Center for Urban Policy Research. New Brunswick, N.J.: Transaction Books, 1971.

Sundquist, James L., and Davis, David W. *Making Federalism Work.* Washington, D.C.: The Brookings Institution, 1969.

Till, Charles. "Migration and Negro Relocation." In *The Metropolitan Enigma: Inquiries into the Nature and Dimensions of America's "Urban Crisis."* Volume II. Washington, D.C.: Chamber of Commerce of the United States, 1967.

Tocqueville, Alexis de. *Democracy in America.* Volumes I and II. New York: Vintage Books, 1954.

———. *Recollections.* Garden City, N.Y.: Doubleday, 1970.

University of Kentucky, Department of Architecture. "A Case Study Located in Eastern Kentucky." In *New Towns: A Proposal for the Appalachian Region.* Lexington: University of Kentucky, 1960.

University of Wisconsin, Industrial Relations Research Institute. *Retraining and Migration as Factors in Regional Economic Development.* Madison: University of Wisconsin, 1966.

Walker, Robert. *The Planning Function in Urban Government.* Chicago: University of Chicago Press, 1941.

Walter, Benjamin. "Political Decision Making in Arcadia." In *Urban Growth Dynamics in a Regional Cluster of Cities,* edited by Stuart F. Chapin and Shirley F. Weiss. New York: John Wiley, 1962.

Whelpton, Pascal K.; Campbell, Arthur A.; and Patterson, John E. *Fertility and Family Planning in the United States.* Princeton, N.J.: Princeton University Press, 1966.

Williams, Norman, Jr. *American Planning Law: Land Use and The Police Power.* Chicago: Callaghan, 1975.

Wingo, Lowden, Jr. "Urban Renewal: Objectives, Analyses and Information Systems." In *Regional Accounts for Policy Decisions,* edited by Werner Z. Hirsch. Baltimore: The Johns Hopkins Press, 1965.

Wise, Harold F. *Planning 1965.* Chicago: American Society of Planning Officials, 1965.

Wood, Robert C. "A Federal Policy for Metropolitan Areas." In *Metropolitan Politics: A Reader,* edited by Michael N. Danielson. Boston: Little, Brown, 1966.

______. *1400 Governments, New York Metropolitan Region Study.* Cambridge, Mass.: Harvard University Press, 1961.

ARTICLES AND PERIODICALS

Adrian, Charles R. "State and Local Government Participation in the Design and Administration of Intergovernmental Programs." *The Annals* 359 (May 1965): 36–37.

"Back-Into-Balance Britain." *Sunday Times* (London). November 5, 1967, p. 34.

Ball, Claiborne M. "Employment Effects of Construction Expenditures." *Monthly Labor Review* 88 (February 1965): 154–55.

Banfield, Edward C. "The Political Implications of Metropolitan Growth." *Daedalus,* Winter 1961.

Barnes, Ralph M., and Raymond, George M. "The Fiscal Approach to Land Use Planning." *Journal of the American Institute of Planners,* Spring-Summer 1955.

Beckman, Norman. "For a New Perspective in Federal-State Relations." *State Government* 39, no. 4 (Autumn 1966): 260–70.

______. "The Planner as a Bureaucrat." *Journal of the American Institute of Planners* 30, no. 4 (November 1964): 325–27.

Bellush, Jewel, and Hausknecht, Murray. "Entrepreneurs and Urban Renewal." *Journal of the American Institute of Planners* 32 (September 1966): 289–97.

Benson, George C. S. "Trends in Intergovernmental Relations." *The Annals* 359 (May 1965): 5.

Bogue, Donald J. "The End of the Population Explosion." *The Public Interest* 7 (Spring 1967).

Boston *Herald.* April 3, 1938, and January 3, 1967.

Boston *Post.* September 4, 1937.

Business Week. July 15, 1967.

Chelstowski, Stanislaw. "Deglomeration." *Polish Perspectives Monthly Review* (Warsaw). November 1966.

Chinitz, Benjamin. "Appropriate Goals for Regional Economic Policy." *Urban Studies* (Glasgow) 3, no. 1 (February 1966).

———. "Regional Economic Policy in Great Britain." *Urban Affairs Quarterly* 1, no. 2 (December 1965), and 1, no. 3 (March 1966).

Christian Science Monitor, March 8, 10, 1966, and January 31, 1968.

Cohen, Wilbur J. "Education and Learning." *The Annals* 373 (September 1967): 87–88.

Colman, William G. "The Federal Government in Intergovernmental Programs." *The Annals* 359 (May 1965).

Congressional Quarterly Weekly Report, March 13, 1965; 24, no. 5 (February 4, 1966); no. 14 (April 8, 1966); no. 42 (October 21, 1966); 27, no. 11 (March 13, 1970); no. 12 (March 20, 1970); 29, no. 7 (February 12, 1971); no. 8 (February 19, 1971).

Dallis, Robert. "Wave of Service Cutbacks Hits Rich, Poor Communities." Trenton *Sunday Times Advertiser,* August 15, 1976, p. B14.

Davidoff, Paul. "Advocacy and Pluralism in Planning." *Journal of the American Institute of Planners* 31, no. 6 (November 1965): 331–38.

DeMuth, Christopher C. "Deregulating the Cities." *The Public Interest,* no. 44 (Summer 1976): 115–28.

Dorfman, Robert. "Measuring Benefits of Government Investments." Washington, D.C.: Brookings Institution Studies in Finance, 1965.

Downs, Anthony. "Alternative Forms of Future Urban Growth in the United States." *Journal of the American Institute of Planners* 36 (January 1970).

Duhl, Leonard J. "Planning and Predicting: Or What to Do When You Don't Know the Names of the Variables." *Daedalus* (issue entitled *Toward the Year 2,000: Work in Progress*) 96, no. 3 (Summer 1967): 779–88.

Dyckman, John. "Social Planning, Social Planners, and Planned Societies." *Journal of the American Institute of Planners* 32 (March 1966): 70–71.

Eckaus, R. S. "Investment in Human Capital." *Journal of Political Economy* 71 (October 1963): 501–04.

Frankel, Charles. "Being In and Being Out." *The Public Interest* 17 (Fall 1969).

Franklin, Ben A. "In Appalachia: Vast Aid, Scant Relief." New York *Times,* November 29, 1970, p. 1.

______. "Kennedy Calls Antipoverty Program a Failure." New York *Times,* February 15, 1968, p. 1.

Freeman, Howard E., and Sherwood, Clarence C. "Research in Large Scale Intervention Programs." *Journal of Social Issues,* January 1965.

Friedmann, John. "The Concept of a Planning Region—The Evolution of an Idea in the United States." *Land Economics* 32, no. 3 (February 1956): 213–27.

______. "Planning as Innovation: The Chilean Case." *Journal of the American Institute of Planners* 32, no. 4 (July 1966): 779–88.

______. "Regional Planning as a Field of Study." *Journal of the American Institute of Planners* 29, no. 3 (August 1963): 168–75.

Glazer, Nathan. "The Grand Design of the Poverty Program." *New York Times Magazine* (February 27, 1966).

Gold, S. M. "Nonuse of Neighborhood Parks." *Journal of the American Institute of Planners* 38, no. 6 (November 1972).

Goodwin, Richard N. "The Shape of American Politics." *Commentary* 43, no. 6 (June 1967): 25–40.

Gorham, William. "Notes of a Practitioner." *The Public Interest* 8 (Summer 1967): 408.

Gross, Bertram M., and Springer, Michael. "A New Orientation in American Government." *The Annals* 1 (issue entitled *Social Goals and Indicators in American Society*) (May 1967): 10.

Grossman, David A., and Levin, Melvin R. "The Appalachian Region: A National Problem Area." *Land Economics* 37, no. 2 (May 1961): 133–41.

Hechinger, Fred M. "Call for the 'Urban-Grant' College." New York *Times,* October 22, 1967.

Herbers, John. "Big-City Mayors Leave Conference Concerned by Shift of Power to the Suburbs." New York *Times,* June 13, 1970, p. 34.

Hess, John L. "The Poverty Programs for Politicians, Too." New York *Times,* August 15, 1976, p. E5.

Horowitz, Irving Louis, and Rainwater, Lee. "Social Accounting for the Nation." *Trans-Action* 4, no. 6 (May 1967): 2–3.

Houstoun, Lawrence O., Jr. "The Revenue Sharing Debate: Simply Sending Money Down Will Worsen the Situation by Postponing Essential Reforms." *City* 5, no. 3 (May/June 1971): 15–18.

Iden, George. "Industrial Growth in Areas of Chronic Unemployment." *Monthly Labor Review,* May 1966.

Kalachek, Edward K. "Automation and Full Employment." *Trans-Action* 4, no. 4 (March 1967): 24–29.

Karmin, Monroe W. "A Not-So-Model Cities Program." *Wall Street Journal,* February 26, 1971.

Keyserling, Herman. "Genius Locii." *Atlantic Monthly* 144 (September 1929): 302–11. (Quoted in Odum, Howard W., and Moore, Harry Estill, *American Regionalism.* New York: Henry Holt and Company, 1938).

Kifner, John. New York *Times,* June 14, 1966.

Kristol, Irving. "The Negro Today Is the Immigrant of Yesterday." *New York Times Magazine,* September 11, 1966, pp. 50–51.

Kuehn, John A., and Bender, Lloyd D. *Growth and Change* 6, no. 2 (April 1975).

Lewis, Anthony. New York *Times,* June 21, 1961.

Loftus, Joseph A. "City Poverty Grants Linked to Aggressiveness." New York *Times,* August 18, 1966.

Long, Norton E. "Citizenship or Consumership in Metropolitan Areas." *Journal of the American Institute of Planners* 31 (February 1965).

———. "Politicians for Hire—The Dilemmas of Education and the Task of Research." *Public Administration Review* 25, no. 2 (June 1965).

McKinley, Charles. "The Valley Authority and Its Alternatives." *American Political Science Review,* September 1950. (Included as Chapter 28 in Friedmann, John, and Alonso, William. *Regional Development and Planning: A Reader.* Cambridge, Mass.: M.I.T. Press, 1964.)

Mann, Lawrence C., and Pillorge, George J. "French Regional Planning." *Journal of the American Institute of Planners* 30, no. 2 (May 1964): 64–74.

Mao, James C. T. "Efficiency in Public Urban Renewal Expenditures Through Benefit-Cost Analysis." *Journal of the American Institute of Planners* 32 (March 1966): 95–106.

Mills, Thomas J. "Scientific Personnel and the Professions." *The Annals* 367 (September 1966): 33–42.

Moynihan, Daniel P. "The Moynihan Report and Its Critics." *Commentary* 43 (February 1967): 31–45.

———. *The Public Interest* 5 (Fall 1966).

———. "Toward a National Urban Policy." *The Public Interest* 17 (Fall 1969).

______. "Urban Conditions: General." *The Annals* 371 (May 1967): 160–61.

______. "You Can't Run the Nation from Washington." Boston *Globe,* October 28, 1967.

Muskie, Edmund S. "Manpower: The Achilles Heel of Creative Federalism." *Public Administration Review* 27, no. 2 (June 1967): 193–94.

Needleman, L., and Scott, B. "Regional Problems and Location of Industry Policy in Britain." *Urban Studies* (Glasgow) 1, no. 2 (November 1964): 153–69.

New York *Times,* March 26, 1958; January 16, 23, 1966; February 10, 1966; March 6, 13, 25, 1966; March 26, 1967; June 22, 1967; August 27, 1967; January 13, 1968; February 2, 1968; January 10, 1970; July 12, 21, 1970; January 11, 23, 24, 1971.

Nixon, John H. "Jobs for Low-Income Areas of the Inner-City." *Economic Development* 3, no. 12 (December 1966).

O'Harrow, Dennis. "A Broad Brush With A Sharp Edge." *American Society of Planning Officials Newsletter,* June 1967.

______. "A New Tune for the Piper." *American Society of Planning Officials Newsletter* 32, no. 3 (March 1966): 21–22.

Okun, Bernard. "Regional Income Inequality and Internal Population Migration." *Economic Development and Cultural Change,* January 1961, pp. 128–43.

Parr, John B. "Outmigration and the Depressed Area Problem." *Land Economics* 42, no. 2 (May 1966): 158–67.

Petshek, Kirk R. "A New Role for City Universities—Urban Extension Programs." *Journal of the American Institute of Planners,* November 1964.

Population Reference Bureau. "Boom Babies Come of Age: The American Family at the Crossroads." *Population Bulletin* 22, no. 3 (August 1966).

Press, Charles, and Adrian, Charles R. "Why Our State Governments Are Sick." *The Antioch Review,* Summer 1964, pp. 156–57.

Pynchon, Thomas. "A Journey Into the Mind of Watts." *New York Times Magazine,* June 23, 1966.

Rein, Martin, and Miller, S. M. "Poverty Programs and Policy Priorities." *Trans-Action* 4, no. 9 (September 1967).

Robock, Stefan. "Strategies for Regional Economic Development." *Regional Science Association Papers,* 17 (1966).

Rogers, David. "New York City Schools: A Sick Bureaucracy." *Saturday Review of Literature,* July 20, 1968, pp. 47–49, 59–61.

Rossi, Peter. "Evaluating Social Action Programs." *Trans-Action* 4, no. 7 (June 1967): 51–53.

Schick, Allen. "The Road to PPBS: The Stages of Budget Reform." *Public Administration Review* 26, no. 4 (December 1966): 243–58.

Schultz, Theodore W. "Capital Formation in Education." *Journal of Political Economy* 51, no. 1 (December 1960): 1–17.

———. "Education and Economic Growth." *1961 Yearbook of the National Society for the Study of Education,* Chap. 3.

———, ed. "Investment in Human Beings." *The Journal of Political Economy* 70, no. 5 (October 1962): 1–8.

Sheehan, Neil. "You Don't Know Where Johnson Ends and McNamara Begins." *New York Times Magazine,* October 22, 1967.

Shorr, Alvin L. "Program for the Social Orphans." *New York Times Magazine,* March 13, 1966.

Shriver, Sargent. New York *Times,* March 9, 1966, p. 24; November 6, 1966, p. 6E.

Sjaastad, L. A. "The Costs and Returns of Human Migration." *The Journal of Political Economy* 70, no. 5 (1962): 80–93.

Stillman, Richard J. "The Bureaucracy Problem at DOJ." *Public Administration Review,* no. 4 (July/August 1976), pp. 429–39.

Wall Street Journal, March 7, 1966, p. 1.

Wildavsky, Aaron. "The Political Economy of Efficiency: Cost-Benefit Analysis, Systems Analysis and Program Budgeting." *Public Administration Review* 8 (December 1966): 297–98.

———. "The Political Economy of Efficiency." *The Public Interest* 8 (Summer 1967): 30–48.

Wilson, James Q. "The Bureaucracy Problem." *The Public Interest* 6 (Winter 1967): 3–9.

Winston, Oliver C. "An Urbanization Pattern for the United States—Some Considerations for the Decentralization of Excellence." *Land Economics,* February 1967.

Wirtz, Willard. "War on Poverty." *Congressional Quarterly* 24, no. 11 (March 18, 1966): 603.

Wood, Robert. "Government and the Intellectual: The Necessary Alliance for Effective Action to Meet Urban Needs." *Governing Urban Society: New Scientific Approaches.* Monograph 7 in a series sponsored by the American Academy of Political and Social Science, pp. 3–14.

Zimmerman, Joseph F. "Metropolitan Reform in the U.S.: An Overview." *Public Administration Review* 30, no. 5 (September–October 1970).

PUBLIC DOCUMENTS

Kaufman, J. J. "Labor Mobility, Training, and Retraining." *Studies in Unemployment.* U.S. Senate Special Committee on Unemployment Problems. Washington, D.C., 1960.

Litton Industries. *Preliminary Analysis for Economic Development Plan for the Appalachian Region.* Prepared for the Area Redevelopment Administration, Washington, D.C., 1965.

Massachusetts. Board of Regional Community Colleges. *Access to Quality Community College Opportunity: A Master Plan for Massachusetts Community Colleges Through 1975.* Boston, 1967.

______. Governor's Management Engineering Task Force. *Survey Report and Recommendations.* Boston, 1965.

______. Special Commission on Audit of State Needs. *Needs in Massachusetts Higher Education.* Boston, 1958.

______. State Planning Board. *Progress Report.* Boston, 1936.

Moynihan, Daniel Patrick. *The Negro Family.* Washington, D.C.: U.S. Department of Labor, 1965.

Ribicoff, Abraham. "The Competent City: An Action Program for Urban America." *Congressional Record,* 89th Cong., 1st Sess., January 23, 1967.

Schultze, Charles L. "The Role of Incentives, Penalties and Rewards in Attaining Effective Policy." *The Analysis and Evaluation of Public Expenditures: The PPB System.* A compendium of papers submitted by the Subcommittee on Economy in Government of the Joint Economic Committee, Washington, D.C., 1969.

Superior Court of New Jersey, Middlesex County, Chancery Division. *Urban League of Greater New Brunswick v. Borough of Carteret et. al.* Decided May 4, 1976.

U.S. Advisory Commission on Intergovernmental Relations. *Factors Affecting Governmental Reorganization in Metropolitan Areas.* Washington, D.C., 1962.

U.S. Advisory Commission on Intergovernmental Relations. 14th Annual Report. *Striking a Better Balance: Federalism in 1972.* Washington, D.C.: U.S. Government Printing Office, 1972.

______. Advisory Commission on Intergovernmental Relations. *Revenue Sharing—An Idea Whose Time Has Come.* Washington, D.C., 1970.

______. The Appalachian Regional Development Commission. *Executive Director's Semi-Annual Report.* Washington, D.C., 1966.

______. Area Redevelopment Administration. *Area Redevelopment Policies in Britain and the Countries of the Common Market.* Washington, D.C., 1965.

______. Area Redevelopment Administration. *Population, Labor Force and Unemployment in Chronically Distressed Areas.* Washington, D.C., 1964.

______. Area Redevelopment Administration. *The Propensity to Move.* Washington, D.C., 1964.

______. Bureau of the Budget. *Bulletin No. 66–3, Planning-Programming-Budgeting.* Washington, D.C., 1965; *Supplement to Bulletin No. 66–3.* Washington, D.C., 1966.

______. Bureau of the Census. *Census.* Washington, D.C., 1960.

———. Bureau of the Census. *1963 Census of Transportation.* "Home-to-Work Travel." TC63 (a)-P5.

———. Bureau of the Census. *Current Population Reports, Population Estimates.* Series P-25, Nos. 326 and 347. Washington, D.C., 1966.

———. Bureau of the Census. *Statistical Abstract of the United States.* Washington, D.C., 1965–67, 1970.

———. Committee on Government Operations. Subcommittee on Intergovernmental Relations. "Federal Expenditures to States and Regions." Washington, D.C., 1966.

———. Committee on Government Operations. Subcommittee on Intergovernmental Relations. "The Federal System as Seen by Federal Aid Officials." Washington, D.C., 1965.

———. Congress. Public Law 89–4, "Appalachian Regional Development Act of 1965," 89th Cong., 1st sess., 1965.

U.S. Congress. Senate. Report of Appalachian Regional Commission presented in *Extension of the Appalachian Regional Development Act.* Hearings before the Subcommittee on Economic Development of the Committee on Public Works. S. 1513, March 10, 11, 12, and June 3, 1975. Washington, D.C.: U.S. Government Printing Office, 1975.

———. Department of Commerce. *Survey of Current Business.* Washington, D.C., 1967.

———. Department of Labor. *Manpower Implications of Automation.* Washington, D.C., 1964.

———. Department of Labor. *Manpower Report of the President.* Washington, D.C., 1964, 1966, 1973.

———. Department of Labor. *Projections 1970, Interindustry Relationships, Potential Demand, Employment.* Bulletin No. 1536. Washington, D.C., 1966.

———. Department of Labor. *Social and Economic Conditions of Negroes in the United States.* Bureau of Labor Statistics Report No. 332. Washington, D.C., 1967.

———. Economic Development Administration. *Economic Development.* Washington, D.C., January and February 1968.

———. Economic Development Administration. *Jobs for America.* Annual Report, Fiscal 1969. Washington, D.C., 1969.

———. *Hearings* before the Committee on Public Works (Senate) and Committee on Public Works (House of Representatives). "Public Works and Economic Development Act of 1965." 89th Cong., 1st sess., 1965.

———. *Hearings* before the Subcommittee on Air and Water Pollution of the Committee on Public Works (Senate). "Air Pollution—1970." 91st Cong., 2d sess., 1970.

———. *Hearings* before the Subcommittee of the Committee on Banking and Currency. "Area Redevelopment Act." 86th Cong., 1st sess., 1959.

______. *Hearings* before the Subcommittee on Fiscal Policy of the Joint Economic Committee. Statement of Rep. Henry S. Reuss, "Revenue Sharing and Its Alternatives." 90th Cong., 1st sess., 1967.

______. *Hearings* before the Subcommittee on Intergovernmental Relations. "Creative Federalism." 90th Cong., 1st sess., 1967.

______. Joint Economic Committee. Subcommittee on Economic Progress. *Federal Programs for the Development of Human Resources.* Washington, D.C., 1966.

______. National Aeronautics and Space Administration. *Electronic Research Center.* Washington, D.C., 1964.

______. National Commission on Technology, Automation and Economic Progress. *Technology and the American Economy.* Washington, D.C., 1966.

______. National Resources Planning Board. Committee on Long-Range Work and Relief Policies. *Security, Work and Relief Policies.* Washington, D.C., 1942.

______. National Science Foundation. "Geographic Distribution of Funds for Research and Development, 1963." *Reviews of Data on Science Resources.* Washington, D.C., 1965.

______. Office of Economic Opportunity. *Community Action Program Guide.* Washington, D.C., 1965.

______. Office of Economic Opportunity. *Office of Economic Opportunity Memorandum.* Nos. 23 and 28. Washington, D.C., 1966.

______. President's Advisory Committee on Labor Management Policy. *The Benefits and Problems Incidental to Automation and Other Technological Advances.* Washington, D.C., 1962.

______. President's Appalachian Regional Commission. *Appalachia.* Washington, D.C., 1964.

______. President's Commission on National Goals. *Goals for Americans.* Washington, D.C., 1960.

______. President's Committee on Administrative Management. *Report of the Committee.* Washington, D.C., 1937.

______. President's Message. "City Demonstration Programs." 89th Cong., 2nd Sess., 1966.

______. Senate. Committee on Labor and Public Welfare. *Selected Readings in Employment and Manpower.* 6 Vols. Washington, D.C., 1964 and 1965.

Wheaton, William L. C., and Schussheim, Morton J. *The Cost of Municipal Services in Residential Areas.* Prepared for the Housing and Home Finance Agency. Washington, D.C., 1955.

Wolfle, Dael. "Can Professional Manpower Trends Be Predicted?" *Seminar on Manpower Policy and Program.* Prepared for the U.S. Department of Labor, Manpower Administration. Washington, D.C., 1967.

REPORTS

American Institute of Planners Committee on Metropolitan Planning. *Workshop Report. Proceedings of the 1964 Annual Conference.* American Institute of Planners, 1964.

Fischer, Victor A. *Proceedings of the 1964 Annual Conference.* American Institute of Planners, 1965.

Hayes, Frederick O'Reilly. *Urban Planning and the Transportation Study. Proceedings of the 1963 Annual Conference.* American Institute of Planners, 1964.

Lepawsky, Albert. *State Planning and Economic Development in the South.* Report No. 4. Washington, D.C.: National Planning Association, Committee of the South, 1949.

Levin, Melvin R. *Recreational Needs in the Providence Model City Area.* Report prepared for the Providence Model City Agency by the Economic and Social Development Institute. Washington, D.C., May 1971.

Loeks, C. David. *Where Metropolitan Planning Stands Today. Proceedings of the 1958 Annual Conference.* American Institute of Planners, 1959, pp. 31–33.

Mushkin, Selma J. *National Policy on Urban Finance.* Washington, D.C.: The Urban Institute, 1970.

National Recreation and Park Association. *Open Space and Recreation Opportunity in America's Inner Cities.* Prepared for Department of Housing and Urban Development, July 1974.

University Training in PPB for State and Local Officials. A Synopsis of the Airlie House Institute of University Training (Selma J. Mushkin, Chairman). Washington, D.C.: The Urban Institute, 1970.

UNPUBLISHED MATERIAL

Levin, Melvin R. "The Depressed Area: A Study of Southern Illinois." Ph.D. dissertation, University of Chicago, 1956.

———. "Government and the Depressed Area." Ph.D. dissertation, Division of Social Sciences, University of Chicago, 1956.

———, and Moscowitz, Harvey M. "South Plainfield: An Industrial Core City in a Region: A Fair Share Analysis of Housing." Analysis prepared for litigation in *Urban League of Greater New Brunswick v. Borough of Carteret.* May 1976.

Listokin, David. "An Analysis of the Fair Share Approach to Housing," Undated ms., Center for Urban Policy Research, Rutgers University.

Zimmerman, Joseph F. "Solving Metropolitan Problems Through Direct State Action." Paper presented at the Northeastern Conference, American Society for Public Administration, 1970.

INDEX

ABOUT THE AUTHOR

MELVIN R. LEVIN, Professor of Urban Planning at Rutgers University, has had extensive experience in many aspects of urban planning. He has been a consultant in both government agencies and universities. Before joining the Rutgers faculty, Dr. Levin was Director of Boston University's Urban Affairs Program, a planning consultant, a transportation planner for the Commonwealth of Massachusetts, a program analyst for the Illinois welfare agency, and a senior economist with the Midwest Research Institute.

Professor Levin received his Ph.D. from the University of Chicago. He is the author of a number of books, including studies of state land use planning, continuing education, and transportation planning, and an introductory text to urban planning.

RELATED TITLES

Published by

Praeger Special Studies

INNOVATIONS FOR FUTURE CITIES

edited by Gideon Golany

THE SUBURBAN ECONOMIC NETWORK: Economic Activity, Resource Use, and the Great Sprawl

edited by John E. Ullmann

SYSTEMATIC URBAN PLANNING

Darwin G. Stuart

URBAN NONGROWTH: City Planning for People

Earl Finkler, William J. Toner, and Frank J. Popper